INFORMATION PROCESSING
IN MOTOR CONTROL
AND LEARNING

Contributors

Jack A. Adams
Sheldon Baron
Gordon L. Diewert
Carol A. Fowler
James S. Frank
Barry H. Kantowitz
J. A. Scott Kelso
Beth Kerr
James L. Knight, Jr.
Ronald L. Knoll
Ronald G. Marteniuk
Stephen Monsell
K. M. Newell
Richard W. Pew
Richard A. Schmidt
Judith L. Smith
Waneen Wyrick Spirduso
George E. Stelmach
Saul Sternberg
M. T. Turvey
Stephen A. Wallace
Alan M. Wing
Charles E. Wright
Howard N. Zelaznik

INFORMATION PROCESSING IN MOTOR CONTROL AND LEARNING

Edited by

George E. Stelmach

Motor Behavior Laboratory
University of Wisconsin—Madison
Madison, Wisconsin

ACADEMIC PRESS   New York   San Francisco   London   1978

A Subsidiary of Harcourt Brace Jovanovich, Publishers

ACADEMIC PRESS, INC.
111 Fifth Avenue, New York, New York 10003

United Kingdom Edition published by
ACADEMIC PRESS, INC. (LONDON) LTD.
24/28 Oval Road, London NW1 7DX

Library of Congress Cataloging in Publication Data

Main entry under title:

Information processing in motor control and learning.

Includes bibliographies.
1. Perceptual–motor learning. 2. Human information
processing. 3. Sensory–motor integration. 4. Physical
education and training. I. Stelmach, George E.
BF295.M67   152.3'34   77–25736
ISBN 0–12–665960–5

PRINTED IN THE UNITED STATES OF AMERICA

Contents

1 Skill Acquisition: An Event Approach with Special Reference to Searching for the Optimum of a Function of Several Variables

Carol A. Fowler and M. T. Turvey

2 Some Issues on Action Plans

K. M. Newell

3 Task Factors That Influence Selection and Preparation for Voluntary Movements

Beth Kerr

13 The Role of Eye and Head Positions in Slow Movement Execution

Ronald G. Marteniuk

14 Hemispheric Lateralization and Orientation in Compensatory and Voluntary Movement

Waneen Wyrick Spirduso

List of Contributors

Numbers in parentheses indicate the pages on which the authors' contributions begin.

Jack A. Adams (229), Department of Psychology, University of Illinois at Urbana–Champaign, Champaign, Illinois 61820

Sheldon Baron (71), Bolt Beranek and Newman Inc., 50 Moulton Street, Cambridge, Massachusetts 02138

Gordon L. Diewert * (241), Motor Behavior Laboratory, University of Wisconsin—Madison, Madison, Wisconsin 53706

Carol A. Fowler (1), Department of Psychology, Dartmouth College, Hanover, New Hampshire 03755

James S. Frank † (183), Department of Physical Education, University of Southern California, Los Angeles, California 90007

Barry H. Kantowitz (205), Department of Psychology, Purdue University, West Lafayette, Indiana 47907

J. A. Scott Kelso (79), Motor Behavior Laboratory, University of Iowa, Iowa City, Iowa 52242

Beth Kerr (55), School of Physical and Health Education, University of Washington, Seattle, Washington 98105

James L. Knight, Jr. (205), School of Industrial Engineering, Purdue University, West Lafayette, Indiana 47907

Ronald L. Knoll (117), Human Information-Processing Research Department, Bell Laboratories, Murray Hill, New Jersey 07974

Ronald G. Marteniuk (267), Department of Kinesiology, University of Waterloo, Waterloo, Ontario, Canada

Stephen Monsell (117), Department of Experimental Psychology, University of Oxford, Oxford OX1 30D, England

---

* Present address: Human Motor Learning and Performance Laboratory, University of Windsor, Windsor, Ontario N9B 3P4, Canada

† Present address: School of Physical Education and Athletics, McMaster University, Hamilton, Ontario L8S 4K1, Canada

K. M. Newell (41), Institute for Child Behavior and Development, University of Illinois at Urbana–Champaign, Champaign, Illinois 61820

Richard W. Pew (71), Bolt Beranek and Newman Inc., 50 Moulton Street, Cambridge, Massachusetts 02138

Richard A. Schmidt (183), Department of Physical Education, University of Southern California, Los Angeles, California 90007

Judith L. Smith (173), Department of Kinesiology and Brain Research Institute, University of California, Los Angeles, Los Angeles, California 90405

Waneen Wyrick Spirduso (289), Department of Physical and Health Education, University of Texas at Austin, Austin, Texas 78712

George E. Stelmach (241), Motor Behavior Laboratory, University of Wisconsin—Madison, Madison, Wisconsin 53706

Saul Sternberg (117), Human Information-Processing Research Department, Bell Laboratories, Murray Hill, New Jersey 07974

M. T. Turvey (1), Department of Psychology, University of Connecticut, Storrs, Connecticut 06268

Stephen A. Wallace (79), Department of Physical Education, University of California at Davis, Davis, California 95616

Alan M. Wing (153), Medical Research Council, Applied Psychology Unit, 15 Chaucer Road, Cambridge CB2 2EF, England

Charles E. Wright (117), Human Information-Processing Research Department, Bell Laboratories, Murray Hill, New Jersey 07974

Howard N. Zelaznik (183), Department of Physical Education, University of Southern California, Los Angeles, California 90007

Preface

The swing of the pendulum back toward the study of the basic processes that subserve behavior is nowhere as apparent as in the theoretical shift observed in motor behavior research since the late 1960s. The study of skill acquisition and motor control is one of the most rapidly expanding areas in psychology and neurophysiology. This research expansion has been brought about by the interest generated from new approaches to rather old problems that now focus not only on the effector responses, but on the entire processing system. Rather than viewing only a small part of total behavior, contemporary approaches to motor behavior are stressing a complete conceptualization of behavior through the description of the mental operations that characterize motor acts. It has become clear to all serious students of motor behavior that basic to the understanding of how motor learning takes place is a thorough knowledge of the function of the central nervous system. As a result, the marked growth has been accompanied by changes in experimental paradigms and theoretical postulations. While it was as recent as the late 1960s that motor behaviorists searched for the empirical relations that governed learning, performance, retention, and transfer behavior, contemporary motor behavior scientists are seeking an understanding of how the brain functions during the processes of learning, control, and memory.

This volume provides an organized and up-to-date picture of the current status of the theoretical and technical developments in the field of motor behavior; and will be of interest both to the advanced student in the field as well as to anyone possessing a basic scientific background.

This book grew indirectly out of a 2-day symposium held under the auspices of the University of Wisconsin—Madison Motor Behavior Laboratory and sponsored by the Committee on Institutional Cooperation for the Big Ten Universities and the Dean's office, School of Education, University of Wisconsin—Madison. As with most conferences, it began with only the general topic and the invited speakers fixed. Everything else, the nature of the presentations, the exact coverage of the topics, and the overall format of the conference, developed spontaneously. Therefore, this volume is what it is not because of careful planning on my part, but rather because of the different paths taken by the contributors.

The purpose of this book is to disseminate the theoretical ideas and empirical findings of a small group of scientists who are actively engaged in motor behavior research. The authors point out and define problems in need of further study in the hope that this will stimulate further research in this area.

The fourteen chapters are not grouped in any manner. Each chapter presents a comprehensive up-to-date review of the pertinent literature. The volume as a whole represents a good blend of theory and empirical data on motor control and learning. Some of the early chapters discuss the several theoretical issues surrounding skill acquisition. However, for the most part the chapters focus on motor programming topics including the nature and significance of preparation, rapid movement sequences, attentional demands, and sensorimotor integration in voluntary movements. These chapters combine to give an excellent overview of the motor programming area and raise some rather controversial points as well.

Editing a book of this nature involves a cooperative venture between the contributors, the editor, and the publisher. I am indebted to many for their efforts on this volume especially to the busy and often overcommitted scientists who took the time to express their ideas in a clear and concise manner, to Academic Press who so willingly and efficiently went about publishing this book, and to Virginia Diggles for her efforts to steer this project through much detail, which kept me from giving up the laborious task long ago. Finally, I would like to offer my sincere appreciation to all those in my Motor Behavior Laboratory who sacrificed their time to critique many of the chapters.

1

Skill Acquisition: An Event Approach with Special Reference to Searching for the Optimum of a Function of Several Variables

Carol A. Fowler

M. T. Turvey

This work was supported by NIH grant HD01994 and NSF grant NSI3617 to Haskins Laboratories.

1

I. Introduction

Our chapter divides into three parts. The first is a roughly hewn statement of the general orientation we wish to take toward the problem of skill acquisition. The second part develops a level of analysis that, in our view, is optimal for the examination of the problem; essentially, it is an ecological level of analysis that promotes the event rather than the performer as the minimal system that will permit an adequate explanation of the regulation and acquisition of skilled activity. The principal claims of the first two parts are highlighted in the third and final part through a detailed examination of a specific but prototypical coordination problem, namely, the problem of how one learns optimally to constrain an aggregate of relatively independent muscles so as to regulate a simple change in a single variable.

II. Motor Tasks, Acquisition Processes, and Actors: A General Orientation

It is prudent to preface a theoretical analysis of learning by some general comments on what the incipient theorist takes to be the nature of tasks that are learned, the nature of the processes that support the learning, and the nature of the agent doing the learning. In the vocabulary of Shaw and McIntyre (1974), those three topics refer, respectively, to the three primary analytic concepts of psychology, namely, the *what, how,* and *who* concepts. One can argue that this set of analytic concepts is closed, that is, that the concepts are logically co-implicative (Shaw & McIntyre, 1974; Turvey & Prindle, 1977). The closure of the set is illustrated by the following example.

> The degree of hardness of a sheet of metal tells us something about the nature of the saw we must use to cut it (i.e., something about *what* is to be done); a blueprint or pattern must be selected in the light of what can be cut from the materials with a given degree of tolerance (i.e., *how* it is to be done); while both of these factors must enter into our equations to determine the amount of work that must be done to complete the job within a reasonable amount of time. This latter information provides a job description that hopefully gets an equivalence class of existing machines rather than a class that might accomplish the feat in principle but not in practice (i.e., implies the nature of the *who* or *what* required to do the task) [Shaw & McIntyre, 1974, p. 311].

A. A Parallel between Evolution and Learning

In search of a general orientation to the nature of tasks, processes, and agents as they bear on the issue of skill acquisition, we are drawn to the parallel between a species participating in the slow processes of evolution and an individual animal participating in the comparatively rapid process of learning.

From a perspective that encompasses the whole evolving world of living systems, any given species appears to be a "special-purpose device" whose salient properties are those that distinguish the given species from other species. These salient properties, synchronically described, mark the state of adaptation of the species to the special and relatively invariant properties of its environment. In the course of time the species maintains its special attunement by coupling its evolution to that of its changing environment.

If the perspective is considerably narrower, encompassing only the lifetime and habitat of an individual animal, then the system being observed appears to be a "general-purpose device" to the extent that the individual animal can enter into various temporary relationships with its environment. In the course of ontogeny the individual animal adds to its repertoire of skilled acts.

It is roughly apparent that the "evolution" in ontogeny of a skilled act parallels the evolution of a species. Adaptation to an environment is synonymous with the evolution of special biological and behavioral features that are compatible (symmetrical) with special features of the environment. Similarly, we may claim that facility with a skill is synonymous with the ontogeny of special coordinative features that are compatible with the special features of the skill. Insofar as an environment has structure that provides the criteria for adaptations, so we may expect, not surprisingly, a task to have structure that provides the source of constraint on skilled solutions. And insofar as a species is said to be a particular biological attunement to a particular niche, we may wish to say, perhaps curiously, that the individual animal, as skilled performer, is a particular attunement to the particular task it performs skillfully. This last and cryptic parallel must be commented on further, for aside from requiring clarification it contains within it a potentially useful metaphor for the understanding of coordinated activity.

Consider the proposition that an animal and its environment are not logically separable, that one always implies the other. An animal's environment should not be construed in terms of the variables of physics as we commonly understand them; a considerably more useful conception is in terms of *affordances* (Gibson, 1977). An affordance is not easily defined, but the following may be taken as a working approximation: "The affordance of anything is a specific combination of the properties of its substance and its surfaces taken with reference to an animal [Gibson, 1977, p. 67]." Thus, for example, the combination of the surface and substance properties of rigidity, levelness, flatness, and extendedness identifies a surface of support for the upright posture and locomotory activity of humans. Put another way, an object or situation, as an invariant combination of surface and substance variables, affords a certain activity for a given animal if and only if there is a mutual compatability between the animal, on the one hand, and the object or situation on the other.

Affordances are the aspects of the world to which adaptations occur. Consequently, we can now identify the special features of the environment referred to

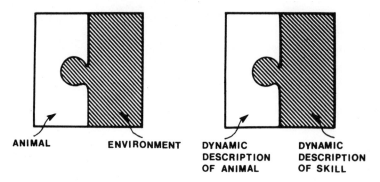

ANIMAL   ENVIRONMENT   DYNAMIC DESCRIPTION OF ANIMAL   DYNAMIC DESCRIPTION OF SKILL

Figure 1. The jigsaw puzzle metaphor.

above as a set of affordances, equate a "set of affordances" with a "niche" (Gibson, 1977), and recognize that a set of affordances is perceptually and behaviorally occupied by an animal. It is in this sense that an animal and an environment are not logically separable, for a niche implies a particular kind of animal and a species implies a particular kind of niche (Gibson, 1977).

A crude but useful metaphor is that the fit between an animal and its niche is like the fit between the pieces of a jigsaw puzzle. Figure 1 depicts the fit for a minimally complex puzzle. On the jigsaw puzzle metaphor, adaptation and attunement are synonyms for the fit of a species to a niche. It is in this same metaphorical sense that skill acquisition can be understood as attunement: In terms of a two-piece jigsaw puzzle, one piece is an appropriate dynamic description of the skill and the other piece is an appropriate and complementary dynamic description of the animal.

B. The Actor as a Mimicking Automaton

To pursue further the idea of skill acquisition as attunement, let us return to the notion of the individual animal as a general-purpose device. The animal of interest to us is, of course, human. In deliberations on perception the human is often referred to as *the perceiver,* in deliberations on action, therefore, it seems appropriate to refer to the human as *the actor.*

We wish to claim that the individual actor is a general-purpose device not because he or she has the capacity to apply a single, general-purpose action strategy to the skill problems encountered, but because he or she has the capacity to become a variety of special-purpose devices, that is, a variety of specific automata. The distinction between these two kinds of general-purpose devices is depicted crudely in Figure 2. One device can accept only one program and generalizes that program across a variety of tasks. The other device can accept a variety of pro-

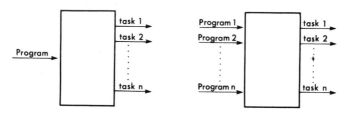

Figure 2. Two kinds of general-purpose devices. The one on the left accepts only one program and generalizes that program across a variety of tasks. The one on the right accepts a variety of programs, one program for each of a variety of tasks.

grams, one program for each of a variety of tasks.[1] The familiar paradigm for learning theory, associationism, identifies the actor as a general-purpose device of the first kind. It can be shown that a formal statement of associationism, the Terminal Meta-Postulate (Bever, Fodor, & Garrett, 1968), is formally equivalent to a strictly finite-state automaton that accepts only one-sided (right or left) linear grammars (Suppes, 1969). Such an automaton is formally incapable of natural language and complex coordinated movements, to name but a few limitations. A person, on the other hand, is obviously capable of such things and more besides. Nevertheless, it is reasonably fair to claim that, on the grounds of mortality and finite computing capacity, our actor, a person, is a machine with finite states. How, then, does he behave as if he were a machine of a more powerful kind such as a linear-bounded automaton that accepts context-sensitive grammars? One hypothesis (Shaw, Halwes, & Jenkins, Note 1) is that the class of finite-state machines that best characterizes the individual person is that of *finite-state transducers*. These machines transduce the behavior of more powerful machines into equivalent finite-state behaviors; they are capable of processing the same inputs as more powerful machines, but only up to some finite limit. In short, the individual actor as a finite-state transducer can "mimic" the competency of more powerful automata; that is, he or she can become, within limits, any one of a variety of special-purpose devices whose complexity is compatible with the complexity of the task it must perform.

We would not wish to push the interpretation of the actor as a finite-state transducer too far. We wish to view it more as an analogy, for there are reasons to believe that the general machine conception, of which finite-state transducers and the like are examples, may well be inappropriate for biology (Shaw, Note 2). Nevertheless, the preceding is sufficiently instructive for our current purposes: It

---

[1] Turvey, Shaw, and Mace (in press) have introduced a similar distinction between "hierarchies" and "coalitions." In the context of the present discussion, a hierarchy is a general-purpose device of the first type and a coalition a general-purpose device of the second type.

identifies our general orientation to the agent—that is, the actor—as a mimicking automaton. We can now make a further comment on the idea of skill acquisition as attunement: It is, in large part, the idea that an actor becomes that particular kind of machine that is consonant with the essential features of the particular skill that the actor is performing.

C. Summary

We summarize these prefatory remarks with a tentative answer to the question: What is it about an actor and about the skills that he seeks to perform such that he can (learn to) make of himself a variety of special-purpose devices? First, in reference to the nature of the actor: The relationships among muscles are sufficiently plastic so that within limits actors are able to constrain or organize their musculature into different systems. On this perspective, learning a skill involves discovering an optimal self-organization. Second, in reference to the nature of skills: Skills have structure, and discovering an optimal self-organization is in reference to those variables of stimulation corresponding to environmental and biokinematic relations that specify the essential features of the skill the actor is to perform. This raises the important question of what are the useful skill-specific variables of stimulation that, in the course of acquiring a skill, guide and regulate the current approximation and prescribe the next approximation to the desired performance (attunement). Third, in reference to the nature of the processes supporting learning: Insofar as the useful skill-related information must be discovered, the actor must engage certain "search methods" that reveal that useful information to him. These search methods must be compatible with the actor; that is, they must be compatible with, for example, real-world mechanical and temporal constraints that natural (as opposed to abstract) actors must obey.

III. Defining the Domain of Skill Acquisition for a Theorist

In seeking an explanation of anything it is important that the forms of theoretical and investigatory attention be a domain of entities and functions that is optimal to the particular problem under investigation. "Optimal domain" means two things. First, any decision to investigate a problem involves selecting some system (some collective of entities and functions) as the minimal one that is relevant to the problem's explanation. If the selected system excludes some entities and functions that are in fact crucial to the explanation, they exert an influence on the selected system that, from the observer's perspective, is random (cf. Bohm, 1957). Consequently, the system's behavior in relation to those perturbations may be inexplicable.

Equally important is the second sense of "optimal domain." Any given system may be described at several different *levels* where each level is distinguished by the entities and functions to which its vocabulary refers. Different levels of description of a system make different concepts available to the theorist that he can invoke in his explanation (Medawar, 1973; Putnam, 1973). Which concepts are most useful to the theorist depends on what problems he has elected to explain.

What should be the minimal system for a theory of the acquisition and performance of skilled activity? At first glance, the *actor* seems to be the appropriate unit deserving observation and systematic measurement. With the actor as the minimal system the concept of coordination can be judiciously defined in terms of relationships defined over the muscles and joints of the body. The locus of movement control can be given relatively precise coordinates, namely, the nervous system of the actor. However, in taking the actor as the minimal system we adopt a myopic view of the contribution of the environment to coordinated activity. This is not to say that an actor-oriented approach to the theory rejects the environment's contribution, but rather that it detracts from a serious analysis of the environment as the necessary support for coordinated, skilled movements. An actor-oriented perspective on skill, with its pinpointing of the actor as the source of control, encourages the impoverished description of information about the environment as sensory signals whose meaning is contributed wholly by the actor (cf. Schmidt, 1975).

The claim we wish to make is that a superordinate system, one that encompasses the actor, his actions, and the environmental support for his actions, is the minimal system whose observation will permit an adequate explanation of the regulation and acquisition of skilled performance. To anticipate, this minimal system will be referred to as an *event*. From the perspective of this system, coordination is a relation defined over the actor and the environment, and control is the exclusive prerogative of neither.

What should be the level of description for this minimal system? Putatively the theorist who aims to explain the acquisition and performance of skilled activities should select a level of description that is compatible with an actor's self-descriptions and descriptions of the environment. The theorist should select a grain-size of vocabulary that, in reference to skilled activity, includes those entities and functions that are regulated by actors and those entities and functions that are regulative of actors.

Our previous discussions of coordinated movement (Turvey, 1977b; Turvey, Shaw, & Mace, in press; Fowler, Note 3) may be characterized as attempts to select and define an appropriate level of description of acting animals and of the environments in which they act. We will summarize and elaborate on those attempts in the remarks that follow.

A. Events as Significant Units of Observation in a Theory of Skilled Action

An act performed in a natural context has two sources of control: One is the actor himself, and the other is the environment in which the act occurs.

To achieve some aim, whatever it may be, an actor engages in a systemic relationship with the environment. That is, he regulates his body in relation to environmental sources of control, such as gravitational and frictional forces. His task, then, is quite different from one of producing an act *in vacuo;* it is to generate a set of forces that, *together with* the environmental forces impinging on him, are sufficient to achieve his aim. In the sense of the jigsaw puzzle metaphor, the forces supplied by the actor complement those supplied by the environment. Furthermore, the actor's aim itself is not entirely a product of his own will. Rather, it must be some selection on his part among the limited possibilities afforded by the environment.

In short, we can say that actors and their environments participate in a larger system that we will call an "event" following the usage of Shaw, McIntyre, and Mace (1974). Structurally described, an event includes the actor and the environmental support for his actions. "Environmental support" includes the surfaces, objects, and living systems in relation to which the actor governs his behavior and, in addition, the structured media (such as the ambient light and air) that provide the actor with an event's functional description—that is, with a specification of what is happening in the course of an act.

Two principles derive from the foregoing discussion. First, an actor controls the functional description of an event rather than the functional description of his own body; second, an appropriate observational perspective of a theorist of skilled action is a perspective that encompasses events rather than actors only. The two principles are illustrated in the following example.

Consider a person changing a flat tire on his car. The tire-changing event includes the actor removing the spare tire and the jack from the trunk of his car, jacking up the car, and replacing the flat tire with the spare. The actor's movements in the course of the tire-changing event and his (inferred) self-commands to movement have no apparent rationale if they are observed in isolation. For instance, the rhythmic up and down gestures of the actor's arms during one phase of the event may be rationalized by an observer only if he recognizes that the arms are operating the handle of the jack and that the flat tire is being raised off of the ground.

More than simply controlling his own movements, an actor controls the character of the event in which one of the participants is himself and the other is the environment. He deems his performance successful if he imposes his intentions on the character of the event. Put another way, an actor has achieved his aim if an observer's description of the event in which the actor participates is synonymous with the actor's description of his intentions.

In sum, an appropriate observational perspective for a theorist includes both the actor and the environment in which he acts. A more limited perspective that excludes or minimizes the environment is likely to remove the means by which an observer can either detect the actor's intent or rationalize aspects of his performance.

B. An Appropriate Level of Description of Events, Actors, and Environment

Events have been promoted as the minimal systems to be observed for the development of an adequate theory of skilled action. Primarily, the grounds for this selection are that no systems smaller than events encompass those entities and functions over which actors exert their control. The same kind of selection criterion may be invoked in a choice of "level of description." Having selected an observational unit, it is necessary to choose a descriptive vocabulary for it. Again, it seems most appropriate to select a grain-size of vocabulary such that its referent entities and functions are those that populate the actor's habitat from his observational perspective, because those are the things with which he deals in the course of his actions.

In the following sections we will select a level of description of an actor and of his habitat. In the case of an actor, our aim is to select a vocabulary that mimics the effective *self*-descriptions putatively invoked by actors as a means of controlling their actions. Similarly, our aim is to select a level of description of the environmental media that is isomorphic with the grain-size of the information detected by actors. Hypothetically, a description of the structured media that captures the significant information for actors is concomitantly a description of the environmental entities and functions that, from the actor's perspective, constitute his habitat (cf. Gibson, 1977; Shaw, McIntyre, & Mace, 1974).

1. The Actor

An actor can be described exhaustively in several ways where each "way" is defined by the primitive entities to which its vocabulary refers. These ways are significantly restricted if we assume that the aim of a theory of coordinated activity is to specify what an actor controls when he performs an act. In this respect, it is not surprising that no one has ever devised a theory of coordinated activity in which the primitive units of vocabulary are the individual cells or molecules of the actor's body.

Presumably two reasons why neither cells nor molecules have been proposed as the primitive entities of a theory of action are, on the one hand, that an actor could not possibly control those microscopic entities and, on the other hand, that even if he could he would not choose to do so. For each cell trajectory he wished to control, an actor would have to provide values for as many as 6 degrees of freedom(df).[2] It is inconceivable that he could continuously set and reset the values of the 6 df of the millions of cells whose state trajectories are regulated in the course of an act.

Even if he could control that many degrees of freedom, to do so would constitute a gross violation of a principle of least effort. The cells in the actor's body are constrained to act as systems of cells. The degrees of freedom of these collectives are orders of magnitude fewer than the summed degrees of freedom of the individual cells in the collectives. A more abstract level of description of an actor than one whose primitive entities are cells captures these constraints on classes of cells by treating each class or collective as an irreducible unit. Thus, "deltoid muscle" refers to a collective of cells that are constrained to act as a unit.

If an actor exploits an abstract level of self-description on which muscles are irreducible units, he indirectly takes care of the vast multitudes of degrees of freedom of his individual cells by directly controlling the many fewer degrees of freedom of collectives of them.

What is more, the "muscular" level of description is less powerful, but in a useful way, than a microscopic level. If an actor were to control his individual cells directly, he could specify values for their trajectories that he could never achieve because they violate the constraints on collectives of cells (e.g., the combined trajectories might entail the disintegration of a muscle). To preclude such violations, the actor would have to know a set of rules for combining cell trajectories. But he can avoid knowing anything about these rules if he selects a more abstract way of describing himself.

We have belabored the obvious point that actors control larger entities than cells and molecules to bring out some reasons why one level of description of an actor may be more useful to a theorist than another. Let us summarize these arguments before suggesting a less obvious point—that a level of description on which muscles are the irreducible units may not be sufficiently coarse-grained to be useful either to an actor or to a theorist.

Some levels of self-description are impossible for an actor to use because they demand that he provide values for vast numbers of degrees of freedom. Relatively macroscopic or abstract levels of self-description help to solve the "degrees of freedom problem" (see Turvey *et al.*, in press) by classifying the entities of the microscopic level and hence their degrees of freedom. The abstract levels provide one label for large numbers of elementary units that are constrained to act as a collective. By controlling the few degrees of freedom of the collective, the actor thereby regulates the many degrees of freedom of the components. The more abstract description is the less powerful one, but it is less powerful in a useful way. It allows the actor to know less of the details of the system that he controls,

---

[2] The 6 df are the values of the instantaneous positions and velocities of a cell on each of the three spatial coordinate axes.

but to regulate it more easily and effectively (cf. Greene, 1969, 1972). Finally, concepts emerge (e.g., "muscles") at a macroscopic level of description that do not exist on microscopic levels because the concepts refer to constraints on, or patternings of, entities that are treated as individuals on a microscopic level (cf. Medawar, 1973; Putnam, 1973).

Several theorists and investigators have proposed that an actor controls *groups* of muscles rather than individual muscles (e.g., Easton, 1972; Turvey, 1977b; Weiss, 1941). Their reasons for preferring the more abstract description of an actor are those given above. An actor *cannot* govern his muscles individually because to specify values for their total number of degrees of freedom would be impractical if relevant cost variables are considered (Shaw & McIntyre, 1974; Turvey *et al.,* in press). Greene (1969) estimates that there are over 40 *df* in the hand, arm, and shoulder alone and dozens more in the trunk, shoulders, and neck. Furthermore, the relationships between a central command to a muscle, the muscle's behavior, and the movements of a limb are indeterminate both physiologically and mechanically (cf. Bernstein, 1967; Grillner, 1975; Hubbard, 1960; Turvey, 1977b). Commands to individual muscles would appear to constitute an inappropriate vocabulary of control for an actor.

Yet, even if an actor could control his individual muscles, there are reasons for believing that he would not choose to do so. First, the actor's muscles are organized into functional collectives. Some collectives, the reflexes, appear to be "prefabricated" (Easton, 1972), but many, those involved in locomotion for instance (e.g., Grillner, 1975; Shik & Orlovskii, 1976), are marshaled temporarily and expressly for the purpose of performing a particular act. There is ample evidence that these systems of muscles that we have called "coordinative structures" (Turvey, 1977b; Turvey *et al.,* in press; Fowler, Note 3) after Easton (1972) are invoked by actors in the performance of large varieties of acts [e.g., speech, see Fowler (Note 3) for a review; locomotion, see Grillner (1975) for a review; swallowing and chewing, see Doty (1968) and Sessle & Hannam (1975)]. The actor's organization of his musculature into coordinative structures that are especially appropriate to the performance of a *limited* class of acts is what we mean when we describe an organism as a general-purpose device by virtue of its capacity to become a variety of special-purpose devices.

The constraints on groups of muscles that organize them into collectives are different in kind from those on some groups of cells—for instance, those that constitute a bone and perhaps those that constitute a muscle. The label "bone" refers to a group of cells constrained to adopt a particular macroscopic form. It seems clear in this case that the constraints have exhausted the *configurational* degrees of freedom of those cells. The result is a rigid body. In contrast, the constraints that yield a coordinative structure appear to be a kind that Pattee (1973) calls "control constraints." Control constraints, like structural constraints, are classifications of the degrees of freedom of elementary components of a system, but they regulate the *trajectories* of a system rather than its configuration. Hence, a coordinative structure is a four-dimensional system that may be identified by what it *does*.

If the actor's vocabulary of self-description or self-control refers to coordinative structures rather than to muscles or, equivalently, if it refers to the control constraints on this musculature, then apparently his descriptions are functional in nature.

A level of self-description on which the coordinative structure constitutes the elemental unit of vocabulary is less powerful than one on which muscles are described, but, again, the loss of power is beneficial to the actor. If muscles are the primitive units of description for the actor, then he can prescribe combinations of muscle contractions that never occur because they violate the constraints on groups of muscles. In the terms of Weiss (1941), the too-microscopic level of description cannot explain why actors limit themselves to coordinated movements and avoid "unorganized convulsions." The macroscopic level allows an actor to exploit the constraints on groups of muscles that putatively limit him to performing coordinated movements.

Finally, on the coarse-grained level of description, concepts or properties emerge (e.g., coordinative structures) that do not exist on the more detailed levels of description. These concepts or properties derive from the constraints on the individual elements of those detailed levels. For instance, the coordinative structures are nested. This property is well documented again for the relatively simple act of locomotion (e.g., Easton, 1972; Grillner, 1975). Each coordinative structure governs an activity. A nested set of coordinative structures may govern a long sequence of movements with little detailed executive control being required of the actor. In fact, the sequence of autonomously generated movements may be indefinitely long (as in walking, chewing, or breathing) if the "repertoire" of the nested coordinative structures regenerates itself cyclically (see Fowler, Note 3).

Since many of the coordinative structures are not "prefabricated," the problem for an actor is to marshal those groups of muscles that will accomplish his purposes. The view of an actor provided by a coarse-grained description of him suggests the forming of relevant coordinative structures as a primary problem of skill acquisition.

2. The Environment in Relation to an Actor

a. Environmental Affordances. A component of an environment populates an actor's world only if the actor can engage in some relationship with it that has significance for him. More simply, the meaning of the component for an actor is captured by specifying the set of events in which the actor and component may participate (cf. Gibson, 1977; Sperry, 1952; Shaw *et al.*, 1974). These potential relationships between actors and environment components are what we called earlier the "affordances" of the components for the actor.

We can provide a different perspective on the concept of "affordance" by re-examining the nature of an event. The character of an event, in particular its functional description, is determined by the totality of the forces exerted by and on the various event participants. Among the forces that shape the character of an event are gravitational forces, which are extrinsic to the actor, and frictional and contact forces, which are generated by the actor's encounter with the environment. In addition to these, there are the forces that enable an actor to regulate the character of an event more directly. They are the forces generated by the actor's own muscular activity.

Clearly, actors cannot achieve an aim to perform an act by generating all of the forces necessary to get the job done. Rather, they must contribute to the totality of extant forces just those muscular forces that will *bend* the character of an event in the desired direction.

By hypothesis, the affordances of an environment for an actor, as given in the structured environmental media, are the sets of forces (of adaptive significance to him) that the actor can generate in collaboration with the extant forces and in relation to the environment. The totality of forces that the actor selects from among the potential ones defines his intent. For a skilled actor, the intent becomes, through his muscular efforts, the functional description of the event.

b. The Structured Media. The structured media, that is, the ambient light and air, etc., apprise actors of the properties of an event; they are said to contain *information about* events in the sense of *specificity to* events.

The media are components of an environment that, relative to other components, are compliant. Thus, for example, when light contacts some surface, the light but not the surface is significantly altered. In particular, the amounts of light reflected from a surface in a given direction and the wavelengths of the light are specific to various properties of the surfaces: the slant of the surface relative to the source of radiant light, its composition, and so on. Hence, the light, on contact with the surface, is *constrained* (or is patterned) in its subsequent behavior by the properties of the surface. Furthermore, the patterning of the rays of light is *specific* to the source of its patterning. Therefore, the structure in the light is isomorphic, though abstractly so, with the properties of the structure's source. Just as an environment is constituted of nestings of entities and functions, a medium contains structures of various grain sizes. But the structure of interest to an actor and to a theorist is only that which is specific to, or isomorphic with, the properties of the *event* in which the actor is participating. The environmental entities and functions that are specified *to an actor* by the structure of a medium are just those whose properties are of adaptive signficance to him.

We believe that this is a crucial observation. The light to an eye is amenable, as is the actor himself, to various levels of descriptions (cf. Mace, 1977). Typically, as Gibson has noted (e.g., 1961), theorists take as their unit of description the individual ray of light, which has only the properties of wavelength and intensity. The individual rays are meaningless to an actor; pursued through his nervous system, they excite receptors on the retina and are transformed into still-meaningless "raw" sensory signals (e.g., Schmidt, 1975). They are supposed to acquire significance only as the actor learns to 'assign meaning to them via the efforts of his community of co-actors who provide him with "knowledge of results."

This view is fostered by a too microscopic level of description of the light and of its neural consequences. In particular, it is too fine-grained to represent what in the light is genuinely informative and significant to an actor, just as the levels of description of an actor in which cells or muscles are the descriptive units are too fine-grained to capture the properties of the muscle systems that actors exploit. That level of description of the light that considers only two variables (intensity and wavelength) fails to capture any of the constraints on the paths, spectral compositions, and intensities of *bundles* of light rays that are specific to (and hence that specify to a perceiver) the environmental sources of the constraints. In contrast, if the sensitivity of perceptual systems is not to the microscopic properties of a structured medium, but rather to the constraints or to the structure itself— that is, to a macroscopic level of description of the medium—then actors need not learn to manufacture a significance for stimulation. The meaning or significance is the set of properties in the environment that structured the light and therefore that are specified by it with reference to an actor.

Other investigators have catalogued some of the information in the structured light available to an actor (e.g., Gibson, 1958, 1961, 1966, 1968; Lee, 1974, 1976; Turvey, 1975, 1977a, 1977b). We provide only a brief description here; but one that is sufficient for our later consideration of the role of higher order variables of stimulation in the control and acquisition of skilled acts.

The patterning of the ambient light to an eye provides an actor with information about (*i*) the layout of environmental surfaces and objects, (*ii*) what is happening in the course of an event, (*iii*) what is about to happen and when it will occur, and (*iv*) the possibilities for control by the actor over what happens. We will consider each in turn.

i. Information about layout provided at a stationary point of observation. The optic array is the set of light rays that reflect off of environmental surfaces and converge at all possible points of observation in the environment (Gibson, 1961). The portions of the array that converge at a single point of observation may be described as a nested set of "visual solid angles" (Gibson, Note 4). A visual solid angle is a closed sector of the array with its apex at the point of observation. It is set off from its neighboring angles by differences from them in the intensity and spectral composition of its component rays of light. Each visual solid angle corresponds to a component of the environment where a component may differ from its neighbors in shape, slant relative to the source of illumination, distance from the observer, and properties of its material composition that determine its spectral and nonspectral reflectance.

Some properties of the environmental correlates of a visual solid angle are specified by the angle's cross-sectional shape, its intensity, and its spectral composition. The borders of an angle typically correspond to the edges of an object in the environment.

Visual solid angles are nested because environmental surfaces and objects are textured. That is, the structure of an environmental surface or object is specified by a corresponding patterning of visual solid angles in the optic array.

More information about structure, as well as information about change, is given in a transforming, rather than a static, optic array.

ii. The structural and functional descriptions of events given by a transforming optic array. According to Pittenger and Shaw (1975), two kinds of information exhaust the information types provided by the structured media of an event. A *structural invariant* is information about shape or, more accurately, about persistent identity, which is preserved across (physical) transformation. A *transformational invariant* is information about physical change, which is preserved across the different structures that may support the change (see also Turvey, 1977a). These two kinds of information provide an actor with an event's structural and functional descriptions.

As an actor moves through an environment, he continually changes his observational perspective on it. If (solely for convenience) we describe this continuous change of perspective as a succession of discrete changes, we may say that the moving observer successively intercepts new observation points as he moves. The optic array at each of these fictitiously abstracted observation points constitutes information about layout of the sort described in the preceding section. The information at one observation point may or may not be sufficient to specify unambiguously to an observer the layout of environmental surfaces and other components relative to him. However, there is only one environmental layout that is consistently possible *across* a set of connected observation points (Gibson, 1966). More accurately, the layout of environmental surfaces that is given in a transforming optic array is just that one layout whose persistent identity is specified throughout the transformation.

A global transformation of the optic array is effected when an actor changes his perspective on the environment. What is invariant (or what has persistent identity) across perspectives is the environmental layout. What changes with observation point is information about the actor's perspective on the environment. That is, a global transformation of the optical structure is effected by the actor's movements and continually provides information on his relationship to the components of the environment. In short, global transformations of the optic array are specific to an observer and to his path through the environment (Lee & Aaronson, 1974; Lee, 1976; Lishman & Lee, 1973; Warren, 1976).

Consider now object motion from a stationary perspective. As an object in the environment changes its location relative to a stationary point of observation, its corresponding visual solid angle in the optic array undergoes transformation. The nature of the changing relationship between observer and observed is specified in part by the nature of the angle's transformation (i.e., by the symmetrical or asymmetrical magnification or reduction of the angle's cross-sectional area). But more than this, it is specified too by the angle's progressive occlusion and disocclusion of those components of the optical structure that correspond to foreground and background components of the environment (Gibson, 1968).

For example, as an object approaches an observer head on, the cross-sectional area of the corresponding visual solid angle at the place of observation expands symmetrically. The bottom or leading edge of the angle progressively occludes foreground optical texture, whereas the top, or trailing edge, disoccludes the optical texture corresponding to the object's background. The lateral edges effect a shearing of optical texture.

Both kinds of transformations (i.e., symmetrical magnification of a visual solid angle and occlusion, disocclusion, and shearing of optical texture) specify motion in a *restricted* part of the environment and, in the absence of additional information that the actor is pulling the object toward him, they specify motion that is due to forces extrinsic to the actor.

iii. The specification of future events. If an actor approaches a barrier or other object head on, the visual solid angle corresponding to it undergoes symmetrical magnification. Its rate of magnification specifies the actor's rate of approach. The fact that the magnification is symmetrical indicates to an appropriately attuned actor that he will collide with the barrier if the current inertial conditions continue. (A nonsymmetrical expansion indicates, depending on the degree of asymmetry, that the actor will bypass the barrier or that he will collide with it to the left or right of its center.) But more than the fact of imminent collision, Schiff (1965) and Lee (1974, 1976) show that the *time to collision* is also specified to an observer by the transforming optical structure.

Thus, the macroscopic patterning of the transforming optic array provides the actor with information about what is currently happening and about *what will* happen if the current conditions persist (cf. Lee, 1976).

iv. The affordance structure of events. Of major importance to an actor attempting to impose his intentions on the character of an event is information that prescribes to him the directions in which his contributions of muscular force can alter the current inertial conditions. To take a simple example, when we say that a surface affords locomotion for an actor, we mean in part that the ambient light (or some other structured medium) specifies to the actor the nature of the reactive forces (the frictional and contact forces) that the surface will supply given his attempts to walk on it. Information about the rigidity of a surface and about its slant and composition is concomitantly information about the surface's potential to participate in an event that includes the actor's walking on it.

This information is only information about walk-on ability in relation to additional information about the actor's somatotype, however. That is, the affordances of a surface (or object) are the events in which the surface and the actor may participate, and they are contingent on the properties of the surface considered not absolutely, but relative to properties of an actor. Hence, to detect the affordances of an environment component, the actor has to detect *body-scaled* information—that is, information about the component's properties relative to his own.

Lee's (1974) analysis of the optical information available to a locomoting observer indicates that information about the position coordinates of objects in the environment and information about the actor's rate and acceleration of movement are provided in units of the observer's own height. Is it possible that information about the actor's general build and perhaps, therefore, about his potential to contribute to the forces governing an event is provided in global transformations of the optic array? When he is walking, there are global transformations due to his sinusoidally shifting center of gravity. The extent of shift in the left–right and up–down directions as well as in the direction of walking may correlate with an actor's size and weight.

These shifts in center of gravity effect rhythmic changes in the horizontal and vertical distance of the actor's head from components of the ground plane. Hence, the actor effects a transformation of optical structure that is specific to his rhythmically changing perspective on the environment. If the transformation in turn is specific to the actor's somatotype, it also provides information about his potential to contribute muscular force to an event.

C. Concluding Remarks: Increasing Controllable Degrees of Freedom so as to Secure Certain Reactive Forces

We began by selecting an observational domain for a theory of skilled action, which we labeled an "event." We considered events to be the minimal observational domains that include, on the one hand, all of the entities and functions over which actors exert their control and, on the other hand, the entities and functions that are regulative of actors. Following that, we selected compatible descriptive vocabularies for the different components of an event. Our selections are more coarse-grained than the vocabularies typically adopted by theorists of skilled action. We defended them on the grounds that it is precisely the *patternings over* microscopic entities and functions that are signified to actors and not the microscopic components themselves.

Our method of selecting the descriptive vocabularies was one that fractionated the event into its components. We will conclude this section of the chapter by reconstructing the event concept and by describing one way in which it enriches a developing theory of skilled action and skill acquisition.

One orientation to coordinated activity, as cited above, is that acts are produced through the fitting together of autonomous subsystems (coordinative structures), each of which "solves" a limited aspect of the action problem. In this orientation, the actor's plan, that is, his abstract self-description, is regarded as the specification of that which remains when the contribution of the autonomous subsystems is subtracted out. The action plan supplies the coordination that is not supplied by the coordinative structures.

Precisely what is it that coordinative structures supply? One answer might be that they autonomously supply certain relations among various parts of the body. The difficulty with this answer is that, left unqualified, it steers dangerously close to an "air theory" formulation of coordinated activity in which the actor, for all intents and purposes, is construed as being suspended in a vacuum, oblivious to external environmental forces. An "air theory" formulation speaks more to the *miming* of coordinated activity than to coordinated activity itself, for coordinated activity requires environmental support for its proper functioning.

Necessarily, an event perspective expresses the contribution of the environment to coordination. Coordination in the event perspective is defined not in terms of biokinematic relationships (which would be so if the actor were taken as the unit of analysis) but in terms of relationships among forces, those forces supplied muscularly by the actor and those supplied reactively and otherwise by the environment. The surfaces of support, the participating structures (such as other actors, striking implements, etc.), the biokinematic links, and gravity provide the actor with a large potential of reactive forces. This emphasis on what the environment provides characterizes the event perspective as a "ground theory" formulation of coordinated activity: An activity cannot logically be separated from its environmental support.

Consider environmental surfaces. These afford reactive forces that are opposite and approximately equal (although not always equal—it depends on the composition of the surface) to the forces generated by muscle activity. Thus, in walking, the actor secures by his muscular efforts reactive forces that propel the body forward at one moment and restrain the forward motion of the trunk at the next. In leaping a high barrier, the actor applies his muscular forces in such a fashion as to secure reactive forces that are more nearly vertical than horizontal.

Of course, when the actor is not in contact with a supporting surface but is moving in the air, then the equal and opposite reaction to a motion of parts of the body occurs within the body itself. Swiftly moving the arm at shoulder level from a sideward to a forward position will rotate the body about its longitudinal axis in the direction of the moving arm. This aside bears significantly on the contrast between the actor/air theory formulation and the event/ground theory formulation in that the same movement performed when the body is in the air and when it is in contact with a rigid surface secures very different reactive forces with very different coordinative consequences.

Consider biokinematic chains. These obey the principles of kinematic chains in general; for example, a controlled movement of one link of the chain will be accompanied by relatively uncontrolled movements in the other, passive links of the chain. Obviously, for a biokinematic chain such as an arm or a leg, muscular forces are not the only forces acting on the chain; besides gravity, there are the kinetic energies and moments of force that necessarily accompany movements of the individual links.

A further and related principle of kinematic chains is that the design of a chain—the lengths and masses of its links, the manner of their joining, and the degrees of freedom of the joints—determines the kinds of curves that the chain can trace out over time. Now an actor can modify the design of a biokinematic chain, and therefore its potential trajectories, in a very simple way: He can selectively freeze the degrees of freedom and vary the range of joint movement. The significance of this is that, for any desired trajectory of a limb, elaborate control on the part of the actor—even moment-to-moment computation—may be needed to secure the trajectory given one "design" of the limb yet very little computation may be needed given another, very different "design." The point is that, with an appropriate design, the reactive forces that are concomitant to movement of the chain as a whole may contribute significantly to the production of the trajectory, but with an inappropriate design the reactive forces that accompany the chain's movement may contribute little to the desired trajectory and may even oppose it.

In this regard, consider the emergence of an effective sidearm strike pattern (hitting a baseball) in preschool children. The development of the skill is realized through the following changes: a more liberal swing due to an increase in the range of motion of the participating joints, increasing usage of the forward step or forward weight shift to initiate the strike pattern, and increasing pelvic and trunk rotation prior to the swing of the arms (in the earliest stages of acquisition pelvic and trunk rotations occur as a result of the strike, with the pattern being initiated by the arm motion). One way of looking at these changes is that they index transformations in the "design" of biokinematic chains. The two arms, coupled at the bat, constitute a biokinematic chain whose design is made more effective for the task by increased uncocking of the wrists and greater flexion at the elbows. The body as a whole is a biokinematic chain, the design of which is made more effective for striking by adding the degrees of freedom of trunk rotation and pelvic rotation. To paraphrase our remarks above, a more effective design of a limb or a body is one in which the reactive forces concomitant to movement are largely responsible for the achievement of the desired trajectory.

Another way of looking at these changes, however, observes that an actor, naive to a particular skill, curtails biokinematic degrees of freedom—through the complete immobilization of some joints that are used when the skill is performed expertly and a restriction on the range of motion of other joints—because he or she lacks a means of controlling the biokinematic degrees of freedom in the manner that the skill demands. It then follows that increasing expertise is indexed by a gradual raising of the ban on degrees of freedom (to borrow Bernstein's most apt phrase). To put it slightly differently, increasing the number of *controllable* biokinematic degrees of freedom is synonymous with becoming more expert. As Bernstein (1967) remarks: "The coordination of movement is the process of mastering redundant degrees of freedom of the moving organ, in other words its conversion to a controllable system [p. 127]."

In short, the changes indexing the acquisition of the batting skill can be interpreted in at least two ways: in one, as the converting of biokinematic degrees of freedom into controllable systems (coordinative structures) and, in the other, as the designing of biokinematic chains so as to secure certain reactive forces. But surely these two interpretations are dual. By increasing the controllable degrees of freedom, the actor increases the potential variability of reactive forces that accompany the activity, thereby increasing the opportunity to discover what the activity-relevant reactive forces might afford by way of control. In the discovery of activity-relevant reactive forces the actor prescribes the conversion of redundant degrees of freedom into controllable systems.

Let us summarize the tenor of these remarks. On the "air theory" formulation of coordinated activity an executive must supply that control that the coordinative structures do not supply. On the "ground theory" formulation an actor must supply that control that the external force field does not supply. In a blend of the two formulations we can say that, in the performance of an athletic skill, coordinative structures are organized so as to secure certain reactive forces; by the felicitous organization of coordinative structures the actor *bends* the force function that is given to yield the force function that is desired. In the grain-size of analysis prescribed by the event perspective, it is neither muscles nor joints that are coordinated in the performance of athletic skill, but forces—those supplied by the actor and those supplied by the environment.

IV. On Converting Biokinematic Free Variables into a Controllable System

In this section we address the question of how an actor forms a controllable system, in Bernstein's (1967) terms, or a coordinative structure, in our terms. In the description of the actor developed in Section III it was concluded that an act is more optimally described in terms of autonomous collectives of free variables than in terms of the free variables themselves, that is, the individual muscles or joints. To lay the groundwork for the analysis that follows, we identify three aspects of the problem of forming such collectives. These aspects are described abstractly; they are, however, reasonably intuitive. Moreover, they may be considered as fundamental aspects of all coordinative problems and we will attempt to show how they relate closely to the summary remarks of Section II.

A. Three Intuitions Relating to Action Problems

First, we believe that in a general but nontrivial sense the problem of forming a coordinative structure or controllable system may be characterized, in part, in the following fashion. Given an aggregate of relatively independent biokinematic degrees of freedom, how can the aggregate be so constrained and the individual degrees of freedom so harnessed as to produce a particular, simple change in a particular single variable ? [3] Thus, for example, to minimize the displacement of the point of intersection of the line of aiming with the target, experienced marksmen constrain the joints of the weapon arm in such a fashion that the horizontal displacements of the individual kinematic links are reciprocally related (a form of constraint that is not at the disposal of the novice) (Arutyunyan, Gurfinkel, & Mirskii, 1968, 1969). To paraphrase this description, we may say, therefore, that the problem of forming a coordinative structure or controllable system is, in part, the problem of discovering the relevant constraint for or, in a somewhat different vernacular, the equivalence class of optimal combinations of (Greene, 1969) a collection of many (fine-grained) variables, such as individual joints, that will realize the actor's intentions with regard to a particular (coarse-grained) variable, such as a limb trajectory.

One easily appreciates that during the acquisition of a skill the fine-grained variables do not present themselves in precisely the same way every time. The specific details, that is, the initial conditions of the fine-grained variables, are not standardized. Nevertheless, the actor must select, on each occasion of the problem, one combination of the variables from the set of all possible combinations; ideally, on each successive occasion the combination selected should approximate more closely the desired objective.

It is often remarked that the felicitous solution of problems of coordination is made possible by "knowledge of results" identified as information about whether an attempted solution (say, a particular movement) was right or wrong (qualitative knowledge of results) and, if wrong, by how much (quantitative knowledge of results). Thus, Adams (1976a) comments: "The human learning of motor movement is based on knowledge of results, or information about error in responding. Knowledge of results can be coarse, like 'Right' or 'Wrong,' or it can be fine grain, like 'You moved 2.5 inches too long' [p. 216]." In our view, this is a gratuitous claim. In the general case, information about degree of nearness to a desired outcome will be insufficient informational support for arriving at a solution to the coordination problem. Let us elaborate.

We identify the general case as discovering an optimal organization of, or constraint for, a number of free biokinematic variables. The argument can be made—

---

[3] We owe this manner of describing controllable systems to Pattee (e.g., 1970, 1973). He considers the existence of control constraints an essential and distinguishing property of a living system.

consonant with the jigsaw puzzle metaphor—that for a system with η biokinematical degrees of freedom there ought to be at least η degrees of freedom in the information that supports the control of that system (Turvey et al., in press). These informational degrees of freedom can be most usefully understood as degrees of constraint (Turvey et al., in press). We can suppose, therefore, that discovering an optimal relation on η free-varying biokinematic degrees of freedom requires that at least η degrees of constraint be available perceptually. We may hypothesize that, *in general, the ease and probability of discovering an optimal organization (that is, learning) relate directly to the extent to which degrees of constraint match degrees of freedom.*

Now, in discrete movement tasks (e.g., Trowbridge & Cason, 1932), the actor must learn to move a limb or a limb segment a fixed distance. It is not difficult to imagine that in the acquisition of such simple tasks the actor freezes all of the free variables (joints) but one; that is, the actor manipulates a single biokinematic degree of freedom. The quantitative knowledge of results about how closely the movement approximated the desired distance is one degree of constraint that matches the one degree of freedom of the movement. Hence, in this case, quantitative knowledge of results is sufficient informational support for learning (see Adams, 1971). However, in the acquisition of an activity involving the regulation of more than one biokinematic degree of freedom, the single degree of constraint provided by quantitative knowledge of results would be inadequate. The fundamental point is this: Quantitative knowledge of results specifies, in a limited sense, what *not* to do next, but, significantly, it does not specify *what* to do next. The novice golfer who putts 2 m to the right of the hole sees that he has erred, but this information, *in and of itself,* cannot tell him *how* to change the organization of his biokinematic free variables so as to err less on the next occasion. If quantitative knowledge of results were the only source of constraint on selecting combinations of biokinematic free variables, then we may suppose that the search for the optimum combination would be essentially blind (that is, the combinations would be chosen at random) and, in principle, the search could proceed indefinitely.

A remedy to the inadequacy of quantitative knowledge of results is suggested by the two remaining notions. On the acceptance of the actor as a special-purpose problem solver, Gel'fand and Tsetlin (1962, 1971) asked what it is that might characterize, in general, the problems posed to the actor so that he might bring to bear *specialized* search procedures, tailor-made (presumably in the course of evolution) for such problems. They suggest that the actor might operate on the tacit assumption that the problems he encounters are *well organized* in the sense (a) that the variables indigenous to a problem may be partitioned into essential (intensive) and nonessential (extensive) variables and (b) that a variable is consistently a member of one or the other class. Given the assumption that the problem is well organized, the actor can successfully apply a certain method of search through the space of constraints (for Gel'fand and Tsetlin it is the ravine method, which is described below). The actor initiates the specialized search method ignorant of the actual pattern of organization of the problem, and it is only in the course of the search that the pattern is disclosed (Gel'fand & Tsetlin, 1962).

Our second intuition, therefore, is that in a general but nontrivial sense each and every problem confronting the skill acquirer may be characterized as follows. *With reference to the objective,* there is an organization defined on the participating elements. The organization may be described as a function that is preserved invariantly over changes in the specific values of its variables. We will speak, therefore, of the *organizational invariant* of a coordination problem. An invariant may be usefully defined for our purposes as *information about* something, in the sense of *specificity to* that something, that is preserved over relevant transformations (see Gibson, 1966; Shaw, McIntyre, & Mace, 1974). By implication, the style of change imposed by an actor on the aggregate of variables is significant to the determination (detection) of the organizational invariant; put bluntly, not all classes of change will reveal the organizational invariant (see Footnote 6).

The third intuition relates to the issue of how a search through combinations of many variables may be guided. Whatever we imagine the search method to be, it must necessarily be the case that the successive "experiments" conducted on the variables exploit information realized by the experiments. Our third intuition, therefore, is that in a general but nontrivial sense there is avaiable to the actor seeking to solve a coordination problem information that specifies, relatively precisely, what to do next. We believe that such information may often take the form of abstract relations defined over variables of stimulation over time and that becoming attuned to such information is part of the solution, developing at a rate equal to that of the isolating of the organizational invariant.

Let us relate these three essential components of the problem of acquiring a controllable system to the concluding remarks of Section II as follows.

1. An actor learns to make of himself a "special-purpose device" designed optimally for the task at hand. He does so by discovering an appropriate organization of his musculature, which differs for different acts (e.g., walking versus swimming). Several sets of muscle organizations may suffice to get a given job done, but some may be more efficient than others. That is, for example, an actor learns to swim before he learns to swim skillfully. Following the work of Gel'fand and Tsetlin (1962, 1971) cited earlier, we suppose that species have evolved special strategies for selecting the most harmonious organization of muscle systems among the restricted set of possible ones. Thus, the idea of the actor as a special-purpose device applies not only to the individual actor acquiring a particular skill, but also to the class of actors acquiring any skilled act. At this more coarse-grained level of description, any problem of skilled action may be described in part as a problem of optimizing a function of several variables (see above).

2. The skill to be acquired may be described as a set of potential constraints on

the character of an event (as an organizational invariant). These constraints set boundary conditions on the possible muscle organizations that the actor can invoke to achieve his performance aims. Therefore, the actor's discovery of the organizational regularities of a task vastly simplifies his search for an optimal self-organization.

3. The efforts of a novice to perform an act may be viewed in part as discovery or search tactics aimed at revealing the organizational structure of the task.

B. The Experimental Task

The task that we have been investigating was designed by Krinskiy and Shik (1964). A subject is seated before a scale and he is instructed to make the scale indicator point to zero. He controls the indicator position in this way: Two of his joint angles (typically his elbow joints) are monitored continuously. The values of the two angles are input to a computer, which transforms them according to the mapping $E = |x - y - (a - b)| + \alpha|x - a| + \alpha|y - b|$; x and y are variables that take on the values of the joint angles each time they are sampled, and a, b, and α are parameters that are changed across, but not within, experiments or trials. The equation controls the needle position on the scale. That is, the needle position corresponds in some simple way to E. The subject can make the needle on the scale go to zero by finding the angles of his joints for which the mapping takes on the value $E = 0$. The needle points to zero when the subject has minimized the mapping.

The subject is unaware of the specific nature of the control that he has over the needle. He knows that by changing his joint angles he changes the needle position, but he does not know that his joint angles are the x and y coordinates of some mapping whose output corresponds to the position of the scale indicator. The starting position of the subject's joint angles may be varied or kept the same over trials. The target values (the values of his joint angles at which the function is minimized) also may be varied or maintained over trials.

Krinskiy and Shik provide a limited quantity of data in the form of graphs depicting the solution strategies of their subjects. Sample graphs are shown in Figure 3. The x-axis represents the value of one elbow-joint angle and the y-axis the value of the other. A diagonal line on the graph represents simultaneous changes of the joint angles on the part of the subject, whereas horizontal or vertical lines represent a change in just one angle. (That the rates of change of the two joint angles are the same is indicated by the slopes of the lines in Figures 3; the slopes are approximately equal to unity.) As the subjects approach the solution they begin changing the values of the two joint angles individually.

Although the minimization task may seem an artificial one, it does have the essential components of a problem of skill acquisition that we have outlined. First, the equal velocities of the movement of the two forearms suggest an or-

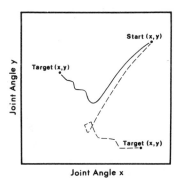

Figure 3. Exemplary solution strategies for two Krinskiy and Shik problems. The starting coordinates represent the angles of the subject's joints at the outset of the task and the target coordinates represent the values that minimize the function.

ganization of the subject's musculature that spans both joints (see Kots & Syrovegin, 1966). In addition, an attractive property of the task for the purposes of investigation is that its organizational invariant is known to the investigator. [It is the mapping $E = |x - y - (a - b)| + \alpha|x - a| + \alpha|y - b|$.] However, it is not known to the subject until his own movements reveal it to him as a lawful, though complex, relationship between the changes of his joint angles and the movement of the needle on the scale. Apparently when the actor has learned the task, he controls the performance of a muscle system. He does so, we will suggest, by detecting the higher-order properties of optical stimulation that prescribe what he should do next given his aim to set the scale indicator to zero.

A final attractive property of the task is that it engages the subject in a search for the minimum of a function of several variables. In this regard, it mimics a task that Gel'fand and Tsetlin (1962, 1971; see also Gel'fand, Gurfinkel, Tsetlin, & Shik, 1971, pp. 329–345) argue is characteristic of muscle systems as they seek a maximally harmonious self-organization. An organization of muscle systems that is maximally harmonious may be one in which the activities governed by the different muscle systems do not compete. If we represent the interactions among the muscle systems as variables, then the search for a harmonious self-organization may be conceptualized as the search for the minmum of a function that encompasses the variables. Gel'fand and Tsetlin suggest that a set of search tactics has evolved, which they call ravine tactics, that are tailored to this kind of optimization task, although they may be ill-suited to other ones. We will describe these search tactics in Section E. Here we merely note that the task of Krinskiy and Shik may not be, in fact, an artificial one for an actor to engage in. Indeed, it was devised to assess whether or not actors employ ravine tactics when given a task for which the tactics are especially suited.

Our contribution to the investigation of the minimization task has been to ask how a subject might learn to solve it efficiently. We have done so by modeling, with the aid of a computer, a skilled performer of the task. Instead of modeling directly the superficial properties of the strategy depicted in Figure 3, we attempted more simply to design a model that could perform the task without invoking blind or random search tactics. Our model uses a strategy that in its superficial properties is similar to the one depicted in Figure 3. The model initially changes both angles at a constant equal rate and, as it nears the target values, changes the angles individually. However, it adopts this way of doing the task as a by-product of a deeper strategy, which is to exploit the higher-order variables of optical stimulation offered by the changes in the scale indicator over time, in preference to the relatively uninformative value E given by the instantaneous needle position.

Before looking at this model, it is instructive to look at one that evidently cannot perform the task without invoking random search tactics. (Hence, the model never becomes a skilled performer.) This latter model is of interest because it is the model of Powers (1973) and it is consistent with the models of closed-loop motor performance proposed, for instance, by Adams (1971, 1976b) and described by Greenwald (1970).

By showing that a model consistent with these theories cannot solve the task in a plausible way, we do not mean to imply that actors never use quantitative knowledge of results (here the value E) to regulate their motor performances. Indeed, the results cited by Adams (1971) and by Greenwald (1970) suggest this as a potent source of information in the acquisition of some skilled movements. We only wish to propose that actors are flexible and can adapt their acquisition strategies, within limits, to the useful dimensions of information provided by a particular problem.

We have selected the model of an actor/perceiver developed by Powers (1973) to serve as a prototypical model of closed-loop motor performance. This and other models of closed-loop performance evidently are general-purpose devices by virtue of having a single general-purpose acquisition strategy. We will show that the strategy is inappropriate to the solution of the task devised by Krinskiy and Shik, and we will suggest that its inapplicability extends to any skilled performance in which higher-order variables of stimulation provide the useful and controlling dimensions of information to an actor.

C. A Model of Closed-Loop Motor Control: Powers, 1973

For Powers, the nervous system of an actor/perceiver may be characterized as a hierarchy of control systems. Figure 4 depicts the structure of an individual control system. Each system works to realize a particular *perceptual* state of affairs and it accomplishes its aim in the way that a mechanical homeostatic device does. Its intent (its intended perceptual state of affairs) constitutes a reference

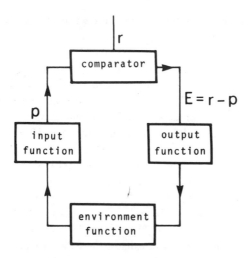

Figure 4. An individual control system.

signal r for the system. That signal is compared periodically with the actual perceptual state of affairs, p. Both sources of information to the control system, the reference signal and the perceptual signal, are conceptualized as quantities, in particular, as rates of neural firing.

The two quantities r and p are subtracted in a comparator and the difference constitutes an error signal E. If the value of E is nonzero, it is transformed into an output signal, or correction procedure, which effects changes in the environment of the control system. (E constitutes the address in memory of a stored correction procedure.) In turn, the environmental changes alter the perceptual input to the control system in the direction of the reference signal. If the actual and intended perceptual states of affairs are the same, $E = 0$, and the control system has achieved its intent.

A condition for the successful performance of the model is that an error signal must correspond in a one-to-one or in a nearly one-to-one way with an appropriate correction procedure. That is, an error signal must specify what needs to be done to nullify it. Apparently this condition is met in the positioning tasks investigated by Adams (1971) and in the line drawing tasks of Trowbridge and Cason (1932). In these tasks, when the experimenter provides quantitative knowledge of results, the subject is given information that specifies what he must do to rectify his error. Similarly, in the tracking tasks described by Powers (1973), the perceived difference in location between a target spot of light and a cursor specifies what must be done to close the gap.

However, the condition is not met in the minimization task of Krinskiy and Shik. In that experiment, the error signal E does not specify to the subject what he must do to correct it. To take just one example, consider the values of E when *a, b,* and *α,* the parameters of the mapping, are set to 15, 10, and 0.2, respectively. The mapping is minimized when $x = a = 15$ and $y = b = 10$. Table I gives a set of values of *x* and *y* for which the error signal is invariantly 6. In the first case, the joint angle corresponding to the value of *y* is at its target position. For the joint angle corresponding to the variable *x* to reach its target position of 15, *x* has to be increased in value by 5. Hence, the correction procedure that is stored in a memory location whose address is $E = 6$ should specify no change in the variable *y* and an increase of 5 units in the value of *x.* However, this correction procedure is inappropriate to all of the other cases listed in Table I. To correct an error of 6 when $x = 12$ and $y = 12$, for instance, *x* has to be increased in value by 3 and *y* decreased by 2. To correct an error of 6 when $x = 15$ and $y = 15$, *x* has to remain unaltered and *y* has to be decreased in value by 5. To correct an error of 6 when $x = 18$ and $y = 8$, *x* has to be *decreased* by 3 and *y* increased by 2. Finally, when $x = 30$ and $y = 25$, both have to be decreased in value by 15. These examples do not exhaust the ways in which an error of 6 can be obtained, nor is 6 the only ambiguous error signal.

In short, for the cases presented in Table I, different correction procedures appropriately correspond to the same error signal of 6. The quantitative knowledge of results that the error signal provides gives little or no information about how it can be nullified; hence, knowledge of results in this task is of limited utility to a subject. On the other hand, ΔE, the velocity of the moving needle on the scale, does provide useful information to a subject, as we will show. However, ΔE information is provided only over successive movements of the actor and over successive loops around the control system, and the individual control system of the kind that Powers describes uses only the current value of *E* to guide its behavior.

Table I
Some Ways of Obtaining an Error of 6 in the Mapping
$$E = |x - y - (15 - 10)| + 0.2|x - 15| + 0.2|y - 10|$$

Component of the mapping			Correction procedure	
x	*y*	*E*	*x*	*y*
10	10	6	$x = x + 5$	
11	11	6	$x = x + 4$	$y = y - 1$
12	12	6	$x = x + 3$	$y = y - 2$
13	13	6	$x = x + 2$	$y = y - 3$
14	14	6	$x = x + 1$	$y = y - 4$
15	15	6		$y = y - 5$
18	8	6	$x = x - 3$	$y = y + 2$
17	7	6	$x = x - 2$	$y = y + 3$
16	6	6	$x = x - 1$	$y = y + 4$
15	5	6		$y = y + 5$
30	25	6	$x = x - 15$	$y = y - 15$

Powers' model and other closed-loop models appear to exclude the use of higher-order relationships that are revealed over relatively long stretches of time between the movements of the actor and their optical or other perceptual concomitants. Furthermore, we can show that the ambiguity, and therefore uninformativeness, of quantitative knowledge of results is not peculiar to the task of Krinskiy and Shik. Instead, it is general to most complex tasks, particularly if the tasks are considered to be performed by a *hierarchy* of closed-loop systems.

D. Quantitative Knowledge of Results is Equivocal in Hierarchial Closed-Loop Systems

In the model of Powers, the nervous system is a nested set of control systems of which only the lowest-level (first-order) systems are in direct contact with the environment. The first-order systems extract information about intensity of stimulation at the receptors. More abstract properties of stimulation (for instance, its form or temporal properties) are constructed by the second- to ninth-order systems based on the first-order perceptual signals. Each superordinate system receives input from several systems on the next level down. It combines these data according to some linear transformation that is peculiar to it. The outcome of the linear transformation is a higher-order property of the stimulus input than had been extracted by any of the subordinate systems.[4]

At every level of the system, perceptual signals are subtracted from reference signals, the latter representing an intended perceptual state of affairs. The resulting error signal constitutes the address of a stored correction procedure. For a first-order system, the correction procedure effects real changes in the environment

---

[4] Powers' claim is not unlike that of feature-based theories of visual perception. It is that the abstract, higher-order properties of the world are constructed (rather than being detected) by perceptual systems. The raw material for the constructions are lower-order, primitive properties of the world, which perceptual systems detect directly. This claim is in contrast to that of Gibson (1966) and others (e.g., Turvey, 1977a). Gibson holds that any properties of a world that an organism *perceives*, however abstract they may be, are detected by him directly.

We should point out an apparent flaw in Powers' and the feature-based views. Consider a perceptual system that has detected *n* primitive elements and that is now given the task of constructing a higher-order percept from them. Even if the domain of possible combinations of the *n* primitive elements is confined to those in two space and to ordinal relationships among them, there are *n!* possible organizations of the elements. If we expand the domain to include the third spatial dimension and if we assign significance to the distances between elements, the number of possible organizations of the *n* primitives must escalate dramatically. Powers' theory has to endow an organism with the means of selecting the single *actual* organization of the elements out of the potentially astronomical number of possibilities. A theory can avoid endowing an organism with this mystical ability if it recognizes that the sector of the world being observed gives these hypothetical primitives only one organization. A plausible proposal is that the observer *detects* the abstract properties themselves rather than having to build them out of a number of primitives.

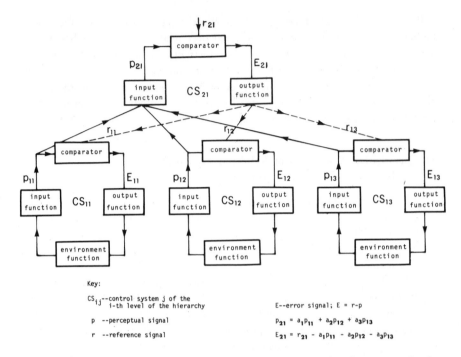

Figure 5. A stack of control systems: three first-order systems nested under one second-order system.

of the actor. However, the correction procedures of the higher-order control systems constitute reference signals for lower-order systems. That is, higher-order systems effect changes in the world only indirectly by changing the reference signals of lower-order systems.

It is easy to show that error signals must almost invariably be ambiguous with respect to their appropriate correction procedures in a hierarchical model of this sort. Figure 5 demonstrates this with a two-tiered nervous system.

Consider a nervous system composed of three first-order systems (CS_{11}, CS_{12}, and CS_{13}) and one second-order system (CS_{21}). Each first-order system supplies CS_{21} with a perceptual signal. According to the model, the perceptual signal of the second-order system p_{21} is a linear transformation of the three first-order perceptual signals p_{11}, p_{12}, and p_{13}. Thus, $p_{21} = a_1p_{11} + a_2p_{12} + a_3p_{13}$. That signal is subtracted from the reference signal r_{21} of the second-order system. The result, $E = r_{21} - a_1p_{11} - a_2p_{12} - a_3p_{13}$, is the error signal of the second-order system. It constitutes the address of a stored correction procedure that will provide the reference signals r_{11}, r_{12}, and r_{13} of the first-order systems.

For concreteness, consider an error signal, $E = 6$. There are many possible combinations of values for r_{21}, p_{11}, p_{12}, and p_{13} that might yield a value of 6 even if some boundaries are set on the possible ranges of values that each might take on. The error signal might be entirely due to an error of one of the first-order systems, or it could be due to various combinations of pairs of first-order systems, or it could be one of many combinations of errors on the part of all three first-order systems.

Quantitative knowledge of results must rarely be informative in a hierarchical closed-loop system because, typically, there is a one-to-many mapping between an error signal and the conditions that may have provoked it. We can conclude from that, perhaps, that the actor/perceiver is not appropriately characterized as a hierarchy of control systems at least when he is performing tasks in which he must exploit the abstract information putatively extracted by the superordinate levels of the system.

The closed-loop model of Powers characterizes the actor as an inflexible general-purpose device. Let us turn now to a different type of model that purports to govern only a limited class of activities. Its performance strategy is tailored to the special features of that limited class of acts but is inappropriate to activities outside of that class. The model that performs the minimization task characterizes just one among the many special-purpose devices that an actor can become depending on his performance aims.[5]

E. Searching the Two-Variable Space: The Ravine Method

For Gel'fand and Tsetlin (1962, 1971), a strategy that is tailored to the minimization problems of muscle systems is the ravine method. It combines local and nonlocal search tactics and thereby avoids the tendency of strictly local search methods to be deceived by local minima of a search space.

The method works in the following way. A local search strategy is selected. [In the problem of Krinskiy & Shik (1964) the actor selects some way of altering the values of his joint angles.] The strategy is maintained until the value $\Delta E/E$ reaches some preselected lower bound. A small value of $\Delta E/E$ implies that the current strategy has reached a point of diminishing returns. When the criterial $\Delta E/E$ is attained for the first time, the actor alters his strategy randomly. The new strategy is maintained until $\Delta E/E$ again reaches its criterial value. The next strategy shift (ravine step) is selected based on which of the previous two was the more successful in approximating the function's minimum. The ravine step is taken in a direction that is nearer to whichever of the first two strategies was the

---

[5] We should point out that the current model is of a skilled performer of the task. An aim of our preliminary efforts was to characterize the state toward which a novice is working. By establishing the ways in which a skilled performer coordinates the movements of his limbs in relation to the variables of stimulation provided him by the scale indicator, we can specify the variables of stimulation to which the novice must become sensitive if he is to learn to perform the task skillfully. Clearly the discovery tactics of the novice must be such that they reveal that organizational invariant (that is, the invariant relationship between what he does and what he sees).

more successful. The procedure is continued until the minimum is reached.

This optimization procedure exploits the special properties of those multivariable functions that, according to Gel'fand and Tsetlin, characterize the muscle systems of an actor. (One special property is that the mapping is "well organized" in the sense described above.) The form of the search methods used by the subjects of Krinskiy and Shik and depicted in Figure 3 is compatible with the hypothesis that they use ravine tactics.

A similar search procedure is also compatible with the graphs in Figure 3. We devised this latter procedure initially as a way of translating the principles of the ravine method, expressed as a set of computational procedures by Gel'fand and Tsetlin, into a set of principles of joint-angle movement that could be implemented by an actor. In doing so, we discovered information provided by the scale indicator that may be more useful to a performer of the task than is $\Delta E/E$. The final model that we will describe rarely shifts its search strategy blindly as that of Gel'fand and Tsetlin does on the first ravine step. It avoids having to do so by exploiting maximally the information provided by the values ΔE and $\Delta(\Delta E)$, the velocity, and the acceleration of the scale indicator. These properties of the event in which the performer participates prescribe to him what he should do next given his performance aims.

F. Searching the Two-Variable Space: Sensitivity to Rate of Change and Rate of Rate of Change

The model is instantiated as a computer program that has eight possible strategies of joint-angle movement available. Four strategies change both joint angles simultaneously and the other four change just one of the angles. The four strategies of simultaneous movement are to increment both angles, decrement both, increment the angle corresponding to the variable x and to decrement y, and to decrement x and increment y. The four strategies of the second type are to increment or decrement x or y.

On each pass, the program alters the value of x and/or of y in the direction dictated by its current muscular organization—that is, by its choice of movement strategy. The two joints are potentially a single coordinative structure; hence, it is simplest for the model/performer to move his two forearms at the same rate.

After altering the values of x and y by equivalent amounts on each pass, the new value of E is computed. If $E = 0$, the program halts because the function has been minimized. If E is nonzero, the values of ΔE (the current value of E subtracted from its previous value) and of $\Delta(\Delta E)$ (the current value of ΔE subtracted from its previous value) are computed. These higher-order properties of the moving scale indicator provide a fairly rich source of information to the model, which uses it to guide its next step.

1. The Information Provided by ΔE.

Let us look separately at the three components of the organizational invariant $E \doteq |x - y - (a - b)| + \alpha|x - a| + \alpha|y - b|$ as a way of seeing how the various higher-order variables of stimulation specify to a skilled performer what he is to do next. The first component of the mapping $C_1 = |x - y - (a - b)|$ is least useful because its contribution to the movement of the needle on the scale provides "proprioceptive" information primarily and little information about whether or not the movement strategy is working. In contrast, $C_2 = \alpha|x - a|$ and $C_3 = \alpha|y - b|$ provide "exteroceptive" information; the coefficients, α, of C_2 and C_3 are different from that of C_1, and therefore their contribution to the value of ΔE can be distinguished from the contribution of C_1.

Table II provides some examples of the information provided by ΔE. Six cases are represented in the table. Three correspond to a movement strategy in which the performer increments the values of both joint angles and three correspond to a strategy in which he increments x and decrements y. The remaining strategies of simultaneous movement may be observed by reading the cases from bottom to top. For each strategy, in one instance represented in the table, the strategy is correct for both joint angles (1a and 2a in Table II). That is, both angles are approaching their target values. (In the examples given, the target values are $x = 15$ and $y = 10$.) In a second instance (1b and 2b), the strategy is appropriate for x, but not for y, and in the last instance (1c and 2c) it is appropriate for neither. The first component of the mapping, $C_1 = |x - y - (a - b)|$, contributes a value of 0 to the scale-indicator velocity (ΔE), if both joint angles are incrementing or if both are decrementing (1a–c in Table II). It contributes a value of 2 (more generally, twice the value of the coefficient of C_1) if one angle is being incremented and one decremented (2a–c). Thus, the proprioceptive information that the subject obtains from the scale indicator tells him whether or not his joint angles are moving in parallel. The *sign* of the contribution of C_1 to ΔE (that is, the direction of needle movement) provides general information about whether or not the current strategy is working to make the needle point to zero.

The other two components of the mapping, $C_2 = \alpha|x - a|$ and $C_3 = \alpha|y - b|$, contribute exterospecific information to the value ΔE. Independently of the particular movement strategy that the performer has adopted, they contribute values to ΔE that are different depending on whether neither joint angle, just one joint angle, or both joint angles are approaching the target. If both angles are approaching their targets (1a and 2a in the table), C_2 and C_3 contribute a value of -2α. When one angle is moving toward its target (1b and 2b), then the contribution of C_2 and C_3 is zero because one contributes α and the other $-\alpha$. The contributions of C_2 and C_3 can be distinguished from that of C_1 because their coefficients are different from the coefficient of C_1 (here $\alpha = 0.2$).

Let us briefly consider an example that illustrates how the value of ΔE can guide the movements of a skilled performer of the task. If the value of ΔE is 2,

Table II
Information Provided by Scale-Indicator Velocity, ΔE

Pass through the computer program	x	y	C_1	C_2	C_3	E	ΔE	$\Delta(\Delta E)$
			1a. Incrementing x, y: appropriate strategy					
1	10	5	0	1	1	2		
							0.4	
2	11	6	0	0.8	0.8	1.6		0
							0.4	
3	12	7	0	0.6	0.6	1.2		
			1b. Incrementing x, y: appropriate only for x					
1	10	11	6	1	0.2	7.2		
							0	
2	11	12	6	0.8	0.4	7.2		0
							0	
3	12	13	6	0.6	0.6	7.2		
			1c. Incrementing x, y: inappropriate strategy					
1	16	12	1	0.2	0.4	1.6		
							−0.4	
2	17	13	1	0.4	0.6	2.0		0
							−0.4	
3	18	14	1	0.6	0.8	2.4		
			2a. Incrementing x, decrementing y: appropriate strategy					
1	10	14	9	1	0.8	10.8		
							2.4	
2	11	13	7	0.8	0.6	8.4		
							2.4	
3	12	12	5	0.6	0.4	6.4		
			2b. Incrementing x, decrementing y: appropriate only for x					
1	10	4	1	1	1.2	3.2		
							2	
2	11	3	3	0.8	1.4	5.2		0
							2	
3	12	2	5	0.6	1.6	7.2		
			2c. Incrementing x, decrementing y: inappropriate strategy					
1	17	5	7	0.4	1	8.4		
							−2.4	
2	18	4	9	0.6	1.2	10.8		0
							−2.4	
3	19	3	11	0.8	1.4	13.2		

Table III

Information Provided by Scale-Indicator

Deceleration, $\Delta(\Delta E)$

Pass through the computer program	Component of the mapping				
	x	y	E	ΔE	$\Delta(\Delta E)$
1	14	6	4		
				0.4	
2	15	7	3.6		0.4
				0	
3	16	8	3.6		

the skilled performer knows two things. First, he knows that his joint angles are changing in opposite directions (one is incrementing and one is decrementing). In addition, because C_2 and C_3 are not represented in the needle velocity, he knows that only one of his joint angles is moving toward its target value. He then should alter the direction of movement of just one angle. Which one should be altered cannot be determined because the coefficients of C_2 and C_3 are the same. If the performer happens to choose the correct angle to change, on the next pass ΔE will equal 0.4 (i.e., 2α), indicating that the angles are now changing in parallel and that both are moving toward their targets. If the choice was incorrect, $\Delta E = -0.4$, and the performer knows to shift the direction of movement of both angles.

2. The Contribution of $\Delta(\Delta E)$

The velocity of needle movement changes when one of the actor's joint angles reaches and goes beyond its target value. Consider the example in Table III. In the example, both joint angles are being incremented. Hence, C_1 contributes a value of 0 to ΔE. In addition, on going from the first pass to the second, both angles are approaching their target values; hence, C_2 and C_3 contribute a value of 0.4 to ΔE. Going from the second pass to the third, however, x moves away from its target value of 15, whereas y continues to approach its target value of 10. Therefore, C_2 contributes -0.2 and C_3 contributes $+0.2$ to the value of ΔE. The new ΔE is 0, and $\Delta(\Delta E)$ is 0.4. This deceleration of the needle is an indication that one of the two angles has reached and surpassed its target. When that occurs, the model shifts from a strategy of simultaneous movement of both joint angles to one of changing a single joint angle.[6]

---

[6] The human subjects in the experiments of Krinskiy and Shik typically shifted from a strategy of simultaneous change of the two joint angles to one of successive change as they neared the target. The strategy of simultaneous change best reveals the "organizational invariant" of the task and therefore is an optimal strategy of movement until one target value is reached.

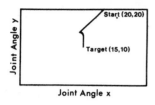

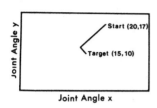

Figure 6. Movement strategies of the computer model (compare with Figure 3).

Figure 6 displays the movement strategies of our model. They are similar in form to but more efficient than those of the subjects of Krinskiy and Shik depicted in Figure 3.

G. Concluding Remarks

Both our model and the mathematical model of Gel'fand and Tsetlin perform the minimization task successfully. Furthermore, in their superficial properties, the strategies of these two models match the performance of the subjects of Krinskiy and Shik. Both models perform the minimization task by adopting procedures that are tailored to the special features of that task but that are inappropriate to the features of other tasks. We can perhaps conclude from these observations, and from the apparent incapacity of Powers' model to solve the task in an efficient way, that the human subjects in the experiment of Krinskiy and Shik likewise adopted a task-specific strategy. Given that those human subjects presumably are capable of performing other kinds of acts for which these tactics must be inappropriate [e.g., the positioning task of Adams (1971)], we may consider this work to provide preliminary support for our conception of the actor as a general-purpose device by virtue of the capacity to become a variety of special-purpose devices.

The procedures of our model are distinguished from the mathematical optimization procedures of Gel'fand and Tsetlin in a way that seems significant to us. We suggested a principle (see also Turvey *et al.,* in press) that holds that for the degrees of freedom necessitating control there must be at least as many degrees of constraint in the information supporting that control. We suggested also that the two *sources* of control constraints are the environment and the actor (Section III).

In the model of Gel'fand and Tsetlin, as applied to the minimization task of Krinskiy and Shik, degrees of constraint are largely supplied by the actor. The environment supplies the values ΔE and E, the ratio of which guides the actor's selection of a new strategy. However, its guidance is minimal. That is, the ratio $\Delta E/E$ tells the actor *when* he should adopt a new strategy of movement, but it does not prescribe *which* strategy he should select. The actor selects a ravine step based on calculations on his part that compare the degrees of success of the two preceding sets of local search tactics.

Relative to this minimal use of environmental sources of constraint, our model yields more of the responsibility for control. The environmentally given values ΔE and $\Delta(\Delta E)$ not only tell the actor *when* to shift strategies, they also prescribe *how* he should alter his strategy to achieve his aim. In short, in this model, relative to that of Gel'fand and Tsetlin, the actor supplies few degrees of constraint and the environment supplies correspondingly many.

We find it intriguing to speculate that these two models may characterize actors at different phases of the skill-acquisition process. Gel'fand and Tsetlin's model may characterize an actor who is sufficiently skilled to solve the task but who does not yet perform it in the most efficient way. The actor provides some degrees of constraint that the environment would provide were he organized or attuned to detect them. Our model, in contrast, yields to the environment as much of the responsibility for control as we have been able to uncover.

In Section III of this chapter, we sought to outline the kinds of information available to an actor given an optimal level of description of the environmentally structured energy distributions that surround him. The potential sources of controlling information available to an actor in a natural environment exceed in number and in level of abstraction those sources made available to the actor in the experiment of Krinskiy and Shik. Nevertheless, as we have shown, the relatively limited information manifest in the Krinskiy and Shik task can tightly constrain the performance of that task. Collectively, these concluding remarks reiterate a major theme of the present chapter, namely, that a careful examination of the environment as a perceptually specified source of constraint is mandatory to the understanding of the acquisition and performance of skilled activity.

Reference Notes

1. Shaw, R., Halwes, T., & Jenkins, J. *The organism as a mimicking automaton.* Unpublished manuscript, Center for Research in Human Learning, University of Minnesota, 1966.
2. Shaw, R. Personal communication, 1977.
3. Fowler, C. A. *Timing control in speech production.* Unpublished Ph.D. dissertation, University of Connecticut, 1977.
4. Gibson, J. J. *On the concept of the "Visual Solid Angle" in an optic array and its history.* Unpublished manuscript, Cornell University, 1972.

References

Adams, J. A closed-loop theory of motor learning. *Journal of Motor Behavior*, 1971, *3*, 111–149.

Adams, J. A. *Learning and memory*. Homewood, Illinois: Dorsey Press, 1976(a)

Adams, J. A. Issues for a closed-loop theory of motor learning. In G. Stelmach (Ed.), *Motor control: Issues and trends*. New York: Academic Press, 1976. (b)

Arutyunyan, G. A., Gurfinkel, V. S., & Mirskii, M. L. Investigation of aiming at a target. *Biophysics*, 1968, *13*, 642–645.

Arutyunyan, G. A., Gurfinkel, V. S., & Mirskii, M. L. Organization of movements on execution by man of an exact postural task. *Biophysics*, 1969, *14*, 1162–1167.

Bernstein, N. *The coordination and regulation of movement*. London: Pergamon Press, 1967.

Bever, T. G., Fodor, J. A., & Garrett, M. A. Formal limitations of associationism. In T. R. Dixon & D. L. Horton (Eds.), *Verbal behavior and general behavior theory*. Englewood Cliffs, New Jersey: Prentice Hall, 1968.

Bohm, D. *Causality and chance in modern physics*. New York: Harper Torchbooks, 1957.

Doty, R. W. Neural organization of deglutition. In C. F. Code (Ed.), *Handbook of physiology* vol. 6, Section 6). Washington: American Physiological Society, 1968.

Easton, T. A. On the normal use of reflexes. *American Scientist*, 1972, *60*, 591–599.

Gel'fand, I. M., Gurfinkel, V. S., Tsetlin, H. L., & Shik, M. L. Some problems in the analysis of movements. In I. M. Gel'fand, V. S. Fomin, & M. T. Tsetlin (Eds.), *Models of the structural-functional organization of certain biological systems*. Cambridge, Massachusetts: MIT Press, 1971.

Gel'fand, I. M., & Tsetlin, M. L. Some methods of control for complex systems. *Russian Mathematical Surveys*, 1962, *17*, 95–116.

Gel'fand, I. M., & Tsetlin, M. L. Mathematical modeling of mechanisms of the central nervous system. In I. M. Gel'fand, V. S. Gurfinkel, S. V. Fomin, & M. T. Tsetlin (Eds.), *Models of the structural-functional organization of certain biological systems*. Cambridge, Massachusetts: MIT Press, 1971.

Gibson, J. J. Visually controlled locomotion and visual orientation in animals. *British Journal of Psychology*, 1958, *49*, 182–194.

Gibson, J. J. Ecological optics. *Vision Research*, 1961, *1*, 253–262.

Gibson, J. J. *The senses considered as perceptual systems*. Boston: Houghton Mifflin, 1966.

Gibson, J. J. What gives rise to the perception of motion? *Psychological Review*, 1968, *75*, 335–346.

Gibson, J. J. The theory of affordances. In R. Shaw & J. Bransford (Eds.), *Perceiving, acting and knowing: Toward an ecological psychology*. Hillsdale, New Jersey: Erlbaum, 1977.

Greene, P. H. Seeking mathematical models for skilled actions. In D. Bootzin & H. C. Muffley (Eds.), *Biomechanics*. New York: Plenum Press, 1969.

Greene, P. H. Problems of organization of motor systems. In R. Rosen & F. Snell (Eds.), *Progress in theoretical biology* (Vol. 2). New York: Academic Press, 1972.

Greenwald, A. Sensory feedback mechanisms in performance control: With special reference to the ideo-motor mechanism. *Psychological Review*, 1970, *77*, 73–99.

Grillner, S. Locomotion in vertebrates. *Physiological Reviews*, 1975, *55*, 247–304.

Hubbard, A. W. Homokinetics: Muscular function in human movement. In W. R. Johnson (Ed.), *Science and medicine of exercise and sport*. New York: Harper, 1960.

Kots, Ya M., & Syrovegin, A. V. Fixed set of variants of interactions in the muscles of two joints in the execution of simple voluntary movements. *Biophysics*, 1966, *11*, 1212–1219.

Krinskiy, V. I., & Shik, M. L. A simple motor task. *Biophysics*, 1964, *9*, 661–666.

Lee, D. N. Visual information during locomotion. In R. B. MacLeod & H. L. Pick (Eds.), *Perception: Essays in honor of J. J. Gibson*. Ithaca, New York: Cornell University Press, 1974.

Lee, D. A theory of visual control of braking based on information about time-to-collision. *Perception*, 1976, *5*, 437–459.

Lee, D., & Aaronson, E. Visual proprioceptive standing in human infants. *Perception and Psychophysics*, 1974, *15*, 529–532.

Lishman, J. R., & Lee, D. N. The autonomy of visual kinaesthesis. *Perception*, 1973, *2*, 287–294.

Mace, W. James J. Gibson's strategy for perceiving: Ask not what's inside your head, but what your head's inside of. In R. Shaw & J. Bransford (Eds.), *Perceiving, acting and knowing: Toward an ecological psychology*. Hillsdale, New Jersey: Erlbaum, 1977.

Medawar, P. A geometrical model of reduction and emergence. In F. Ayala & T. Dobzhansky (Eds.), *Studies in the philosophy of biology*. Los Angeles: University of California Press, 1973.

Pattee, H. H. The problem of biological hierarchy. In C. H. Waddington (Ed.), *Toward a theoretical biology* (Vol. 3). Chicago: Aldine, 1970.

Pattee, H. H. The physical basis and origin of hierarchical control. In H. H. Pattee (Ed.), *Hierarchy theory: The challenge of complex systems*. New York: Braziller, 1973.

Pittenger, J., & Shaw, R. Aging faces as viscal-elastic events: Implications for a theory of non-rigid shape perception. *Journal of Experimental Psychology: Human Perception and Performance*, 1975, *1*, 374–382.

Powers, W. T. *Behavior: The control of perception*. Chicago: Aldine, 1973.

Putnam, H. Reductionism and the nature of psychology. *Cognition*, 1973, *2*, 131–146.

Schiff, W. Perception of impending collison: A study of visually directed avoidance behavior. *Psychological Monographs*, 1965, *79* (Whole No. 604).

Schmidt, R. A. A schema theory of discrete motor skill learning. *Psychological Review*, 1975, *82*, 225–260.

Sessle, B. J., & Hannam, A. G. *Mastication and swallowing: Biological and clinical correlates*. Toronto: University of Toronto Press, 1975.

Shaw, R., & McIntyre, M. Algoristic foundations to cognitive psychology. In W. Weimer & D. S. Palermo (Eds.), *Cognition and the symbolic processes*. Hillsdale, New Jersey: Erlbaum, 1974.

Shaw, R., McIntyre, M., & Mace, W. The role of symmetry in event perception. In R. B. MacLeod & H. L. Pick, Jr. (Eds.), *Perception: Essays in honor of J. J. Gibson*. Ithaca, New York: Cornell University Press, 1974.

Shik, M. L., & Orlovskii, G. N. Neurophysiology of locomotor automatism. *Physiological Reviews*, 1976, *56*, 465–501.

Sperry, R. Neurology and the mind–brain problem. *American Scientist*, 1952, *40*, 291–312.

Suppes, P. Stimulus–response theory of finite automatia. *Journal of Mathematical Psychology*, 1969, *6*, 327–355.

Trowbridge, M. H., & Cason, H. An experimental study of Thorndike's theory of learning. *Journal of General Psychology*, 1932, *7*, 245–258.

Turvey, M. T. Perspectives in vision: Conception or perception? In D. Duane & M. Rawson (Eds.), *Reading, perception and language*. Baltimore, Maryland: York, 1975.

Turvey, M. T. Contrasting orientations to a theory of visual information processing. *Psychological Review*, 1977, *84*, 67–88. (a)

Turvey, M. T. Preliminaries to a theory of action with reference to vision. In R. Shaw & J. Bransford (Eds.) *Perceiving, acting and knowing: Toward an ecological psychology*. Hillsdale, New Jersey: Erlbaum, 1977. (b)

Turvey, M. T., & Prindle, S. Modes of perceiving: Abstracts, comments, and notes. In H. Pick & E. Saltzman (Eds.), *Psychological modes of perceiving and processing of information*. Hillsdale, New Jersey: Erlbaum, 1977.

Turvey, M. T., Shaw, R., & Mace, W. Issues in the theory of action: Degrees of freedom, coordinative structures and coalitions. In J. Requin (Ed.), *Attention and performance* (Vol. 7). Hillsdale, New Jersey: Erlbaum, in press.

Warren, R. The perception of egomotion. *Journal of Experimental Psychology: Human Perception and Performance*, 1976, *2*, 448–456.

Weiss, P. Self-differentiation of the basic pattern of coordination. *Comparative Psychology Monograph*, 1941, *17*, 21–96.

𝒬2

Some Issues on Action Plans

K. M. Newell

I. Introduction

Knowing and doing are intricately related, and yet we do things that we do not know about and, by the same token, we have knowledge of acts that we cannot construct. It is surprising, therefore, that the theoretical gap between knowledge of action and execution of action remains as wide in the late 1970s as it was to Miller, Galanter, and Pribram in 1960. This is so despite the infusion, or shall I say intrusion, of concepts from cognitive psychology into the domain of motor skills and the rather liberal acceptance of information-processing notions.

In the 1970s research efforts focus principally on movement regulation and the relative contribution of central and peripheral mechanisms in the control process (cf. Stelmach, 1976). The acquisition, organization, and use of knowledge in action are issues rarely referred to, and, when they are, they appear so nebulous as to be trivial (Gentile & Nacson, 1976). Yet, as Lewis (1946, p. 3), among others, has elucidated, knowing is for the sake of doing and the significance of knowledge lies in its guidance of action. Fortunately, there are indications that psychologists are at last beginning to awaken to the importance of the dynamic relationship between knowledge and action (Neisser, 1976; Turvey, 1977; Weimer, 1977). In addition, the revitalization of schema as a construct for motor acts (Pew, 1974; Schmidt, 1975, 1976b) lends hope that we will continue to move away from the mechanistic S–R position, which has dominated motor learning throughout the twentieth century.

Information Processing in
Motor Control and Learning

This chapter discusses briefly a number of issues associated with the link between knowledge and action. The focus will be on action plans, particularly their representation, function, conscious implementation, and development. The role of plans in motor learning is an issue that has received very little direct attention in the literature although plans are often alluded to in theoretical formulations of skill acquisition (e.g., Adams, 1971; Gentile, 1972). The hope is that this chapter will contribute toward stimulating an interest in action plans and the role they play in the construction and execution of acts. Before we advance further, however, we should distinguish between actions and movements.

II. Actions and Movements

Movements generally refer to the motion of the body and limbs produced as a consequence of the spatial and temporal pattern of muscular contractions. Body movement can also occur, however, independently of the performer's efforts through the creation of an imbalance of forces acting externally on the body. Regardless of the cause of movement, the spatial and temporal pattern can be described rather precisely through kinematics. In contrast, space and time are not usually relevant criteria for actions. Rather, actions are identified by the goal to which they are directed (e.g., open the door, lift the weight, etc.) or by specifying certain criteria to which the performer complies in what he does (e.g., walking, hopping, etc.). As a consequence, a variety of potential movements may be *generated* to complete any one act (Bernstein, 1967), and, by the same token, a variety of movements may be *identified* as a particular act (Mischel, 1969).

This distinction between actions and movements may not, however, be as universally clear-cut as indicated above. Consider the case of closed skills (Poulton, 1957) and, in particular, those in which the goal of the task or act requires the production of a set movement pattern, such as in gymnastics, and highboard diving. In this situation, the act the performer attempts to complete is the production of a set movement pattern of a template of motion, and, as a consequence, the distinction between action and movement on the basis of kinematics becomes ambiguous. Presumably only biological variation will bring about different movement patterns from the same executive command, as by definition the initial environmental conditions remain constant in a closed skill. As an aside, it is worth noting that in this class of tasks the relationship between movement outcome and muscle activity as denoted by EMG recordings may not be as variant as Mac-Neilage (1970) and others (e.g., Gentile & Nacson, 1976; Turvey, 1977) would have us believe, particularly with highly skilled performers.

Of greater significance perhaps is the fact that actions are usually characterized by some intention on the part of the performer to reach a desired goal (Lewis, 1946); if the goal or criteria of an act are accidentally achieved by the performer, we would not describe this as an action. For example, if a person leaned against a door to rest and it suddenly opened due to a faulty door catch, we could not describe this as the act of opening the door on the part of the performer, even if the kinematics and end product of the movement were identical to those produced in the normal act of opening the door. We need to know what was intended by the performer, because it is the thought behind it that differentiates action from movement (Knox, 1968). Although intention may be a troublesome philosophical concept (cf. Brand, 1970), it has several identifiable behavioral features (Bruner, 1973). These include anticipation of the outcome of the act, selection among appropriate means for achievement of the act, and sustained direction of behavior during deployment of the means (Bruner, 1973, p. 2). In addition, some physiological consequences such as a corollary discharge (Sperry, 1950; Teuber, 1964) or efference copy (von Holst, 1954) may well arise from voluntary movement. In summary, we see that the concept of action differs from that of movement on a number of counts. Movement can be characterized as being a necessary but not sufficient condition for motor action.

III. Plans for Action

The previous section implied that we require knowledge and plans for acts but not for movements. This assumption needs to be justified, however, because a good deal of theorizing in motor learning has not taken this perspective. Although Thorndike (1931) gave direct recognition to the concept of acts, a number of traditional and current theories of motor learning (e.g., Adams, 1971; Guthrie, 1935; Schmidt, 1975) have focused on the movement pattern to be generated in order to solve a particular motor problem, rather than the concept of action. Although movement outcome has usually been the primary dependent measure, as in the linear positioning task, the backdrop for this work has been movements rather than acts, which has contributed toward the emergence of a certain line of theorizing with respect to motor control and learning.

From this viewpoint, the performer attempts to solve the motor act through the production of a set movement pattern, and only if an error in response selection or execution is detected will closed-loop control be invoked in the form of response modification (Adams, 1971; Schmidt, 1975). In contrast, acts, as we have seen, do not generally require a specific movement pattern for their completion although the movement generated may possess certain lawful characteristics. Thus, a general but reasonably accurate response for the act at hand may be initiated with the knowledge that it can be biased or tuned to some degree during movement execution (Easton, 1972; Greene, 1972). One might argue from this perspective that these modifications are not error corrections in the traditional sense because the generalized response initiated by the performer was never in-

tended to carry the precision required to complete the motor act. This may appear
to be a play on words, but it is a subtle difference that has important implications
for the representation of actions in the brain and the subsequent control processes
during movement production.

Early notions regarding the representation of actions in the brain held that
muscles were represented in a one-to-one correspondence, similar to a keyboard
arrangement. This metaphor was given prominence by Fritsch and Hitzig (1870),
who showed that electrical stimulation of certain centers of the brain elicited
movement and that the contractions could be localized to narrow delineated
groups of muscles. A more general interpretation of the localization finding is
that stimulation of a cortical unit initiates groups of muscles that operate collectively around an individual joint. This has led many to argue that movements,
not muscles, are represented in the motor cortex (e.g., Walshe, 1943), although
the exact movement produced will vary according to the intensity of the electrical
stimulation applied and the initial conditions of the organism in relation to the
environment.

There are compelling theoretical arguments and increasing empirical evidence
against the position that it is movements that are represented in the brain. Theoretically, the most persuasive has been Bernstein (1967), who detailed several
lines of argument against the one-to-one correspondence of initial impulse and
movement produced (see also Turvey, 1977). To account for the constancy that
may be produced in action, Bernstein suggested that there must be some higher
level engram that topologically but not metrically represents an abstract motor
image of space and that is structurally far removed from the joint–muscle
schemata. That is, the higher motor centers contain some projection of external
space in the form present in the motor field. This postulation sounds rather
esoteric, but it is one that appealed to Bernstein more than the traditional view
of the central nervous system containing projections of joints and muscles.

Experiments by Evarts (1967, 1968, 1969), however, suggest that force rather
than space may be the environmental property that becomes encoded. He showed
that electrical activity in the motor cortex of monkeys learning to displace a lever
proved to be a function of the force required and, in particular, of the change in
force required, rather than the degree of displacement of the lever. In contrast,
Brooks and Stoney (1971) have suggested that the parameters of velocity and
displacement may be coded more directly than the Evarts data indicated. The
parameters of movement specified by the efferent command are not unequivocally
established at this time, but the position emerging (Turvey, 1977), in the absence
of empirical confirmation, is that the plan generated is for action and the environment contingencies (Pribram, 1971), such as forces, necessary to complete the
motor act. A system of this nature is also attractive because it brings economy to
storage and allows for flexibility in the movement generated to complete the act.

It is conceivable that our lack of understanding of the detail required of the
efferent command or motor program is contributed to in part by the different

skill levels of the subjects performing the motor tasks across experiments. Evarts' (1968) monkeys, for example, performed at least 3000 trials per day for several months prior to surgery and the experimental trials. It is difficult to ascertain, however, the exact amount of practice of the monkeys used by Humphrey, Schmidt, and Thompson (1970), which is the study that Brooks and Stoney (1971) in part base their inferences upon. The problem that arises from this situation is that the level of analysis or the parameters encoded in the action plan may change as the performer becomes more proficient in the act. This is consistent with the progression–regression hypothesis (Fuchs, 1962) formulated for tracking, where it has been shown that, as the tracker becomes more proficient, he operates on or progresses to a higher level derivative of the error amplitude signal. That is, the performer progresses in response programming from displacement through velocity to acceleration parameters. The corollary to this also holds in that the skilled tracker often regresses from acceleration cues to a lower level derivative of the error signal when subjected to undue stress during performance of the primary task. It appears, therefore, that the action plan needs to be dynamic to account for, at a minimum, the continual interaction of the skill level of the performer and the environmental conditions.

Further evidence for the representation of action comes from Pribram, Kruger, Robinson, and Berman (1955–1956), who showed that precentral lesions of the motor cortex of monkeys interfered with skilled acts and not individual muscles or movements. They found that acts were not abolished through the removal of the locus of a habit, but rather a scotoma of action resulted, as Pribram and his associates called it, after its visual counterpart. Of related interest is the fact that a good number of patients suffering from apraxia have trouble completing an act, although they often know what it is they have to do and are quite capable under certain circumstances of generating a movement that would complete the act (Geschwind, 1965, 1975).

In review, the position emerging holds that the performer requires plans for actions rather than for movements. Again, it should be emphasized that the distinction is not as trivial as it may appear at first sight. Indeed, it forces a rather different theoretical perspective of motor learning than is currently in vogue (e.g. Adams, 1971; Schmidt, 1975). Furthermore, it holds the key to understanding the detail required of the action plan and, as a consequence, the relative contribution of central and peripheral processes to movement control. Let us now turn to the detail required of the action plan.

IV. How Detailed Is an Action Plan?

The role of an action plan and the particulars required of it will depend to large extent on our view of how the human system operates. If we view the system as an open-loop mode, where the movement is run off in response to an executive command that contains all the necessary detail for complete execution of the act, including its ability to withstand environmental contingencies, then the plan will inevitably be very detailed and comprehensive. On the other hand, if we view the system as a closed-loop mode, where the organism has the time and machinery to modify the ongoing movement, then the detail required of the action plan to generate the response initially becomes less cumbersome. Although the closed-loop mode is more complex than the open-loop mode, it is the process that is usually preferred for describing how humans operate, and we will consider the action plan in this light.

Closed-loop interpretations of movement control generally fall back on the assumption that the system is controlled hierarchically (Bruner & Bruner, 1968; Elliott & Connolly, 1974; Miller et al., 1960). From this viewpoint, the highest level of the system structure, often termed the executive, is responsible for making the fundamental decisions regarding the action plan and dictates the lesser decisions or details of the plan to appropriate structures at lower levels of the hierarchy. Indeed, Miller et al. (1960, p. 16) defined a plan as any hierarchical process in the organism that can control the order in which a sequence of operations is to be performed. This system places considerable responsibility on the executive as the highest decision process in the hierarchy, for ensuring that the response unfolds as planned. Yet, as Bernstein (1967) has argued, the executive is limited in many respects, particularly with regard to the degrees of freedom it possesses relative to the lower levels of the system.

The detail required of the executive command is reduced if we view the system not as a hierarchy, but as a heterarchy or coalition (McCulloch, 1945; von Forester, 1960). From this viewpoint, which has been postulated as a viable system for human action (Greene, 1972; Turvey, 1977), substructures are not necessarily subordinate to structures at a higher level in the hierarchy. Indeed, at any one point in time, a lower structure in the nervous system may act as the executive because the roles of structures in the system are potentially interchangeable. Greene (1972) has proposed that such a system allows the executive to initiate a general "ball-park" response with the understanding that lower levels of the system will have the capacity to modify the response through rapid tuning systems. This has the effect of reducing the complexity of the initial action plan, along with the demands on the executive, and allows for updating of the plan during the course of response execution. An important question arising from this position is how specific the ball-park response must be for the act to be completed. Presumably, the plan must be sufficiently detailed so that the ball-park response does not end up in left field. Expressed another way, and in the language of Schmidt (1976a): What degree of response variability, or error from the motor program perspective, can be tolerated before an execution problem becomes a selection problem? In any event, the prevailing view of a heterarchy is that the executive command does not need to contain all the details of the action plan

(Greene, 1972; Turvey, 1977), although it will probably contain all the ingredients invariant to the act.

The detail required of the initial action plan will naturally vary as a function of the demands placed upon the performer by the motor act. In short rapid movements, for example, the opportunity for tuning or biasing of the ball-park response is limited, and the emphasis on the precision of the initial command is, therefore, at a premium. In contrast, slow movements to a location (e.g., the linear positioning task) allow ample time and opportunity for response tuning, and as a consequence the ball-park response could presumably fall into left field and yet the act will still be completed. In addition, the skill level of the performer may modify the degree to which the action is controlled centrally (Pew, 1966), as we shall see in the later section on the development of action plans.

It should be apparent that the concept of motor program, which has received a good deal of theoretical and empirical attention (e.g., Keele & Summers, 1976), could be viewed as analogous to an action plan. Indeed, throughout their treatise of the subject, Miller et al. (1960) proposed that a program could be substituted for a plan, although there was no real evidence for the convergence of these concepts. One problem is that the motor program has been interpreted as having a rather rigid organization, due in large part to Keele (1968), who defined it as a prestructured set of muscle commands that determines the completion of the act uninfluenced by peripheral feedback. Although this conception of the motor program has been modified to account for rapid tuning of execution errors and the general character that parameters of the program may take (Pew, 1974; Schmidt, 1975, 1976a), the concept of motor program still seems far too inflexible to be considered analogous to a plan as outlined above, particularly if the system is viewed as a heterarchy. Some rapproachment between an action plan and a motor program may be achieved, however, by viewing the generalized motor program as being derived from the action plan in the final stage of its differentiation from an abstract representation to a relatively precise muscle–joint combination.

Drawing on our general knowledge to formulate an action plan specific to the situation is an integral part of the total action process. An intriguing issue is the awareness of the individual with respect to the changing character of the action plan. Indeed, how explicit is an action plan and to what extent does cognition play a role in action? It is to these issues that we now turn.

V. How Conscious Is an Action Plan?

A good number of motor skills textbooks give action plans a very static and conscious role in the construction and execution of an action. The scenario is often portrayed as follows. The performer assesses the relevant environmental cues, constructs an appropriate action plan, and then generates a response that is congruent with that plan. If task characteristics allow, he may be able to modify the response during its execution. On completion of the response he evaluates response-produced feedback and, finally, he may update the action plan before attempting the act the next time (e.g., Gentile, 1972; Marteniuk, 1976). The implication is that the performer consciously undergoes all of the processes or operations outlined in a rigid and orderly sequence. Our experience, however, surely suggests otherwise.

Have you ever thought what it is you say to yourself in the construction and execution of an act or whether inner speech (Sokolov, 1972) is involved in this process at all? Eccles (1972) has suggested that, with simple well-learned acts, a general command such as "place finger on nose" or "pick up glass" is all that is required for the act to be run off automatically. Occasions arise, however, in the humdrum of daily life, when you are probably unaware of how you decided to perform a certain act and how you constructed and completed the relevant action. Similarly, skilled sportsmen are often ignorant of the precise details of action by which they perform a particular sports skill. This may be a blessing in disguise, however, because it appears that the less aware, or more subconscious, you are of the production of a particular act, the better it is (Eccles, 1972). For example, we know that if a pianist focuses his attention on his finger movements, which generate a particular segment of an overall action sequence, rather than on the piece he is playing, then the act of piano playing is often interrupted or marred in some way.

Cognitive explanations for the construction and execution of actions imply an active conscious involvement on the part of the performer. This involvement is often characterized in the form of planning, hypothesis formulation, hypothesis testing, and so on (Gentile, 1972) or in the progression of stages postulated to occur from input to output along the information-processing continuum (Marteniuk, 1976). This explicit planful behavior is usually considered to be more prevalent in the early stages of learning a particular act (Adams, 1971; Fitts, 1964; Gentile, 1972), because with practice the action usually appears to be more automatic. On many occasions, however, we learn and perform an act unaware of even the general rules that govern our actions. Polayni's (1958) classic example of the rule governing bicycle riding exemplifies this point as well as, if not better than, any other example. Clearly, we have no idea of the rule we are observing in bicycle riding, and knowledge of it would not help us learn to ride or enable us to teach the skill of bicycle riding any better. How then is this tacit knowledge (Polayni, 1958, 1966) derived and how do we draw upon it to construct and execute motor acts?

It is often argued that the particular or concrete knowledge must be present before the general or abstract knowledge can be created. Hayek (1969) has advanced the reverse position in proposing that a disposition or general rule for a certain action develops first and then is followed by an amalgamation of many such dispositions, which leads to the characteristics of a particular action. This emphasis on "the primacy of the abstract," as Hayek labeled it, also generates an interesting paradox. That is, we are unaware of the abstract, not because it operates at too low a functional level in conscious experiences, but rather because it proceeds at a higher or so-called "superconscious" level.

The view that there is knowledge we can talk about, and that which we cannot, provides a background against which to consider the changing face of an action plan. That is, the change of the abstract action plan to a concrete configuration of muscle–joint arrangements may be viewed as the passing from the abstract to the particular. Interestingly, Evarts (1973) has indicated that the representation of an action at the motor cortex is more concrete than is usually given credence. This implies that structures physically below the level of the motor cortex, which provide the necessary knowledge base for the eventual action representation, are at a higher functional level of the system. On this account, one might posit that the term 'lowerarchy' [1] affords a more veridical description of the action system than the traditionally held hierarchy. Nevertheless, the suggestion is that the plan progresses through a series of stages and representations or, as Turvey (1977, p. 230) has stated, that the action plan unfolds as a series of progressively less abstract projections of the environment.

Our discussion so far has made the implicit assumption that the performer has at his disposal the appropriate action plan for any particular act. Clearly, though, action plans develop with experience in the same way that execution of an action improves with practice. How, then, do action plans evolve? Has nature provided us with the appropriate abstract knowledge on which rather precise action plans can be differentiated and muscle–joint relationships developed, or does the abstract knowledge develop with the increasing maturity and experience of the individual? The principal approach to this and related questions has been to describe the development of the action plan from a behavioral perspective.

VI. Development of an Action Plan

To some extent, every action is a repetition of actions performed previously because the environmental contingencies that determine the act, and confine the means by which the act may be executed, contain similarities from situation to situation. It is logical, therefore, to suggest that new action plans are developed from old plans. Underlying this perspective is the assumption that at some point in time there must be an original plan or plans on which to build. Generally, these have been considered to be inherited or instinctual, and, in fact, instincts have even been thought of as plans themselves (Miller et al., 1960). That plans or

---

[1] I would like to thank Les Carlton for pointing out this analogy.

rules for action may be inherited does not necessarily dictate that the overt behavior or action is also innate. It is one thing to know explicitly or implicitly what
to do, but quite another to be able to actually do it.

From a behavioral perspective, we can describe a number of aspects associated
with the development of an action plan. For example, in the neonate, acts fundamental to survival, such as breathing, sucking, and swallowing, appear to be the
most well developed and controlled. The newborn can modify these automatic
actions, however, given access to information relating to the outcome of his responses. For example, Bruner and Bruner (1968) have reported that neonates as
young as 4 weeks will adapt their sucking behavior to keep a motion picture in
focus. Indeed, the infant can generate an adaptive strategy in sucking to simultaneously maximize the availability of milk and the clarity of the picture. Thus,
voluntary control may be obtained over automatic responses early in a child's
development, although it appears that if the new act becomes too demanding, the
infant will fall back into his normal sucking plan, which can be run off successfully. In other words, when the infant cannot establish an appropriate action plan
or differentiate it into the compatible muscle–joint schema, he will invariably
regress to a plan that is well ingrained from which he can generate a partially
successful action. Interestingly, this finding parallels the progression–regression
hypothesis (Fuchs, 1962) discussed in Section III.

Once basic manipulations of body parts, or so-called anatomical acts (Elliott &
Connolly, 1974), have been mastered by the child to a reasonable degree, they can
be included as an element or subroutine (Connolly, 1970) in a variety of actions.
As an illustration, a precision grip once obtained will be tailored to meet the
demands of a range of acts whether it be picking up a pencil or placing a peg
in a hole (Connolly, 1973). Initially, the inclusion of this new element into a
complex action sequence can cause the subroutine, and indeed the whole action
sequence, to appear ungainly. With practice, however, the subroutine usually becomes coordinated into the act to form what Bruner (1973) has called a higher-
order action. Subroutine in this context refers to the functional aspects of the
movement in relation to its consequences, as opposed to its anatomical or neurological state. Intuitively, it appears that the development of the rules or motor
syntax (Connolly, 1973) governing the linking of subroutines will determine in
large part the quality of the action sequence produced. In addition, the degree
to which a subroutine can be modularized reflects another fundamental constraint
on skill acquisition. These intuitions have been advanced principally from a
descriptive stance that leaves open a comprehensive examination of the development of action sequences.

The maturing individual must generalize actions not only to acts that might
be deemed to coexist within the same action class, but also to acts that might fall
outside the designated action class. Generalization, or transfer, is a central concern to schema accounts of motor learning (Pew, 1974; Schmidt, 1975) that

postulate that the performer abstracts parameters or response specifications invariant to a given class of movements. When the performer is faced with a new task within a given movement class (to use the vocabulary of Schmidt), reasonable transfer to the new motor task will occur. Because we are conceptually unsure of what constitutes an action or movement class, the question of how generalizable the schema or action plan is has to be begged in large part. Is it merely the metrical prescriptions of the action that are generalizable or is it the fundamental elements of the coordinative structure or motor program that can be modularized to complete a variety of acts?

Observation suggests that action plans are generalizable and flexible and that they have the capacity to produce very automatic responses and structured action sequences. Indeed, a well-practiced act presumably has a plan that can be changed rapidly from its abstract representation to the precise joint–muscle combination. In other words, the motor program can be generated instantaneously to provide a well-established action solution to a familiar motor act. Furthermore, observation suggests that practice produces a more comprehensive plan so that it encompasses larger units of a complex sequential action. A familiar example is the ability of typists to increase the string of letters that they can combine automatically until a word or segment of a word can be literally run off with a flourish (Book, 1908). In a similar vein, Pew (1966) has demonstrated that a longer temporal sequence of open-loop control is possible with extended practice in a two-hand tracking task. The developing action plan, therefore, seems to increasingly incorporate elements of expectancy with respect to the features of the ongoing action, in addition to being open to modification as a consequence of preceding actions or subroutines of actions.

A fundamental issue for theorists of skill acquisition is *how* the developing action plan incorporates longer segments of an act and has the capability to generalize to other acts. After all, it is one thing to describe and specify the development of an action plan behaviorally, but quite another to understand how this development materializes. Presumably, if the action plan represents the parameters or rules for translating an intention into an action, and this projection relates topologically but not metrically to the environment, then it is the development of these rule relationships that we need to comprehend. This process is a continuous process in the form of a search for the optimal motor solution to the motor act (Bernstein, 1967).

We have a very poor understanding of the rules involved in action and the manner in which plans for action develop. Work on action plans has taken place at a very gross level (Gentile, 1972; Gentile & Nacson, 1976), with its focus being primarily on the general strategy the performer employs to modify his movement pattern in an attempt to achieve the goal of the task. Although this work has provided a necessary and useful beginning, it has done little more than confirm what is apparent to the careful observer. What is required is a much finer grained analysis of the parameters that are fundamental to action and the relationships that develop between biokinematic links. In addition, these rules or relationships need to be established with respect to the performer in the environment (see Chapter 1). Too much of the research conducted in motor learning has the performer operating in an impoverished environment, so that he is often devoid of vision and confined to rather static and unnatural conditions. While these sterile laboratory conditions have helped us to develop a rudimentary understanding of the effect of specific variables on motor learning and performance, it may well be that, on issues such as action plans, these rather artificial conditions have generated rather artificial answers. The performer needs to be an active participant or doer in experiments as opposed to a relatively passive performer constrained by a barren environment.

In summary, it must be emphasized that the development of an action plan is unlikely to reflect a rigid and orderly sequence, but rather the flexible buildup and modularization of any particular action. Action plans are continually being updated as a consequence of the interaction of the performer with the environment. There is a dynamic link between perception and action, in which knowing facilitates doing, and doing fosters knowing. Neisser (1976) succinctly captures this cyclical relationship when, in regarding action plans as being somewhat analogous to schemata, he says: "The schema is not only the plan but also the executor of the plan. It is a pattern of action as well as a pattern for action [p. 56]."

References

Adams, J. A. A closed-loop theory of motor learning. *Journal of Motor Behavior*, 1971, *3*, 111–149.

Bernstein, N. *The coordination and regulation of movement*, New York: Pegamon Press, 1967.

Book, W. F. *The psychology of skill*. Missoula, Montana: Montana Press, 1908.

Brand, M. (Ed.). *The nature of human action.* Glenview, Illinois: Scott, Foresman, 1970.

Brooks, V. B., & Stoney, S. D. Motor mechanisms: The role of the pyramidal system in motor control. *Annual Review of Physiology*, 1971, *33*, 337–392.

Bruner, J. S. Organization of early skilled action. *Child Development*, 1973, *44*, 1–11.

Bruner, J. S., & Bruner, B. M. On voluntary action and its hierarchical structure. *International Journal of Psychology*, 1968, *3*, 239–255.

Connolly, K. J. Skill development: Problems and plans. In K. J. Connolly (Ed.), *Mechanisms of motor skill development*. London: Academic Press, 1970.

Connolly, K. Factors influencing the learning of manual skills by young children. In R. A. Hinde & J. Stevenson-Hinde (Eds.), *Constraints on learning*. New York: Academic Press, 1973.

Easton, T. A. On the normal use of reflexes. *American Scientist*, 1972, *60*, 591–599.

Eccles, J. C. *The understanding of the brain*. New York: McGraw-Hill, 1972.

Elliott, J., & Connolly, K. Hierarchical structure in the development of skill. In K. Connolly & J. Bruner (Eds.), *The development of competence in childhood*. London: Academic Press, 1974.

Evarts, E. V. Representation of movements and muscles by pyramidal tract neurons of the perceptual motor cortex. In M. D. Yahr & D. P. Purpura (Eds.), *Neurophysiological basis of normal and abnormal motor activities.* New York: Raven, 1967.

Evarts, E. V. Relation of pyramidal tract activity to force exerted during voluntary movement. *Journal of Neurophysiology,* 1968, *31,* 14–27.

Evarts, E. V. Activity of pyramidal tract neurons during postural fixation. *Journal of Neurophysiology,* 1969, *32,* 375–385.

Evarts, E. V. Brain mechanisms in movement. *Scientific American,* 1973, *229,* 96–103.

Fitts, P. M. Perceptual-motor skill learning. In A. W. Melton (Ed.), *Categories of human learning.* New York: Academic Press, 1964.

Fritsch, G., & Hitzig, E. [Ueber die elektrische Erregbarkeit des Grosshirns.] *Archiv für Anatomie, Physiologic, und Wissenschaftliche Medicin,* 1870, 308–314. (In K. H. Pribam (Ed.). *Brain and behavior* 2: *Preception and action.* Hammonsworth, Middx., Eng.: Penguin Books, 1969)

Fuchs, A. H. The progression–regression hypothesis in perceptual motor skill learning. *Journal of Experimental Psychology,* 1962, *63,* 177–183.

Gentile, A. M. A working model of skill acquisition with application to teaching. *Quest,* 1972, *17,* 3–23.

Gentile, A. M., & Nacson, J. Organizational processes in motor learning and motor memory. In J. Keogh & R. S. Hutton (Eds.), *Exercise and sport sciences reviews* (Vol. 4). Santa Barbara, California: Journal Publishing Affiliates, 1976.

Geschwind, N. Disconnexion syndromes in animals and man, Part II. *Brain,* 1965, *88,* 585–644.

Geschwind, N. The apraxias: Neural mechanisms of disorders of learned movement. *American Scientist,* 1975, *63,* 144–149.

Greene, P. M. Problems of organization of motor systems. In R. Rosen & F. M. Snell (Eds.), *Progress in theoretical biology* (Vol. 2). New York: Academic Press, 1972.

Guthrie, E. R. *The psychology of learning.* New York: Harper, 1935.

Hayek, F. A. The primacy of the abstract. In A. Koestler & J. R. Smythies (Eds.), *Beyond reductionism.* Boston: Beacon, 1969.

Humphrey, D. R., Schmidt, E. M., & Thompson, W. D. Predicting measures of motor performance from multiple cortical spike trains. *Science,* 1970, *170,* 758–762.

Keele, S. W. Movement control in skilled motor performance. *Psychological Bulletin,* 1968, *70,* 387–403.

Keele, S. W., & Summers, J. J. The structure of motor programs. In G. E. Stelmach (Ed.), *Motor control of issues and trends.* New York: Academic Press, 1976.

Knox, M. *Action.* London: Allen and Unwin, 1968.

Lewis, C. I. *An analysis of knowledge and valuation.* La Salle, Illinois: Open Court, 1946.

Marteniuk, R. G. *Information processing in motor skills.* New York: Holt, 1976.

MacNeilage, P. F. Motor control of serial ordering of speech. *Psychological Review,* 1970, *77,* 182–196.

McCulloch, W. S. A heterarchy of values determined by the topology of nervous nets. *Bulletin of Mathematical Biophysics,* 1945, *7,* 89–93.

Miller, G. A., Galanter, E., & Pribram, K. H. *Plans and the structure of behavior.* New York: Holt, 1960.

Mischel, T. Scientific and philosophical psychology: A historical introduction. In T. Mischel (Ed.), *Human action.* New York: Academic Press, 1969.

Neisser, I. *Cognition and reality.* San Francisco: Freeman, 1976.

Pew, R. W. Acquisition of hierarchical control over the temporal organization of a skill. *Journal of Experimental Psychology,* 1966, *71,* 764–771.

Pew, R. W. Human perceptual-motor performance. In B. H. Kantowitz (Ed.), *Human information processing:* Tutorials in performance and cognition. New York: Erlbaum, 1974.

Polanyi, M. *Personal knowledge: Towards a post-critical philosophy.* London: Routledge and Kegan Paul, 1958.

Polanyi, M. *The tacit dimension.* Garden City, New York: Doubleday & Co., 1966.

Poulton, E. C. On prediction in skilled movements. *Psychological Bulletin,* 1957, *54,* 467–479.

Pribram, K. H. *Languages of the brain.* Englewood Cliffs, New Jersey: Prentice-Hall 1971.

Pribram, K. H., Kruger, L., Robinson, R., & Berman, A. J. The effects of precentral lesions on the behavior of monkeys. *Yale Journal of Biology and Medicine,* 1955–1956, *28,* 428–443.

Schmidt, R. A. A schema theory of discrete motor skill learning. *Psychological Review,* 1975, *82,* 225–260.

Schmidt, R. A. Control processes in motor skills. In J. Keogh & R. S. Hutton (Eds.), *Exercise and sport sciences reviews* (Vol. 4). Santa Barbara, California: Journal Publishing Affiliates, 1976(a)

Schmidt, R. A. The schema as a solution to some persistent problems in motor learning theory. In G. E. Stelmach (Ed.), *Motor control: Issues and trends.* New York: Academic Press, 1976(b)

Sokolov, A. N. *Inner speech and thought.* New York: Plenum, 1972.

Sperry, R. W. Neural basis of the spontaneous optokinetic response produced by visual inversion. *Journal of Comparative and Physiological Psychology,* 1950, *43,* 482–489.

Stelmach, G. E. (Ed.). *Motor control: Issues and trends.* New York: Academic Press, 1976.

Teuber, H. L. Comment on E. H. Lenneberg's paper—Speech as a motor skill with special reference on nonphasic disorders. *Monographs of the Society for Research in Child Development,* 1964, *29,* 131–138.

Thorndike, E. L. *Human learning.* New York: Century, 1931.

Turvey, M. T. Preliminaries to a theory of action with reference to vision. In R. Shaw & J. Bransford (Eds.), *Perceiving, acting and knowing: Toward an ecological psychology.* Hillsdale, New Jersey: Erlbaum, 1977.

von Foerster, H. On self-organizing systems and their environments. In M. C. Yorits & S. Cameron (Eds.), *Self-organizing systems.* New York: Pergamon Press, 1960.

von Holst, E. Relations between the central nervous system and the peripheral organs. *British Journal of Animal Behavior,* 1954, *2,* 89–94.

Walshe, F. M. R. On the mode of representation of movements in the motor cortex, with special reference to "convulsions beginning unilaterally" (Jackson). *Brain,* 1943, *66,* 104–139.

Weimer, W. B. A conceptual framework for cognitive psychology: Motor theories of the mind. In R. Shaw & J. Bransford (Eds.), *Perceiving, acting and knowing: Toward an ecological psychology.* Hillsdale, New Jersey: Erlbaum, 1977.

3

Task Factors That Influence Selection and Preparation for Voluntary Movements

Beth Kerr

I. Introduction

Many movement situations demand a quick reaction in response to an external event. The performer, who must try to respond as quickly as possible, makes a number of decisions about the movement that is to be employed. Limb, direction, torque, sequencing: All must be appropriate to the task at hand. Decisions require time. The length of time that precedes movement execution often reflects the complexity of decisions required to select and prepare the necessary voluntary response. This planning period includes decisions at many levels or stages. First, the stimulus must be encoded, identified, and associated with the appropriate task-defined outcome, for example, red light equals right key. The response needed for this outcome is usually defined in terms of an environmental goal, for example, push button 6 in. to right of center, as fast as possible, with right index finger. At this point the performer may identify task-defined values that distinguish the correct movement from other possible alternatives, such as right not left, forward not backward, long not short. This first global memory stage encompasses the processes normally identified with stimulus preprocessing, stimulus identification, and response determination or selection in standard reaction time

Information Processing in
Motor Control and Learning

paradigms (Smith, 1968; Theios, 1975). Second, motor control parameter values must be computed for the intended movement, for example, abduct right arm, flex right index finger, etc. This second stage requires a shift from a task-defined external perspective to one that is internal to the motor control system. In a third stage, motor control parameter values are elaborated and translated into a format appropriate for force production for the actual response. Structuring the actual movement commands occurs in this stage. Finally, the response is executed. My labels for the two final initiation stages are *response selection* and *response preparation*. Taken together, selection and preparation are often called *programming*. Since response selection and response preparation are difficult to separate experimentally, the global programming label will often be appropriate.

We have often questioned the degree to which full movements are programmed prior to movement onset and then executed without ongoing correction or sequencing procedures that depend on peripheral feedback (Keele, 1968). Advance programming and ongoing control are also difficult to separate. However, it is possible to test the notion that movement programming occurs. One approach focuses on the role of feedback in control by considering changes in movement when feedback is altered or eliminated (see Keele & Summers, 1976). Evidence that movement can occur when feedback has been eliminated supports the position that the movements are centrally controlled by motor programs. This approach, however, is beset both by procedural questions surrounding surgical and nonsurgical means for eliminating feedback and by theoretical questions surrounding the potential roles of feedback, including internal feedback, at different levels (Evarts, 1971). A second approach focuses on the possibility that motor commands can be structured prior to movement onset (see Klapp, 1976). The extent to which commands can be prepared in advance of movement is of interest, whether or not feedback plays a role. This second approach involves the assumption that response selection and preparation will require time and that the length of time needed will vary as programming demands change. We manipulate the task goal parameters and observe the effects on movement initiation time. The best strategy is to hold the number of possible movement task choices constant and then compare the time to initiation movements for different levels of one task parameter, for example, long versus short duration movements that cover the same distance. Admittedly, the notion that starting time reflects programming time is difficult to disprove. A failure to find differences between initiation times for different conditions does not preclude programming for these responses: The times associated with different parameters might not differ. However, there is evidence that some different task requirements affect response initiation time differentially (see Klapp, 1976). These differences suggest that variable amounts of time must be necessary to select and prepare the movements associated with the varying parameter demands.

This chapter is not intended to document motor programs or to compare open-loop and closed-loop systems. Instead, it reviews the factors that influence the time to initiate short voluntary movements and thus may be inferred to influence programming, that is, response selection and preparation. This chapter includes three main sections in addition to the concluding remarks. The first describes discrete movement paradigms and discusses methodological and procedural issues. The second section considers the relationship between movement initiation and execution stages. The third section analyzes the task factors that influence the movement programming process.

II. Discrete Movement Paradigms

Fortunately, tasks that require rapid short movements lend themselves easily to the laboratory environment, possess face-value external validity, and appeal to most subjects. As a result, reaction time–movement time paradigms have a long-standing history in the study of information processing during voluntary movements (see Woodworth, 1938). Even though these tasks are highly familiar, a brief review of common procedures and the time measures that serve as dependent variables is in order. In most tasks, the subject moves a single limb through a distance to a target. Two time components are measured. Initiation time is the time duration between signal onset and overt response initiation. Movement time is the time duration between response initiation and response completion, the actual time at which the subject reaches the intended target.[1] These two times added together, initiation time plus movement time, equal the total time duration between signal onset and movement completion. Some prefer to label the starting time as reaction time rather than initiation time. Here, however, the reaction time label will be reserved for tasks that require a kinematically simple and discrete response, for example, a keypress involving finger flexion, whereas the initiation time label will refer to time to begin kinematically more complex motions, for example, the coordinated shoulder–elbow–wrist–finger movements needed to move between widely separated targets, turn a crank, or control a tracking level. Initiation time and movement time will be used to delimit the two task-imposed stages: initiation and execution.

As a rule, subjects respond as fast as possible, and initiation and movement

---

[1] The apparent simplicity of initiation time and movement time measures is somewhat misleading. Initiation time and movement time divide what is really a continuous process into two discrete components. The division point may be one of convenience rather than of theoretical significance. An additional procedural problem is that initiation time often includes time for some overt movement associated with switch closure or release. Now that sophisticated measurement and data reduction techniques are available, fractionated reaction time (Weiss, 1965) and force, acceleration, and displacement records in conjunction with EMG records measuring both voluntary EMG onset and onset of premovement agonist reflex modulation (Kots, 1969) will often be in order.

times measure ability to minimize total response time. However, only one of the two components need be speeded. For example, some tasks require that subjects initiate movements as fast as possible and time-control overt movements (Klapp & Erwin, 1976). In this case, movement time is an independent variable and movement times are monitored to guarantee that task demands are met in different conditions. Other tasks allow subjects unlimited time to prepare and initiate the response but require that the movement itself be executed as fast as possible (Fitts & Radford, 1966). Specific time parameter controls for initiation time have not as yet been employed but may be appropriate in future work.

Tasks may or may not require choice at signal onset. In the choice-response case, several movements are possible and the signal to begin designates the correct movement for that trial (e.g., red means move right; green means move left). In the simple-response case, one movement remains valid throughout a block of trials or a precue designates the appropriate movement before each trial. Consider the design for a study comparing short-duration and long-duration movements. Subjects could be asked to perform (*a*) fixed blocks of trials of long-duration responses and fixed blocks of trials of short-duration responses (simple) or (*b*) mixed blocks of trials including both long-duration responses to one signal and short-duration responses to a second signal (choice). An alternate choice procedure is to vary the parameter of interest across blocks but require another choice within blocks. For example, subjects might perform fixed blocks of long-duration or short-duration trials that require a choice between two possible directions. The number of choices, the number of factors that vary, and the presence or absence of choice between levels for a factor may affect attempts to pinpoint the locus of programming effects (see page 64).

As always, errors can be both informative and inconvenient. Certainly they cannot be ignored (see Pachella, 1974). Well-designed hardware and software systems now allow one to prevent false starts, to abort "suspiciously long" trials, and to repeat immediately or in the same experimental session trials on which subjects reach the wrong target or fail to reach any target. Careful signal randomization procedures, variable warning intervals, and/or catch trials are employed to control subject anticipation strategies. Nevertheless, errors will still occur and will bring with them problems of interpretation.[2] Will we associate the error with initiation time, movement time, or both? At this point the type of error becomes important: Errors such as starting to move in the wrong direction seem to be tied to initiation time; undershooting a target, however, could be associated with a fast movement time and/or initiation time. Differences

---

[2] Correct response trials with inordinately short initiation times (e.g., a 15–msec trial in a condition with a mean time of 200 msec) become an interpretation problem. There is no standardized procedure for dealing with these extreme scores. However, strict experimental procedures that discourage false starts and fast guesses in all conditions seem preferable to post hoc analyses that selectively eliminate trials with short initiation times.

between initiation time and movement time across error and nonerror trials may help identify the locus of errors. Speed–accuracy trade-offs often exist both for errors and initiation time and for errors and movement time. There may be additional trade-offs between the two times themselves. One might find, for example, that movements to the right have faster initiation times but slower movement times than movements to the left (e.g., Simon, 1969). Correlational techniques are often used to evaluate such trade-offs.

One correlational procedure compares dependent variables across subjects (see, e.g., Klapp, 1975). Negative correlations are viewed as cause for concern that subject strategy has come into play. For example, a negative correlation between initiation time and error rate would indicate that those subjects most able to achieve fast times do so at the expense of errors. This procedure does not control for differences that might occur in association with different levels of an independent variable. Thus, an alternative procedure is to correlate mean scores across experimental conditions (see Rosenbaum, Note 1). Here, negative correlations stand out as a warning that differences among condition means for a single dependent variable, taken alone, could be misleading. For example, a negative correlation between initiation time and movement time across conditions suggests that the conditions with fast initiation times have slower movement times. Subjects may have accepted long movement times in trade for short initiation times in some but not all conditions.

Obviously, formal tests for differences among condition means will be conducted for each dependent variable. A full report that combines tests for differences among means for initiation time, movement time, and errors with correlational checking procedures permits the most complete interpretation of the influence patterns for the different levels of the independent variables.

III. The Relationship between Initiation and Execution Stages

Do parameters associated with the required movement influence the time needed to initiate that movement? A survey of the contemporary literature immediately points up an inconsistency: For the past 20 years physical education and experimental psychology have approached this question in different ways. Research has proceeded from two different perspectives that did not begin to converge until the past few years. In psychology, the work by Paul Fitts and his associates (see Fitts & Peterson, 1964) prompted the widely accepted conclusion that initiation and execution stages are independent. In physical education, Franklin Henry and his associates (see Henry & Rogers, 1960) have promoted the position, commonly known as the "memory drum" theory, that the time to initiate a movement varies directly with the complexity of the movement.

There is little reason to dwell on differences between the two approaches, but quick reviews for both provide a historical overview for recent work.

The basic Fitts task requires moving a stylus back and forth between two targets as quickly as possible (continuous version) or moving a stylus, on signal, to one of several possible targets (discrete version). Fitts and coworkers (Fitts, 1954; Fitts & Peterson, 1964; Fitts & Radford, 1966) found a systematic relationship between the combined influence of target distance and target width on movement time. However, neither distance nor target width affected initiation time to any degree. Conversely, the signal probability affected initiation time but failed to show much influence on movement time. Supporting evidence has suggested that the attention demands during initiation and execution stages are also influenced by different factors. Ells (1973) reported that attention demands during movement initiation vary with the number of possible choices but not with target width, whereas attention demands during the execution stage vary with width requirements but fail to reflect the number of possible choices. These findings have been interpreted as showing that movement control parameters such as distance do not influence initiation time. Fitts and Peterson (1964) themselves suggested that perceptual and motor processes are serial and independent in nature.

In contrast, studies conducted or inspired by Franklin Henry have varied task demands in order to observe the effects of movement complexity on initiation time. Results in this type of study have often been contradictory. However, there is ample evidence, dating in fact from the beginning of the twentieth century (see Woodworth, 1938), that initiation time can vary in response to movement task demands. For example, the widely cited Henry and Rogers paper (1960) reported that simple initiation time for an upward key release was faster than initiation time preceding a movement forward to grasp an object suspended in front of the body and that this reaching movement could be initiated more quickly than a movement that required pauses on several intermediate targets. The finding that movements that require some degree of terminal accuracy are initiated more slowly than those that do not is fairly standard (Glencross, 1972; Laszlo & Livesey, 1977; Wrisberg & Pushkin, 1976). Other work suggests that initiation time (a) increases as required movement duration increases (Klapp & Erwin, 1976), (b) fails to increase as resistance increases (Glencross, 1973), (c) may (Glencross, 1973; Klapp, 1975) or may not (Brown & Slater-Hammel, 1949; Glencross, 1976; Klapp, 1975; Lagasse & Hayes, 1973) increase as distance increases, (d) may or may not increase as target width decreases (Glencross, 1976; Klapp, 1976), (e) increases as the number of responding limbs increases (Glencross, 1973), and (f) in comparison to a direct forward movement to a single target, increases for a movement that requires a pause or pause and reversal in route to a final target (Norrie, 1967, 1974; Glencross, 1972) but not for movements that require reversals without a pause on a definite target (Glencross, 1972,

1973). Admittedly, clear-cut patterns have remained elusive. However, initiation time must be considered to be sensitive to differences in movement parameters.[3]

To return to the question of initiation and execution stage independence: Initiation time as well as movement time may change in response to task changes that manipulate movement time via task complexity. Will movement time, in turn, show differences in response to changes intended to influence initiation time? Suppose the actual physical movement remains constant while other conditions (e.g., the number of possible choices) change? A common assumption has been that movement time will not be influenced by changes expected to affect initiation time. However, there are a number of situations in which the same independent variables affect both initiation and movement times:

1. The Simon spatial S–R compatability effect occurs for movement time as well as initiation time (Simon, 1968).

2. Small but significant changes in movement as well as initiation time occur in response to both stimulus uncertainty and the number of possible choices (Fitts & Peterson, 1964).

3. Movement time as well as initiation time increase with the number of possible choices of direction (Ells, 1973; Kerr, 1976), extent (Kerr, 1976) and, in general, the number of movement features to be selected (Rosenbaum, Note 1).

4. Both movement time and initiation time increases occur with the addition of a second stimulus (S_2) that does not require a response in the S_1–R_1, S_2 version of the psychological refractory period paradigm (Herman & Israel, 1967; Kantowitz, 1969).

Retaining the assumption that initiation time and movement time will vary independently would be naive.

One additional set of findings is often cited to buttress claims that initiation and execution stages are independent: Across subjects, initiation time and movement time within a given task are not highly correlated (see, e.g., Henry & Rogers, 1960; Henry, 1961a; Smith, 1961b). In the same manner, correlations between movement time and initiation time for individual subjects are often low (Henry, 1961b). A fast initiation time does not predict a fast movement time. In retrospect, a failure to find high correlations between trial initiation time and movement time is not surprising. Other attempts to correlate the dependent variables associated with reaction time trials have been equally frustrating [see Posner (1974) for a discussion of attempts to find correlations between reaction time and physiological measures]. However, neither these findings nor low

---

[3] Hindsight permits the observation that studies using the "memory drum" paradigm often varied more than one dimension at the same time. Care must be taken to change one parameter singly while holding others constant.

cross-task correlations (Lotter, 1961; Smith, 1961a), which have supported the position that abilities are task specific (see Marteniuk, 1974), should discourage attempts to test for relationships between initiation and movement execution stages in other ways. Low correlations between initiation time and movement time (measures that assess ability to minimize response duration) need not imply that initiation and execution stages incorporate independent processes, nor should they discourage attempts to manipulate task parameters and measure their influence on initiation time.

IV. Factors That Influence Programming Time

This section contains a review of studies that examined the influence of different task factors on initiation time and a discussion of strategies for studying these factors. As a first step, objections are raised to the assertion that motor programming only occurs with speed-maximized movements and/or movements with very short movement times. This opens the way for the consideration of evidence from studies that do not require speeded movements or short movement times. Second, the influence of physical task dimensions and task timing requirements on programming time is evaluated. Third, means to discriminate between response selection and response preparation processes are considered. A short final paragraph discusses studies that manipulate the levels of two or more parameters to test for possible parallel processing strategies.

Several temporal conditions have been proposed as criteria for the occurrence of programming. Some argue that movements will not be programmed in advance unless the task requires that they be executed as rapidly as possible (Henry & Rogers, 1960; Henry & Harrison, 1961). However, the finding that initiation time varies for different controlled durations counters the assumption that speed must be maximized for programming to occur (Klapp & Erwin, 1976). One might still hypothesize that short movement time, which may or may not reflect maximum speed requirements, is a necessary condition for movement programming. Many believe that short movement times fail to allow a sufficient period for ongoing control and correction so that such movements, of necessity, must be programmed in advance. Movements with short movement times do seem to be less subject to correction procedures (Schmidt, 1972; Schmidt & Russell, 1972). However, while movements with short movement times may be likely candidates for advance programming as opposed to ongoing control, this does not constitute evidence that short movement times are a necessary condition for programming. In fact, when differences are present, initiation time increases as movement times become longer, suggesting that programming demands increase as the necessary movement time increases. There may be an upper limit on the duration of movements that are programmed in advance (see Klapp & Erwin, 1976). However, the 100- to 200-msec range often noted as the minimum to permit corrections to occur (see Schmidt, 1976) does not qualify as a maximum for advance programming to occur.

What task-related factors appear to be important in dictating the length of the programming process? The two most frequently tested factors, movement distance and target width, do not appear to be critical or at least fail to influence initiation time in a consistent fashion. Distance fails to influence initiation time when movement terminates on small, well-defined targets (Brown & Slater-Hammel, 1949; Fitts & Peterson, 1964; Klapp, 1975) but may cause initiation time to increase as distance increases for movement with no target-defined endpoint (e.g., as in passing through a photoelectric make-and-break) or very wide targets (Klapp, 1975). Yet, even when precision demands have been low, initiation time failed to increase with distance when distance varied as a choice within blocks (Glencross, 1972). Initiation time did increase with distance when distance demands varied instead across blocks in two cases that both also involved a choice along another dimension: arm (Glencross, 1973) and direction (Klapp, 1975). Likewise, precision requirements may or may not influence initiation time. Target width does affect initiation time for very short-distance, speeded movements. Klapp (1975) employed the Fitts discrete tapping task to show that initiation time for short (2 and 11 mm) distances but not long (70 and 336 mm) distances varied with target diameter. However, movement times (which were around 150 msec) for short distances failed to increase as diameter decreased, suggesting that for short distances subjects opted to increase initiation time rather than increase movement time to permit ongoing correction. With the exclusion of these very short distance movements, the influence of target width on initiation time has been very small (Fitts & Peterson, 1964; Glencross, 1976; Klapp, 1975). In general, distance and precision effects are interdependent and appear only in highly specialized situations. Task parameters that define external physical movement dimensions are probably not the primary causal factors in determining movement programming times.

Instead, the critical variable determining initiation time appears to be the *complexity of timing requirements*. Evidence that timing requirements influence programming is available from studies that show that initiation time (*a*) is longer for the longer of two possible required durations, (*b*) increases as the number of timed movement segments increases, and (*c*) varies in response to timing requirements for the components of the movement. Initiation times for movements that differ only in required duration have been tested in two different ways. One task required a duration-controlled 10-cm lever movement. Here, Klapp and Erwin (1976) found longer initiation times for the longer of two learned durations in tests that included a number of different duration pairs. In the second task, using the so-called "Morse code" paradigm, reaction time for the "held-down" keypress "dah" exceeded reaction time for the short keypress "dit" (Klapp, Wyatt, & Lingo, 1974). Evidence for the relationship between initiation time and the number of response components rests primarily on verbal response times. Choice initiation time preceding pronunciation for an item increases with the number of syllables in the item to be pronounced (Eriksen, Pollack, & Montague, 1970; Klapp, Anderson, & Berrian, 1973). This increase is independent of the time needed for perception (Klapp *et al.*, 1973) and the actual duration of the produced response (Klapp & Erwin, 1976). Simple initiation time for the first item in a precued string of items to be pronounced (e.g., Monday, Monday–Wednesday, or Monday–Wednesday–Friday) increases with the number of items in the string (Monsell & Sternberg, Note 2). A parallel finding occurs for typed strings of letters; the time to initiate the first letter in a precued string increases with the number of letters in the string (see Chapter 6 of this volume). Support comes from the memory drum paradigm; one consistent finding has been that movements that require intermediate pauses on targets require longer to initiate than those that do not (Henry & Rogers, 1960; Glencross, 1973; Norrie, 1967, 1974). Formal pauses may break the movement into natural segments. Two findings suggest that within-response timing is important. Klapp and Erwin (1976) showed that time to start a timed lever movement that must incorporate a second movement, namely, a button press and release, was longer than the time to start a timed lever movement without a second component. Rosenbaum (Note 3) required that subjects control the time interval between two keypresses. The reaction time for the first response increased as the time required between responses increased from 10 to 220 msec. This suggests that within-task timing demands were important during the original programming process.[4] Temporal organization appears to be critical. Timing requirements are the primary task-imposed components that influence the time needed for movement selection and preparation processes.

Suppose one hopes to separate response selection and response preparation stages from one another. There is a preliminary step before this distinction can be considered: The time for encoding and identifying stimuli and for associating stimuli with task-appropriate responses must remain constant across conditions so that differences in initiation time can be identified with movement programming stages rather than processes that occur before programming (e.g., remembering that red means move right). The most straightforward approach standardizes the number of task alternatives across conditions. Other variables known to affect reaction time (e.g., signal intensity, warning interval duration) must also be controlled. Only when one is comfortable with the assumption that initial processing times remain equal across conditions should differences in initiation time be attributed to programming stages.

---

[4] One study appears at first to contradict this point. Klapp and Wyatt (1976) found that the time to initiate a response with a long-duration second component (e.g., dit–*dah*) did not exceed the time to initiate a response with a short-duration second component (e.g., dit–*dit*). However, the interval between the two components did reflect the expected time differences.

The most conservative approach is to consider the two programming stages together. Yet there are cases where one might guess that response selection times remain constant and response preparation times vary. If a parameter dimension is known before signal onset, it may be possible to bypass the response selection stage for that parameter. If selection is not a consideration, the response preparation stage will be the locus for differences in initiation time. This type of test requires that the parameter of interest be manipulated across (fixed) rather than within (mixed) blocks of trials. All one-choice tasks and choice tasks that vary the parameter of interest across rather than within blocks meet this criterion. The latter tasks, however, require the assumption that choice on a second parameter within blocks (e.g., right versus left choice at signal onset) does not affect the selection for the parameter manipulated across blocks (e.g., long versus short duration). Unfortunately, this assumption is one that is not easily tested. Differences between parameter dimensions do occur in fixed block testing (e.g., Klapp & Erwin, 1976, Experiments II and III). The comparison of times for mixed and fixed blocks may be an appropriate strategy for isolating stages in future work.

One-choice tasks also present problems. These may permit subjects to bypass both stages. Subjects might hold a completely *pre*programmed response in readiness so that a one-choice stimulus serves merely to trigger the fully *pre*programmed response rather than to initiate selection and/or preparation procedures (Klapp, 1976). Klapp *et al.* (1974) found that reaction time differences between long-duration and short-duration keypresses that were present for a choice case disappeared with sufficient motivation and practice in a one-choice condition. Yet, as differences between conditions have been present for a number of one-choice movements, it seems unlikely that both selection and preparation are bypassed in all one-choice cases. There is also no guarantee that subjects fail to hold more than one completely *pre*programmed response in readiness. Stimuli might trigger *pre*programmed responses in choice as well as simple conditions.

One additional set of studies deserves a few comments. These studies manipulated several task parameters simultaneously, tested for additive versus interactive effects (Sternberg, 1969; Taylor, 1976), and attempted to determine whether processing occurs in serial or in parallel (e.g., Kerr, 1976; Klapp, 1977; Rosenbaum, Note 1). One disadvantage inherent in this methodology is that, since the total number of possible alternatives may change under different conditions, the locus of obtained effects is particularly difficult to pinpoint. Identifying the stimuli and determining appropriate task goals as well as response selection and response preparationn may be implicated. We can say that the number of possible directions (Gibbs, 1965; Kerr, 1976; Megaw, 1972), the number of possible distances (Kerr, 1976), and, in general, the number of parameters that require decisions (Rosenbaum, Note 1) affect initiation time. When choice is involved for more than one parameter (e.g., arm, direction, and extent), subjects are able to utilize precued information on one dimension (or on two of three dimensions) to reduce the time to initiation the full response when it is cued. This reduction accompanies cues for responding member (Klapp, 1977; Rosenbaum, Note 1), duration (Klapp, 1977), distance (Rosenbaum, Note 1), and direction (Rosenbaum, Note 1). Is processing serial or parallel when all task parameters are presented simultaneously? Rosenbaum (Note 1) argues that arm, direction, and distance are prepared in serial. Klapp (1977), however, suggests that the responding member (finger) need not be identified before duration can be considered. The answer is not clear. One serious problem may be that these task-defined parameters (distance, direction, etc.) that we identify as important may be very different from the internal values that truly affect the motor control system; the parameters we define may not be considered singly, as we would like to think (Kerr, 1976).

V. Concluding Remarks

This chapter argues that the time to initiate movements provides clues to response selection and preparation processes. Past findings that initiation time and movement time are not highly correlated and the belief that initiation and movement stages are independent may have discouraged designs that manipulate task parameters to study their effect on initiation time. This methodology, however, is an appropriate one. It is also important to realize that programming does not require speeded-movement conditions or movement times below some minimal cutoff. Programming can be evaluated using a variety of conditions, including those interesting situations that call for duration control. An overview of the task factors that prove to influence programming indicates that temporal complexity and organization, as opposed to physical task dimensions (e.g., distance), may dictate the length of movement selection and preparation processes.

Acknowledgments

I would like to thank Elliot Saltzman and Marcy Lansman for their comments on early drafts of this chapter.

Reference Notes

1. Rosenbaum, D. A. *Stages of human movement initiation.* Manuscript submitted for publication.
2. Monsell, S., & Sternberg, S. *The latency of short and rapid utterances; Evidence for response preprogramming.* Paper presented at the Seventh International Symposium on Attention and Performance, Senanque, France, August, 1976.
3. Rosenbaum, D. A. *Mental time and real time in the production of manual responses.* Paper presented at the Psychonomic Society, Saint Louis, Missouri, November, 1976.

References

Brown, J. S., & Slater-Hammel, A. T. Discrete movements in the horizontal plane as a function of their length and direction. *Journal of Experimental Psychology*, 1949, *39*, 84–95.

Ells, J. G. Analysis of temporal and attentional aspects of movement control. *Journal of Experimental Psychology*, 1973, *99*, 10–21.

Ericksen, C. W., Pollack, M. D., & Montague, W. E. Implicit speech: Mechanism in perceptual encoding? *Journal of Experimental Psychology*, 1970, *84*, 502–507.

Evarts, E. V. Feedback and corollary discharge: A merging of the concepts. *Neurosciences Research Program Bulletin*, 1971, *9*, 86–112.

Fitts, P. M. The information capacity of the human motor system in controlling the amplitude of movement. *Journal of Experimental Psychology*, 1954, *47*, 381–391.

Fitts, P. M., & Peterson, J. R. Information capacity of discrete motor responses. *Journal of Experimental Psychology*, 1964, *67*, 103–112.

Fitts, P. M., & Radford, B. K. Information capacity of discrete motor responses under different cognitive sets. *Journal of Experimental Psychology*, 1966, *71*, 475–482.

Gibbs, C. B. Probability learning in step-input tracking. *British Journal of Psychology*, 1965, *56*, 233–242.

Glencross, D. J. Latency and response complexity. *Journal of Motor Behavior*, 1972, *4*, 241–256.

Glencross, D. J. Responses complexity and the latency of different movement patterns. *Journal of Motor Behavior*, 1973, *5*, 95–104.

Glencross, D. J. The latency of aiming movements. *Journal of Motor Behavior*, 1976, *8*, 27–34.

Henry, F. M. Reaction time–movement time correlations. *Perceptual and Motor Skills*, 1961, *12*, 63–66. (a)

Henry, F. M. Stimulus complexity, movement complexity, age, and sex in relation to reaction latency and speed in limb movements. *Research Quarterly*, 1961, *32*, 353–356. (b)

Henry, F. M., & Harrison, J. S. Refractoriness of a fast movement. *Perceptual and Motor Skills*, 1961, *13*, 351–354.

Henry, F. M., & Rogers, D. E. Increased response latency for complicated movements and a "memory drum" theory of neuromotor reaction. *Research Quarterly*, 1960, *31*, 448–458.

Herman, L. M., & Israel, A. Decremental and facilitatory effects of second signals on response time to first signals under different levels of uncertainty. *Proceedings of the 75th Annual Convention of the American Psychological Association* 1967, *2*, 27–28.

Kantowitz, B. H. Double stimulation with varying response information. *Journal of Experimental Psychology*, 1969, *82*, 347–352.

Keele, S. W. Movement control in skilled motor performance. *Psychological Bulletin*, 1968, *70*, 387–403.

Keele, S. W., & Summers, J. J. The structure of motor programs. In G. E. Stelmach (Ed.), *Motor control: Issues and trends*. New York: Academic Press, 1976.

Kerr, B. Decisions about movement direction and extent. *Journal of Human Movement Studies*, 1976, *3*, 199–213.

Klapp, S. T. Feedback versus motor programming in the control of aimed movements. *Journal of Experimental Psychology: Human Perception and Performance*, 1975, *104*, 147–153.

Klapp, S. T. Short-term memory as a response preparation state. *Memory and Cognition*, 1976, *4*, 721–729.

Klapp, S. T. Response programming, as assessed by reaction time does not establish commands for particular muscles. *Journal of Motor Behavior*, 1977, *9*, 301–312.

Klapp, S. T., Anderson, W. G., & Berrian, R. W. Implicit speech in reading, reconsidered. *Journal of Experimental Psychology*, 1973, *100*, 368–374.

Klapp, S. T., & Erwin, I. Relation between programming time and duration of the response being programmed. *Journal of Experimental Psychology: Human Perception and Performance*, 1976, *2*, 591–598.

Klapp, S. T., & Wyatt, E. P. Motor programming within a sequence of responses. *Journal of Motor Behavior*, 1976, *8*, 19–26.

Klapp, S. T., Wyatt, E. P., & Lingo, W. M. Response programming in simple and choice reactions. *Journal of Motor Behavior*, 1974, *6*, 263–271.

Kots, Ya. M. Supraspinal control of the segmental centres of muscle antagonists in man. I. Reflex excitability of the motor neurones of muscle antagonists in the period of organization of voluntary movement. *Biophysics*, 1969, *14*, 176–183.

Lagasse, P. P., & Hayes, K. C. Premotor and motor reaction time as a function of movement extent. *Journal of Motor Behavior*, 1973, *5*, 25–32.

Laszlo, J. I., & Livesey, J. P. Task complexity, accuracy, and reaction time. *Journal of Motor Behavior*, 1977, *9*, 171–177.

Lotter, W. S. Specificity or generality of speed of systematically related movements. *Research Quarterly*, 1961, *32*, 55–62.

Marteniuk, R. G. Individual differences in motor performance and learning. In J. A. Wilmore (Ed.), *Exercise and sport sciences reviews* (Vol. 2). New York: Academic Press, 1974.

Megaw, E. D. Direction and extent uncertainty in step-input tracking. *Journal of Motor Behavior*, 1972, *4*, 171–186.

Norrie, M. L. Practice effects on reaction latency for simple and complex movements. *Research Quarterly*, 1967, *38*, 79–85.

Norrie, M. L. Effects of movement complexity on choice reaction and movement times. *Research Quarterly*, 1974, *45*, 154–161.

Pachella, R. G. The interpretation of reaction time in information-processing research. In B. H. Kantowitz (Ed.), *Human information processing: Tutorials in performance and cognition*. Hillsdale, New Jersey: Erlbaum, 1974.

Posner, M. I. Psychobiology of Attention. In C. Blakemore & M. S. Gassaniga (Eds.), *The handbook of psychobiology*. New York: Academic Press, 1974.

Schmidt, R. A. The index of preprogramming (IP): A statistical method for evaluating the role of feedback in simple movements. *Psychonomic Science*, 1972, *27*, 83–85.

Schmidt, R. A. Control processes in motor skills. In J. Keogh & R. S. Hutton (Eds.), *Exercise and sport sciences reviews* (Vol. 4). Santa Barbara, California: Journal Publishing Affiliates, 1976.

Schmidt, R. A., & Russell, D. G. Movement velocity and movement time as determiners of degree of preprogramming in simple movements. *Journal of Experimental Psychology*. 1972, *96*, 315–320.

Simon, J. R. Effect of ear stimulated on reaction time and movement time. *Journal of Experimental Psychology*, 1968, *78*, 344–346.

Simon, J. R. Reactions toward the source of stimulation. *Journal of Experimental Psychology*, 1969, *81*, 174–176.

Smith, E. E. Choice reaction time: An analysis of the major theoretical positions. *Psychological Bulletin*, 1968, *69*, 77–110.

Smith, L. E. Individual differences in strength, reaction latency, mass and length of limb and their relation to maximal speed of movements. *Research Quarterly*, 1961, *32*, 208–220(a)

Smith, L. E. Reaction time and movement time in four large muscle movements. *Research Quarterly*, 1961, *31*, 88–92. (b)

Sternberg S. The discovery of processing stages: Extension of Donders' method. In W. G. Koster (Ed.), *Attention and performance* (Vol. 2). Amsterdam: North-Holland, 1969.

Taylor, D. A. Stage analysis of reaction time. *Psychological Bulletin*, 1976, *83*, 161–191.

Theios J. The components of response latency in simple human information processing tasks. In P. M. A. Robbitt & S. Dornic (Eds.), *Attention and performance* (Vol. 5). New York: Academic Press, 1975.

Weiss, A. D. The locus of reaction time change with set, motivation, and age. *Journal of Gerontology,* 1965, *20,* 60–64.

Woodworth, R. S. *Experimental psychology.* New York: Holt, 1938.

Wrisberg, C. A., & Pushkin, M. H. Preparatory set, response complexity, and reaction latency. *Journal of Motor Behavior,* 1976, *8,* 203–207.

4

The Components of an Information Processing Theory of Skilled Performance Based on an Optimal Control Perspective

Richard W. Pew
Sheldon Baron

I. Introduction

The spurt in theory development in motor performance and motor learning has produced largely qualitative theories. Such developments as Adams's closed-loop theory (1971) and Schmidt's schema theory (1975) provide verbal–analytic statements of the functional specifications of a system that could learn to produce movements of particular types. These theories permit the formulation of alternative hypotheses and make it possible to accept or reject the hypotheses on the basis of empirical data. In general, they do not provide sufficient detail to make

Information Processing in
Motor Control and Learning

it possible to produce a mathematical model or write a computer program that would predict the behavior of real subjects. While science should progress from the general to the specific and verbal–analytic theories are a natural step in that progression, we should be searching continually for formal means of representing theory in sufficient quantitative detail that our intuitions may be aided by formalisms that force implicit assumptions into the open and expose the logical consistencies and inconsistencies in our theories. Said another way, these popular theories leave so many degrees of freedom unconstrained that one is at a loss to know whether they could be translated into representations of motor performance in a natural setting.

One highly developed formalism that appears to be uniquely applicable to the study and representation of motor performance is that of optimal control theory. The leverage of optimal control theory to model human performance derives from one fundamental assumption, namely, that a well-trained subject will act in a near-optimal manner that is contingent on his internal limitations and his understanding of the task. The appropriateness of that assumption has been evaluated repeatedly in studies of manual control systems and has been shown to be remarkably robust. Models based on it produce predictions of a variety of dimensions of performance that typically lie within 1 SD of the mean in terms of the sampling variability of a group of subjects evaluated on the same measures. That is, the model is at least as good a predictor as another subject would be. The optimality assumption is used in a manner exactly analogous to the application of the ideal observer in signal detection theory. The theory is prescriptive of what a subject *should* do and a subject's limitations may be introduced to degrade ideal performance so that the model becomes descriptive of what real subjects actually do. In a sense, the optimal control model may be regarded as a generalization of a Bayesian decision model to incorporate control as well as decision behavior, to deal with continuous functions of time, and to accommodate multiple sensory inputs.

It is interesting that, as a model of human performance, the optimal control model has, for the most part, been treated as a "black box." It has been shown to be predictive of performance in practical control tasks, but little attention has been given to the isomorphisms between the components of the model and the activities that a theorist having an information-processing view of motor performance might hypothesize. In fact, it now appears that a good case can be made for at least some correspondences between the model and information-processing theory, and the purpose of this chapter is to describe these correspondences and to begin to formulate theoretical questions about motor performance that may be addressed by the model. Because the model can simulate real performance, no degrees of freedom of representation are left unspecified, and we stand to learn a lot from the model about the features of the environment that must serve as inputs and about the behavioral concomitants of the model itself.

II. Environmental Description

In order to apply the optimal control model, the following features of the environment must be described.

1. The sources of sensory information to be utilized in the control task must be represented in the form of an "output vector," which describes, for example, position, velocity, and acceleration as a function of time as it may be perceived by the subject. A signal-to-noise ratio is assigned to each output variable, analogous to a signal detection representation of its detectability. This sensory representation is not limited to visual inputs but may include auditory, proprioceptive, vestibular, or tactile inputs if they are considered important for the task in question.

2. A stochastic or deterministic representation of the driving function or environmental disturbances over which the subject will exert control must be formulated.

3. A state-variable representation or model of the system being controlled must be used. This system may be an external plant such as an aircraft or automobile or it may simply be the dynamics of a limb or control stick if they are believed to impose limitations on the subject's control strategy.

4. A quantitative statement of the criterion or performance index against which the subject's performance will be judged must be developed. Criteria such as minimizing error, minimizing effort (where effort can be defined in terms of force or movement), minimizing time to return to an equilibrium state, or combinations of such variables are all possible metrics that may be employed as performance critieria. The requirement of a performance index is one important way in which the optimal control model departs from more familiar models of manual control. The theorist must either make assumptions about the performance index being employed by a subject or test the implications of different possible metrics for performance of the model.

III. Model Description

Given this environmental description, the model of the subject's behavior incorporates the elements shown in Figure 1. For a mathematical description of the model, the reader is referred to Kleinman, Baron, and Levison (1971). The figure illustrates only a single-dimensional control task, but the variables illustrated should be regarded as multidimensional vectors.

First, the displayed variables are assumed to be corrupted by "observation noise" introduced by the human subject. This noise is exactly analogous to the internal noise level postulated in signal detection theory. It is the way the model introduces human limitations in processing and attentional capacity. Different

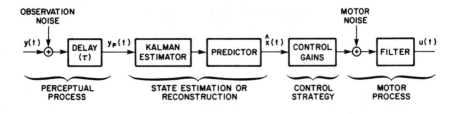

Figure 1 Structure of the optimal control model.

noise levels may be assumed for different displayed variables and, for example, if several visual displays are providing useful information, the noise level associated with each may be adjusted to account for the distribution of attention assigned by the operator. Alternatively, a model of attentional scanning may be introduced to predict the noise level associated with each variable in order to produce optimal performance with respect to the criterion variable.

At this point the model is dealing with a noisy representation of the displayed quantities. That representation is then delayed by an amount τ to represent internal human processing delays. Again it is possible to assume differential delays for different sensory channels, but this will complicate the model substantially and has not been done in manual control applications.

The central elements of the model are represented in the blocks described as the Kalman estimator and predictor. Their purpose is to generate the best estimate of the *current* state of the displayed variables at time t based on the noisy, delayed perceptual information available. These blocks compute the estimate of this state so as to minimize the residual estimation uncertainty. What is being captured is a representation of the subject's ability to construct from his understanding of the system and his incomplete knowledge of the moment-by-moment state of the system a set of expectancies concerning the system behavior at the next moment in time. It is in these blocks that it is assumed that the subject has an internal model of the dynamics of the system being controlled and a representation of the statistics of the system forcing function or disturbances. This representation is analogous to the schema of current theories, and it is interesting to note that, in this formulation, the schema must incorporate knowledge of both the expected signals and the system dynamics being controlled.

Given the best estimate of the current system state, which may include components representing the error between the current and the desired state, the next block, labeled control gains, assigns a set of weighting factors to the elements of this estimated state in order to produce control actions that will minimize the defined performance criterion. This is sometimes referred to as the "control law" and the analogy with detection theory can be applied here as well. Just as the costs and payoffs associated with detection performance influence decision criteria, the choice of performance index influences the weighting matrix assigned. The separation between detection sensitivity and response bias corresponds to the separation here between estimation and control weighting assignments. Changes in the performance criterion affect the control law but not the estimation process. This may be an important distinction in thinking about motor performance as well.

Just as an observation noise is postulated to account for processing inadequacies, a motor noise is introduced to account for the subject's inability to generate control actions corresponding exactly to his intentions. In many applications this noise level is insignificant in comparison with the observation noise, but where precise control is important to the conditions being analyzed this could become an important variable and has received little attention.

Finally, motor output is assumed to be filtered or smoothed by the inherent sluggishness in the motor response system, and this filter, together with the motor noise, represents the limited output capabilities of the subject.

This, then, provides an intuitive description of the elements of the optimal control model. It should be emphasized that the parameter values that must be provided by the investigator correspond to the human limitations that constrain behavior. The model, taking these limitations as the constraints within which performance is produced, predicts the best that the subject can do, depending on his own limitations. A large backlog of empirical research provides the data necessary to make realistic estimates of these parameter settings in the manual control context, and many of these results should, in turn, be useful for studies of motor performance per se.

To illustrate the manual control results, the model has been shown to predict the effects on performance of introducing different forcing functions, different plant dynamics, two-dimensional versus one-dimensional tracking, of tracking with peripherally versus centrally fixated displays, and of introducing motion cues as a source of sensory information. In an experiment by Levison (personal communication, 1977), it was demonstrated with the model and confirmed empirically that the provision of visual cues to motion in the peripheral field of view of a stationary subject produced the same performance effects as corresponding physical movement of the subject's platform.

IV. Issues That May Be Addressed by the Model

More important to the goals of this chapter is the formulation of as yet unanswered questions concerning motor performance that could be addressed by the optimal control model. The topic of greatest interest to this group is perhaps the question of how to represent changes in behavior resulting from practice. Thus far, essentially no work has been done on this problem, but several hypotheses suggest themselves.

A. Shifting Attentional Allocation

It has been argued, particularly by Fleishman and Hempel (1954), that subjects allocate their attention to various available sensory cues early in practice differently than later in practice. The optimal control model would represent this by assigning different observation noise levels to the display variables as a function of practice and would examine the implications of these variables for both the quality of performance and the particular features of that performance as embodied in such dependent variables as frequency response characteristics.

B. Development of the "Perceptual Trace"

As was mentioned, the optimal estimator and predictor make use of an "internal" representation of the driving function or disturbances against which the subject is exerting control. In the usual case, these functions are random appearing and are known only statistically. If the forcing function is represented deterministically, then the output of the predictor will be a perfect representation of the signal and the only performance degradation would result from limitations in the motor end of the model. However, if we wish to represent the acquisition of control of a deterministic signal for which the subject learns the pattern as a result of practice, it would be possible to add uncertainty to the representation of this deterministic signal in the Kalman estimator and predictor and to postulate and to test empirically the ways in which this uncertainty is reduced with practice. An important point is that with this kind of paradigm one can depart from strict tracking studies and begin to explore conditions more like those associated with voluntary movement. Depending upon individual biases, one may want to identify these manipulations with either perceptual trace formation (Adams, 1971) or schema formation (Schmidt, 1975).

C. Development of the Internal Model of System Dynamics

The optimal control model also requires a representation of the system that is constraining the subject's performance. In manual control applications it is usually assumed that a well-trained subject has a perfect representation of his own limb dynamics and of the system being controlled. However, some pilot work has examined the implications of assuming that the subject has an incorrect or oversimplified model of those dynamics. It has been shown that the optimal control model will make discriminably different predictions when that model is changed. This suggests the possibility of tracing the acquisition of this representation of system behavior. In the terminology used in studies of motor control and learning, we believe that is another component of the subject's schema that could be explored quantitatively by postulating the ways in which the specificity of this model might change with practice and by testing the model predictions of these hypotheses against empirical observations.

D. Impact of Choice of Performance Criterion

A question that is often finessed in studies of skilled performance is the subject's implicit criterion of good performance. Since that criterion must be made explicit in the optimal control model, it is possible to explore theoretically the implications of assuming different performance criteria. It seems likely that this is a further dimension of behavior that might change during the course of skill acquisition.

V. A Possible Experiment

To make this discussion more concrete, consider the following experimental conditions that might provide a starting point for exploring the acquisition of control behavior using the model. The system forcing function would be a sinusoidal waveform with a frequency of about 0.25 Hz. The plant being controlled would be a simulated, lightly damped, second-order system, a control task of considerable difficulty. Two control stick conditions would be studied. The first condition would employ a force stick that provides no positional cues and no proprioceptive cues to the feel of the second-order plant. The second condition would provide direct proprioceptive feel of the plant either by building a control stick having those physical dynamics directly or by using a stick incorporating a torque motor and building in artificially the force and positional feedback cues associated with control of the second-order plant. A disturbance input would be added to the plant output that randomly perturbs the positional output. In the case of the control feel condition, this disturbance would actually apply forces to the stick itself.

By examining the model parameters that best represent performance in the force feel condition and assuming that the force feedback provides the subject with a well-defined and accurate representation of the plant, it would be possible to trace the model parameter changes as the subject learns the characteristics of the sine-wave input. In the force stick condition, one could examine the acquisition of the internal model of the plant by using the parameter settings for the force feel condition to describe changes in the forcing function model and to focus attention on parameter changes associated with the buildup of a good representation of the subject's internal model of the second-order plant dynamics.

In this way, we might begin to get a quantitative description of changes in the subject's schema representing this control task.

VI. Summary

We have introduced the conceptual framework of the optimal control model for perceptual–motor performance to illustrate the potential correspondences between it and the currently popular concepts of information processing in skills. The environmental and behavioral specifications that the model uses tell us some important things about the components of a theory of skill. The model also has the potential, if used in conjunction with empirical work formulated in the context of the model, to illuminate further our understanding of skill acquisition.

References

Adams, J. A. A closed-loop theory of motor learning. *Journal of Motor Behavior*, 1971, *3*, 111–150.

Fleishman, E. A., & Hempel, W. E. Changes in the factor structure of a complex psychomotor task as a function of practice. *Psychometrika*, 1954, *19*, 239–252.

Kleinman, D. L., Baron, S., & Levison, W. H. A control theoretic approach to manned-vehicle systems analysis. *IEEE Transactions on Automatic Control*, 1971, *AC–16*, 824–832.

Schmidt, R. A. A schema theory of discrete-motor skill learning. *Psychological Review*, 1975, *82*, 225–260.

5

Conscious Mechanisms in Movement[1]

J. A. Scott Kelso
Stephen A. Wallace

I. Introduction

Although the conscious correlates of voluntary acts have intrigued psychologists and physiologists at least since the time of Duchenne (1883), our understanding is still at a rather primitive level. While it is generally accepted that certain effector and receptor mechanisms may subserve the conscious apprecia-

[1] Much of the research reported here and the preparation of the paper were supported by a Laura Spelman Rockefeller award from the University of Iowa and a biomedical research support grant (FR–07035) from the General Research Support Branch, Division of Research Resources, the Bureau of Health Professions, Education and Manpower Training, National Institutes of Health to J. A. Scott Kelso. Stephen A. Wallace was supported by Grant 704–01 from the Illinois Department of Mental Health and Developmental Disabilities. We express our thanks to David Goodman, who assisted in the background work for this paper.

Information Processing in
Motor Control and Learning

tion of movement, there is little consensus as to the nature and utility of the information that each provides to the performer (Goodwin, McCloskey, & Matthews, 1972; McCloskey, Ebeling, & Goodwin, 1974). This is by no means a new state of affairs. Renowned scientists and philosophers of the nineteenth century ferociously argued about the relationship of voluntary action to what Hyslop (1895) termed the "so-called 'ideas of motion' which precede the actual motion and to the so-called 'kinesthetic sensation' or 'sense of effort' which follows the motion [p. 421]."

We should note Hyslop's equation of "sense of effort" and "kinesthetic sensation" and the obvious peripheral origin of each. However, many others [including Muller, Hughlings-Jackson, and Crichton-Browne (reviewed in Hyslop, 1895)] believed the "sense of effort" to be purely central, consisting of an efferent motor discharge accompanying rather than following muscular action. Clearly, this debate continues among psychologists and physiologists alike. On the behavioral side, some have argued that voluntary movements are based on purely centrifugal mechanisms (e.g., Jones, 1974) whereas others stress the role of sensory feedback (Adams, 1976, pp. 87–108). In the area of neurophysiology, some evidence has been provided for the neural counterparts of "sense of effort" (for reviews, see Evarts, 1971; Kelso & Stelmach, 1976, pp. 1–40), although other researchers have argued that "to postulate such sensations in a normal subject with normal limbs means to abstain from chances of progress and prefer a 'dead end' of research to a 'live wire' [Granit, 1972, p. 654]."

While debate and argument are usually excellent stimulants to scientific research, why has it taken us so long to come up with a unified conceptualization of "movement" information processing? We believe that at least part of the answer lies in the very nature of the information with which we have to deal. As elegantly pointed out by Neisser (1976), nothing in "active touch" corresponds to the retinal image or the spectrum of continuous sound, which provide the basic input in studies of vision and psychoacoustics. When we prepare for and execute movements, a flow of information is generated from so many diverse sources that the distinction between input and output becomes a cloudy one. In essence, we are moving and perceiving the results of our movements at the same time.

Although some would argue that we have to control the input in order to obtain knowledge on how movement information is "perceived, coded, and retrieved [Stelmach, Note 1]," and while this would seem an admirable goal in light of visual and auditory information processing, it seems rather questionable whether the study of movement should or even can progress via such an approach. Passive, psychophysical techniques used to examine motor information fail to account for the fact that the active component plays a significant role in the conscious perception of movement (Gibson, 1962; Kelso, 1977a; Paillard & Brouchon, 1968, pp. 37–55; Weimer, 1977, 267–314); they also fail to tap the nature of the cognitive mechanisms preceding the production of movement. By examining the nature of active goal-oriented movements, we propose that more can be learned about movement processes than by stimulating the tip of a finger with a vibrotactile input, for example. As Sperry (1952) remarked over a quarter of a century ago, and has reiterated (Sperry, 1976, pp. 163–178), analysis of the motor output may tell us much more about internal mental processes than analysis of the input.

In this chapter we wish to pursue an empirical finding that has intrigued us and that reflects to some degree the philosophical position presented above. We refer to the almost invariant finding that when a blindfolded individual makes a voluntary movement of his/her own choice and is later asked to reproduce that movement, considerable enhancement of performance occurs relative to conditions where the subject moves or is moved passively to an experimenter-defined constrained location. In previous reports, we have addressed various aspects of this problem, which we will term the *preselection effect* (Kelso, 1975, 1977a,b,c; Kelso & Stelmach, 1976; Stelmach, Kelso, & Wallace, 1975; Stelmach, Kelso, & McCullagh, 1976; Wallace & Stelmach, 1975). In this chapter and in the traditions of midwestern empiricism, we wish to present data relevant to the generality of the preselection effect. We want to emphasize that the basic finding has led us into a variety of areas within the realm of experimental psychology concerning the voluntary control of movement.

In pursuing the nature of the preselection effect, many questions have arisen that extend beyond the basic finding and appear to present potential avenues for research. For example, we shall show that the presence of afferent movement cues is not crucial for the accuracy of preselected movement and, furthermore, that the availability of preselection reduces the dominance effects of visual input concurrent with movement. Finally, we shall focus on the theoretical mechanisms postulated for the preselection effect and attempt to present what we believe to be the optimum account for the data. Throughout this chapter we shall try to intertwine relevant neurophysiological work with behavioral data for the purpose of supporting our position and suggesting future directions.

II. Empirical Basis

A. The Generality of the Preselection Effect

There can be no question regarding the generality of the preselection effect—the evidence speaks for itself. The superior reproduction accuracy of preselected movement has been demonstrated with slow to moderate paced movements (Kelso, 1977a; Marteniuk, 1973; Stelmach, Kelso, & McCullagh, 1976; Wallace & Stelmach, 1975), rapid movements (Jones, 1972, 1974; Stelmach, Kelso, & Wallace, 1975), and semicontinuous movements (Russell, Note 2) and across a variety of movement amplitudes. Furthermore, preselected reproduction has been superior to constrained reproduction with both distance and location cues available (Jones, 1972, 1974, Expt. 1; Jones & Hulme, 1976, Expt. 1; Kelso, 1977a; Stelmach *et al.*, 1976), location cues only (Marteniuk, 1973; Stelmach *et al.*, 1975, Expts. 2 and 3; Wallace & Stelmach, 1975, Expt. 2), and distance cues only (Jones & Hulme, 1976, Expt. 2; Marteniuk, 1973; Stelmach & Kelso, 1977, Expt. 1). We have obtained data that serve to emphasize the tremendous generality of the foregoing findings as well as their potential (but largely unexplored) sensitivity to developmental trends.

The initial issues surrounding this work had to do with how children code kinesthetic information and whether they can maintain what is coded over short periods of time. Although movement-produced information is given a dominant role in conceptualizations of skill development (Bruner, 1973), process-oriented research on the problem is conspicuous by its absence. As a starting point, we chose the terminal location of the movement as the cue to be reproduced, since research on adults has clearly shown that location can be maintained if retention intervals are not filled with verbal information-processing activity (e.g., Laabs, 1973). The question was: Can the developmentally young rehearse [2] location? A large body of data indicates that deliberate mnemonic strategies are absent in the immature (for reviews, see Brown, 1974; Flavell, 1970), but the bulk of that work is limited to the view that rehearsal processes involve covert speech. Location information, on the other hand, may possibly be stored as an image or relatively direct representation of the stimulus input rather than a verbal description of the stimulus (Posner, 1973, pp. 35–73). It becomes of interest then to determine whether the rehearsal strategy deficiency hypothesis is generalizable to this type of representational activity and, if it is, what procedures can be adopted to overcome such deficiences.

Our subjects for these studies consisted of two groups of educably mentally retarded children varying in mean mental age (8.9 years, range = 8.3–9.7 years, and 5.8 years, range = 4.7–6.9 years). Our initial experiments, details of which can be obtained elsewhere (Kelso, Goodman, Hayes, & Stamm, Note 3), showed that the older group reproduced location [3] more accurately both immediately and after a 15-sec interval delay. However, there was no differential effect of retention interval for either developmental group; both showed an inability to rehearse location, in contrast to the evidence obtained using adults (e.g., Keele & Ells, 1972; Laabs, 1973). While there are several possible reasons for this finding,

---

[2] Rehearsal here is not restricted to situations in which processing is verbal, but rather to situations for which it can be shown that retention requires central processing (Posner & Rossman, 1965).

[3] We should note that this work was on *constrained* location, mainly because we felt it important to obtain comparisons with a basically secure adult finding (e.g., Laabs, 1973; Marteniuk & Roy, 1972). Location cues were manipulated in the standard manner.

it may be that our subjects were characterized by a rather passive acceptance of the task (Brown, 1974, 1975, pp. 103–152), a factor that would inhibit any active transformation of the input into a mnemonic code.

How, then, might we enhance the codability of movement-produced information? A number of potential (but as yet untried) procedures might be adopted, such as providing verbal or visual strategies to assist in categorizing the movements (e.g., Shea, Note 4). However, we argued that, if the developmentally young are capable of accurate movement planning, improved performance under preselected conditions might also be expected. This turned out to be precisely what happened. The two age groups (14 subjects in each) performed preselected and constrained movements under each of three retention interval conditions (immediate and 7- and 15-sec delays). The results, demonstrating the preselection effect, are shown in Figure 1. The superiority of preselection was not differential as a function of age and prevailed over all three retention intervals. Furthermore, there was evidence that both groups could retain location over 7

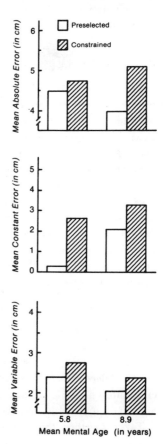

Figure 1 Mean absolute, constant, and variable errors for preselected and constrained conditions as a function of mental age.

sec but not over 15 sec—a finding that warrants further study. The main point, however, is that the facilitatory effects arising from preselecting a movement are not restricted to adult findings. If preselection enables the performer to plan the movement prior to its execution, as we have argued elsewhere (Kelso, 1977a,b; Kelso & Stelmach, 1976; Stelmach *et al.,* 1975; see also the following discussion), it seems that the developmentally immature are perfectly capable of such operations. However, the intention to plan performance is a general factor previously not found in the developmentally young (Brown, 1974, 1975; Smirnov & Zinchenko, 1969, pp. 452–502). It therefore remains to be seen whether our findings, which appear to be indicative of "planfullness" (Brown, 1975) and strategic behavior, are unique to the movement domain. Although we have often referred to the importance of plans and strategies in motor learning (e.g., Miller, Galanter, & Pribram, 1960), much remains to be learned on how the young child utilizes strategic control to meet the changing task demands required of most skill situations. In addition, we need to ask if and how strategies influence the control of movement. The work on preselection may be a starting point for further investigation of issues of this nature.

B. Preselection and Conscious Proprioception

The robustness of the preselection effect certainly cannot be questioned. Of further concern to us, however, was whether the preselection effect was dependent upon or influenced by the presence or absence of proprioceptive and visual information. Let us first consider the role of proprioceptive input in preselected and constrained movements. In previous reports, data were presented indicating that simple preselected finger movements were unaffected by the removal of joint and cutaneous sources of input using the wrist-cuff technique (Goodwin *et al.,* 1972; Merton, 1964, pp. 387–400), whereas constrained movements showed dramatic decrements in performance (Kelso, 1977b,c). The data for preselected movements under cuff conditions appear to concur with the hypothesis borrowed from investigators in speech control, namely, that the greater the ability of the central nervous system (CNS) to "predictively determine" a motor response, the less the need for peripheral sensory feedback (MacNeilage & MacNeilage, 1973). Indeed, there appears to be considerable generality to this notion, as evident in neurophysiological work on monkeys using limb and eye movements (Bizzi, 1974; Brooks, 1975). Briefly, when the animal is in a predictive mode of performance, the movement pattern generated shows evidence of a substantial central programming component and an apparent independence of peripheral feedback (Kelso, 1977b). In contrast, in the exploratory performance mode, the opposite pattern of results occurs; movements are clearly updated by feedback for successful execution.

Taken together, the data suggest that preselected movements contain a substantial motor programming component not hitherto acknowledged by those espousing closed-loop notions (Adams, 1971, 1976; Newell, 1974; Stelmach, 1973). On the other hand, under constrained exploratory conditions, feedback about the location of the limb appears to be crucial for accurate movement reproduction.

There were other rather interesting aspects of the data obtained via the wrist-cuff technique that first, may tell us more about the nature of preselection and second, force us to consider more fully the role of the various receptor systems mediating the conscious appreciation of movement. Witness the following situation. During cuff trials when loss of movement-position sensitivity had occurred, the subject was instructed to preselect a given movement but was prevented from executing it by the experimenter restraining the finger at the starting position. This condition occurred 12 times for each subject throughout the testing session and was designed to reveal whether the obstructed movement was perceived on the basis of proprioception—particularly the unaffected muscle receptors lying in the forearm. However, not a single subject ($N = 12$) perceived that the movement had been obstructed. Rather, they proceeded to reproduce what was essentially an "illusory" movement, that is, one that had been planned but never executed (see Figure 2). Thus, under wrist-cuff conditions, the subject appears to perceive preselected movement on the basis of what he/she *expects* to occur rather than the actual consequences of action, which are unavailable. Preselection, then, appears to involve an internal signal conveying the expected consequences of action, a point to which we will return later.

Of course this finding also suggests that muscle receptors are not providing

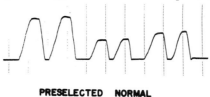

PRESELECTED   NORMAL

PRESELECTED   CUFF

Figure 2   Potentiometer output for preselected normal and wrist-cuff performance demonstrating the illusory movement phenomenon (see the text for the details).

useful information to the performer. The unexpected obstruction should have led to an above-normal firing level in both tendon organs and muscle spindles (Goodwin *et al.,* 1972; Vallbo, 1972, pp. 317–324), thus increasing their potential to access central awareness. Indeed, Granit (1972) has argued that such a mismatch between the "demand" of the motor system (as reflected in α–γ co-activation) and its "accomplishment" (the 1A discharge from muscle spindles) is the *necessary condition* for muscle afferents to mediate perception. The normal checking of the outcome of the movement in relation to commands generated is assumed to be an automatic process, not reaching awareness unless something unexpected occurs.

Given that a mismatch has been created by obstructing the planned displacement, why then did the subject not perceive it as such if Granit's (1972) hypothesis is correct? A possible answer to this problem, and one that has led us to consider more fully the nature of the information provided by different types of proprioceptors, may lie in the Marsden, Merton, and Morton (1972) finding that ischemia severely depresses the muscle afferent response to stretch. The implication of this result is that a combination of joint and cutaneous inputs is necessary for muscle afferent signals to reach consciousness. While not detracting from the interpretation that subjects perceived preselected movements to take place on the basis of a central "intention," it seems rather clear that, by using the wrist-cuff technique, the possible perceptual effects of muscle spindle information are largely removed. Very similar findings have been obtained by Gandevia and McCloskey (1976) using drug infiltration techniques to anesthize the joints.

We have converged on the foregoing interpretation by examining movement reproduction under a variety of conditions in patients in whom the finger joints have been completely removed and replaced. This procedure eliminates joint capsular afferents but usually leaves cutaneous inputs intact. The data for these patients, who performed 12 preselected and 12 constrained movements into each of three response sectors, are presented in Figure 3. The most interesting contrast is for constrained performance between joint replacement and wrist-cuff groups. In terms of absolute accuracy, the mean reproduction error is 3.13° compared to a mean of 13.33° for subjects in the constrained–cuff condition.

This is a rather fascinating finding in light of the classical role given by most physiologists and psychologists to joint receptors in the perception of movement and position (Marteniuk, Shields, & Campbell, 1972; Marteniuk & Roy, 1972; Skoglund, 1956, 1973, pp. 111–136). That is, "classical" conceptions of kinesthesis are built upon the angular specificity notion, namely, that receptors in the joints fire maximally at specific angles throughout the full range of limb position and that these signals are relayed to higher levels in such a way as to enhance specificity of information (Somjen, 1972). Such a position no longer appears tenable in light of data indicating a relative lack of activity from articular nerves when

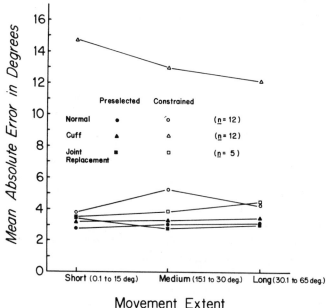

Figure 3   Mean absolute error as a function of movement extent for normal, wrist-cuff, and joint replacement groups performing under preselected and constrained movement conditions.

the joint is held at or near its midposition compared to when it approaches maximum flexion or extension (Clark & Burgess, 1975; Lynn, 1975; Miller, 1973). Indeed, Grigg (1976) has shown that a sizable proportion of afferents in cat medial articular nerve fire as a function of the degree of torque developed at a fixed joint position. This finding suggests that muscular contractions activate joint neurons and that joint afferents can function as *load detectors*. Furthermore, it appears to strengthen other reports (e.g., Clark & Burgess, 1975) that sense of position depends upon receptors other than joint afferents.

Clearly, we may have to reassess previous behavioral predictions based on apparently erroneous neurophysiological data. But what are the alternatives to joint receptors? Whether tactile information per se is sufficient to account for the performance of joint replacement patients shown in Figure 3 is open to question. Goldscheider's (1889) work, in which the skin was anesthetized via induction currents, revealed no disturbing effects on movement perception, a result that has been corroborated (Browne, Lee, & Ring, 1954; Provins, 1958). An alternative interpretation is that cutaneous inputs facilitate access to the CNS (cortical motoneurons) by muscle receptors. If this is the case, a strong argument would be generated for the role of muscle receptors in the conscious appreciation of movement—a stance that is receiving increasing support (Goodwin,

1977, pp. 87–124); Goodwin *et al.,* 1972; Gandevia & McCloskey, 1976; Horch, Clark, & Burgess, 1975). A more systematic assessment of movement-position sense in joint replacement patients with and without skin input may clarify this issue.

Perhaps an even more challenging question for movement control pertains to the structures responsible for affecting the reflex responses of muscle spindles. No evidence exists as to whether it is skin receptors, joint receptors, or both. One of us (Kelso) is preparing to explore these alternatives by examining the muscle response to unexpected changes in load in patients who have had the joint capsule removed. If joint capsular inputs are important, as suggested by Grigg's (1976) work and clinical observations of poor load compensation following prosthetic replacement, we would expect at best a greatly diminished response to muscle perturbations.

It is clear that many interesting and challenging questions remain to be answered with regard to the function of the various receptor mechanisms mediating proprioceptive information and to their role in movement control. The studies presented here were the first to examine movement reproduction following the removal of joint receptors and precipitated some of the follow-up problems that we have discussed. It seems obvious that if we are not to give proprioception an almost mythical status in the regulation of voluntary movement we must delineate its role more completely (Taub, 1977, pp. 335–374). By specifying the behavioral significance of peripheral mechanisms in movement perception and control, we should be in a stronger position to infer the contribution of central programming operations.

In summary, our initial question concerning the dependence or independence of preselected movement reproduction on conscious proprioceptive information has led us to a further and in-depth assessment of proprioceptors per se. We do not wish to lose sight of the basic finding, however—that preselected movements may be accurately reproduced whether or not cues for motion are present. We turn now to an attempted series of converging operations on this interpretation. Basically, the approach was not to *remove* information arising from preselected movements but rather to adopt a complementary procedure of providing additional information—in this case, vision.

C. Preselection, Attention, and Visual Dominance

The assumptions underlying the manipulation of vision in these experiments are identical to those pertaining to feedback deprivation techniques. If preselection involves primarily central response organization processes (whatever their nature) operating prior to movement initiation, neither the removal nor the addition of sensory information should facilitate movement accuracy to any major degree. On the other hand, if constrained movements are feedback dependent (as the wrist-cuff data suggest), they may benefit from additional visual input, as indeed indicated in the studies by Adams and Goetz (1973) and Stelmach (1973). This set of predictions formed the main basis for the experiments to be described here, details of which can be obtained elsewhere (Kelso & Frekany, in press). As you will see, we were also forced to consider the role of attentional variables and visual dominance (Posner, Nissen, & Klein, 1976) in determining response accuracy under conditions where visual and movement information are concurrent. Such factors appear to have been largely ignored in previous research designed to test closed-loop theory via visual feedback manipulations.

In the initial set of experiments, subjects ($N = 40$ in each experiment) performed preselected and constrained movements on a linear slide with and without vision on the criterion movement. Reproduction movements were always carried out in the absence of vision. To provide a valid comparison of reproduction errors, the movements chosen by subjects in the preselected conditions were presented to their yoked counterparts in the constrained conditions. In the first experiment, vision was manipulated by allowing the subject to see the terminal position of the limb for 3 sec. At the end of this period, vision was removed by closing the front of a "black box" suspended from the ceiling of the testing room but not resting on the subject's shoulders. The slide was returned to the starting position (which remained constant throughout) and the subject reproduced accordingly. In the no-vision conditions, subjects simply rested at the endpoint for 3 sec prior to reproduction. The design then consisted of four independent groups (preselected and constrained; with and without terminal vision) who performed 30 trials into three response sectors (short, 0–20 cm; medium, 20.1–40.0 cm; long, 40.1–60.0 cm).

The results shown in Figures 4 and 5 did not completely fulfill the expecta-

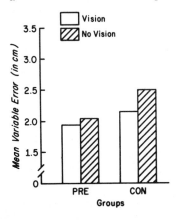

Figure 4 Mean variable error for preselected and constrained groups with and without terminal visual information.

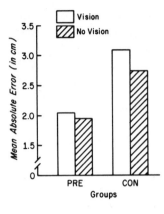

Figure 5   Mean absolute error for preselected and constrained groups with and without terminal visual information.

tions of our original hypotheses. The preselected conditions were clearly significantly more accurate than constrained for absolute and variable error. The visual manipulation, however, was not particularly effective. Preselected movements were reproduced equally well with and without terminal visual input, thus fulfilling one-half of our initial prediction. However, although there was an apparent improvement in response accuracy for the constrained–vision condition in terms of mean variability (which just failed significance, $0.05 > p < 0.10$), the trend was reversed when absolute accuracy was examined (see Figures 4 and 5). These findings were somewhat disappointing in terms of other investigations that have reported facilitatory effects of vision on movement accuracy (e.g., Adams & Goetz, 1973; Posner, 1967; Stelmach, 1973; Stelmach & Kelso, 1975).

An obvious drawback to the present experiment was that there may have been an insufficient amount of visual information available to augment motor accuracy. To test this notion, we employed an identical design (i.e., same conditions and same number of subjects) and procedures similar to those of the previous study except that visual information was available throughout the performance of the criterion movement rather than merely at the end location. We expected this manipulation to provide an even stronger test of the notion that additional peripheral inputs are less important in preselected than constrained movements.

As can be seen in the absolute error data shown in Figure 6, however, vision does *not* aid the reproduction accuracy of either constrained or preselected movements. Indeed, under preselected conditions there appears to be a *detrimental* effect of concurrent vision, a finding surely not predicted on the basis of closed-loop theory. Why might this occur? One reason might be that the subject attends simultaneously to incoming visual information and to the execution of the motor plan. Since both operations presumably require attention, increased reproduction errors may reflect an overload in the limited-capacity processing

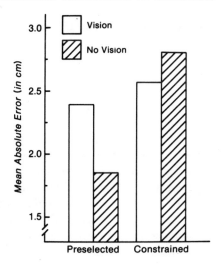

Figure 6 Mean absolute error for preselected and constrained groups with and without concurrent vision.

system (Klein & Posner, 1974). The presence of visual interference in preselected but not constrained movements might then be explained by the greater central-processing requirements of the former (Jones, 1974; Stelmach *et al.*, 1976). Another, rather intriguing but speculative possibility pertains to the nature of preselection per se. If one aspect of preselecting a movement involves the generation of what Pribram (1971, 1976, pp. 303–322) and others before him (e.g., James, 1890) have termed an "image of achievement," and if the hypothetical image and the visual input arising from movement are discrepant, interference might be expected to occur. While we have no data to offer on this point at present, it might be possible to evaluate relative biasing effects of "plan" or "image" on visual input and vice versa using prism techniques in a manner similar to that employed for the assessment of visual–auditory discrepancy (e.g., Warren & Cleaves, 1971).

We have confirmed the interfering effect of vision on preselection in a brief follow-up experiment. Ten subjects made a total of 30 preselected movements with concurrent vision into three response sectors in a manner identical to the preselected–vision condition of the foregoing experiment. In addition, each subject received six randomly presented "catch" trials in which vision was also provided during the reproduction movement. The results were revealing in two respects. First, reproduction errors were again sizable, with a mean absolute error of 3.3 cm, providing further support for the visual interference effect shown in Figure 6. Second, reproduction errors in the catch trials were much smaller ($M = 2.13$ cm), indicating that if vision is to be useful it must be available for both presentation and reproduction movements. Indeed, the research on positioning responses that has shown vision to contribute more to reproduction performance than any other feedback channel (e.g., Adams & Goetz, 1973; Stelmach, 1973; Stelmach & Kelso, 1975) has always fulfilled this condition. The problem with such studies is that visual reference points obtained from the task display during the criterion movement may have been used at reproduction to inform subjects of the movement location (Newell & Chew, 1975). This may well have been the case in the catch trial data reported here.

More important, however, is the strong suggestion that subjects were attending to visual information in these experiments in spite of the fact that it was not usually available for reproduction. Thus, the attentional biases of the subject appeared to influence the results to a major degree. In the final experiment of this series, we wanted to determine if the interfering effect of vision on preselected movements could be reduced by specifically informing the subject of the reproduction modality prior to the presentation of the criterion movement. Our assumption was that, if vision is spontaneously attended in preselected movements, prior knowledge of the output modality should not have a facilitatory effect on reproduction.

Two experimental groups were employed (18 subjects in each). In one condition (preselected–vision informed), subjects were cued to the modality of reproduction prior to the start of each trial, whereas in the other condition (preselected–vision uninformed) subjects were not cued until after the criterion movement. Reproduction was by vision only (V), in which the experimenter moved the slide until instructed to stop by the subject, movement only (M), or with both vision and movement available. Thirty-six trials were performed by each subject into three response sectors with a different random order of reproduction modality and sectors employed for each subject. Of major interest was the groups × modality of output interaction, which was significant for

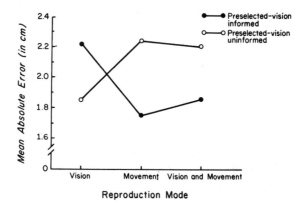

Figure 7 Mean absolute error for preselected–vision groups when informed and uninformed of modality of reproduction.

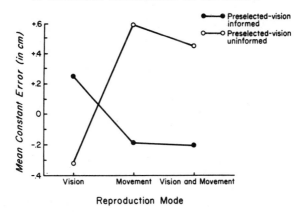

Figure 8 Mean constant error for preselected–vision groups when informed and uninformed of modality of reproduction.

absolute and signed error ($p < 0.05$) and is shown in Figures 7 and 8. The pattern of results is identical for each dependent variable with post hoc analysis revealing that the major difference between informed and uninformed groups arises in the movement-only condition. The superiority of the informed group suggests that subjects were capable of selectively processing movement information, whereas subjects in the uninformed group appear to have maintained their attention on vision. The nonsignificant differences between the groups under vision-only and vision-plus-movement conditions further indicate that vision is primarily processed, just what one would expect from the extensive literature on visual dominance (see Posner *et al.*, 1976).

The important point to emphasize from the present data is that prior knowledge of the response modality is effective in reducing the deleterious effects of vision on movement reproduction. At first this finding appears to be in conflict with the previous experiments (see Figure 6 and the following discussion). Since vision was available on the criterion but not the reproduction movement, why, after the first few practice trials, did subjects not process movement information selectively and ignore the visual input?

The information-processing analysis of visual dominance by Posner and his associates (Klein, 1976, pp. 143–174; Posner *et al.*, 1976) provides a possible solution to this dilemma. Posner *et al.* (1976) propose that, under conditions where information about an event is available from vision and another modality and where vision is quite adequate for responding, attention to vision predominates. This situation especially prevails if the subject is in a "neutral set," as would exist in a situation where no specific instructions as to reproduction modality are given. In contrast, where explicit procedures are adopted to direct the subject's attention to nonvisual input with the purpose of improving response accuracy (Posner *et al.*, 1976, p. 168), the basis toward vision can be reversed. Such a situation prevailed in our precuing experiment (see Figures 7 and 8) as well as in other work on short-term visual–kinesthetic conflict (Kelso, Cook, Olson, & Epstein, 1975) and appears to explain the selective effects found for movement over visual information.

Our data concur with the view that subjects can program their conscious attention to (a) receive information from a desired source and (b) perform specific operations on received information (Posner & Snyder, 1975). The consequence of this viewpoint is that conscious attention to one source of information limits the availability of the limited processing system to handle other inputs. Hence, the attentional effects shown in Figures 7 and 8 but not in other instructional manipulations (Klein & Posner, 1974, Expt. 2) may be interpreted in light of the fact that we used active–preselected movements, which, because of their preplanned nature, are processed at a higher level of conscious attention than passive movements (Klein & Posner, 1974). Consequently, given a predisposition to attend to the preselection aspect of the movement, inhibition in processing visual signals is more likely to occur than under purely passive conditions.

The foregoing analysis might act as a starting point in the resolution of at least two problems. First, it has the potential to clarify, at least partially, one of the mysteries in the motor domain, namely, why active movements are perceived and processed differently than passive movements. It has been argued in a largely forgotten paper that a receptive system of higher order is excited during active movement rather than passive (Gibson, 1962). This may be another way of saying that conscious attention can be more easily directed to active than passive movement, as we have proposed. An investigation of attention demands might resolve this issue. If movement-produced stimuli have a different "excitatory capacity" (Gibson, 1962) in active rather than passive movement, corresponding effects on attentional measures [e.g., probe reaction time (Ells, 1973)] should be evident.

A second and largely unexplored problem has to do with the relationship between informational discrepancy and the relative dominance effects of visual and proprioceptive information. Warren and Cleaves (1971) varied the discrepancy between the seen and felt position of the limb from 10° to 60° using prismatic displacement techniques. Visual biasing decreased significantly as the sources of information were moved farther apart. There was also a tendency for the proprioceptive biasing of vision to increase as discrepancy increased. What these data seem to indicate is that the more discriminable the two sources of input the easier it is to reduce visual biasing. Put another way, we might expect that by enhancing movement-generated information (i.e., by making it more discriminable) we can reduce dominance effects on proprioception and hence particular types of performance deficits (e.g., Jordan, 1972; Klein & Posner, 1974). One of the most effective techniques for doing this may be to allow the subject to preselect a movement of his/her own choice (as in most real-life situations). If, as we propose, preselection demands a high level of conscious attention, we might predict a reversal of the usual visual dominance of proprioception. Indeed, as in previous work (Canon, 1971; Kelso *et al.,* 1975), we might expect to show that visual dominance is not as immutable as some would have us believe (e.g., Rock & Victor, 1964). These speculations warrant further study since the apparent "enhancing" effect of preselecting a movement may have important practical and theoretical implications.

D. Summary

In the last three sections we have presented empirical data from studies directed at obtaining further information on the "uniqueness" of preselection. Clearly our approach has been a pluralistic one, and we have on occasion wavered away from investigating the preselection effect, per se, to what appeared to be interesting sidetracks. Of course, each of the sidetracks tends to become a major issue in itself, and certainly the topics that we have alluded to, for example, attentional factors and dominance relationships in vision and movement, are important research endeavors in their own right. We have as yet only tentatively discussed the theoretical processes underlying the accuracy of preselected movement. Instead, we have pointed to the generality of the preselection effect and to its potential application, but we have not strayed too far from describing the data. Researchers in motor skill learning have been criticized for remaining at this level of analysis for too long. It has been said, for example, that Woodworth's (1899) descriptive conclusions are as correct today as they were then. However, paraphrastic redescriptions of the data are not explanations (Weimer, 1977). It remains for us now to present the theoretical issues surrounding the preselection effect. Specifically, we want to theorize upon the psychological processes involved in preselection and speculate on its neural correlates. In line with our empirical work, we propose to argue that preselection represents a principal conscious mechanism in the control of movement and the acquisition of skill.

III. Theoretical Accounts

A. Methodological Considerations

Before scrutinizing the possible theoretical mechanisms underlying the preselection effect, it is necessary to dispel certain methodological problems that exist within the preselected–constrained experimental paradigm (Wallace, Kelso, & Goodman, Note 5). The first potential problem is that, in every study to date, constrained trials have always been yoked to preselected trials—a factor creating an obvious treatment-order artifact. A second consideration is that subjects in preselected trials perform criterion and reproduction movements under *identical* conditions, whereas constrained subjects have to switch from arrested conditions on the criterion to a free or voluntary situation at reproduction. A final and perhaps most important factor is that the presence of a mechanical stop during constrained production may have adverse effects on the encoding process due to impact. Hollingworth (1909) demonstrated with the constrained procedure that constant errors at reproduction were directly related to the force of impact at the stop that defined the criterion movement—the larger the force at impact, the greater the positive constant errors. Granit (1972) suggested that this "illusion" may be due to an increase in muscle spindle firing after impact. We have argued elsewhere (Stelmach *et al.*, 1975; Kelso & Stelmach, 1976) that the impact problem was not important in one of our studies where subjects in both preselected and constrained conditions reproduced the endpoint of the criterion movement with distance cues reduced (Stelmach *et al.*, 1975, Expts. 1 and 2).

Our original argument was based on the lack of a significant groups effect for constant error in both experiments. While our findings tend to dismiss the impact problem, at least for consistent directional biases, there is no reason why impact at the stop could not increase response variability over the course of an experiment. Increases in response variability would obviously inflate variable error, and thus absolute error, accounting for poorer constrained reproduction. We have assessed the potency of the foregoing problems by (*a*) counterbalancing treatment order; (*b*) substituting a mechanical stop with an auditory tone on constrained criterion production (Experiment 1); and (*c*) requiring subjects

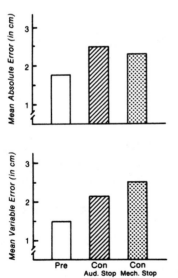

Figure 9 Mean absolute and variable errors for preselected, constrained–auditory stop, and constrained–mechanical stop conditions.

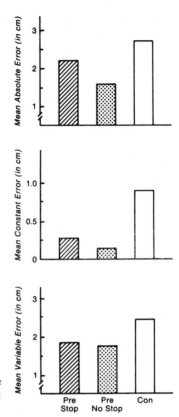

Figure 10 Mean absolute, constant, and variable errors for preselected–stop, preselected–no-stop, and constrained conditions.

during preselected trials to also impact into the mechanical stop whose position was preselected (Experiment 2). The results from both experiments discounted a methodological interpretation of the preselection effect. First, it mattered little whether preselected trials preceded or succeeded constrained trials; the preselection effect remained, thus ruling out a treatment-order artifact. Second, as shown in Figure 9, removing a mechanical stop during constrained criterion production and replacing it by an auditory tone stop did not improve reproduction. Preselected reproduction was still superior. Third, requiring subjects during preselected trials to impact into a mechanical stop only marginally reduced the preselection effect (see Figure 10). Thus, the overall results suggest that the preselection effect is not due to a fault in the methodology and that some underlying theoretical mechanism or process unique to preselected movement is operating to enhance reproduction.

With the methodological explanations of the preselection effect appearing improbable, we turn now to theoretical accounts of the phenomenon. There have been two general mechanisms posited for the superior reproduction accuracy of preselected over constrained and passive movements. The first of these emphasizes the cognitive aspects of preselection, stressing, for example, the possible differences in the attention demands of preselected versus constrained movements. The so-called "cognitive" view further points to the greater availability of "task-related" information that may allow preselected subjects to formulate encoding strategies. Unique to the latter notion is the rejection of the role of efferent information in producing the preselection effect.

In dramatic contrast to the cognitive position, "motor" theorists stress the importance of internal efferent monitoring operations available in preselected but not constrained movements. However, little reference is made to the planning process that must precede the discharge of motor commands.

From our point of view, neither of these dichotomous accounts is sufficient *alone* to explain the preselection effect. Following a critical examination of cognitive and motor hypotheses and their incumbent predictions, we will develop a theoretical position stressing the mutual relationship between planning and efferent components of preselected movement. At this point, we see little benefit to be derived from considering such important elements in the organization of movement in independent terms.

B. Cognitive Mechanisms

1. Attention Differences

According to this account, when the subject preselects the criterion movement, more attention is allocated to the task, hence facilitating the pickup of relevant movement cues. Thus, the prediction is that more central capacity is allocated during a preselected than a nonpreselected criterion movement. Using the probe reaction time (RT) technique as a measure of attention demands (Kahneman, 1973; Kerr, 1973), two studies by Roy (Roy, Note 6; Roy & Diewert, 1975) do not support an attentional explanation of the preselection effect. In the Roy and Diewert study, it was found that while probe RT was inflated (relative to control) during preselected and constrained criterion movements, there were no probe RT differences between the two conditions. This finding suggests that the monitoring of movement information in both preselected and constrained movements requires the same amount of central capacity.

The problem with the foregoing study, however, was that constrained subjects were given prior information that allowed them to predict the extent of the criterion movement. Essentially, then, they performed preselected movements. A follow-up study by Roy (Note 6) compared probe RT performance during preselected movements to that of a typical constrained situation where subjects had no prior knowledge of the criterion movement to be produced. Similar to the Roy and Diewert (1975) finding, the results indicated no differences between probe RT performance on preselected and constrained trials. In fact, there was some suggestion that the probe RTs on constrained trials were higher than on preselected trials. This finding suggests that greater central capacity may be allocated to monitoring movement information during constrained movements, a view also supported by Jones and Hulme (1976). Jones and Hulme showed that a visual detection task performed during criterion movement production adversely affected reproduction accuracy of a constrained–passive movement, but not of a preselected–active movement. This finding suggests that more attention was allocated to input monitoring during constrained–passive conditions.

The above findings do not support the notion that superior preselected reproduction is due to increased attention allocation during the input monitoring of criterion movement information. It is quite likely, however, that attentional effects may be operating *prior to* the initiation of a preselected movement when the subject is asked to formulate a plan of action. Some evidence has been generated for this proposal using voluntary movements outside the reproduction paradigm (Ells, 1973; Posner & Keele, 1969; Wilke & Vaughn, 1976). Thus, because of the greater planning component in preselected than in constrained movements, more attention may be required prior to movement than during the movement itself. It seems fair to say that previous investigators have failed to consider or at least examine the central capacity requirements of planning operations. Surely this step is necessary to delineate the possible role of attention in the preselection process.

2. Encoding Strategy Differences

This view, advanced by Marteniuk (1976), Roy and Diewert (1975), and Roy (Note 6), states that the preselection effect is entirely due to the use of a more effective encoding strategy on preselected trials. Although global in definition, the encoding strategy pertains to having more information of the movement to be produced during the preselection process. At least three specific predictions can be generated from this hypothesis. One of these is that, if preselection aids in the initial registration or encoding of movement-related information, superior preselected over nonpreselected performance should be obtained after immediate reproduction, where the act of rehearsal is minimal. There is some supporting evidence for this prediction (e.g., Jones, 1974, Expt. 1; Kelso, 1977a; Stelmach *et al.*, 1975, Expts. 2 and 3; Wallace & Stelmach, 1975, Expt. 2; Roy, Note 6).

A second prediction of this hypothesis is that, if an encoding strategy is the explanation of superior preselected reproduction, providing a similar strategy during constrained trials should result in equivalent performance. The results of two studies previously mentioned support this prediction (Roy, Note 6; Roy & Diewert, 1975). In the Roy and Diewert study, subjects in preselected conditions were first presented a movement range or orienting movement and subsequently asked to produce half of that movement. This procedure allowed subjects to predict the extent of the criterion movement. The subject's estimation of half of the orienting movement served as the criterion movement to be reproduced later. Subjects in the constrained condition were also presented an orienting movement followed by the criterion movement to a mechanical stop, which they were told would always be one-half of the orienting movement. Given this strategy, subjects in the constrained condition were able to reproduce the criterion movement as accurately as preselected subjects.

While the latter two predictions of the encoding strategy hypothesis have been supported reasonably well, the third prediction has not been supported. According to Roy (Note 6), a necessary and sufficient condition for the preselection effect is that the subject must have an available encoding strategy. Since the strategy is viewed as purely cognitive in nature, its active implementation is not a prerequisite to accurate performance. Thus, a third prediction of the hypothesis is that the manner in which the criterion movement is produced is irrelevant as long as strategy is available. Roy (Note 6) showed that subjects in both active– and passive–constrained conditions supplied with an encoding strategy performed as well as those in a preselected condition and that all three conditions were superior to a constrained condition where no such prior knowledge was available. In contrast, data from a study by Kelso (1977a) conflict with Roy's findings. In the Kelso study, subjects in a preselected–passive condition were asked to select a movement covertly and were then passively moved by the experimenter to their desired position. Electromyographic recordings were taken to ensure the passivity of the subject's criterion movement. Following the passive, yet preselected, movement, the subject actively estimated the criterion movement. The results (which were replicated in a follow-up experiment) showed significantly poorer reproduction under passive–preselected than active–preselected conditions. Methodological differences between the Roy and Kelso studies could account for the discrepant results. For example, subjects in Roy's passive–constrained with strategy condition may not have been completely passive on criterion presentation. Using electromyographic recordings, Kelso observed that most subjects have difficulty in remaining passive during a preselected movement and considerable practice is required to achieve the passive state.

In further conflict with the third prediction of the encoding strategy notion are data from the Wallace *et al.* (Note 5) study discussed earlier. In Experiment 2 (see absolute error in Figure 10), it was shown that subject-terminated preselected movements were reproduced more accurately than preselected movements to a mechanical stop. While this finding certainly does not support the encoding strategy hypothesis, it is in agreement with our position that the efferent component of preselected movement at least partially contributes to the preselection effect.

To synthesize, the independence of encoding strategy from mode of execution is in considerable doubt. Furthermore, the first two predictions of the strategy hypothesis can be handled via mechanisms involving cognitive and motor components (see Section III, D). Finally, serious concerns must be expressed regarding the vagueness of the encoding strategy concept as stated (Roy, Note 6; Roy & Diewert, 1975). We do not find it particularly satisfactory that advance information of various kinds differentiates preselected and constrained movements. What are the contents of such information and the nature of the operations involved? We shall return to questions of this kind when we present our own position (see Section III,D).

C. Motor Mechanisms

1. Central Monitoring of Efference Hypothesis (CME)

That the memory of preselected movements is solely based on the central storage of efferent signals is a view defended by Jones (1972, 1974; Jones & Hulme, 1976). According to the CME hypothesis, the preselection process results in the central monitoring and storage of an efference copy—a motor memory system operating without peripheral feedback. As such, the CME concept as expressed by Jones represents the most extreme view of the motor mechanisms underlying the preselection effect.

The CME hypothesis states that preselected movements are more accurately reproduced because the efferent commands can be more efficiently monitored and stored. In addition, Jones is quite explicit in stating that it is the efferent commands regarding *movement extent* that are centrally stored in preselected movements. Thus, inferior reproduction of nonpreselected movements is due to the lack of or inefficient monitoring of efference for movement extent. Because of this inability to store relevant efferent information, nonpreselected reproduction is based on afferent cues that, according to Jones, have no access to central processing.

By changing starting positions of the criterion and reproduction movements (Laabs, 1973), Jones (1974, Expt. 2) tested the hypothesis that the commands for extent can be centrally processed in preselected movements. In this experiment, it was shown that subjects could reproduce the extent of a preselected movement equally well from variable and constant starting positions. Hence, as long as the efferent commands for movement extent were the same for criterion and recall movements, no deficits in reproduction occurred, regardless of initial starting positions.

Kelso and Stelmach (1976), however, reviewed evidence contrary to the Jones hypothesis. In an experiment by Stelmach *et al.* (1975, Expt. 1), for example, subjects were forced to generate a different efferent output at reproduction from that employed on the criterion movement. This was accomplished by requiring the subjects to reproduce the endpoint rather than the distance of criterion movement. According to the Jones hypothesis, this procedure should have resulted in less accurate reproduction, whereas distance reproduction should have been superior since the efferent output for criterion and reproduction movements remained the same. Contrary to the CME notion, subjects reproducing preselected endpoints were more accurate even though a different efferent command had to be generated on the reproduction movement. While these data indicate the potency of preselectd location over distance, they also strike a strong blow against the CME hypothesis.

An even more convincing test of the Jones (1974) hypothesis would be to examine motor reproduction under conditions where afferent movement cues are rendered unavailable via the wrist-cuff technique (Kelso, 1977d). As long as movement extent is unaltered, no deficits in accuracy should occur according to the Jones (1974) model. In this situation, any information coded in the efference (such as duration and velocity) would remain unaffected. However, were the starting position to be altered and the subject asked to reproduce spatial location, stored extent information would not be reliable for reproduction purposes since the movement parameters required for accurate reproduction would of course be altered.

Kelso (1977d) examined distance and location reproduction under normal and wrist-cuff conditions. The results showed that preselected location reproduction was unaffected by the cuff manipulation, whereas reproduction of distance deteriorated dramatically from normal (see Figure 11). The superiority of location was all the more significant in light of the failure of subjects to report any per-

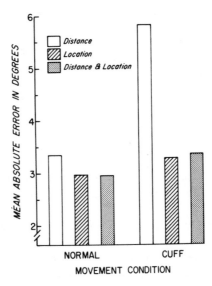

Figure 11 Mean absolute error for normal and wrist-cuff groups performing under distance, location, and distance-plus-location conditions.

ception of changed starting position under cuff conditions (see also Section II,B). Precisely the opposite result would have been predicted had subjects been relying on central command signals coded in terms of extent, as Jones (1974) has argued. Rather, an internal representation of spatial location seems a more likely alternative.[4]

In summary, little if any support exists for the CME hypothesis as stated by Jones (1974). Its major flaws lie in a failure both to emphasize the cognitive component and to recognize the peripheral component of normal, preselected movement.

2. Corollary Discharge Hypothesis

Borrowing from Teuber's (1966, pp. 182–216, 1974) account of motor control, Kelso (1975) and Stelmach et al. (1975) initially proposed that preselection may facilitate the encoding of proprioceptive information via an efference-based mechanism. According to the corollary discharge hypothesis, as a result of pre-selection a corollary motor signal activates appropriate or relevant sensory areas, thereby presetting them for the sensory consequences of the motor act. Thus, under preselected conditions, sensory-processing centers in the central nervous system are prepared to receive peripheral information, whereas under nonpre-selected conditions this is not possible. Allen and Tsukahara (1974) have re-viewed cerebrocerebellar pathways that could conduct a corollary discharge operation.

The corollary discharge hypothesis advocates the importance of efferent in-formation, as does the CME hypothesis. A key difference between the two hypotheses is the function of the efferent commands and the type of movement information actually stored by the central nervous system. The CME hypothesis proposes that the efferent commands are centrally stored, whereas the corollary discharge hypothesis suggests that *afferent* information is more efficiently stored in sensory centers that have been sensitized by a corollary discharge.

In our opinion, the corollary discharge hypothesis has more validity than the CME view because it is not specifically aligned with and does not give special treatment to the parameter of movement extent. The findings that preselected location reproduction is superior to preselected distance under normal condi-tions (Stelmach et al., 1975, Expt. 1), although difficult to handle by the CME account, are easily explained by the corollary discharge hypothesis. The ex-planation is that, as a result of initiating a preselected movement, a corollary discharge can sensitize the sensory centers in the central nervous system for the receipt of a more potent movement cue, namely, location information. In other words, by preselecting, the image or anticipated sensory consequences of the final

---

[4] The challenging question of how the finger attains a desired location in the absence of starting position and motion cues is dealt with more fully in the Kelso (1977d) paper.

limb position can be forwarded to sensory centers by a corollary discharge, which prepares them for the actual sensory consequences. While this process may occur for preselected distance information, preselected location reproduction is superior because positional cues are better represented in memory than distance cues (e.g., Laabs, 1973; Marteniuk, 1973).

An important limitation to the corollary discharge view as initially conceptualized is that the anticipated sensory consequences arise *simultaneously* with the discharge of efferent commands to the muscles (Teuber, 1960). This view ignores the planning process occurring prior to the generation of output signals. In the next section we will present a case that the anticipated sensory consequences of intended movements are formulated *before* the participation of effector mechanisms in the CNS. Indeed, we will argue that such expectancies are the basis on which motor commands are generated.

D. Our Position

Given that we are not particularly enamored with present theoretical accounts of the preselection effect, what can we offer in their place? One concept that we feel cannot be avoided is that of the *image*. Russian investigators have long viewed voluntary (preselected) movement as based upon an image (e.g., Anokhin, 1969, pp. 830–856; Sokolov, 1969, pp. 671–704; Zaporozhets, 1965, pp. 434–440) and, while the notion fell into disrepute in this country with the advent of conditioning analyses of behavior (e.g., Hull, 1931), it is certainly still at large in present theories of motor behavior. Adams (1976), for example, refers to his perceptual trace concept, which is aroused once movement is initiated, as a "motor image" whose strength is a positive function of experience with the various sources of sensory feedback associated with movement. In contrast, Gentile (1972), whose work is based largely on the work of Konorski (1967) and Miller *et al.* (1960), views an "image or plan" existing prior to movement whose role is to guide execution. Similarly, the term "expected sensory consequences" (Pew, 1974; Schmidt, 1975), though not cited as such, is no more than what William James (1890) termed "an anticipatory image of the sensorial consequences of movement which . . . is the only psychic state which introspection lets us discern as the forerunner of our voluntary acts [p. 501]." Thus, the image is alive and well in motor behavior circles whether we like the term or not.

The experiments that used preselected movements seem to demand the concept of an image as the precursor to movement. The Stelmach *et al.* (1975) paper, for example, in which preselected location was superior to constrained location, points to this conclusion. If proprioceptive location information per se was the primary determinant of reproduction performance (e.g., Laabs, 1973; Marteniuk & Roy, 1972), no benefits of preselection should have been apparent.

There are two major questions that we must address. First, what do we mean by an image? Second, what function does it play in contributing to a theoretical account of the preselection effect? The former problem really has to do with the nature of motoric representation in the brain—a subject of much debate in neurophysiology since the late nineteenth century, but which can only be dealt with briefly here [see Evarts (1973) and Turvey (1977, pp. 211–266) for a fuller treatment]. In accord with Pribram (1976), we feel that the *level of analysis* has much to do with how we envisage motor representation. Anatomically, one can demonstrate using discrete stimulation techniques that muscles are represented in the motor cortex (e.g., Woolsey & Chang, 1948). At the physiological level, cortical representation can be shown to consist of *movements* centered around a joint (e.g., Phillips, 1965, pp. 389–421). At the behavioral level of analysis, however, neither of these views suffices. Ultimately, action itself, defined as the environmental consequences of movement, must be represented in the brain. How else might we solve the now familiar problem of motor equivalence (see Schmidt, 1975; Turvey, 1977)? The image, or motor representation, in the brain has to be in terms of completed action, an image of achievement as it were (Pribram, 1971, 1976; Teuber, 1974).

It should be emphasized that this notion of the image is in contrast to that posited in closed-loop formulations (e.g., Adams, 1971; Bernstein, 1967), in which the image serves as a template for comparison with current feedback but is not activated prior to performance. The present conceptualization is more in agreement with an ideomotor model where the response is selected on the basis of its own anticipated feedback (Greenwald, 1970). This brings us to the crux of the problem. *The role of the image in preselected movement is to generate anticipatory signals that prepare the actor to accept certain kinds of information.* This view bears some similarity to the notion of corollary discharge discussed earlier as a plausible mechanism underlying the preselection effect. Perhaps a literal interpretation of corollary discharge might argue that the anticipated sensory consequences are "left behind" in sensory centers following the generation of movement commands. Certainly, the early papers of Teuber (e.g., 1960) give this impression. However, corollary discharges have also been discussed in terms of the *preparation of movement,* preceding voluntary movement as "central predictors of impending motor acts, together with their expected sensory consequences [Teuber, 1974, p. 522]." This view of corollary discharge as an internal representation of intended action is compatible with that presented here. The anticipatory signals, then, are the *basis on which commands are organized,* one of their functions being to serve as a referent for the interpretation of incoming feedback.

The important implication of this proposal is that when we preselect a movement we *obtain* information that is in terms of our expectations. In a sense, we predict the way things ought to be (in a spatial task, for example, where our limbs will terminate) as a result of effecting a movement and hence establish a *context* for movement-produced information. In constrained movement, however, an appropriate context cannot be specified because no anticipatory image is available; we are thus forced to remain in a passive *receptive* mode.

What evidence supports our anticipatory image idea and what type of information might be coded in these signals? Consider the experiment presented in Section II, B in which subjects with anesthetized digits felt they had executed planned movements in spite of being restrained from doing so. A logical interpretation of this finding is that the subject perceived movement to occur on the basis of what he *expected* to happen (i.e., the anticipatory image) as a result of generating an intended movement. Indeed, under preselected, voluntary conditions, it can be argued that subjects rely on the internal signal containing the anticipated sensory consequences, rather than on the actual sensory input, which is redundant if the movement has been accurately preplanned. A similar interpretation can be made of the "phantom limb" phenomenon, where amputees perceive movement to occur following a volitional effort to move the nonexistent limbs (Henderson & Smyth, 1948; James, 1890; Simmel, 1966).

Other data in support of internal anticipatory signals come from an experiment by Liu (1968) in which subjects, following practice at exerting a pressure of 1000 or 500 g a distance of 3.5 cm, were tested (unknown to them) at a lighter or heavier pressure, respectively. In each case, characteristic overshoots and undershoots resulted. It seems likely that practice at a certain pressure led to the development of an expectation for certain inputs associated with the learned response. Actions based on the same set of anticipatory signals would clearly be ineffective if the force to be produced is changed without informing the performer.[5]

Long ago, William James (1890) argued that representations of a movement's different sensory effects are "delicately foreshadowed" in the brain. We clearly can anticipate the sensory consequences of lifting a cannon ball versus a hollow sphere and program our actions based on such expectancies. With unknown objects, however, we initiate movement on the basis of an anticipatory image made probable by the object's appearance. A beautiful example of this phenomenon comes from Bower's (1976) work on weight conservation in young children, and the results further support the present postulations when interpreted as follows. A ball of clay is placed in the infant's hand and then removed and rolled into an elongated sausage. The new shape completely alters the infant's anticipated sensory consequences because a program of action is generated on the

---

[5] It can be argued that the Liu (1968) data can be handled rather well by a motor program view. That is, the subject simply initiated the learned program when the pressure was changed, thus leading to characteristic errors. We would like to think that this is only part of the story. Programming operations, in our view, are based upon the expected sensory consequences of the intended movement.

basis of an expectation that the object is much heavier. That is, the child flexes the elbow forcefully in response to the misperceived weight of the object. An opposite effect occurs when the clay is returned to its original spherical shape; the limb supporting the object is momentarily extended. This points to the conclusion that the child determines the pattern of action based on an anticipation of sensory consequences, albeit in this case an erroneous one.

A final datum from our laboratory illustrates the possible role of an anticipatory image of achievement in the perception of movement.[6] The question was as follows. When we produce preselected movements, are we attending primarily to the expected sensory consequences of action or to the actual sensory input arising as a result of movement? Consider a situation in which the subject first informs the experimenter of the locus of his/her preselected movement by placing a mechanical stop at some location on a linear positioning device. This condition is identical to that employed in the previously mentioned "impact" experiment (Wallace et al., Note 5). The subject's task is to move to the stop and reproduce accordingly. However, we created a "conflict" situation by altering the location of the stop to a position 10 cm *before* the position preselected. On the first of these conflict trials the subject was instructed to reproduce the actual location of the stop (i.e., on the basis of the actual sensory input), whereas on the second conflict trial the subject was asked to reproduce the originally planned movement. Thus, in the first conflict situation a positive constant or signed error (CE) would indicate a bias in the direction of the anticipated sensory consequences of the movement. The average CE of 12 subjects was +3.52 cm, as opposed to the average CE of +0.17 cm for the same subjects with no conflict between the preselected and presented criterion movements. This was statistically significant ($p < 0.05$) and suggested that the image or plan did indeed exert a powerful bias. The second conflict condition allowed us to examine the influence of the actual sensory consequences on those expected following a preselected movement. That is, we wanted to assess the possible biasing effect of the movement actually presented on the reproduction of the original plan. The appropriate control condition for this comparison is the subject's ability to reproduce the preselected left arm movement with the contralateral limb. Subjects consistently undershot in this situation (mean CE = -2.38 cm), a finding in agreement with Wallace (1977 Expt. 1). If the biasing effect of the presented movement on the reproduction of the preselected movement is a potent one, the CE should be even more negative than the control CE value. However, this was not the case [mean CE = -2.6 cm, $t(11) < 1.0$]. Thus, a conflict criterion movement (and its associated sensory consequences) appears not to exert an influence on the reproduction of the movement originally preselected. That is, our perception of movement, as reflected in the reproduction responses, is influenced more by

---

[6] These data are not published elsewhere.

central expectations of sensory input than by the actual input itself. Weimer (1977) and others before him (e.g., Sperry, 1952) have developed a strong case for this position for perception as a whole.

We have argued that the role of the motor image is to create an expectancy or readiness for certain kinds of information, but what is the nature of the input that is anticipated? One suggestion is that the image of achievement encodes environmental contingencies (e.g., forces) rather than patterns of muscle contraction (Pribram, 1971, 1976). This conclusion is based largely on Evarts' (1967, pp. 215-254) data showing that the output of pyramidal tract neurons in motor cortex is more closely related to the amount of force required than to displacement. Investigators in biomechanics would argue that this is a logical necessity, for unless the output of the motor system is specified in force parameters there can be no displacement.[7] However, to say that the image or central motor representation is composed of "learned anticipations of the force and changes in force required to perform a task [Pribram, 1971, p. 250]" is not correct from our viewpoint. Ultimately our actions require accurate displacement, and, as Turvey (1977) has pointed out, the "image" that Pribram is referring to must "represent the action plan at a fairly late state in its differentiation [p. 229]." If the goal of our movements is to reach a desired position in space, then it would seem equally clear that one of the primary inputs expected is specified in terms of final limb position. Indeed, evidence is accumulating that terminal limb position may be centrally programmed (e.g., see Bizzi, Polit, & Morasso, 1976; Kelso, 1977d).

Our thesis here is that the internal representation of anticipated sensory consequences may contain primarily locational information. Certainly the wrist-cuff data on location reproduction (see Figure 11 and the following discussion in Section III,c) support this view. A reasonable interpretation is that, in the absence of afferent cues, an internal representation of location was available under preselected conditions to mediate reproduction performance. On largely intuitive grounds, since the primary *input* code seems to be positional in nature (e.g., Keele & Ells, 1972; Laabs, 1973), it seems reasonable to suggest that the CNS may prepare itself for that input by having available the expected sensory consequences of movement coded in locational terms. A main advantage of this proposal is that the referent signal and the input are compatible codes. Of course, this analysis applies primarily to spatial tasks, which nevertheless constitute an important part of the movement repertoire.

IV. Predictions and Conclusions

Obviously the previous discussion of anticipatory images comprises only a single component of the total process of movement initiation and execution. However, we believe it to be an important and largely neglected aspect and one

---

[7] We would like to thank Carol Putnam for her discussion on this point.

that is crucial to our understanding of motor control. Our speculations lead us to suggest that the availability of such images constitutes one of the major differences between preselected and constrained movements. To postulate internal representations of expected sensory consequences, however, does not contribute much to knowledge unless we attach some predictions about our hypothetical construct. Aside from obvious (but important) questions as to the nature of the programming operations based upon such internal representations, we believe a number of testable predictions arise from the foregoing analysis.

First, as a result of having prior knowledge of the sensory consequences of our actions, input processing should be facilitated. We have already suggested that, in the spatial tasks used in most of the experiments reported here, the pickup of location cues may be enhanced. However, we do not as yet have experiments that address this hypothesized sensitization or tuning process in preselected movement. A second and related prediction is that not only should certain input signals receive more efficient processing, but we should also be biased toward accepting particular movement information. Sperry (1952) expresses this point nicely in discussing perceptual processes. He points out that humans have a general tendency to perceive selectively what they are already looking for and expect to see, a view amplified by Neisser (1976). Such decision biases may have decremental effects on performance, as in the situation where the program of action based on an "expectancy" is incorrect (e.g., Liu, 1968). A third prediction is that, because the actual sensory consequences are, in a sense, "predictable," we may be able to more easily pick up environmental information relevant to successful movement completion. A study by Dyhre-Poulsen (1975) supports this notion. In this experiment a sinusoidal vibration was applied to the right index fingertip at various intervals prior to flexion, and the sensory threshold was determined. The latter was found to increase approximately 200 msec before flexion of the stimulated finger and was specific to the digit being moved. In line with other data on cats and monkeys (Coulter, 1974; Dyhre-Poulsen & Hounsgaard, 1973) showing that somatosensory evoked potentials were significantly depressed prior to and during free limb movements (but not passive movements), this finding suggests that sensory signals are inhibited as a result of voluntary movement. The possibility exists then that the modulation of centripetal afferent signals arising from self-produced movement enhances the intake of other information, a prediction supported for visual signals during preselected movement (Jones & Hulme, 1976).

A final but probably most important prediction of the present conceptualization is that the internal, anticipatory image and the organization and discharge of motor commands (efference) are intrinsically bound together. We cannot divorce the image or "strategy" from the efference, as some would have us do (Roy, Note 6). Such prior imaging is the means to an end, where the end is better regulation of the overt response (Sperry, 1952). In preselecting a movement, an internal representation of the anticipated sensory consequences of that movement is available. As long as the sensory consequences of movement are predictable, the program to move can be executed smoothly. It does not matter whether a mechanical stop is located at the preselected location (Roy & Diewert, 1975) as long as the performer is allowed to regulate the movement to coincide with the stop rather than impact into it (Wallace *et al.*, Note 5). We have preliminary data on movement characteristics (e.g., velocity and acceleration) that suggest that the availability of preselection (regardless of whether the movement is subject-terminated or to a stop) affects *how* the movement is executed. Unless some neurological disturbance has occurred to isolate the "plan" from its execution (as in certain kinds of apraxias), we see no need to separate the two. The internal representation of anticipated sensory consequences of intended actions *determines* the program for movement. How else can the expected and actual sensory consequences ever match?

In conclusion, this chapter has dealt with a diverse body of theory and data that have one feature in common, namely, what we have called "the preselection effect." Clearly, a great deal has yet to be learned about the nature of preselection, but such a quest might prove ultimately important, if for no other reason than its empirical implications. However, we would like to think that preselection is at the heart of what is often termed "volition" (Buchanan, 1812; Kimble & Perlmuter, 1970)—that much-maligned concept that has been shunned by experimental psychologists in the past. We believe that some of the approaches and predictions suggested in this paper represent a promising start to an experimental analysis of a major component of voluntary motor behavior.

Throughout this chapter we have also tended toward a particular philosophical position on how the psychology of movement might proceed. Perhaps it is best summed up in the expression that what we sense affects what we do and what we do affects what we sense.[8] In our opinion, only the first half of this rather trite statement has been emphasized in psychological conceptualizations of behavior, *including* information-processing models. Perhaps in the latter part of this chapter we have overemphasized the second half of the statement. If this is so, we are still a long way from redressing the balance. We would like to place the emphasis on the organization of central brain states, which control and modulate input and output, rather than on the transmission of signals from receptors to effectors (Pribram, 1976). This is not to deny entirely the traditional role given to sensory input in the ongoing regulation of movement. Such information is probably important for the development of internal motor representations. However, the internal motor representations serve as the *context* within which subsequent input becomes processed. In other words, when we consciously preselect a movement, we are in a sense imposing the past upon the

---

[8] A similar sentiment is prevalent in Turvey's (1977) paper, which stresses a dualistic approach to perception and action.

future. Information already acquired *determines* what will be picked up. Our "anticipatory image" or internal model is already available to us for interpreting the results of our actions.

Reference Notes

1. Stelmach, G. E. *Toward an information processing approach in motor behavior research.* Paper presented at the joint meeting of the National College of Physical Education Association for Men and Women, Florida State University, Talahasee, Florida, January 1977.
2. Russell, K. R. E. *The influence of movement intent on short term motor memory.* Unpublished Ph.D. dissertation, University of Wisconsin, 1975.
3. Kelso, J. A. S., Goodman, D., Hayes, C., & Stamm, C. L. *Coding and retention characteristics of kinesthetic information in the developmentally young.* Manuscript in preparation.
4. Shea, J. B. *The effects of labeling on motor short-term memory.* Paper presented at the Sixth Canadian Symposium for Psychomotor Learning and Sport Psychology, Halifax, October 1974.
5. Wallace, S. A., Kelso, J. A. S., & Goodman, D. *The preselection effect reconsidered.* Unpublished data.
6. Roy, E. A. *An assessment of the role of preselection in memory for movement extent.* Unpublished Ph.D. dissertation, University of Waterloo, 1976.

References

Adams, J. A. A closed-loop theory of motor learning. *Journal of Motor Behavior*, 1971, *3*, 111–149.

Adams, J. A. Issues for a closed-loop theory of motor learning. In G. E. Stelmach (Ed.), *Motor control: Issues and trends*, New York: Academic Press, 1976.

Adams, J. A., & Goetz, E. T. Feedback and practice as variables in error correction and detection. *Journal of Motor Behavior*, 1973, *5*, 217–226.

Allen, G .I., & Tsukahara, N. Cerebrocerebellar communication systems. *Physiological Review*, 1974, *54*, 957–1006.

Anokhin, P. K. Cybernetics and the integrative activity of the brain. In M. Cole & I. Maltzman (Eds.), *A handbook of contemporary Soviet psychology.* New York: Basic Books, 1969.

Bernstein, H. *The coordination and regulation of movement.* New York: Pergamon, 1967.

Bizzi, E. Common problems confronting eye movement physiologists and investigators of somatic motor functions. *Brain Research*, 1974, *71*, 191–194.

Bizzi, E., Polit, A., & Morasso, P. Mechanisms underlying achievement of final head position. *Journal of Neurophysiology*, 1976, *39*(2), 435–444.

Bower, T. G. R. Repetitive processes in child development. *Scientific American*, 1976, *235*, 38–47.

Brooks, V. B. Roles of cerebellum and basal ganglia in initiation and control of movements. *Le Journal Canadien Des Sciences Neurologiques*, 1975, *2*(3), 265–277.

Brown, A. L. The role of strategic behavior in retardate memory. In N. R. Ellis (Ed.), *International review of research in mental retardation* (Vol. 7). New York: Academic Press, 1974.

Brown, A. L. The development of memory: Knowing, knowing about knowing and knowing how to know. In H. W. Reese (Ed.), *Advances in child development and behavior* (Vol. 10). New York: Academic Press, 1975.

Browne, K., Lee, J., & Ring, P. A. The sensation of passive movement at the metatarsophalangeal joint of the great toe in man. *Journal of Physiology, London*, 1954, *126*, 448–458.

Bruner, J. Organization of early skilled action. *Child Development*, 1973, *44*, 1–11.

Buchanan, J. *The philosophy of human nature*. Richmond, Kentucky: Grimes, 1812.

Canon, L. K. Directed attention and maladaptive "adaptation" of displacement of the visual field. *Journal of Experimental Psychology*, 1971, *88*, 403–408.

Clark, F. J., & Burgess, P. R. Slowly adapting receptors in cat knee joint: Can they signal joint angle? *Journal of Neurophysiology*, 1975, *38*, 1448–1463.

Coulter, J. Sensory transmission through lemniscal pathway during voluntary movement in the cat. *Journal of Neurophysiology*, 1974, *37*, 831–845.

Dyhre-Poulsen, P. Increased vibration threshold movements in human subjects. *Experimental Neurology*, 1975, *47*, 516–522.

Dyhre-Poulsen, P., & Hounsgaard, J. Transmission of afferent impulses through the lemniscal system during a conditioned movement in the monkey. *Acta Physiologica Scandinavica*, 1973, Supplement *396*: 68.

Duchenne, G. B. *Selections from the clinical works of Dr. Duchenne*. London: New Lydenham Society, 1883.

Ells, J. G. Analysis of temporal and attentional aspects of movement. *Journal of Experimental Psychology*, 1973, *99*, 10–21.

Evarts, E. V. Representation of movements and muscles by pyramidal tract neurons of the precentral motor cortex. In M. D. Yahr & D. P. Purpura (Eds.), *Neurophysiological basis of normal and abnormal motor activities*. New York: Raven, 1967.

Evarts, E. V. Feedback and corollary discharge: A merging of the concepts. *Neurosciences Research Program Bulletin*, 1971, *9*, 86–112.

Evarts, E. V. Brain mechanisms in movement. *Scientific American*, 1973, *229*, 96–103.

Flavell, J. H. Developmental studies of mediated memory. In L. P. Lipsitt & H. W. Reese (Eds.), *Advances in child development and behavior* (Vol. 5). New York: Academic Press, 1970.

Gandevia, S. C., & McCloskey, D. I. Joint sense, muscle sense, and their combination as position sense, measured at the distal interphalangeal joint of the middle finger. *Journal of Physiology*, 1976, *260*, 387–407.

Gentile, A. M. A working model of skill acquisition with application to teaching. *Quest*, 1972, *XVII*, 3–23.

Gibson, J. J. Observations on active touch. *Psychological Review*, 1962, *69*, 477–491.

Goldscheider, A. Untersuchen über den Muskelsinn. *Archiv für Anatomie und Physiologie, Leipzig*, 1889, *3*, 369–502.

Goodwin, G. M. The sense of limb position and movement. In J. Keogh & R. S. Hutton (Eds.), *Exercise and sport sciences reviews* (Vol. 4). Santa Barbara, California: Journal Publication Affiliates, 1977.

Goodwin, G. M., McCloskey, D. I., & Matthews, P. B. C. The contribution of muscle afferents to kinaesthesia shown by vibration induced illusions of movement and by the effects of paralyzing joint afferents. *Brain*, 1972, *95*, 705–748.

Granit, R. Constant errors in the execution and appreciation of movement. *Brain*, 1972, *95*, 649–660.

Greenwald, A. G. Sensory feedback mechanisms in performance control: With special reference to the ideo-motor mechanisms. *Psychological Review*, 1970, *77*, 73–99.

Grigg, P. Response of joint afferent neurons in cat medial articular nerve to active and passive movements of the knee. *Brain Research*, 1976, *118*, 482–485.

Henderson, W. R., & Smyth, G. E. Phantom limbs. *Journal of Neurology, Neurosurgery and Psychiatry*, 1948, *11*, 88–112.

Hollingworth, H. L. The inaccuracy of voluntary movement. *Archives of Psychology*, 1909, *2*, 1–87.

Horch, K. W., Clark, F. J., & Burgess, P. R. Awareness of knee joint angle under static conditions. *Journal of Neurophysiology*, 1975, *38*, 1436–1447.

Hull, C. L. Goal attraction and directing ideas conceived as habit phenomena. *Psychological Review*, 1931, *38*, 487–506.

Hyslop, T. B. *Mental physiology*, London: Churchill, 1895.

James, W. *Principles of psychology* (Vol. 1). New York: Holt, 1890.

Jones, B. Outflow and inflow in movement duplication. *Perception & Psychophysics*, 1972, *12*, 95–96.

Jones, B. The role of central monitoring of efference in motor short-term memory for movements. *Journal of Experimental Psychology*, 1974, *102*, 37–43.

Jones, B., & Hulme, M. R. Evidence for an outflow theory of skill. *Acta Psychologica*, 1976, *40*, 49–56.

Jordan, T. C. Characteristics of visual and proprioceptive response times in the learning of a motor skill. *Quarterly Journal of Experimental Psychology*, 1972, *24*, 536–543.

Kahneman, D. *Attention and effort*. Englewood Cliffs, New Jersey: Prentice-Hall, 1973.

Keele, S. W., & Ells, J. C. Memory characteristics of kinesthetic information. *Journal of Motor Behavior*, 1972, *4*, 127–134.

Kelso, J. A. S. Central and peripheral information in motor control. In J. King & W. W. Spirduso (Eds.), *Motor control symposium*. Austin: University of Texas Press, 1975.

Kelso, J. A. S. Planning and efferent components in the coding of movement. *Journal of Motor Behavior*, 1977, *9*, 33–47. (a).

Kelso, J. A. S. Motor control mechanisms in timing behavior. In R. E. Stadulis, C. O. Dotson, V. L. Katch, & J. Shick (Eds.), *Research and practice in physical education*. Champaign, Illinois: Human Kinetics, 1977, 231–254. (b)

Kelso, J. A. S. Coding processes and motor control: An integrated approach. In R. W. Christina & D. Landers (Eds.), *Psychology of motor behavior and sport*. Champaign, Illinois: Human Kinetics, 1977, 225–242. (c)

Kelso, J. A. S. Motor control mechanisms underlying human movement reproduction. *Journal of Experimental Psychology: Human Perception and Performance*, 1977, *3*, 529–543.(d)

Kelso, J. A. S., Cook, E., Olson, M. E., & Epstein, W. Allocation of attention and the locus of adaptation to displaced vision. *Journal of Experimental Psychology: Human Perception and Performance*, 1975, *1*, 237–245.

Kelso, J. A. S., & Frekany, G. A. Coding processes in preselected and constrained movements—Effect of vision. *Acta Psychologica*, in press.

Kelso, J. A. S., & Stelmach, G. E. Central and peripheral mechanisms in motor control. In G. E. Stelmach (Ed.), *Motor control: Issues and Trends*. New York: Academic Press, 1976.

Kerr, B. Processing demands during mental operations. *Memory and Cognition*, 1973, *1*, 401–412.

Kimble, G. A., & Perlmuter, L. C. The problem of volition. *Psychological Review*, 1970, *77*, 361–384.

Klein, R. M. Attention and movement. In G. E. Stelmach (Ed.), *Motor control: Issues and trends*. New York: Academic Press, 1976.

Klein, R., & Posner, M. I. Attention to visual and kinesthetic components of skills. *Brain Research*, 1974, *71*, 401–411.

Konorski, J. *Integrative activity of the brain*. Chicago: University of Chicago Press, 1967.

Laabs, G. J. Retention characteristics of different cues in motor short-term memory. *Journal of Experimental Psychology*, 1973, *100*, 168–177.

Liu, I. Effects of repetition of voluntary responses: From voluntary to involuntary. *Journal of Experimental Psychology*, 1968, *76*, 398–406.

Lynn, B. Somatosensory receptors and their CNS connections. *Annual Reviews of Physiology,* 1975, 105–127.

MacNeilage, P. F., & MacNeilage, L. A. Central processes controlling speech production in sleep and waking. In F. J. McGuigan (Ed.), *The psychophysiology of thinking.* New York: Academic Press, 1973.

Marsden, C. D., Merton, P. A., & Morton, H. B. Servo action in human voluntary movement. *Nature, London,* 1972, *238,* 140–143.

Marteniuk, R. G. Retention characteristics of motor short-term memory cues. *Journal of Motor Behavior,* 1973, *5,* 249–259.

Marteniuk, R. G. *Information processing in motor skills.* New York: Holt, 1976.

Marteniuk, R. G., & Roy, E. A. The codability of kinesthetic location and distance information. *Acta Psychologica,* 1972, *36,* 471–479.

Marteniuk, R. G., Shields, K. W., & Campbell, S. C. Amplitude, position, timing and velocity as cues in reproduction of movement. *Perceptual and Motor Skills,* 1972, *35,* 51–58.

McCloskey, D. I., Ebeling, P., & Goodwin, G. M. Estimation of weights and tensions and apparent involvement of a "sense of effort." *Experimental Neurology,* 1974, *42,* 220–232.

Merton, P. A. Human position sense and sense of effort. Homeostasis and feedback mechanisms. *18th Symposium of the Society of Experimental Biology.* Cambridge, England: Cambridge University Press, 1964.

Miller, G. A., Galanter, E. G., & Pribram, K. H. *Plans and the structure of behavior.* New York: Holt, 1960.

Miller, S. Joint afferent fibres responding to muscle stretch, vibration and contraction. *Brain Research,* 1973, *63,* 380–383.

Neisser, U. *Cognition and reality.* San Francisco: Freeman, 1976.

Newell, K. M. Knowledge of results and motor learning. *Journal of Motor Behavior,* 1974, *6,* 235–244.

Newell, K. M., & Chew, R. A. Visual feedback and positioning movements. *Journal of Motor Behavior,* 1975, *7*(3), 153–158.

Paillard, J., & Brouchon, M. Active and passive movements in the calibration of position sense. In S. J. Freedman (Ed.), *The neuropsychology of spatially oriented behavior.* Homewood, Illinois: Dorsey, 1968.

Pew, R. W. Human perceptual-motor performance. In B. H. Kantowitz (Ed.), *Human information processing: Tutorials in performance and cognition.* New York: Erlbaum, 1974.

Phillips, C. G. Changing concepts of the precentral motor area. In J. C. Eccles (Ed.), *Brain and conscious experience.* New York: Springer-Verlag, 1965.

Posner, M. I. Characteristics of visual and kinesthetic memory codes. *Journal of Experimental Psychology,* 1967, *75,* 103–107.

Posner, M. I. Coordination of internal codes. In W. G. Chase (Ed.), *Visual information processing.* New York: Academic Press, 1973.

Posner, M. I., & Keele, S. W. Attention demands of movements. In W. G. Koster (Ed.) *Attention and Performance II.* Amsterdam: Swets & Zeitlinger, 1969.

Posner, M. I., Nissen, M. J., & Klein, R. M. Visual dominance: An information-processing account of its origins and significance. *Psychological Review,* 1976, *83*(2), 157–171.

Poser, M. I., & Rossman, E. The effect of size and location of interpolated reducing transformations upon short-term retention. *Journal of Experimental Psychology,* 1965, *70,* 491–505.

Posner, M. I., & Snyder, C. R. R. Attention and cognitive control. In R. L. Solso (Ed.), *Information processing and cognition: The Loyola symposium.* Hillsdale, New Jersey: Erlbaum, 1975.

Pribram, K. *Languages of the brain.* Englewood Cliffs, New Jersey: Prentice Hall, 1971.

Pribram, K. Executive functions of the frontal lobes. In T. Desiraju (Ed.), *Mechanisms in transmission of signals for conscious behaviour*. Amsterdam: Elsevier, 1976.

Provins, K. A. The effect of peripheral nerve block on the appreciation and execution of finger movements. *Journal of Physiology, London*, 1958, *143*, 55–67.

Rock, I., & Victor, J. Vision and touch: An experimentally created conflict between the two senses. *Science*, 1964, *143*, 594–596.

Roy, E. A., & Diewert, G. L. Encoding of kinesthetic extent information. *Perception & Psychophysics*, 1975, *17*, 559–564.

Schmidt, R. A. A schema theory of discrete motor skill learning. *Psychological Review*, 1975, *82*, 225–260.

Simmel, M. L. Developmental aspects of body schema. *Child Development*, 1966, *37*, 83–95.

Skoglund, S. Anatomical and physiological studies of knee joint innervation in the cat. *Acta Physiologica Scandinavia*, 1956, *124*, 1–99. (Monograph Supplement)

Skoglund, S. Joint receptors and kinaesthesis. In I. Iggo (Ed.), *Handbook of sensory physiology: Somatosensory system* (Vol. 2). New York: Springer-Verlag, 1973.

Smirnov, A. A., & Zinchenko, P. I. Problems in the psychology of memory. In M. Cole & I. Maltzman (Eds.), *A handbook of contemporary Soviet psychology*. New York: Basic Books, 1969.

Sokolov, E. N. The modeling properties of the nervous system. In M. Cole & I. Maltzman (Eds.), *A handbook of contemporary Soviet psychology*, New York: Basic Books, 1969.

Somjen, G. *Sensory coding in the mammalian nervous system*. New York: Appleton-Century-Crofts, 1972.

Sperry, R. W. Neurology and the mind-brain problem. *American Scientist*, 1952, *40*, 291–312.

Sperry, R. W. Mental phenomena as causal determinants in brain function. In G. G. Globus, Savodnik, & G. Maxwell (Eds.), *Consciousness and the brain: A scientific and philosophical inquiry*. New York: Plenum, 1976.

Stelmach, G. E. Feedback—a determiner of forgetting in short-term motor memory. *Acta Psychologica*, 1973, *37*, 333–339.

Stelmach, G. E., & Kelso, J. A. S. Memory trace strength and response biasing in short term motor memory. *Memory and Cognition*, 1975, *3*, 58–62.

Stelmach, G. E., & Kelso, J. A. S. Memory processes in motor control. In S. Dornic (Ed.), *Attention and performance* (Vol. 6) Hillsdale, New Jersey: Erlbaum, 1977.

Stelmach, G. E., Kelso, J. A. S., & McCullagh, P. D. Preselection and response biasing in short-term motor memory. *Memory and Cognition*, 1976, *4*, 62–66.

Stelmach, G. E., Kelso, J. A. S., & Wallace, S. A. Preselection in short term motor memory. *Journal of Experimental Psychology: Human Learning and Memory*, 1975, *1*, 745–755.

Taub, E. Movement in nonhuman primates deprived of somatosensory feedback. In J. Keogh & R. S. Hutton (Eds.), *Exercise and sports sciences reviews* (Vol. 4). Santa Barbara, California: Journal Publishing Affiliates, 1977.

Teuber, H. L. Perception. In J. Field, H. W. Magoun, & V. E. Hall (Eds.), *Handbook of physiology (neurophysiology)* (Vol. 3). Washington, D.C.: American Physiological Society, 1960.

Teuber, H. L. Alteration of perception after brain injury. In J. C. Eccles (Ed.), *Brain and conscious experience*. New York: Springer-Verlag, 1966.

Teuber, H. L. Key problems in the programming of movements. *Brain Research*, 1974, *71*, 533–568.

Turvey, M. T. Preliminaries to a theory of action with reference to vision. In R. Shaw & J. Bransford (Eds.), *Perceiving, acting and knowing*, Hillsdale, New Jersey: Erlbaum, 1977.

Vallbo, A. B. Muscle spindle afferent discharge from resting and contracting muscles in normal subjects. In J. E. Desmedt (Ed.), *New developments in electromyography and clinical neurophysiology* (Vol. 3). Basel: Karger, 1972.

von Helmholtz, H. In J. P. C. Southall (Ed.), *Helmholtz's treatise on physiological optics* (Vol. 3). New York: Dover, 1962.

von Holst, E. Relations between the central nervous system and the peripheral organs. *British Journal of Animal Behavior*, 1954, *2*, 89–94.

Wallace, S. A. The coding of location: A test of the target hypothesis. *Journal of Motor Behavior*, 1977, *9*, 157–169.

Wallace, S. A., & Stelmach, G. E. Proprioceptive encoding in preselected and constrained movement. *Mouvement*, 1975, *7*, 147–152.

Warren, D. H., & Cleaves, W. T. Visual proprioceptive interaction under large amounts of conflict. *Journal of Experimental Psychology*, 1971, *90*, 206–214.

Weimer, W. B. A conceptual framework for cognitive psychology: Motor theories of the mind. In R. Shaw & J. Bransford (Eds.), *Perceiving, acting and knowing*. Hillsdale, New Jersey: Erlbaum, 1977.

Wilke, J. T., & Vaughn, S. C. Temporal distribution of attention during a throwing motion. *Journal of Motor Behavior*, 1976, *8*, 83–88.

Woodworth, R. S. The accuracy of voluntary movement. *Psychological Review*, 1899 (Monograph Supplement Whole No. 13).

Woolsey, C. N., & Chang, T. H. Activation of the cerebral cortex by antidromic volleys in the pyramidal tract. *Research Publications Associates Nervous Mental Disorders*, 1948, *27*, 146.

Zaporozhets, A. V. The role of orienting activity and of the image in the formation and performance of voluntary movements. In L. G. Voronin, A. N. Leontiev, A. R. Luria, E. N. Sokolov, & O. S. Vinogradova (Eds.), *Orienting reflex and exploratory behavior*. Washington, D.C.: American Institute of Biological Sciences, 1965.

6

The Latency and Duration of Rapid Movement Sequences: Comparisons of Speech and Typewriting

Saul Sternberg
Stephen Monsell
Ronald L. Knoll
Charles E. Wright

117

Information Processing in
Motor Control and Learning

I. Introduction

We communicate verbal information in three principal ways: We write, we speak, and we use keyboards. Maximum information rates in speech and typing are higher than in writing (Seibel, 1972), and as more of our work uses computers, keyboard entry is becoming increasingly important. This chapter reports some new findings about the temporal patterns of rapid movement sequences in speech and typewriting and what these patterns might mean in relation to the advance planning or "motor programming" of such sequences. We shall be concerned with how response factors affect the time to initiate a prespecified rapid movement sequence after a signal (the "simple-reaction" time) when the goal is to complete the sequence as quickly as possible, as well as how such factors affect the rate at which movements in the sequence are produced.[1] The response factor of central interest will be the number of elements in the sequence.

Most existing research on skilled performance has been concerned with *perceptual*–motor skills. For example, in most studies of typing behavior, performance has been measured when new segments of text are read concurrently with the typing of segments that have just been read (see, e.g., Butsch, 1932; Shaffer, 1976). Nonetheless, it has been argued that a major source of errors in typing is in the control of finger movements rather than in the perception of what is to be typed (see, e.g., Shaffer & Hardwick, 1969; Van Nes, 1976). Partly for this reason and partly because we believe it is desirable to study aspects of skilled performance in isolation, we have tried in these experiments on speech and typewriting to study movement processes uncontaminated by the concurrent perception of new material.

These studies began with two accidental findings (reported in Monsell & Sternberg, Note 1). The first was that the number of words in a brief rapid

---

[1] Some similar questions about handwriting are addressed in Chapter 7.

utterance influenced the time to initiate the utterance, even though the talker knew what he would have to say well in advance of the reaction signal. This finding seemed surprising, particularly in view of the claim based on previous studies (Eriksen, Pollack, & Montague, 1970; Klapp, 1971, 1976) that the latency (or reaction time) for saying a single word, known in advance, is not affected by the number of syllables it contains. The second finding was that the functions relating the duration of these rapid utterances to the number of words they contained were concave upward rather than being linear, indicating that words in longer sequences were produced at slower rates.

Our interest in the effect of the length of a movement sequence on its latency was based partly on the possibility that it reflects a latency component used for advance planning of the entire sequence: The length effect would then measure the extra time required to prepare extra elements. The idea that changes in reaction time might reflect changes in *sequence preparation* in this way seems to have been first proposed by Henry and Rogers (1960), who found that simple-reaction time increased with the number of elements in a sequence of movements made with one arm. According to their model, part of the reaction time includes the time to gain access to stored information concerning the whole sequence: a process akin to loading a program into a motor buffer, with sequences containing more elements requiring larger programs, and larger programs requiring more loading time. Numerous studies have since been made of effects of factors such as the extent, duration, and "complexity" of arm and hand movements on their latency. Both simple-reaction and choice-reaction paradigms have been used. However, as indicated in the reviews of this work by Hayes and Marteniuk (1976) and by Kerr (Chapter 3 of this volume), both paradigms have given rise to conflicting and controversial findings. We consider briefly three issues that are relevant to these conflicts and to the experimental methods we decided to adopt.

A. Element Invariance and the Measurement of Response Complexity

One issue that arises in examining previous work is the proper index of response complexity. An increase in the extent or duration of a movement sequence may not necessarily increase the amount of planning required, as measured by the number of "instructions" or "subprograms" in a "program." (Once this issue is raised, it suggests an explanation for the contrast mentioned above: The latency of an utterance could be influenced by the number of words in the utterance but not by the number of syllables in a word if the "programming unit" were a suprasyllabic sequence such as a word or a stress group, rather than something smaller such as a syllable or an articulatory gesture.)

The aspect of response complexity we have manipulated in our experiments is the number of elements (spoken words, keystrokes) in a movement sequence, which we varied over a wide range (from one to five) relative to previous studies. To minimize the probability that effects of the number of elements in a sequence on its latency or duration are trivial consequences of differences in the elements themselves, we have tried to ensure that the elements are as fixed as possible, regardless of the sequence in which they are embedded. Insofar as the approximation to this *element-invariance requirement* is a good one, the wide range enables us to study the form of the function relating latency to the number of elements and to investigate the relation between the "programming units" and the elements we manipulate. In addition, insofar as the form of the function is simple (e.g., linear), the data would suggest that the invariance requirement is approximately satisfied.

Before leaving this issue it is helpful to be somewhat more precise about the requirement of element invariance. Let us divide elements in a sequence into four classes: interior elements (i) both preceded and followed by other elements, beginning elements (b), terminating elements (t), and single elements (s) neither preceded nor followed by others. Now consider the elements that are present in sequences of increasing length: s, bt, bit, $biit$, $biiit$. To study the form of the function relating latency (or duration) to the number of equivalent elements in a sequence we can restrict ourselves to the *changes* in performance that result from equivalent *increases* in length, starting from a short sequence.

Suppose that we start with sequences of length $n = 2$. Then all increases in length can be regarded as resulting from the addition of i-elements. We therefore need to assume that i-elements are all equivalent. In addition, since elements already present must not change as we increase sequence length, all b-elements must be assumed to be equivalent regardless of sequence length, and similarly for t-elements. There is no need for b- and t-elements to be equivalent to i-elements or to each other.

If we start with sequences of length $n = 1$ rather than $n = 2$, however, we must also assume the equivalence of s- and b-elements and of i- and t-elements (or, alternatively, of s- and t-elements and of i- and b-elements). One can imagine this requirement not being met, especially given the evidence, from speech, of bidirectional coarticulation effects (see Kent & Minifie, 1977). Insofar as our data cause us to question this equivalence, we must restrict our attention to the performance functions for $n \geqslant 2$.

B. Response Effects in Simple Reactions
versus Choice Reactions

A second issue raised by previous work is whether choice reaction or simple reaction is the more appropriate paradigm for investigating the effects of the characteristics of a response on the planning of that response. One argument (e.g., Klapp, 1976) assumes that after sufficient practice one movement sequence (simple reaction) can be fully prepared in advance of the signal, but that more than one (choice reaction) cannot; therefore, choice-reaction latencies are more likely to reflect response-planning operations. However, there is little independent evidence favoring either of the assumptions. Certain response variations have been observed to produce larger effects on latency of the choice reaction, and this fact has been taken as evidence that advance planning between signal and response plays a larger role there than in the simple reaction. However, this inference depends on the idea that the only locus of response-factor effects is response planning; the inference is not justified if response factors also influence additional operations that might be required for choice reactions but not for simple reactions, such as "translation" from stimulus to response or "response selection."

There are two kinds of "compatibility" effects in the choice-reaction paradigm that suggest the influence of response factors on operations other than response planning. Consider first the finding that the latency of a particular response to a particular stimulus depends on the mappings of the other possible responses on the other possible stimuli (e.g., Duncan, 1977). This suggests that changes in latency produced by varying the attributes of a specified response to a specified stimulus are likely to depend on S–R mappings of other pairs—a dependence that might be hard to explain solely in terms of the planning of that response.

Consider second the effects of compatibility of entire stimulus and response ensembles ("SE–RE compatibility," as contrasted with the "S–R compatibility" of mappings of the same stimulus and response ensembles; Brainard, Irby, Fitts, & Alluisi, 1962): The change in latency induced by switching from one R-ensemble to another depends on the S-ensemble. This indicates that at least one of the processing stages between stimulus and response is influenced by the identities of both (Sternberg, 1969a, Section 5.3); hence, any effect of response factors might arise at least in part in that stage and could therefore depend on (interact with) stimulus factors—another dependence that might be hard to explain in terms of response planning.

Considerations like these not only weaken the argument just mentioned for using the choice-reaction paradigm, but also show that the effects of response (or stimulus) factors cannot be assigned conclusively to response (or stimulus) processes without suitable control experiments. While this caveat applies to simple- as well as choice-reaction paradigms, we believe the hazards to be greater in the choice situation, where it is likely that a more complex series of processes determines the latency and that stimulus–response interactions are larger. Indeed, in those studies we know of where the same variations in S–R mapping were examined in both choice-reaction and simple-reaction paradigms, S–R compatibility effects that were substantial in the former proved to be vanishingly small in the latter (Callan, Klisz, & Parsons, 1974; Anzola, Bertoloni, Buchtel, & Rizzolatti, 1977).

Another consideration that arises in the choice-reaction paradigm is the possibility of effects of *response–response compatibility*. Evidence has been accumulating that the other possible responses in an experiment influence the latency of a specified response, not merely by virtue of their number, but also their kind. Thus, in the case of binary choice, the latency of a response is shorter if it is paired with another that could be performed at the same time (Berlyne, 1957), or that is performed by a finger on the opposite hand (Kornblum, 1965), or that involves a movement in the same direction (Megaw, 1972), or that contains the same initial phoneme (Sanders, 1970). Given the available evidence, these effects cannot be unequivocally distinguished from S–R or SE–RE compatibility and conclusively assigned to response processes. But insofar as similar effects are observed with arbitrary stimulus ensembles and arbitrary S–R mappings, an interpretation in terms of response processes is compelling. We believe that ultimately an account of the planning and execution of responses will have to explain R–R compatibility.[2] For the present, however, such considerations complicate the interpretation of response effects: In the choice-reaction paradigm, the influence of altering one of the responses on the latency of that response could depend on the identity of the other (not performed) response.

Our approach, then, has been to study the effects of sequence length on latency in the simple-reaction paradigm; we believe that contributions to these effects from stimulus discrimination and S–R translation processes are minimized in that paradigm, and it permits us to defer the issue of R–R compatibility. If under these conditions there remains an orderly dependence of latency on the nature and number of elements in the entire movement sequence, this dependence would seem particularly worth investigation, since there would appear to be fewer alternatives that compete with the hypothesis of advance planning of the entire sequence than in the choice-reaction paradigm. However, we do not wish to argue that just because we use the simple-reaction paradigm, any effects of response factors on latency can be immediately assigned to a response-planning process that occurs after the signal but before the start of the response. It is still necessary to pit this hypothesis against the promising alternatives that remain, such as delays associated with operations that are required to maintain a description of the response in short-term verbal memory, failure of the invariance requirement discussed above, or effects of sequence length on the time to retrieve the first element from a previously loaded motor-program buffer. Indeed, as we shall attempt to show, the results we have obtained thus far tend to favor a somewhat different hypothesis from the one that first attracted us to the problem.

---

[2] A study by Rosenbaum (Note 2) can be regarded as a first attempt to provide a process model of R–R compatibility effects. He has argued, with experimental support, that under some conditions only the movement "features" not shared by the pair of responses in a binary choice-reaction task are prepared after the signal, whereas the features they do share are prepared before the signal. Note that "R–R compatibility" has usually been applied to simultaneously performed responses.

C. Relation between Advance Planning and Feedback Control

A third issue raised by previous work, and one that dominates much writing on motor processes, is the relation between the advance planning of a movement sequence and the influence of feedback during the execution of that sequence. Clearly the existence of any sensory delay requires that brief movement elements be controlled independently of the peripheral feedback they produce (e.g., Welford, 1974). The idea of a central motor program for the control of entire sequences seems to have arisen from the observation that sensory delays were too great to permit feedback ("closed loop") control even from one element to the next, in rapid performance (e.g., Lashley, 1951; but see also Adams, 1976).

The "program" concept has been restricted in recent years by the idea that the *only* way organisms deal with limited feedback delays in executing rapid movements is to preplan entire sequences (e.g., Schmidt, 1972), rather than, for example, planning some movements concurrently with the execution of earlier movement. Thus, in his influential definition, Keele (1968; see also Russell, 1976) proposed that "a motor program may be viewed as a set of muscle commands that are structured before a movement sequence begins, and that allows the entire sequence to be carried out uninfluenced by peripheral feedback [p. 387]."

This definition has seemed to suggest to some investigators that advance planning generates only command sequences that can be executed without any feedback ("open loop"), rather than, for example, programs that include instructions for sensing and responding to feedback, programs that can themselves be altered in response to feedback, or even programs that consist of ordered sets of "response images" (e.g., Greenwald, 1970; Adams, 1976) to which feedback from the movement sequence is compared.

We believe that it is inappropriate to restrict the "program" concept to cases of sequence control without feedback. Suppose that for a particular kind of movement sequence we had a hierarchical analysis in terms of sequences of units, each consisting of a sequence of subunits, and so forth. At each level of the hierarchy, control would have to be exercised over the selection, sequencing, and timing of the subunits, as well as over other attributes. At each level of the hierarchy and for each attribute, separate and largely independent questions could be raised, first about the roles of central and sensory sources of feedback and second, about the time relations between preparation and execution. Possible roles of feedback include, for example, serving as a cue that triggers the onset of the next subunit in a sequence, or providing information used in an error-correction process. Possibilities for the scheduling of preparation range from preparing each subunit after the previous one has been executed, through preparing later subunits while earlier ones are being executed, to preparing the whole sequence in advance.

We feel that questions about the existence and extent of advance planning are separable from questions about the precise role played by feedback, and we suspect that the methods appropriate for answering them are very different. In our view the experiments to be described in this chapter bear principally on the issue of the time relation between planning and execution.[3]

II. Experiments on Speech

With minor deviations the procedure on each trial of the three speech experiments to be described was as follows: First a short list of digits or words was presented sequentially and visually, at a rate of about 1 sec per item. The lengths and compositions of the lists were varied from trial to trial by means of a different balanced randomization for each subject. The list was followed by a fixed delay of about 4 sec that subjects could use for rehearsing silently and preparing to respond. On about 85% of the trials a visual "recite signal" (an illuminated rectangle) appeared at the end of the delay. This signal was preceded at 1-sec intervals by two brief "countdown" signals (the first signal auditory, and the second visual), which were included to minimize the subject's time uncertainty about when he might be required to respond. On the remaining 15% of the trials the recite signal was omitted; subjects were not to respond on these "catch trials," which were included so as to prevent anticipations on signal trials.

Instructions, feedback, scores, and cash bonuses were designed to encourage subjects to *complete* the reciting of each list as soon as possible after the signal, while maintaining a low error rate. (The error rates were in fact negligible and will not be discussed.) The subjects were four female high school students who were well practiced in experiments requiring rapid reciting.

Using an energy-sensitive speech detector with a low threshold, we made two measures of each response: its *latency,* measured from signal onset to the start of the utterance, and its *duration.* (The subjects were attempting to minimize the sum of these two measures.) Each subject had about 200 trials per day.

A. Numbers in Ascending Sequence

In our initial studies we had used lists of randomly ordered letters or digits. We later observed the same effects with well-learned sequences that place a minimal load on memory. Thus, in the first experiment presented here the lists were subsequences of one to five items drawn from the natural number sequence

---

[3] The experiments on speech were selected from a larger series described in Monsell and Sternberg (Note 1) and to be reported in greater detail elsewhere by Monsell and Sternberg. The experiment on typewriting was selected from a series to be reported in greater detail elsewhere by Sternberg, Knoll, and Wright.

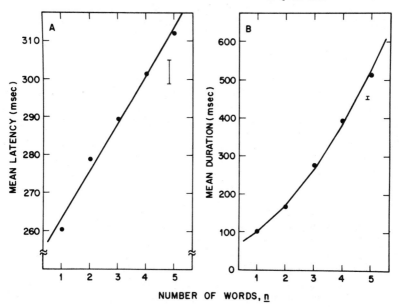

NUMBER OF WORDS, n

Figure 1   Ascending numbers experiment: The results are averaged over four subjects and over starting numbers; about 140 observations per point. (A) Mean latencies, estimate of standard error ($\pm SE$), and fitted linear function (Table I). (B) Mean durations, estimate of $\pm SE$, and fitted quadratic function (Table I). Note the difference between the ordinate scales. See Table I, Footnote a, for the fitting procedures. The SE estimates in Figure 1A–6B were chosen to be appropriate for revealing badness of fit. They are therefore based on mean squares for high-order interactions from analyses of variance in which *subjects* was treated as a fixed effect. Table I appears on p. 139.

$1, 2, \ldots, 9$, and starting with one of the five numbers $1, 2, \ldots, 5$. On the single day of testing there were about seven trials per subject for each of the 25 possible lists.[4]

Figure 1A shows that mean latency increased approximately linearly with the number of words (n) in the list at a rate of 12.6 msec/word. Thus, the time to start saying *two–three–four–five–six*, for example, was about 50 msec greater than the time to start saying *two*. Latency functions were similar across starting digits (slopes of the fitted functions are 10.2, 10.1, 15.3, 14.0, and 13.3 msec/word for lists starting with 1, 2, 3, 4, and 5, repectively) and across subjects (slopes are 10.1, 9.5, 19.4, and 11.3 msec/word for the four subjects). Linear regression

---

[4] A feature that distinguishes this experiment from our other experiments is that, although beginning items are balanced in lists of different lengths, populations of interior and terminating items differ systematically across lengths, thereby violating the element-invariance requirement of Section I,A. This could bias the results somewhat, especially for duration data.

accounts for 98.7% of the variance among mean latencies; deviations from linearity were not statistically significant.[5]

Figure 1B shows that the increase of duration with list length is distinctly nonlinear; the quadratic function shown fits well however, accounting for 99.8% of the variance among mean durations.[6] Acceleration of the duration function implies that the average articulation rate depends on list length: the longer a list, the greater the average time from the beginning of one word to the beginning of the next (this idea is made precise in Section V,A). Subjects responded well to the request that they complete their utterances rapidly: Their average articulation rate of about 9.4 words/sec is high relative to previously reported maximum rates (Hudgins & Stetson, 1937; Landauer, 1962).

B. Weekdays in Normal, Random, and Repeating Sequence

In a second experiment we compared subjects' production of three kinds of weekday sequences: normal (e.g., *Wednesday–Thursday–Friday–Saturday*), random, without replacement (e.g., *Monday–Friday–Wednesday–Sunday*), and repeating (e.g., *Monday–Monday–Monday–Monday*). The cyclic structure of the days of the week allowed us simultaneously to match populations of beginning words, terminating words, and interior words across list lengths (even in the familiar normally ordered lists) and across conditions. Lists contained from one to five words, and the two days of the experiment provided about 25 trials per length per condition per subject.

Mean latency (Figure 2A) again increased approximately linearly with list length. Slopes of the fitted linear functions do not differ significantly across conditions. The average latency slope is actually *smaller* for weekdays (8.8 msec/word) than for digits (12.6 msec/word) despite their greater syllabic length, but this between-experiment difference is not reliable.

Despite the similarity of latency functions, durations were, of course, much greater for lists of weekdays than for lists containing the same number of digits.

---

[5] To test whether the latency effect could result from a small but increasing proportion of extreme observations with longer lists, we examined the latency distributions. Mean quantiles for each list length and mean standard deviations were obtained by averaging separate estimates from latency distributions for each subject and starting digit. The slopes of linear functions fitted to the mean 20 and 80% points of the distributions were 10.2 and 14.1 msec/word, respectively, indicating that the entire distribution, and not simply the upper tail, is affected by list length. The greater rate of change for the higher quantile reflects a small increase in dispersion with list length; mean standard deviations of latencies increase from about 22 msec ($n = 1$) to 30 msec ($n = 5$).

[6] We chose a quadratic function partly because of its success in describing other duration data for $1 < n < 5$. Although departures from the fitted quadratic function are small, they are statistically significant in this experiment (but not in the others to be reported). See Footnote 4 for a possible explanation of this difference between experiments.

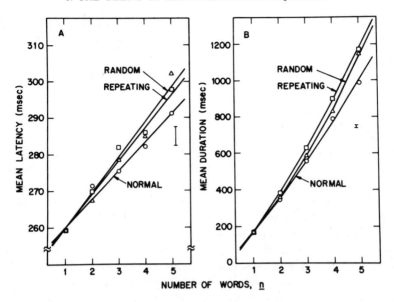

Figure 2 Weekdays in normal, random, and repeating sequences: The results are averaged over four subjects; about 100 observations per point. (A) Mean latencies, estimate of $\pm SE$, and fitted linear functions: normal, $259.9 + 7.8(n-1)$; random, $259.9 + 9.6(n-1)$; and repeating, $259.9 + 9.1(n-1)$. (B) Mean durations, estimate of $\pm SE$, and fitted quadratic functions: normal, $168.8 + 174.1(n-1) + 8.6(n-1)^2$; random, $168.8 + 174.0(n-1) + 16.6(n-1)^2$; and repeating, $168.8 + 201.2(n-1) + 12.7(n-1)^2$. The three fitted functions in each panel were constrained to pass through a common fitted value at $n = 1$.

Mean durations (Figure 2B) are significantly nonlinear, but very well described by quadratic functions [7]; these functions differ significantly across conditions.

For understanding our results, the relation between the repeating condition and the others will be of particular interest. One way to make this comparison is to subtract from each coefficient of the fitted function for the repeating condition the mean of the corresponding coefficients for normal and random conditions. The resulting differences are 0.4 ± 0.9 msec/word for the slope of the latency function, 0.1 ± 4.0 msec/word^2 for the quadratic coefficient of the duration function, and a significant 27.2 ± 3.2 msec/word for the linear coefficient of the duration function.[8] The only reliable effect of constructing an utterance from repetitions of the same word rather than from distinct words is to increase the linear coefficient of the duration function.

---

[7] The percentages of variance among the mean durations accounted for by fitted quadratic functions are 99.92, 99.96, and 99.98% for normal, random, and repeating conditions, respectively, and 99.99% for the means over conditions.

[8] When quantities are stated in the form $a \pm b$, b is an estimate of the standard error of a, based on between-subject variability.

When we compare the duration function for numbers to the average function for the weekdays conditions (see Table I) we find that the large duration difference is localized primarily in the constants (101.1 versus 168.8 msec) and linear coefficients (57.6 versus 183.1 msec/word). The quadratic coefficients (12.2 versus 12.6 msec/word^2) are almost identical.

C. Words of One and Two Syllables

Because they were produced in separate experiments, comparison of the data from number and weekday lists could only suggest whether and how the coefficients of the latency and duration functions depend on number of syllables per word. For more precise estimation of these effects we ran an experiment that was larger and that incorporated deliberate variation of word length.

Lists varied in length from one to four words; the words in a list were either all one-syllable words or all two-syllable words. The vocabulary consisted of 72 common nouns and was constructed so that all the two-syllable words were stressed on the first syllable and contained (an approximation to) one of the one-syllable words as the first syllable. (Examples of such embedded pairs are *bay–baby*, *rum–rumble*, *track–tractor*, *cow–coward*, and *limb–limit*.) Our aim was to bring our manipulation as close as possible to the addition of an unstressed syllable to a given stressed syllable. On each of the eight days of the experiment

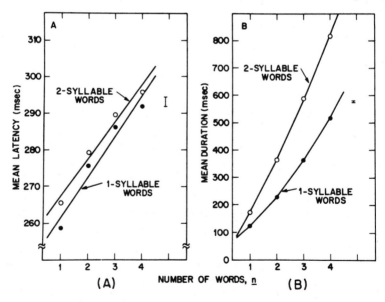

Figure 3 Experiment comparing words of one and two syllables: The results are averaged over four subjects and 8 days; about 400 observations per point. (A) Mean latencies, estimate of ±*SE*, and fitted linear functions (Table I). (B) Mean durations, estimate of ±*SE*, and fitted quadratic functions (Table I).

a subject worked with lists drawn from sets of nine words of each length that were changed from day to day; the sets were chosen so that a subject encountered the two members of any embedded pair on different days.

Each list was presented on three successive trials; because repetitions had little effect on either latency or duration, the data were averaged over repetitions. Each subject contributed about 12 observations per list length per word length per day.

Latency functions in this experiment (Figure 3A) were significantly nonlinear, but since this is the only experiment among many using lists of up to six words, in which we have observed such nonlinearity, we feel justified in describing the latency data in terms of parameters of the fitted linear functions. Slopes of these functions (in units of milliseconds per word) for one-and two-syllable words are almost identical, confirming the suggestion derived from the other two experiments; the difference is 0.9 ± 1.1 msec/word. However, the *mean* latency was influenced to a small but statistically significant extent by number of syllables: Mean latency for lists composed of two-syllable words was 4.5 ± 1.3 msec longer. (Experiments by other investigators have perhaps not been sensitive enough to detect differences as small as this; hence the earlier claim of no effect.) In an idealized description of these data one can take the slope difference to be zero and assert, therefore, that the effects of syllables per word and words per list are *additive:* Each factor has the same effect regardless of the level of the other.

The relation between latency functions for the lists containing one- and two-syllable words is stable with increasing practice, as shown by Figure 4. Both

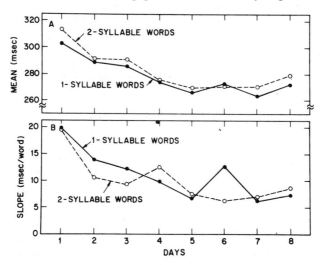

Figure 4 Effects of 8 days of practice on two aspects of latency (Figure 3A) for lists of length one to four of one- and two-syllable words. (A) Mean latency averaged over four list lengths, versus days; about 200 observations per point. (B) Slope of fitted linear latency function, versus days.

means and slopes decrease to what appear to be asymptotes, and, while there is no consistent ordering of slopes across days, the mean latency for lists of one-syllable words is smaller on 7 out of 8 days.

As one would expect, and despite its small effects on latency, number of syllables had a large effect on the duration function (Figure 3B). Data from both conditions are again well described by quadratic functions: The large duration difference is localized (see Table I) primarily in the constants (1-intercepts; 122.4 versus 173.4 msec) and linear coefficients (91.9 versus 180.4 msec/word); the quadratic coefficients (13.6 versus 12.0 msec/word^2, with a difference of 1.6 ± 0.9 msec/word^2) are almost identical, confirming the earlier findings.

D. Some Findings from Other Experiments

Here we list a few of our findings from other experiments that are especially pertinent to the interpretation of the latency effect.

1. Asymptote of the Latency Function

As the length of well-learned sequences is increased beyond about six words, the latency ceases to increase in an orderly manner and tends, instead, to fluctuate about an asymptotic value. (For novel sequences the range of the latency effect is of course limited in a different way: Once the immediate memory span is exceeded, both latency and error rate increase drastically.)

2. Insensitivity to an Additional Load on Short-Term Memory

In one experiment subjects memorized two lists on each trial: The first was to be recited fast, and the second was to be recited at a leisurely pace afterwards. The combined length of the two lists was never greater than five items. The presence and length of the second list had virtually no effect on the latency for reciting the first list (or on its duration). The latency therefore depends not on the load on short-term memory before or after the signal, but on the amount that must be said fast.

3. Invariance across Recite Signals of Different Modalities

In an experiment comparing visual and auditory recite signals, the difference between slopes of the resulting latency functions for lists of one to five words was negligible and nonsignificant.

4. Invariance across Changes in Time Uncertainty

In the experiments described here we attempted to minimize subjects' time uncertainty about when the recite signal might occur by using fixed foreperiods and countdown signals. In an experiment in which this procedure was compared to one with a highly variable foreperiod, we found that although the increase in time uncertainty was effective, in the sense that it caused an increase in the mean of the latency function, the change in its slope was negligible and nonsignificant.

5. Effect of Interpolating Words without Primary Stress

We have studied the effects of inserting unstressed connectives (*and, of, or*) between the successive nouns in a list, and of inserting words with little stress (*by, and, is a, minus*) between the successive (stressed) digits in a list. Neither of these operations increased the slope of the latency function (in milliseconds per noun or per digit) above its normal value; however, they did increase the mean latency. Thus, whether a list is augmented by extra unstressed syllables, or by separate words that carry little or no stress, the result is the same: There is a small increase in the mean, but no effect on the slope.

III. Hypotheses about the Latency Effect

The findings presented thus far provide us with two principal facts to be explained. First, the latency for rapid reciting of a prespecified utterance increases approximately linearly and at a rate of about 10 msec/word (or primary stress), over a range of one to five words. Second, over the same range, the more words in the utterance, the slower the rate at which it is recited. We begin with a discussion of some of the alternative hypotheses that we have considered for the latency effect and that have guided our experiments.

A. Time-Sharing: Readiness versus Rehearsal

The first two hypotheses reflect the possibility that the latency effect results from the load imposed by lists of increasing length on a short-term memory store, as traditionally conceived.[9] Suppose that while the subject awaits the signal he divides his time between maintaining his memory of the list (by covert rehearsal, for example) and being ready to respond to the signal. If the reaction signal occurs when he is in the *maintenance state* then it takes time to shift into the *ready state*. Increasing the list length may increase either the proportion of time spent in the maintenance state or the time taken to switch out of it. Given this hypothesis, and assuming that the subject has conrol over which state he is in, one would expect that increasing the time uncertainty associated with the reaction signal would make it more likely that the subject was in the maintenance state

---

[9] Here and elsewhere (where we use the term "ordinary short-term memory") we refer to the "short-term store" of Atkinson and Shiffrin (1968), or "primary memory" (see, e.g., Craik & Levy, 1976; Crowder, 1976).

when the signal occurred and would therefore increase the size of the latency effect (indexed by the slope of the latency function). The invariance of the slope, found when time uncertainty was manipulated experimentally, argues against this hypothesis. (In addition, the subjects asserted that they were not consciously rehearsing as the time approached when the signal might be presented.)

B. Capacity-Sharing and the Load on Short-Term Memory

A related possibility is that the longer the list, the more of a limited "capacity" (rather than time) has to be devoted to maintaining it in memory, and this reduces the capacity available for either processing the recite signal or having the first item ready. Several of our findings argue against this hypothesis (as well as the previous one). First, the similarity of latency functions for weekdays in normal, random, and repeating sequences shows that the capacity required to retain the list in memory is unimportant. Second, Baddeley, Thomson, and Buchanan (1975) have shown that the limit on the number of unrelated words that can be retained in short-term memory can be described in terms of the time it takes to say those words, so that brief words require less of the memory capacity than long words. Yet we have shown that the slope of the latency function is independent of word duration. Finally, by using an auxiliary memory load, we showed that increasing the number of words to be maintained in short-term memory, without changing the number to be recited fast, does not influence the latency.

C. Competition among Distinct Response Elements

According to the element-competition hypothesis, adequate preparation for the reaction signal requires that all the distinct elements from which the response is to be constructed be mentally "primed" or "activated" before the response begins (Lashley, 1951; Wickelgren, 1969). Suppose that all the primed elements then compete with any element that has to be produced, and that competition increases latency. The first element in a longer list has more competitors and hence a longer latency. Such a mechanism is particularly appealing because it can also readily explain the finding that the average rate at which the elements in longer lists are produced is lower. This hypothesis can be rejected on the basis of the typical latency effect found in the repeated weekdays condition, where list length was increased not by enlarging the set of *types* (and hence the number of *distinct* elements to be primed), but by adding to the number of *tokens* of the same type. Insofar as the primed elements are smaller than words, the absence of an effect of syllables per word on the latency-function slope can also be taken as negative evidence.

D. Information Transmitted

A fourth hypothesis is based on the observation that the amount of selective information in the response, in the sense of Shannon (see Garner, 1962), increases with the length of the list. Suppose that even though the list is specified in advance, the subject must resolve response uncertainty in selecting what to say at the time of response intiation. According to one version of this hypothesis (*sequence uncertainty*), the list must be selected from the set of all lists of the same length drawn from the same vocabulary. According to another version (*first-item uncertainty*), the first word must be selected from among all the words in the list. Under either version, if latency increased with the amount of information transmitted by the response, one would expect that for random lists, latency would increase with length. However, since an increase in the number of *repeated* words should not cause a corresponding increase in the amount of information, results from the weekdays experiment argue against this hypothesis.

E. Sequence Preparation (Version 1): Motor-Program
   Construction or Activation

According to the final and, we think, the most acceptable pair of hypotheses among those we consider, a representation of the entire response appropriate for controlling its execution (a *program*) is constructed before the response starts. The program consists of a set of linked *subprograms,* one for each *unit* of the response. The measure of the length of the program is the number of subprograms it contains. We suppose that the program is retained in a special *motor-program buffer* that is distinct from ordinary short-term memory. This memory state (or code or structure) is not sensitive to factors such as familiarity of the response, similarity or identity among its elements, its duration as such, or the extent to which short-term memory is otherwise occupied.

The first version of the sequence-preparation hypothesis is in the spirit of the "memory drum" model proposed by Henry and Rogers (1960): Either part or all of a process by which the program is constructed, or else a process of activating a previously constructed program (by "loading" it, for example), is not (and perhaps cannot be) started before the signal. Furthermore, this process is completed before the response begins and has a duration that increases linearly with the number of units in the list. Either the duration of the process is independent of subprogram length or subprogram length is independent of unit size; otherwise we would have seen an effect on the latency slope of syllables per word.

Why should a process of program construction or activation not be completed *before* the signal, when the subject knows in advance exactly what has to be said? We offer two speculative reasons:

1. Constructing or activating a motor program might be inherently tied to its execution: Once the program is ready to be used, execution follows automatically and is hard to inhibit. If the preparation process took place before the signal, the subject would then respond on catch trials. To avoid this, preparation must await the signal. If program activation involved loading the program into a delay-line memory, for example, and execution occurred when the information emerged at the other end of the delay line, the system would have the required property that activation causes execution.

2. The contents of the motor buffer might be subject to rapid decay, in which case the program would have to be set up immediately before use. (Furthermore, processing of the reaction signal might interfere with maintenance of information in the motor buffer.) [10]

F. Sequence Preparation (Version 2): Subprogram Retrieval

According to the second version of the sequence-preparation hypothesis, the construction and any necessary activation of the program as a whole are accomplished before the signal. However, only after the signal occurs is the subprogram for the first unit retrieved or located in the program. Mean retrieval time increases linearly with the number of subprograms contained in the buffer. This could arise because the retrieval is accomplished by means of a sequential search (analogous to mental search processes that have been proposed for other domains; e.g., Sternberg, 1969b) through the set of subprograms or through a directory of subprogram "addresses." Alternatively, retrieval time could increase with the number of subprograms because capacity has to be shared between a parallel search or a direct access process, and maintenance of the motor program; the property of linearity is less readily associated with such mechanisms, however. Possible reasons why retrieval of the first subprogram might have to await the signal are similar to the two reasons given above.

The retrieval version of the sequence-preparation hypothesis has a feature not shared with Version I: It not only explains the latency effect, but also leads naturally to an account of the slower production rate for longer lists, if the same retrieval mechanism is assumed to apply to each of the other units in the list as to the first. Insofar as the relations between latency and duration data are consistent (inconsistent) with such an account, they support the retrieval (activation) version.

---

[10] Neurophysiologists have argued that parts of the nervous system that may be implicated in the sequencing and timing of rapid movements can retain information only briefly. Also, certain neural structures, such as the parallel fibers in the cerebellum, appear to function as delay lines—though the delays they generate may be too short for present purposes (see Kornhuber, 1974; Eccles, 1969).

Suppose, for example, that the mechanism responsible for the length effect is a simple search process.[11] Then there are two obvious ways in which latency and duration might be related. If the same set of subprograms is searched, regardless of how many units have already been produced, then we expect that the mean time between the production of one unit and the next will increase linearly and at the same rate with list length as the latency does. On the other hand, if the contents of the buffer shrink as the response proceeds, then it is easy to show that the mean time between one unit and the next (averaged over the list) will again increase linearly, but at half the rate at which the latency increases. (These statements are valid without further assumptions if the search process is *exhaustive* [Sternberg, 1969b]; if it is *self-terminating* they depend on the order of the search meeting certain requirements.) A similar argument can be made if the mechanism is based on capacity sharing; in that case, we have a variety of element competition (see Section III,C) that applies to identical as well as distinct elements. We shall consider the duration data below, in light of these issues.

IV. Elaboration of the Sequence-Preparation Hypotheses

A. Nature of the Programming Unit in Speech

Both versions of the sequence-preparation hypothesis incorporate the idea that the response latency increases by some amount for each part (subprogram) of the motor program, where each subprogram controls one of the *units* in the response.[12] What is the nature of these response units? (They need not correspond to what we have called *elements*—convenient but arbitrary response segments.)

---

[11] The idea that in proceeding through a set of linked subprograms a search is used (rather than a process involving direct access by one subprogram to the next) would be superfluous if subprograms were stored in the same order in which they were to be used. An example of a theory of the control of serial order that is more congenial to the search idea is Wickelgren's (1969) context-sensitive associative theory of speech production, whose units could be stored in a random order and still support an ordered serial response, because each unit is stored with tags that indicate the preceding and following units.

[12] An alternative possibility for the construction version of the hypothesis is that the latency depends on the length of a higher-level program from which the motor program is constructed. Consider the following analogy: There is a "source program" (e.g., a series of coded representations in short-term memory) and an "object program" (the motor program) that is compiled from it and held in the motor buffer. Compiling requires fetching source units, translating them, and sending the resulting object units. Object units need not correspond one to one with source units. The rate of compiling could primarily reflect the rate of fetching, the rate of translating, or the rate of sending. In the construction version of the hypothesis, we cannot assign the latency effect unambiguously to one of these. Thus, the latency might, for example, depend on the number of words (a possible source unit) or the number of stress groups (a possible object unit). For the activation or retrieval versions of the hypothesis, however, the latency effect should reflect object units.

Recall that variation in the number of syllables per word had no effect on the latency increment per word. Since this manipulation indirectly alters the duration of a word, the number of articulatory gestures it contains, and the number of syllables, the unit cannot be a *speech segment of specified duration*, the *articulatory gesture*, or the *syllable*. Two of the remaining alternatives are the *word*, and the *stress group* or "metric foot" (a segment of speech associated with a primary stress). We have seen that the increase in latency with list length depends on the number of words in the list with primary stress and not on whether other words, with little or no stress, are inserted. Our present conclusion is that each subprogram controls a stress group, and we shall tentatively assume this in the following sections. The fact that the unit that underlies performance in our experiments appears to be articulatory rather than semantic seems to us to support further the interpretation of the latency effect in terms of a motor program.

B. A Basis for the Syllables Effect

We have seen (Section II, C and D) that although there was no effect on the latency-function *slope* (in milliseconds per stress group) of increasing the number of syllables per word or of inserting unstressed words, these operations did add an approximately constant increment to the latency for lists of each length, thereby increasing the latency-function *mean*. How can this increase be explained in the context of the sequence-preparation hypotheses? One possibility is that while activation (of the entire program) or retrieval (of the first subprogram) is completed in a time determined by the number of units, each unit has to be further *unpacked* into its constituents (syllables or articulatory gestures, for example) before it can be executed. Unpacking can be regarded either as advance planning or as retrieval, at a lower level of the response hierarchy.

Suppose that duration of the unpacking process increases with the *size* (number of constituents or duration) of a unit. Since only the first unit must be unpacked before the utterance begins, the unpacking operation prolongs the latency by the same amount for all list lengths. The latency function therefore increases in mean, but not in slope, when we increase the unit size. One implication that could be used to test the unpacking idea is that for a list of specified length whose units are of mixed size, the latency should depend only on the size of the first unit.

V. Analysis of the Duration Function

A. Quantitative Representations for Duration Data

Our second principal finding is that the duration function accelerates with sequence length, which suggests that the average interval between the starting times of successive elements is greater for longer sequences; this property also characterizes typewriting (see Section VI). We have seen in Section III,F that the quantitative characterization of the duration effect may help to select among alternative hypotheses for the latency effect. In the present section we introduce some concepts and notation that will facilitate the analysis and comparison of duration data in speech and typing.

The existence of the duration effect suggests that it might be useful to examine the individual time intervals between successive elements that add together to generate the observed duration. Such examination, however, requires measuring the interval between single time points associated in an invariant manner with individual elements (a *measurement-invariance requirement*); this is difficult in experiments involving rapid speech, but easy for typewriting, where the exact time of each key depression can be readily determined.[13] Let these times in a sequence of length n be T_{1n}, T_{2n}, . . . , T_{nn}, with the reaction signal specifying the time origin so that T_{1n} is the latency, L_n. (Note that if we regard each response element as *ending* with the key depression, then the measured latency in typing incorporates the duration of the first element, unlike the latency measure in speech, which does not incorporate the duration of the first word.) The $n - 1$ time intervals between successive elements are then $T_{2n} - T_{1n}$, $T_{3n} - T_{2n}$, . . . , $T_{nn} - T_{n-1,n}$, which we denote R_{2n}, R_{3n}, . . . , R_{nn}, respectively. A useful measure of production rate that can be estimated from the duration, $D_n = T_{nn} - T_{1n}$ of an entire sequence of length n, and which is easy to relate to the $n - 1$ time intervals between successive elements, is the *mean* such time interval,

$$R_{\cdot n} = \frac{1}{n-1} \sum_{k=2}^{n} R_{kn} = \frac{1}{n-1} \sum_{k=2}^{n} (T_{kn} - T_{k-1,n}) = \frac{1}{n-1}(T_{nn} - T_{1n}) = \frac{1}{n-1} D_n, \quad (n \geq 2). \quad (1)$$

We use "R" because $R_{\cdot n}$ and R_{kn} are measures of *rate;* note, however, that they denote time per response element, not elements per unit time.

The rate function $R_{\cdot n}$ provides an alternative representation of duration data that has some useful properties. First, if D_n increases as a quadratic function of length, then, as we shall see below, $R_{\cdot n}$ increases linearly.[14] This simplicity of form, together with the fact that $R_{\cdot n}$ has a smaller range of variation than D_n, makes any systematic deviations from the fitted function more apparent and facilitates comparisons between functions. In addition, in those instances where

---

[13] As a starting point, one can decompose the movement sequence in typing a list of letters into a series of elements, each ending at the moment a key depression is detected. Then, by definition, the single measured time point always marks the end of a movement element, and so the requirement of an invariant relation between time point and element is satisfied. It is possible, however, that this initial decomposition of the movement sequence is not the best one theoretically, even though it facilitates measurement; one test is whether the data are orderly and easily interpretable. We believe that for the movement sequences in rapid speech the appropriateness of any particular decomposition is even less obvious.

[14] An alternative measure with this property but less desirable in other respects is the first difference function, $D_n - D_{n-1}$, which is similar to the derivative.

the duration variance increases most dramatically with n, we have observed the $R_{.n}$ variances to be more homogeneous.

Estimation of $R_{.n}$ as defined in Eq. (1) is straightforward for typing data, but to apply that definition to our speech experiments the duration measures first need correction. Let T^*_{kn} and T_{kn} represent, respectively, the starting and ending times of the kth word in a response of length n. For the response as a whole the measured starting time T^*_{1n} (appropriate for a measure of latency) and the measured ending time T_{nn} do not mark corresponding points in the first and last response elements; these measures therefore fail to meet the measurement-invariance requirement mentioned previously in this section. Let us identify the *end* of each word as the desired (invariant) time point. Then the measured duration $D^*_n = T_{nn} - T^*_{1n}$ includes not only the sum $D_n = T_{nn} - T_{1n}$ of the $n - 1$ intervals from the end of one word to the end of the next, but also the time $T_{1n} - T^*_{1n}$ from the start to the end of the first word. To estimate D_n from D^*_n we must therefore subtract an estimate of this extra time. If we assume that the duration of the first word is independent of n, then $D^*_1 = T_{11} - T^*_{11}$ provides the desired estimate, so that $D_n = D^*_n - D^*_1$, and we have

$$R_{.n} = \frac{1}{n-1} D_n = \frac{1}{n-1} (D^*_n - D^*_1), (n \geqslant 2). \tag{2}$$

If D_n is actually quadratic, but the duration of the first word depends on n, then it is likely that D^*_n would differ systematically from a fitted quadratic function and that $R_{.n}$ would be systematically nonlinear. (A dependence of the duration of the first word on n, particularly on $n = 1$ versus $n > 1$, could come about from failure of the element-invariance requirement discussed in Section I,A.) Note that Eq. (2) can be regarded as a generalization of Eq. (1); in a case such as typewriting, $D^*_1 = 0$, so $D_n = D^*_n$.

Now let us consider a quadratic duration function as fitted to the data in Figures 1B, 2B, and 3B:

$$D^*_n = \alpha + \beta(n - 1) + \gamma(n - 1)^2, (n \geqslant 1). \tag{3}$$

We have written D^*_n as a function of $n - 1$ rather than of n because the parameter α then represents D^*_1 (which is zero for the case of typewriting) and because the rate and duration functions are then related in a simple way; from Eqs. (2) and (3) we get

$$R_{.n} = \beta + \gamma(n - 1), (n \geqslant 2). \tag{4}$$

Thus, a quadratic duration function implies a linear rate function: The quadratic coefficient, γ, in D^*_n represents the amount by which the average interval between one element and the next increases for each element added to the response, whereas the linear coefficient, β, represents a "base" value of the average inter-element time, to which the successive increments are added. If the duration function were linear, we would have $\gamma = 0$, and the rate function would then be a constant.

B. Analysis of Durations in Experiments on Speech

Latency and duration functions that were fitted to the data from the three speech experiments are summarized in the top four lines of Table I. As already noted, the quadratic coefficients in the four duration functions are remarkably similar in magnitude, despite substantial differences in word duration. This implies that the rate at which the mean time between successive words increases with sequence length is the same for words containing different numbers of syllables. To reveal this more clearly, we have displayed the observed and fitted rate functions $R_{\cdot n}$ for our third experiment (see Figure 6A). When we describe the production rate as a function of the number of words (rather than, for example, the number of syllables) the two rate functions are almost perfectly parallel, just as for the latency functions (see Figure 3A), despite their considerable difference in mean: The slope difference between the fitted functions is

Table I
Fitted Latency and Duration Functions
from Four Experiments [a]

Experiment or condition	Latency function, $L(n) = \eta + \theta(n - 1)$	Duration function, $D(n) = \alpha + \beta(n - 1) + \gamma(n - 1)^2$
Speech		
Ascending numbers	$263.3 + 12.6(n - 1)$	$101.1 + 57.6(n - 1) + 12.2(n - 1)^2$
Weekdays (mean)	$259.9 + 8.8(n - 1)$	$168.8 + 183.1(n - 1) + 12.6(n - 1)^2$
Monosyllabic nouns	$261.5 + 11.1(n - 1)$	$122.4 + 91.9(n - 1) + 13.6(n - 1)^2$
Disyllabic nouns	$267.4 + 10.1(n - 1)$	$173.4 + 180.4(n - 1) + 12.0(n - 1)^2$
Typewriting		
Alternating hands	$229.7 + 14.9(n - 2)$	$71.9(n - 1) + 15.2(n - 1)^2$
One hand	$231.2 + 4.1(n - 2)$	$142.9(n - 1) + 14.1(n - 1)^2$

[a] Values are in milliseconds. The element count, n, represents the number of words (speech experiments) or the number of letters (typing experiment) in the response. Parameters θ and η of $L(n)$ were fitted by least squares to data for $n > 1$ (speech) or for $n > 2$ (typing). Estimates of β and γ were determined by least-squares fitting of a line to the rate function $R_{\cdot n}$. For speech, the constant α was then determined by least-squares fitting of a quadratic function with specified β and γ; for typing, α was set at zero, corresponding to the measured duration of a single response.

only 1.6 ± 0.9 msec/word.[15] That is, the effects on the mean time between successive words of the number of syllables per word and the number of words in the response are almost perfectly additive: The first term, β, depends only on word length, whereas the second term, $\gamma(n-1)$, depends only on number of words. The simplicity of our results, when described in this way, supports the view that it is the number of words or stress groups in the response, not the number of syllables or articulatory gestures, that determines the decline in production rate with response length—the same response unit that we have seen (in Section IV,A) to be implicated in the growth of latency.

The results in Table I also show that the rate and latency effects—measured by the parameters γ and θ, respectively—are remarkably close in magnitude. This is consistent with the proposal that the two effects are actually the same and are generated by a common mechanism, as is assumed in the subprogram-retrieval version of the sequence-preparation hypothesis, with a nonshrinking buffer (Section III, F). However, although similar in many ways, our results from measurements of typewriting will force us to question the generality of identical effects.

VI. An Experiment on Typewriting

For several reasons we decided to study the sequences of rapid finger movements in typewriting using essentially the same paradigm as in the speech experiments. First, typing readily permits measurement of the individual time intervals between successive response elements, in addition to overall response duration. Second, although potential artifacts due to measurement error may never be entirely eliminated, they are at least likely to be different in typing than in speech. In speech for example, measurement delays might be influenced by loudness, sequence length might influence the volume of air in the lungs, and it is difficult to apply an objective criterion of response accuracy. These problems are obviously not critical in typing, but others might be, such as variations in the starting position of the hands or in the movements used to press a particular key. Third, we wished to see to what extent our findings generalized to a very different performance with a different training history. It can be argued that the production of a spoken word is much more complex than the pressing of a key, because it requires the exquisitely precise timing and coordination of a large

---

[15] Both sets of data are slightly concave downward and, although we have not found this to be true in all our speech experiments, we have observed this effect often enough to make us suspect that it is real. Examination of the first differences, $D_n - D_{n-1}$, makes us suspect that the nonlinearity of $R._n$ results from a violation of the element-invariance requirement (see Section I,A), which causes the estimation error discussed in Section V,A: The measured duration, D_1^*, of a single isolated word may be somewhat longer than the duration of the first word in a list that contains more than one word.

number of diverse muscle systems that control respiratory, laryngeal, and multiple articulatory mechanisms (see, e.g., Kent & Moll, 1975; MacNeilage & Ladefoged, 1976). Furthermore, while normal speech rates are far slower than those obtained in our experiment, typists are trained to achieve high rates outside the laboratory.

A. Procedure

The procedure was similar to that used in the speech experiments. On each trial a row of from one to five different letters was first displayed for 1.0 sec. The display was followed by a fixed delay of 2.4 sec. On 80% of the trials a brief tone burst occurred at the end of the delay, signaling the subject to start typing the letter list. This reaction signal was preceded at 0.7-sec intervals by two brief noise bursts, which served as "countdown" signals. Keypress responses on the remaining 20% of the trials, on which the reaction signal was omitted, were regarded as errors. Again, the procedure was designed to encourage subjects to complete their responses as soon as possible after the signal while maintaining a low error rate. (The mean percentage of trials on which errors occurred was 2.3%; these few errors will not be considered further.) The time recorded for the depression of a key was determined by when it was detected by an electronic keyboard.[16]

Each letter list was presented on three successive trials; because repetitions had little effect on either latency or duration, the data were averaged over repetitions. Lengths and compositions of the lists were varied from one group of three trials to the next by means of a different balanced randomization for each subject.

Since Lahy's (1924) pioneering "Motion Study in Typewriting" and similar work reported by Coover (1923), it has been known that letter bigrams that are typed by fingers on alternate hands can be produced at faster rates than bigrams typed by fingers of the same hand. To explore responses containing elements whose durations differed, as we did in speech by manipulating the number of syllables per word, we used pure one-hand sequences in some blocks of trials and pure alternating-hand sequences in others; in both conditions, left and right hands were used equally often. All sequences were drawn from the same 16 letters, and average bigram frequencies in English were equated in the two conditions; we used only bigrams that actually occur in English.

The subjects were four female professional typists employed at Bell Laboratories, with test rates in prose typing of about 90 words per minute (or about 7.5 strokes per second). The data to be presented were obtained on 2 days of testing, after 1 day of practice with the same types of material. During the 2

---

[16] Our keyboard had "N-key rollover," which permits it to detect a keypress with a neglible delay after it occurs, regardless of whether other keys remain depressed (see Kallage, 1972).

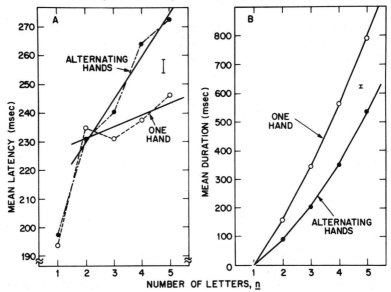

Figure 5 Typewriting of lists of letters typed by fingers on alternating hands and by fingers on one hand only: The results are averaged over four subjects; about 200 observations per point. (A) Mean latencies, estimate of $\pm SE$, and linear functions fitted to data for $n \geqslant 2$ (Table I). (B) Mean durations, estimate of $\pm SE$, and fitted quadratic functions (Table I).

days, each subject provided about 50 observations for each of the five list lengths per condition.

B. Latencies of Typing Responses

Figure 5A and Table I show that response latency again increased with sequence length, but in a different manner in the two conditions. The nonlinearity (latency for $n = 1$ falls below a fitted line) that is present in both sets of data is significant for the one-hand condition only. We have chosen to fit linear functions to the data for $2 \leqslant n \leqslant 5$ in both cases, however, to achieve comparability and because the standard error of the slope for the alternating-hand data, based on between-subject differences, is reduced by a factor of 2 when L_1 is omitted.[17] To emphasize the omission of L_1, in Table I we represent the fitted lines as functions of $n - 2$ instead of $n - 1$; the constant terms then represent intercepts at $n = 2$. Despite the irregularity of the function for the one-hand condition, estimated slopes are very similar across subjects: The mean and standard error are 4.1 ± 1.3 msec/letter for this condition (significantly greater than zero) and 14.9 ± 1.7

---

[17] In a replication of this experiment with different subjects we obtained very similar results.

msec/letter for the other, with a difference of 10.8 ± 1.8 msec/letter that is highly significant.

Why should either of our latency functions show a discontinuity between a single keystroke and multiple keystrokes? And why should such an effect occur more strongly in typing than in speech? One possibility is that as sequence length is changed from $n = 1$ to $n = 2$, the response elements fail to satisfy the element-invariance requirement (see Section I,A). In particular, a single keystroke may not be equivalent to either a beginning or terminating keystroke, especially in the one-hand condition. One possible reason for the contrast with our speech data is that while the production of even a single monosyllabic word typically involves multiple articulatory gestures and therefore requires precise control over timing and coordination, this may be true only of sequences of two or more keystrokes, because of the relative simplicity of a single keystroke.

There is no reason to believe that the letter strings in the two conditions place systematically different loads on ordinary short-term memory; the difference between the latency functions therefore provides further evidence against the time-sharing and capacity-sharing hypotheses discussed in Section III.

C. Response Durations and Interstroke Intervals

Both duration functions, shown in Figure 5B, are significantly nonlinear but are well described by the fitted quadratic functions, in remarkable agreement with the speech data. Our subjects responded well to the exhortation that they complete their responses quickly: In the alternating-hands condition they produced about 9.3 strokes per second—a higher rate for these meaningless letter strings than they averaged in continuous prose. As expected, the one-hand condition produced substantially longer durations, but, as in speech, element duration appears not to affect the quadratic coefficients. The rate functions in Figure 6B again make the simplicity of the duration data more apparent and facilitate comparison to the speech data in Figure 6A. The fitted linear functions that describe both sets of typing data so well are separated by about 70 msec and are almost perfectly parallel, with a mean slope difference of only 1.0 ± 2.5 msec/letter. Thus, the effects on the mean time between successive strokes of the number of strokes and of the nature of the transition from one stroke to the next are almost perfectly additive. More experiments are needed before we can interpret the similarity of rate-function slopes in milliseconds per keystroke for typing and in milliseconds per stress group for speech.

For the alternating-hands condition, we observed still another property of the speech data that also characterizes typing: The sizes of the latency and rate effects, measured by the parameters θ and γ, respectively, are very similar, with $\hat{\gamma} - \hat{\theta} = 0.3 \pm 5.1$ msec/keystroke. However, the conjecture that the two effects

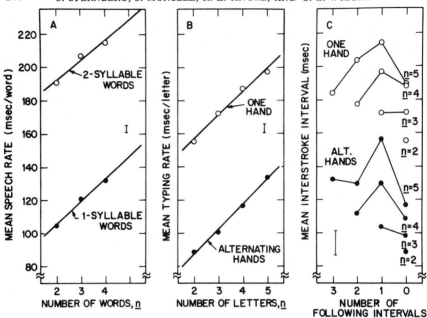

Figure 6   Time intervals between successive response elements in speech and typing. (A) Rate functions (mean interval versus response length) for speech and estimate of $\pm SE$. Fitted lines: $91.9 + 13.6(n - 1)$ for one-syllable words and $180.4 + 12.0(n - 1)$ for two-syllable words. The data are from Figure 3B. (B) Rate functions for typing and estimate of $\pm SE$. Fitted lines: $71.9 + 15.2(n - 1)$ for letter lists typed with alternating hands and $142.9 + 14.1(n - 1)$ for letter lists typed with one hand only. The data are from Figure 5B. (C) Mean interstroke interval for each serial position in letter lists of lengths $n = 2, 3, 4,$ and 5 typed with alternating hands and with one hand only, and estimate of $\pm SE$. The results are averaged over four subjects; about 200 observations per point. Intervals early in a list have more intervals following them and appear toward the left of the plot. The SE estimate is based on the *serial-positions* $\times$ *subjects* interaction. The points in B represent the means of the functions in C.

are in general mediated by the same mechanism, supported by these data as well as by the results from the speech experiments, is called into question by the one-hand data, where we observe a significant difference of $\hat{\gamma} - \hat{\theta} = 10.1 \pm 3.0$ msec/keystroke between these measures of the rate and latency effects. More work is needed to decide whether to give up the conjecture and explain the similarity of γ and θ values in some other way or to seek a special explanation for the dissociation of effects found only in one typing condition.

Figure 6C shows, for responses of length $n = 2, 3, 4,$ and 5 in each condition, the individual intervals, $R_{kn} = T_{kn} - T_{k-1,n}$, between successive keystrokes that contribute to the means, $R_{\cdot n}$, of Figure 6B. The means of each of the $n - 1$ successive interstroke intervals contained in responses of length n are shown as functions of the number of *following* intervals—a number that appears to be a more powerful determinant of the forms of these functions than the number of preceding intervals.[18]

In every case, intervals followed by the same number (0, 1, or 2) of other intervals are longer when they are contained in longer responses, demonstrating the strength of the effect of sequence length on stroke rate. Note that even the time from the first stroke to the second (not lined up in Figure 6C) is systematically greater for longer sequences. For sequences of four and five letters, the stroke rate is slower toward the middle of the sequence than at either end.

The patterns of interstroke intervals are very similar in the two conditions. To a first approximation, then, the two sets of R_{kn} functions differ by just a constant: The effect on interstroke interval of whether interstroke transition is within or between hands is roughly additive with the effect of serial position, at the same time as the effect on *mean* interstroke interval of transition type is almost perfectly additive with the effect of length. One way to explain such instances of additivity is to assume that the effects on interstroke interval of length and serial position, in the first place, and of transition type, in the second, are mediated by different *stages* of processing—separate operations that occur sequentially (Sternberg, 1969a).

An important challenge for any theoretical account of these duration data is to explain jointly the simplicity of performance at the macroscopic level (linearity with length at the level of the means) and the greater complexity at a microscopic level (nonlinearity with serial position).

VII. Summary of Findings and a Tentative Model for the Latency and Duration of Rapid Movement Sequences

A. Summary of Method and Findings

We begin this section by summarizing the main facts about rapid speech and typewriting that our experiments thus far have revealed. Subjects made *responses* composed of short sequences of equivalent *response elements*, either spoken words or keystrokes. They were rewarded for completing these responses as quickly as possible after a reaction signal. We varied the *response length* (number of elements) over a range from $n = 1$ to $n = 5$. We also manipulated *element size* (or duration) by varying either the number of *constituents* (syllables per word) or the nature of the required movements (successive keystrokes by same versus alternating hands). The two main measures were *response latency, L_n*, from the reaction signal to the first element and *response duration, D_n*, from the first element to the last. We found that a useful representation of duration data is provided by a *rate function, $R_{.n}$*, that describes the mean time interval between one

---

[18] This might be taken as further evidence of the influence of advance planning.

element and the next, averaged over the $n-1$ intervals in a response. In typing we also measured the individual time intervals, R_{kn}, between successive elements as a function of serial position, k, within the response.

We shall tentatively assume the correctness of our conclusion that in speech the *stress group* (a segment of speech associated with one primary stress) is the theoretically relevant response *unit*, based on the observation that it is in terms of this unit that our effects on both latencies and durations are most simply described. In typing we shall identify the single keystroke as the response unit.[19] For purposes of this summary, we shall also treat two of our findings as anomalies that, for the present, we shall not seek to explain. One is the shape of the latency function for one-handed typing, which is nonlinear over the $1 \leqslant n \leqslant 5$ range and shallow over the $2 \leqslant n \leqslant 5$ range. The other is the downward concavity of the latency functions in the third speech experiment. Given that we set these exceptions aside, the main facts that we need to explain (for lists of up to at least five units) are as follows:

1. L_n (mean latency) increases with n (response length).
2. The increase is approximately linear.
3. L_n increases with number of constituents per unit.
4. The effects on L_n of number of units and number of constituents per unit are additive (do not interact).
5. $R_{\cdot n}$ (mean time interval from one unit to the next) increases with n.
6. The increase is approximately linear.
7. The effects on $R_{\cdot n}$ of number of units and unit size are additive.
8. The rates at which L_n and $R_{\cdot n}$ increase with n are similar.
9. R_{kn} (mean time interval from unit $k-1$ to unit k in a response of length n) changes nonmonotonically with serial position, k.
10. The effects on R_{kn} of serial position and unit size are approximately additive.

B. A Tentative Model

Based on qualitative aspects of our data, we found the sequence-preparation hypothesis (Sections III,E and III,F) to be the only survivor among the mechanisms we considered for the latency effect. This observation is the starting point for our tentative model. Next, because we are taking the similarity of the slopes of L_n and $R_{\cdot n}$ to be more than a coincidence, we prefer that the model account for both latencies and rates by means of the same mechanism. (If a dissociation

---

[19] Note that for speech we happened to define an *element* (a response segment of arbitrary size) in such a way that it corresponded to what our results later suggested was a *unit* (a theoretically relevant response segment). Thus, in the speech experiments of Sections II,A–II,C our element was a *word* (rather than, for example, a syllable or a segment of specified duration), which was equivalent to a *stress group* in our materials. The convenient result is that response length, n, denotes the number of units as well as the number of elements, and unit size (in number of constituents or duration) is equivalent to element size.

between these slope parameters were discovered in later experiments, our preference might change, of course.) This decision, in turn, favors the second version
of the preparation hypothesis (subprogram retrieval) over the first (program
construction or activation) because Version 1 would require that the entire program be reconstructed or reactivated before the execution of each unit—a requirement that appears implausible to us. Our choice of model for the latency effect
therefore depends on our findings about durations.

The particular retrieval mechanism suggested by our results is *self-terminating*
sequential *search* through a *nonshrinking* buffer, rather than, for example, a
process of direct access whose speed is limited by a capacity that must be shared
among all the subprograms. *Search* seems to lead more naturally to linearity of
time versus length, given the direct-access models of which we are currently
aware. The buffer should be *nonshrinking* because otherwise $R_{\cdot n}$ would have half
the slope of L_n, rather than approximately the same slope. The search is presumably necessary because subprograms are not arranged in the buffer in the order
in which they must be executed. By assuming a *self-terminating* search rather
than an exhaustive one (e.g., see Sternberg, 1969b), we are able to accomodate
a wide variety of effects of serial position on R_{kn} (together with the approximate
linearity and slope equality of L_n *and* $R_{\cdot n}$) by suitable assumptions about search
order.

One aspect of search order is its variation from one trial to the next, which
might depend, for example, on the order in which subprograms are stored in the
buffer. Another aspect is its variation from the search for one subprogram to the
next within a response: The search might start at the same location for each subprogram or at the location of the last subprogram retrieved, for example. In any
case, it is the mean position of a subprogram in the search order when that subprogram is the one to be executed that determines serial-position effects. If the
order is random, then all subprograms have the same mean position, and R_{kn}
functions should be flat: The R_{kn} range, $\max\{R_{kn}\} - \min\{R_{kn}\}$, should be
approximately zero. At the other extreme, if the order is fixed so that a subprogram in some one serial position is always found first and a subprogram in some
other serial position is always found last, position effects are maximized and,
ignoring sampling error, the R_{kn} range can be shown to be $2(n-1)\gamma$. The ratio
of the observed range to its estimated maximum provides a measure of the magnitude of position effects. For the typing data shown in Figure 6C, we find the
average value of this ratio for $n = 3$, 4, and 5 to be 0.04, 0.23, and 0.27, respectively, indicating that position effects were relatively small and implying that the
order of the hypothesized search is closer to being random than fixed.[20] This
finding is consistent with the approximate equality of L_n and $R_{\cdot n}$ slopes, which

---

[20] At present we can offer no convincing explanation for the shapes of the serial position
functions. We can assert, however, that the observed shapes are not incompatible with a self-
terminating search. Indeed, ignoring sampling error, it can be shown that if the R_{kn} range is
no greater than $n\gamma$ then *any* serial-position function can be accommodated by a suitable self-
terminating search order.

requires us to assume that the mean search position of the first subprogram is approximately equal to the mean search position of the others.[21]

The structure of our model is governed, in part, by application of the additive-factor method (Sternberg, 1969a) and is to some extent independent of details of the retrieval and unpacking processes. For the latency, the additivity of effects of length and number of constituents per unit suggests the existence of separate processing stages whose durations are additive components of the latency and which are influenced selectively by these factors. This leads us to propose a *retrieval stage* (influenced by the number of units, but not their sizes) followed by an *unpacking stage* (influenced by the number of constituents in a unit, but not by the number of units; see Section IV,B). Both of these stages follow operations that mediate detection of the reaction signal and the decision to respond.

Our assumption that execution of later units involves the same mechanisms as execution of the first unit leads us to propose that durations of the same retrieval and unpacking stages are included in R_{kn} and hence in $R_{\cdot n}$. That the effect of unit size on $R_{\cdot n}$ (which again is additive with the effect of number of units) is so much larger than its effect on latency is explained by the existence of a *command stage* (again not influenced by the number of units) during which the sequence of commands is issued that cause execution of the constituents of the response unit.

Exactly what the commands specify about the ensuing movements—whether muscle contractions or target positions, for example (MacNeilage & MacNeilage, 1973)—is not critical for the model. But we have to place constraints on the time relations between the command stage for a response unit, which we do not measure directly, and the execution of that unit. According to our model, successive command stages are not only sequential, but are temporally discrete, being separated by search and unpacking operations—operations whose average duration is estimated to be about 40 msec longer in 5-unit responses than in 2-unit responses. Yet the movements produced (and the resulting sounds, in speech) often appear to be smooth, continuous, and even overlapping (Kent & Minifie, 1977). To reconcile our stage model with this observation, let us assume that execution of unit k can be prolonged so as to continue in parallel with the search and unpacking stages associated with unit $k + 1$. We assume further that if it is prolonged, it is nonetheless interrupted or modified by the execution of unit $k + 1$, in such a way that it does not delay the completion of that unit. The execution of the final unit in the response may also outlast its command stage, but the amount by which it is prolonged is independent of response length, n. From these assumptions, it follows that the measured duration of a response differs

---

[21] One-hand typing might be an exception in this respect, where the subprogram for the first unit had a privileged position in the buffer, thereby producing a flatter latency function.

from the time between the beginning of the first command stage and the end of the last by at most a constant that is independent of n.

The model, then, introduces three types of processing stage. Let S_k denote the time to locate the subprogram for response unit k by means of a self-terminating search (or an alternative process, such as one involving direct access, that might later prove more appropriate). S_k depends on the number of units and on the serial position of unit k in the search order, but not on unit size. Let U_k denote the time between locating the subprogram and beginning the command sequence for unit k—the time to unpack the constituents—which depends only on the number of constituents per unit (length of the subprogram). Finally, let C_k denote the time to issue the sequence of commands that control unit k, which depends only on the size of the unit and not on either its serial position or the number of units.[22]

For the speech experiments, where the latency, L_n, is regarded as marking the *start* of the execution of the first response unit, we have

$$L_n = T_{1n}^* = T_b + S_1 + U_1, \tag{5}$$

where T_b denotes a "base time" during which the subject detects the signal and decides to respond. (Symbols are written in the same order as the corresponding stages are assumed to occur; see Section V,A for definitions of T_{kn} and T_{kn}^*.) For the typing experiment, where the latency is regarded as marking the *end* of the execution of the first response unit, we have [23]

$$L_n = T_{1n} = T_b + S_1 + U_1 + C_1. \tag{6}$$

For both kinds of experiment the inter–element time is

$$R_{kn} = T_{kn} - T_{k-1,n} = S_k + U_k + C_k, \, (2 \leqslant k \leqslant n). \tag{7}$$

This tentative model is consistent with all 10 of the facts listed above that our studies have revealed.

---

[22] An elaboration of these assumptions about C_k and/or U_k, for $k \geqslant 2$ is suggested by the weekdays experiment (Section II,B). There we found that responses consisting of repetitions of the same word differed only in duration from responses containing n different words and that this "fatigue" effect was limited to an increased value of the parameter β. Given our model, this finding would require that repetition have an effect on only the duration $U_k + C_k$ of unpacking and command stages of units after the first and that the increase in $U_k + C_k$ be as large on the first repetition as on later repetitions.

[23] The fact that latencies for the one-hand and alternating-hand conditions are ever similar (as they are for $n = 1$ and $n = 2$) may indicate that values of $U_1 + C_1$ are approximately equal in the two kinds of sequence. But the difference between the rate functions for the two conditions shows that even' if this is the case, the values of $U_k + C_k$ $(k > 1)$ must differ.

Acknowledgments

The research reported here could not have been done without the expert hardware and systems-software support provided by A. S. Coriell and W. J. Kropfl. We are also indebted to M. Y. Liberman for advice on phonetics, to J. B. Kruskal and D. E. Meyer for comments on the manuscript, and to the skilled typists from the Word-Processing Center and Secretarial Service at Bell Laboratories, Murray Hill, who served as subjects.

Reference Notes

1. Monsell, S., & Sternberg, S. The latency of short and rapid utterances: Evidence for response preprogramming. Paper presented at the Seventh International Symposium on Attention and Performance, Sénanque, France, August, 1976.
2. Rosenbaum, D. A. Human movement initiation: Selection of arm, direction, and extent. Unpublished manuscript, Bell Laboratories, 1978.

References

Adams, J. A. Issues for a closed-loop theory of motor learning. In G. E. Stelmach (Ed.), *Motor control: Issues and trends*. New York: Academic Press, 1976.

Anzola, G. P., Bertolini, G., Buchtel, H. A., & Rizzolatti, G. Spatial compatibility and anatomical factors in simple and choice reaction time. *Neuropsychologia*, 1977, *15*, 295–302.

Atkinson, R. C., & Shiffrin, R. M. Human memory: A proposed system and its control processes. In K. W. Spence & J. T. Spence (Eds.), *The psychology of learning and motivation: Advances in research and theory* (Vol. 2). New York: Academic Press, 1968.

Baddeley, A. D., Thomson, N., & Buchanan, M. Word length and the structure of short-term memory. *Journal of Verbal Learning and Verbal Behavior*, 1975, *14*, 575–589.

Berlyne, D. E. Conflict and choice time. *British Journal of Psychology*, 1957, *48*, 106–118.

Brainard, R. W., Irby, T. S., Fitts, P. M., & Alluisi, E. A. Some variables influencing the rate of gain of information. *Journal of Experimental Psychology*, 1962, *63*, 105–110.

Butsch, R. L. C. Eye movements and the eye–hand span in typewriting. *Journal of Educational Psychology*, 1932, *23*, 104–121.

Callan, J., Klisz, D., & Parsons, O. A. Strength of auditory stimulus–response compatibility as a function of task complexity. *Journal of Experimental Psychology*, 1974, *102*, 1039–1045.

Coover, J. E. A method of teaching typewriting based on a psychological analysis of expert typing. *National Education Association Addresses and Proceedings*, 1923, *61*, 561–567.

Craik, F. I. M., & Levy, B. A. The concept of primary memory. In W. K. Estes (Ed.), *Handbook of learning and cognitive processes* (Vol. 4). Hillsdale, New Jersey: Erlbaum, 1976.

Crowder, R. G. *Principles of learning and memory*. Hillsdale, New Jersey: Erlbaum, 1976.

Duncan, J. Response selection rules in spatial choice reaction tasks. In S. Dornič (Ed.), *Attention and performance VI*. Hillsdale, New Jersey: Erlbaum, 1977.

Eccles, J. C. The coordination of information by the cerebellar cortex. In S. Locke (Ed.), *Modern neurology*. Boston: Little Brown, 1969.

Eriksen, C. W., Pollack, M. D., & Montague, W. E. Implicit speech: Mechanism in perceptual encoding? *Journal of Experimental Psychology*, 1970, *84*, 502–507.

Garner, W. R. *Uncertainty and structure as psychological concepts*. New York: Wiley, 1962.

Greenwald, A. G., Sensory feedback mechanisms in performance control: With special reference to the ideo-motor mechanism. *Psychological Review*, 1970, *77*, 73–99.

Hayes, K. C., & Marteniuk, R. G. Dimensions of motor task complexity. In G. E. Stelmach (Ed.), *Motor control: Issues and trends.* New York: Academic Press, 1976.

Henry, F. M., & Rogers, E. E. Increased response latency for complicated movements and a "memory drum" theory of neuromotor reaction. *Research Quarterly of the American Association for Health, Physical Education and Recreation*, 1960, *31*, 448–458.

Hudgins, C. V., & Stetson, R. H. Relative speed of articulatory movements. *Archives Néerlandaises de Phonétique Expérimentale*, 1937, *13*, 85–94.

Kallage, R. Electronic keyboard design with N-key rollover. *Computer Design*, 1972 (February), 57–61.

Keele, S. W. Movement control in skilled motor performance. *Psychological Bulletin*, 1968, *70*, 387–403.

Kent, R. D., & Minifie, F. D. Coarticulation in recent speech production models. *Journal of Phonetics*, 1977, *5*, 115–133.

Kent, R. D., & Moll, K. L. Articulatory timing in selected consonant sequences. *Brain and Language*, 1975, *2*, 304–323.

Klapp, S. T. Implicit speech inferred from response latencies in same–different decisions. *Journal of Experimental Psychology*, 1971, *91*, 262–267.

Klapp, S. T. Short-term memory as a response preparation state. *Memory & Cognition*, 1976, *4*, 721–729.

Kornblum, S. Response competition and/or inhibition in two-choice reaction time. *Psychonomic Science*, 1965, *2*, 55–56.

Kornhuber, H. H. Cerebral cortex, cerebellum and basal ganglia: An introduction to their motor functions. In F. O. Schmitt & F. G. Worden (Eds.), *The neurosciences: Third study program*. Cambridge: MIT Press, 1974.

Lahy, J. M. Motion study in typewriting. In *Studies and reports* Series J (Educational) No. 3. Geneva: International Labour Office, 1924.

Landauer, T. K. Rate of implicit speech. *Perceptual and Motor Skills*, 1962, *15*, 646.

Lashley, K. S. The problem of serial order in behavior. In L. A. Jeffress (Ed.), *Cerebral mechanisms in behavior*. New York: Wiley, 1951.

MacNeilage, P., & Ladefoged, P. The production of speech and language. In C. Carterette & M. P. Friedman (Eds.), *Handbook of perception* (Vol. 7). New York: Academic Press, 1976.

MacNeilage, P. F., & MacNeilage, L. A. Central processes controlling speech production during sleep and waking. In F. J. McGuigan (Ed.) *The Psychophysiology of Thinking*. New York: Academic Press, 1973.

Megaw, E. D. Direction and extent uncertainty in step tracking. *Journal of Motor Behavior*, 1972, *4*, 171–186.

Russell, D. G. Spatial location cues and movement production. In G. E. Stelmach (Ed.), *Motor control: Issues and trends*. New York: Academic Press, 1976.

Sanders, A. F. Some variables affecting the relation between relative stimulus frequency and choice reaction time. *Acta Psychologica*, 1970, *33*, 45–55.

Schmidt, R. A. The index of preprogramming (IP): A statistical method for evaluating the role of feedback in simple movements. *Psychonomic Science*, 1972, *27*, 83–85.

Seibel, R. Data entry devices and procedures. In H. P. Van Cott and R. G. Kinkade (Eds.) *Human engineering guide to equipment design*. Washington, D.C.: American Institute for Research, 1972.

Shaffer, L. H. Intention and performance. *Psychological Review*, 1976, *83*, 375–393.

Shaffer, L. H., & Hardwick, J. Errors and error detection in typing. *Quarterly Journal of Experimental Psychology*, 1969, *21*, 209–213.

Sternberg, S. The discovery of processing stages: Extensions of Donders' method. *Acta Psychologica*, 1969, *30*, 276–315.(a)

Sternberg, S. Memory-scanning: Mental processes revealed by reaction-time experiments. *American Scientist*, 1969, *57*, 421–457.(b)

Van Nes, F. L. Analysis of keying errors. *Ergonomics*, 1976, *19*, 165–174.

Welford, A. T. On the sequencing of action. *Brain Research*, 1974, *71*, 381–392.

Wickelgren, W. A. Context-sensitive coding, associative memory, and serial order in (speech) behavior. *Psychological Review*, 1969, *76*, 1–15.

7

Response Timing in Handwriting

Alan M. Wing

I. Introduction

Despite the growing importance of alternative ways of conveying information, handwriting is a skill likely to remain with us for a long time to come. It is generally an overlearned skill that involves very rapid sequencing of movements and so is of considerable theoretical interest for the study of movement control. In this chapter I will describe an experimental approach to the study of handwriting that I am currently pursuing at the Applied Psychology Unit. I believe it is an approach that is applicable to other motor skills and it has suggested, in the case of handwriting, answers to some questions that could usefully be raised about these other skills.

II. Quantitative Variability in Handwriting

A natural taxonomy for handwriting partitions words into letters, letters into their constituent strokes, and strokes into the movements actually used to create the strokes. It is convenient to take this taxonomy and assume that there are

Information Processing in
Motor Control and Learning

corresponding levels of information processing in the production of handwriting. Spelling errors that are "slips of the pen" as opposed to errors of convention reflecting mislearned rules of spelling can provide insight into the operation of the higher levels of such a model (e.g., Van Nes, 1971). While data on this qualitative variability in handwriting are relevant to the overall skill, here I will only be concerned with quantitative variability that reflects the nature of movement control.

An example of the sort of quantitative variation that I will be discussing is given in Figure 1 which shows a number of repetitions of the cursive letter "a" taken from the normal writing of six people. Differences in the size and in the shape of the letters may be seen not only between individuals but also within any one person's handwriting. In this chapter, I will restrict consideration mainly to within-individual variation. While such variation is evidenced in the written trace after the movement is complete, my purpose is to present an account of the variation in terms of the movements as they unfold in time. Specifically, I will describe a model of handwriting that attributes the *spatial* quantitative variation to be seen in Figure 1 to *temporal* variation in control of responses that underlie the movement. As motivation for the model, we will briefly review an experiment by Legge, Steinberg, and Summerfield (1964) that demonstrated an effect of nitrous oxide on the overall size of writing.

Legge and his colleagues required their subjects to copy in cursive script short prose passages while breathing nitrous oxide in oxygen. With an increase in concentration of nitrous oxide they found linear increases in the average height of upward-extended letters and in the average length of words measured along the line of writing. The change in letter height reached 2 mm at 50% concentra-

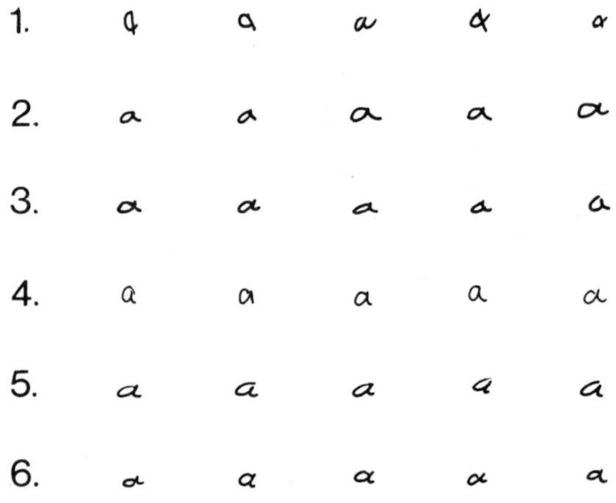

Figure 1 Variation in handwriting within and between six different people. The letter "a" is shown as it was written on the first five occasions in which the letter occurred in the initial position of the word in the course of writing an exam paper.

Figure 2 Effect of change in friction on handwriting. The arrows on the left indicate an increase in friction that lasted until the arrows on the right. Time per letter (approximately 150 msec) was unaffected but average letter height decreased from 12 to 8 mm. Data are from Denier van der Gon and Thuring (1965).

tion, whereas the corresponding width change was closer to 1 mm per letter. Since the ratio of the changes approximates the height-to-width ratio of upward-extended letters, we may say that nitrous oxide produced an overall scaling of the spatial extent of writing movements.

In a later paper, Legge (1965) hypothesized that such changes in the overall size of writing could be due to nitrous oxide-induced changes in the perception of proprioceptive feedback, assuming that feedback is used in maintaining the overall dimensions of writing movements. However, an experiment by Denier van der Gon and Thuring (1965) suggests that, during handwriting, there is no monitoring of proprioceptive feedback information about the size of the movements. In an experiment involving a step increase in the friction between pen and paper at times unexpected by the writer, they observed a sizable reduction in the height of letters but no change in the time taken to write them (see Figure 2). We will now consider an alternative to Legge's interpretation of changes in the overall size of handwriting. It will, in fact, place the source of the effects directly on changes in motor output rather than indirectly on changes in proprioceptive feedback. First, however, we need some information on the nature of muscle activation in handwriting.

III. Discrete Nature of Force Application in Handwriting Movements

A description of handwriting movements and of the biomechanical factors that contribute to the movements may be found in the appendix. Briefly, two separate pairs of muscle groups are responsible for the fluctuating transverse movements (in the direction of the slope of the writing) and the longitudinal fluctuations (in the direction of the writing line). Integrated muscle activity in each group is discontinuous in time during writing. A pulse of activity in the agonist muscle group occurs around the time of a change in the direction of pen travel. Antagonist activity is not observed until just before the time at which there is a reversal in the direction of that same component of the movement.

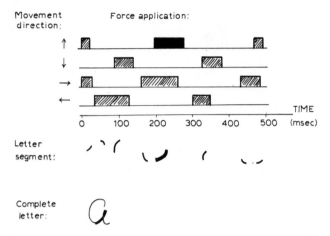

Figure 3 Simulation of cursive letter "a" production using constant amplitude applied forces. The shape was determined by adjusting only the timing of the forces. [From Vredenbregt & Koster (1971); reprinted by permission.]

A mechanical simulation of this mechanism was instantiated by Vredenbregt and Koster (1971). They used two pairs of orthogonally mounted, direct-current electric motors to drive a pen over paper. The voltages they used to control the motors were modeled on EMG records of muscle activity during handwriting and were of fixed amplitude. Cursive script was produced (see the example in Figure 3) by adjusting the time and duration of application of the voltages. Although a time scale for the simulation is shown, it is in a sense arbitrary. The same letter *shape* would be produced even if the unit of time were, for example, greater than the millisecond. That is, overall upward time scaling of the times between all the force onsets and offsets would not change the letter shape. However, it would lead to an increase in overall *size* of each letter. Since each movement component would be allowed to continue longer before a change in direction, the distance traveled in each movement segment would be greater. Such changes would be in proportion to the timings and thus to the movement extents of the letter produced under the "normal" time scale.

IV. Time Scaling as a Determinant of Handwriting Size

Nitrous oxide is a central nervous system depressant. Adam, Rosner, Hosick, and Clark (1971) have shown that low concentrations of anesthetic drugs affect response timing in the following way. Under the influence of the drug the production of time intervals overestimates objective time in that the responses made by a subject to terminate judged intervals occur late. Since the overestimation is proportional to the interval required, the authors made the point that the effects were consistent with an internal clock running at a slower rate under the drug conditions.

Suppose an internal clock responsible for the timing in handwriting of successive onsets and offsets of activity in the muscle groups was likewise affected by the nitrous oxide in the Legge et al. (1964) experiment. Slow running of the clock would in effect result in a rescaling that lengthens all intervals between the successive muscle events shown in Figure 3. Thus, the observed proportional increases in letter height and width could have originated in a proportional lengthening of the time allowed for each movement segment between direction changes.

Spacing of letters within a word involves a steady left to right wrist extension with ulnar abduction of the wrist. Steady background muscle activity is needed to produce this and on it there must be superimposed the pulsed activity for the fluctuating left to right movements. Since time rescaling could not affect such steady activity, our account suggests that spacing between letters will be unchanged. (If the spacing of letters does increase with overall letter size, then we would need to assume that left to right translation velocity is actively adjusted to suit the time scale, perhaps on the basis of visual feedback.)

If time scaling can account for the involuntary scaling of the spatial extent of handwriting movements observed by Legge et al., what happens when a person voluntarily changes the overall size of his handwriting? I will now describe a preliminary experiment that I ran at the APU that suggests that there is a rescaling to longer time intervals in large writing.

In each of 10 trials two subjects had to write a single pre-cued word at a "comfortable" writing speed. However, on each trial before writing the word, they were instructed to write either larger than they would normally write or smaller than normal. Writing was with a pen on paper superimposed on a Computek GT50 graphic tablet.[1] During each trial, position coordinates of the pencil point were sampled every 1.6 msec for 800 msec from the point in time at which the subject first put pen to paper. Examples of plots of the horizontal and vertical displacements as a function of time relative to the starting position are shown in Figure 4. The upper and lower plots show, for one subject, the first 800 msec of the word "electric" written large and small, respectively, on two separate trials. All four of the words (used in random order) began with the three letters "ele." Interactive computer-aided measurement was used to determine the perpendicular height of the "l" and the second "e" and the durations

---

[1] The graphic tablet at the APU uses an interface designed by R. Bloomfield and passes x,y-coordinate data with a resolution of 0.28 mm at rates of up to 1250 Hz to a 16-bit processor word computer with an exchangeable disk that allows data storage in bulk. The tablet uses a writing implement that is an ordinary soft-lead propelling pencil modified by inclusion of a small sensing coil near the tip of the pencil and connected by thin wires through the other end to a control box.

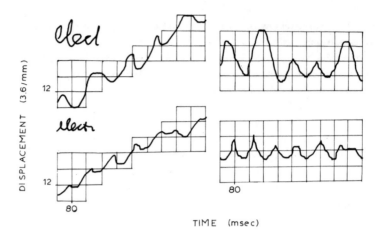

Figure 4 Longitudinal (left to right) and transverse (up and down) displacements as a function of time for the first 800 msec of writing the word "electric." Two representative samples written large and small shown for one subject.

of these letters. (The temporal boundary of a letter was defined as the point in time where the minimum vertical-axis coordinate was first attained at the completion of the downstroke of the preceding letter.)

Time to write as a function of the size of writing instruction is summarized in Table I as an average of the two successive letters. A near doubling of the spatial extent of the handwritten letters is accompanied by a statistically reliable increase in their duration. However, there is not a doubling of duration and so the average pen point velocity must have increased in the larger writing. There seem to be two interpretations of this result. On the one hand, there may be greater muscle activity resulting in increased applied forces in larger writing (cf. Denier van der Gon & Thuring, 1965). Alternatively, it may be that in small writing the reduction in intervals between activation of agonist and antagonist muscles may be sufficient to lead to a reduction in effective force developed by the agonist even though the amount of activity remains unchanged. Resolution of these two alternatives must await further experimentation.

A rather different source of data on time scaling in handwriting may be

Table 1

Time to Write as a Function of Size of Writing

	Instruction		
	Small	Large	
Height (mm)	4.7	8.0	
Duration (msec)	135	154	$(p < .025)$

found in the paper by Vredenbregt and Koster (1971). They also looked at the intervals between times of turning points of transverse movements when a number of different individuals wrote the same letter. Although different people produced differences in the shape of the letter, Vredenbregt and Koster claimed that the ratios of the time intervals were very similar over individuals but that different time-scaling factors were involved. Since people differ in the shape of their handwritten letters and not just in the speed of writing, Vredenbregt and Koster's finding implies that individual differences in formation of letters based on the same underlying letter models must arise from differences in applied forces. These in turn could be a consequence of differences in amplitude of activity in the muscles or in biomechanical factors or both.

V. Timing of Successive Movements in Single-Letter Production

From a consideration of time scaling as a determinant of the spatial extent of letters, we now turn to an investigation of variability in the timing of successive movements within a single letter. The data are drawn from an experiment that was originally designed to determine whether simple auditory reaction time in the written production of single lowercase letters (m, n, v, and w) is a function of the number of transverse movement direction changes, which increases from v, n, w, through m.

A trial was initiated by the subject applying pen pressure on paper on the surface of the graphic tablet (see Figure 5). A visual displayed signal then indicated to the subject which response was required. Three seconds later a sequence

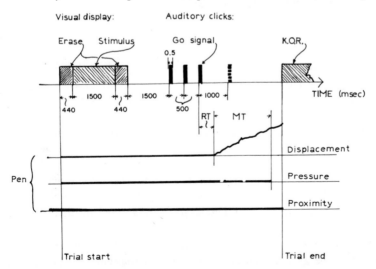

Figure 5 Paradigm for measusement of handwriting latencies. K.O.R., knowledge of results.

of two auditory warning signals 500 msec apart was followed after another 500 msec by the auditory "go" signal. Catch trials without a "go" signal were scheduled on one-fifth of the trials and required the subject to withhold his response until a third click occurred 1000 msec later. (Subjects were required to keep error rates at or below 1 per 100-trial block.) On reaction trials, RT was measured to the instant at which the pen first moved, and then sampling of pen position continued every 1.6 msec until the pen was taken out of proximity to the tablet by a vertical movement exceeding 1 cm. Visual knowledge of results was then given for total time from the signal to start to the last instant at which there was pen pressure preceding pen out of proximity. Pen coordinate data, as well as trial type and latency information, were stored for subsequent analysis. At the end of each 100-trial block the average total times for each of the four responses were displayed and the subject was encouraged to minimize these times. A session comprised three blocks and lasted about 40 min. The data I will report here are from two subjects (one male, one female) based on the last 50 responses of each type from three blocks following several days of practice with this task.

A. Reaction Time Data

The reaction time data are summarized in Figure 6 as a function of number of segments in the response. Only one response, the letter "v" for subject 1, was initiated reliably faster than the other responses. Thus, these data do not support the notion of increased advance preparation time with increase in complexity of the handwriting movement (cf. Chapter 6).

B. Amplitude and Duration of Movements

Duration and amplitude of each movement element except the last were determined for each response from turning points of the transverse component of the movement using the interactive computer-aided procedure mentioned earlier. Figure 7 shows the average times and displacements of successive minima and maxima of the transverse component of the four different responses for the two subjects. The slopes of the lines connecting these points give a measure of the average velocity of each element. It is very noticeable that seven out of eight initial elements share the same average velocity, which is, however, lower than subsequent elements, which also share very similar average velocities. This finding is consistent with equal amplitude forces being used in driving the pen, the lower average velocity in the first segment reflecting the force required to overcome initial static friction. (At subsequent turning points, the pen scalar velocity will usually be greater than zero since there is continual left to right displacement with time.)

In the following summary of the data, segment durations were defined be-

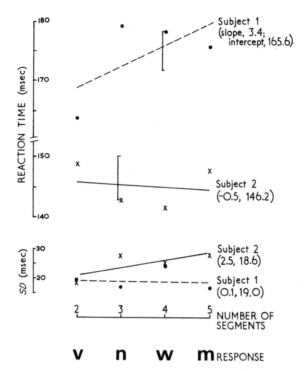

Figure 6   Latency to initiate pen movement following auditory start signal as a function of the number of segments in the four alternative responses. Vertical bars indicate representative 2 *SE*; least-squares fit straight line is shown with slope and intercept alongside. Data are for two subjects based on the last 50 observations of each response.

tween the instants at which the transverse movement minima and maxima were first attained, since these points lie closest in time to the onsets of the underlying controlling forces. The durations and the standard deviations of each of the four segments in sequence from left to right averaged over the different letters are shown in Figure 8. It is interesting to observe that the levels of variability are of the same order as the inter-response interval variability observed by Wing and Kristofferson (1973) in a task where subjects made repetitive responses at rates in the region of three per second. However, as a proportion of the mean interval produced, the variability of timing in handwriting movements is relatively much larger.

C. Correlational Analysis of Segment Durations

What effects will variability in the duration of these segments have on the letter produced? The answer to this question depends critically on the nature of that variation. If chance deviation about the mean duration of one segment is

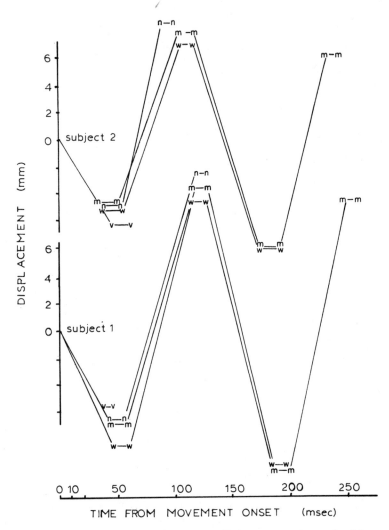

Figure 7 Average displacements of transverse displacement maxima and minima versus average time of arrival at and departure from these points. Data are based on the last 50 observations of each response; 2 *SE* are of the order of 0.5 mm and 3 msec.

usually matched with proportional corresponding deviations in the succeeding segments, this amounts to time rescaling and no letter *shape* distortion will be seen. That is, positive correlation among all segment durations will tend to produce letters that vary in overall size but are not distorted in shape (assuming any variation in force amplitudes is uncorrelated). On the other hand, suppose the durations of successive segments are uncorrelated. There is then no compensa-

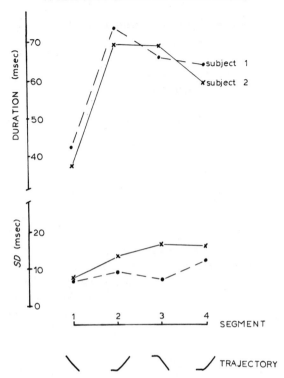

Figure 8 Means and standard deviations of segment durations averaged over response type. Data are based on the last 50 observations of each response.

tion by succeeding segment durations for shape distortion introduced by a deviation about the mean in the duration of an earlier segment.

Negative correlation between succeeding segment durations underlies Vredenbregt and Koster's (1971) simulation of shape distortions in the handwritten letter "a" (see Figure 9). It will be recalled that Figure 3 showed the sequencing of applications of force to produce the letter "a." In that figure the force shown in black was partly responsible for the diagonally upward movement that closes the loop of the "a." Figure 9 shows the effect of a timing "error" on letter shape

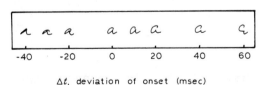

Δt, deviation of onset (msec)

Figure 9 Letter "a" distortion as a function of advanced or retarded time of application of the upward force (see Figure 3) that occurs halfway through production of the letter. Simulation data are from Vredenbregt and Koster (1971).

in the instant of application of that force (with its duration held constant and all other events occurring at the same times as specified in Figure 3). If that pulse is temporally advanced (Δt more negative), the duration of the preceding diagonally downward movement will be shortened and the duration of the diagonally upward movement will be correspondingly lengthened. To the extent that there may be random variation in Δt independent of the times of occurrence of the other events, this mechanism introduces negative correlation between the durations of the two successive movement segments.

A summary of the actual nature of the variability in the timing of the up and down segments in writing the single letters v, n, w, and m is given in Figure 10. The correlations shown are averages. They are based on correlations calculated separately for the two subjects for each of the four types of response. In this chapter we need only consider the six correlations between the four segment durations.

A cluster of three positive correlations involving segments 2, 3, and 4 contrasts in an interesting way with negative and zero correlations involving segment 1. While there is effectively no within-trial compensation for variation in the duration of segment 1, chance deviation in the duration of segment 2 is well matched in segment 3 and, to a smaller degree, in segment 4. That is, these data do not show overall time scaling of successive segments, but certain of the segments do

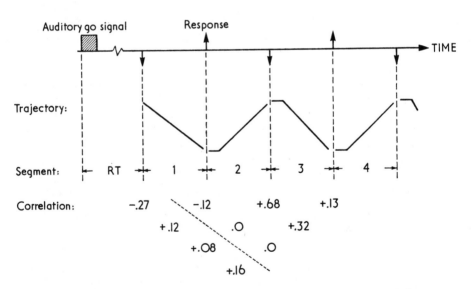

Figure 10 Correlations between durations of segments defined on transverse displacement turning points. From the bottom apex the rows show the correlations between segments separated by three, two, one, and no (i.e., adjacent) intervening segments. Correlations shown are the averages over individual correlations for the two subjects that in turn were computed separately for each of the four responses.

appear to group together. Although we initially characterized the responses as involving up to four segments (excluding the last segment) defined by direction changes, the correlations suggest, at most, three distinct functional units or strokes: down, up and down, and up.

What might be the source of the large correlation between segments 2 and 3, a correlation which was in fact equally large in both "w" and "m" responses of both subjects? Because of the short durations of the segments, it is most unlikely that there is active compensation of the duration of segment 3 on the basis of peripheral feedback about the duration of segment 2. Instead we will suppose that the subject preselects a spatial target that will be the maximum for upward movements, relative to the baseline, or writing line, which corresponds to the horizontal line through the successive minima. We assume that this target is then used to prepare movements that will make up segments 2 with 3 and segment 4 with the final segment (which was not actually measured). Such preparation would involve computation of the two corresponding time intervals between activations of muscle groups that will produce the correct direction changes.[2] If there is variability in the selection of the position of the target, such conversion to a temporal code means that the time specifications would be perfectly positively correlated. The fact that the correlation observed between segments 2 and 3 is less than unity may be interpreted as indicating that there is an additional source of variability. Presumably this arises in the mechanism responsible for actually achieving the specified timing once movement has begun. In a simple two-stage model of timing, this variability may arise in intervals generated by a free-running central timekeeper and/or in the neuromuscular delays that follow activation of the neuromuscular events by the timekeeper and precede actual occurrence of movement. In fact, Wing and Kristofferson (1973) have shown that such a model predicts negative correlation between adjacent intervals defined on successive responses. In the case of handwriting, this would have the effect of further reducing the expected positive correlation between the durations of segments 2 and 3.

The proposed account of the positive correlation between segments 2 and 3 is based on targets for the maxima defined relative to the writing line. Thus, the functional unit of the first up and down stroke begins at the boundary between segments 1 and 2 and ends at the boundary between segments 3 and 4. However, the negative correlation that, under the two-stage timing model, would be expected between the durations defined on such boundaries is not present between segments 3 and 4. The reason for this may lie in the correlation of 0.35 between segments 2 and 4. We assume that this latter correlation is due to use

---

[2] Kornhuber (1974) has argued that rapid ballistic movements are based on a conversion of external spatial referents to a coding that specifies muscle groups and their relative timings. He provides clinical data that suggest the involvement of the cerebellum in such recodings.

of the same target for the second maximum as for the first maximum, but, with additional unrelated variance thrown in by the time segment 4 is actually produced. Because the durations of the two segments 3 and 4 share a mutual dependence on the duration of segment 2, a positive correlation would be expected between segments 3 and 4, which could obscure the expected negative correlation. Indeed, the partial correlation between the durations of segments 3 and 4, which eliminates the effect of the duration of segment 2, is negative (-0.13).

In summary, while there is considerable within-individual variability in the timing of single-letter handwriting movements, that variability is not random. Rather, there is a pattern of underlying correlations that tend to reduce distortions of letter shape. These correlations suggest certain interesting speculations about the nature of movement control. The first step toward provision of further evidence for or against the account of variability in single-letter production advanced in this chapter must be an analysis of the statistical relations between timing and distance traveled. At the same time, it should be realized that any complete solution must eventually take into account the third aspect of movement control, namely, applied force.

VI. Conclusion

The overall conclusion of this chapter is that timing can play an important role in the control of the overall size of handwriting and in the definition of the shape of the characters. In the control of overall size, I have suggested that time scaling may be involved whether size changes occur voluntarily or involuntarily. There is considerable variability in timing of handwriting movements and this variability may arise in peripheral response delays and/or in more central timekeeper intervals. However, not all timing "errors" in the movements are negatively correlated or unrelated. I have shown why those movements whose durations are positively correlated may act to preserve the shape of letters and how such correlations could arise.

VII. Appendix: Biomechanical Considerations in Handwriting

This appendix gives a comprehensive description of handwriting to make behavioral details explicit that might otherwise be taken for granted and, at the same time, to identify physical factors that may limit or interact with motor control. Successive subsections will take up movements used in handwriting, the nature of muscle activity during handwriting, and, finally, the physical nature of pen [3] point dynamics.

---

[3] The term "pen" is used inclusively to refer to any writing implement.

A. Upper Limb Movements in Handwriting

No two individuals will adopt exactly the same posture and movements when writing seated at a table. Even so, a fair degree of consensus on how one should write is found, for example, in leaflets on writing that many pen manufacturers make available to schoolteachers. The following characterization of handwriting movements is thus in a sense prescriptive, although I may add that my own observations of many people suggest that it is descriptive for a majority of right-handed writers using script based on the Roman alphabet.

The forearm rests semiprone on the table surface so that the cupped hand, holding the pen between thumb and first finger with second finger giving support underneath, rests on the outer edge of the little finger. Pen point movement is effected by three muscle/joint systems that are capable of relatively independent operation:

1. Transverse displacements of the pen point (i.e., movement in the direction of the predominant slope of the writing) of from 0.5 to 1 cm in amplitude are the result of simultaneous flexion or extension of thumb, index, and second fingers. The position of rest is with the pen point a little way above the line of writing, about halfway up the small characters.

2. Longitudinal fluctuating movements in the direction of the line of writing (to give characters their width) are achieved by the wrist joint. Wrist flexion with radial abduction produces retrograde motion (to the left), whereas motion to the right is by wrist extension combined with ulnar abduction. Retrograde stroke amplitudes would usually not exceed 0.5 cm. Wrist joint movement also produces some left to right progression, which, however, is typically limited to one word at a time.

3. Gross movement of the pen across the page, usually made intermittently at word boundaries, is achieved by abduction of the humerus at the shoulder (movement of the upper arm away from the body) interspersed with lateral rotation about the shoulder joint.

Handwriting movements of those left-handed writers who position the hand below the writing line are the analog of the above with substitution of the complementary movements about shoulder and wrist joints. However, a second group of left-handed writers is generally recognized comprising those that write with the hand in a hooked position above the line of writing (Smith & Reid, 1961; Levy & Reid, 1976). In the case of hooked-position writers, the roles of wrist and thumb/finger movements in controlling fluctuating pen movements are opposite to the roles in writers with the hand below the line. That is, transverse displacements by hooked-position writers are the product of wrist movements, and longitudinal fluctuations are the result of thumb/finger flexion or extension. That the choice of handwriting hand position by left-handed writers is other than arbitrary is suggested by Levy and Reid's (1976) finding that cerebral lateralization of visuospatial and of linguistic functions in left-handers can be indexed on the basis of hand position. However, it has not yet been shown whether the relation they found may be attributed to differential organization of movement in writing or to differences in information processing as a result of the visual written trace only being covered when produced by left-handers writing with the hand positioned below the line.

B. Muscle Activity during Handwriting

Fortunately for the purpose of making electromyographic (EMG) recordings of activity in muscles associated with transverse handwriting movements, the muscle bodies of the prime movers (extensor digitorum communis and flexor digitorum profundus) are located in the forearm (Landsmeer & Long, 1965). Their anatomical location is distinct from that of flexor carpi radialis and extensor carpi ulnaris (e.g., see Hollinshead, 1969), these latter muscles being associated with radial and ulnar abduction at the wrist producing the longitudinal fluctuations in handwriting. It is therefore possible to use EMG electrodes attached to the surface of the skin to obtain a record of the sequencing of muscle activity, such as that due to Vredenbregt and Rau (1971) show in Figure A1. The subject was required to use a pencil to make circular movements of 1-cm ampli-

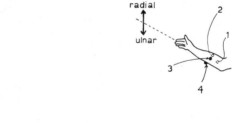

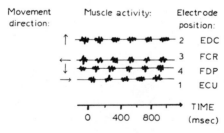

Figure A1 Forearm muscle activity during circular pencil movements of approximately 1-cm amplitude. Electromyographic signals were recorded from bipolar surface electrodes positioned as shown with the likely muscle sources extensor carpi ulnaris (ECU) (1), extensor digitorum communis (EDC) (2), flexor carpi radialis (FCR) (3), and flexor digitorum profundus (FDP) (4). Adapted from Vredenbregt and Rau (1971).

tude while muscle activity was recorded from electrodes attached as shown. Muscle activity at each electrode is shown as a function of time, and the associated directions of movement are also shown.

From this and other similar studies (Denier van der Gon & Thuring, 1965; MacDonald, Note 1; Vredenbregt & Koster, 1971), it has been established that, during handwriting, each participating muscle exhibits well-defined temporal periods of activity and inactivity. Activity in the agonist muscle or muscles (producing a force in the direction of the desired movement) is generally restricted to a small portion of the total movement time near or just before the beginning of the overt movement. Antagonist muscle activity (which serves to reduce or oppose the effect of the agonist muscles) is not typically contemporaneous with agonist activity.[4] Consequently, most of each successive movement within a letter unfolds ballistically and, once the movement is initiated, the actual trajectory will be strongly determined by physical factors rather than under active control. Within words, between-letter spacing is achieved by wrist extension with ulnar abduction, the movement being achieved by a steady background of activity on which the activity to produce the longitudinal fluctuating movements is superimposed (MacDonald, 1966).

C. Pen Point Dynamics

When a point of mass m is acted upon by an impulsive force F_x acting in the direction x, the amount by which it is accelerated, d^2x/dt^2, may be determined from Newton's second law of motion, $F_x = m(d^2x/dt^2)$. In the case of pen point movement, not only must we consider components of force at right angles to x in the direction y, but we must include a number of additional terms representing other physical effects:

1. In writing, not only the pen but also the fingers and the hand move. The equation of motion requires different inertial components, $(m_1 + m_2)(d^2y/dt^2)$ and $m_1(d^2x/dt^2)$, in longitudinal and transverse directions, respectively, since the whole hand (including the fingers) and the pen are involved in the former, but only the fingers and the pen move in the latter.

2. When any two objects are in contact and one moves relative to the other, a force at the plane of contact opposes motion. This force is called friction and is independent of the area of the sliding surface but is proportional to the load between them. The ratio of the frictional force to the load on the plane of contact is known as the coefficient of friction. Bingel and Maier-Leibniz (Note 2) demon-

---

[4] EMG studies of handwriting movement control have considered the timing of agonist muscle electric activity relative to the timing of electrical activity in the antagonist muscle. Strictly speaking, it is not the timing of electrical activity that is important in determining muscle coordination but the timing of the effects of that activity in terms of force onset and termination (cf. Corser, 1974). However, such data do not yet exist for handwriting movements.

strated time-dependent variations of up to a factor of 2 in the contact pressure between pen and paper during writing. These changes in load mean that the coefficient of friction should be expressed as a function of time, $k(t)$.[5]

3. MacDonald (Note 1) has demonstrated that significant effects of static friction can occur in writing. Static friction is a force opposing onset of motion and we will represent it by a function f that drops to zero for scalar velocity $d[(x^2 + y^2)^{1/2}/dt]$ exceeding some relatively small value.

4. Movement of the hand and fingers also requires terms to take account of muscle viscosity (resistance to changes in rate of change of length) and muscle stiffness (resistance to change in length), as Yasuhara (1969) pointed out. Taking account of the fewer and smaller muscle attachments to the joints involved, it is reasonable to suppose that these are less for transverse than for longitudinal displacements. Assuming that the sign of the respective displacements has no effect for the relatively small movements in handwriting, we may represent them by $b_1(dx/dt) + c_1x$ and $(b_1 + b_2)(dy/dt) + (c_1 + c_2)y$. Thus, the complete equation of motion is given by

$$F_x(t) = m_1 \frac{d^2x}{dt^2} + [k(t) + b_1] \frac{dx}{dt} + f \frac{[d(x^2 + y^2)^{1/2}]}{dt} + c_1x$$

and

$$F_y(t) = (m_1 + m_2) \frac{d^2y}{dt^2} + [k(t) + (b_1 + b_2)] \frac{dy}{dt} + f \frac{[d(x^2 + y^2)^{1/2}]}{dt} + (c_1 + c_2)y,$$

where the functions of time $F_x(t)$ and $F_y(t)$ represent the effective driving forces provided by the muscles.

In the literature, there have been two distinct treatments of pen point dynamics that take simplified versions of these equations as their starting points. They differ partly in their assumptions about the form of the muscle forcing functions $F_x(t)$ and $F_y(t)$ but also in the way in which the parameters of the forcing functions are estimated. The earlier work by Denier van der Gon, Thuring, and Strackee (1962), Vredenbregt and Rau (1971), and Vredenbregt and Koster (1971) was carried out in Holland. These workers all assumed that $F_x(t)$ and $F_y(t)$ take only two amplitude values (one of these being zero) and that what varies is the timing and duration of application of the forces. The simulation by Vredenbregt and Koster (1971) exemplifies this approach. Cursive script was produced by varying the time and duration of application of constant voltages to each of two pairs of orthogonally mounted, direct-current electric motors. In addition to inclusion of static and (time invariant) sliding friction terms achieved by using pen in contact with paper, this system also had a property analogous to

---

[5] MacDonald's (Note 1) argument that sliding friction is negligible relative to the inertial component of mass multiplied by acceleration was based, invalidly, only on changes of direction when velocities are at or near a minimum.

the effects of muscle viscosity, *b*. When one motor in a particular pair was being run, the opposing motor was driven backward and the consequent electric generator effect actually made the latter motor act as a brake. With this system, Vredenbregt and Koster were able to obtain a reasonable approximation to normal cursive script.

A different approach from the Dutch work was given by Yasuhara (1969). He suggested that the muscle driving forces should be modeled as continuous exponential functions, with a fixed time constant τ but variable times of onset. Additional free parameters in the model were A, representing force amplitude, and r, which allowed for sliding friction (which Yasuhara assumed was time invariant) and muscle viscosity. Static friction and muscle stiffness were not treated explicitly. While Yasuhara provided two examples of estimation of these parameters from acceleration data of actual handwriting, he did not present data on the adequacy of the physical model he assumed. Indeed, the EMG data described earlier suggest that Yasuhara's model diverges from normal control of forces in handwriting.

In summary, there have been a number of explorations of physical factors affecting pen point movement to the point of simulating the actual dynamics of cursive script. However, none of these has systematically evaluated the contribution to the nature of the written trace of the different physical factors entering into the equations of motion. Thus, we are not yet in a position to quantitatively predict changes in the form of writing that follow for example, an increase in surface roughness, which would increase friction.

Reference Notes

1. MacDonald, J. S. Experimental studies of handwriting signals (Tech. Rep. 433). Massachusetts: Massachusetts Institute of Technology, Res. Lab. Electronics, March 1966.
2. Bingel, A. G. A. & Maier-Leibnitz, H. Investigations of handwriting forces (Project 21–02–070 Report No. 1). Randolph Field, Texas: USAF School of Aviation Medicine, November 1948.

References

Adam, N., Rosner, B. S., Hosick, E. C., & Clark, D. L. Effect of anaesthetic drugs on time production and alpha rhythm. *Perception & Psychophysics*, 1971, *10*, 133–136.
Corser, T. Temporal discrepancies in the electromyographic study of rapid movement. *Ergonomics*, 1974, *17*, 389–400.
Denier van der Gon, J. J., & Thuring, J. Ph. The guiding of human writing movements.*Kybernetik*, 1965, *2*, 145–148.
Denier van der Gon, J. J., Thuring, J. Ph., & Strackee, J. A handwriting simulator. *Physics in Medicine*, 1962, *6*, 407–414.
Hollinshead, W. H. *Functional anatomy of the limbs and back.* Philadelphia: Saunders, 1969.
Kornhuber, H. M. Cerebral cortex, cerebellum, and basal ganglia: An introduction to their

172   *ALAN M. WING*

motor functions. In F. O. Schmitt & F. G. Worden (Eds.), *The neurosciences: Third study program*. Cambridge, Massachusetts: MIT Press, 1974.

Landsmeer, J. M. F., & Long, C. The mechanism of finger control based on electromyograms and location analysis. *Acta Anatomica*, 1965, *60*, 330–347.

Legge, D. Analysis of visual and proprioceptive components of motor skill by means of a drug. *British Journal of Psychology*, 1965, *56*, 243–254.

Legge, D., Steinberg, H., & Summerfield, A. Simple measures of handwriting as indices of drug effects. *Perceptual and Motor Skills*, 1964, *18*, 549–558.

Levy, J., & Reid, M. Variations in writing posture and cerebral organization. *Science*, 1976, *194*, 337–339.

Smith, A. C., & Reid, G. F. Wrist crooking and speed in left-handed writers. *Perceptual and Motor Skills*, 1961, *12*, 94.

Van Nes, F. L. Errors in the motor programme for handwriting. Institut voor Perceptie Onderzoek *Annual Progress Report*, 1971, *6*, 61–63.

Vredenbregt, J., & Koster, W. G. Analysis and synthesis of handwriting. *Philips Technical Review*, 1971, *32*, 73–78.

Vredenbregt, J., & Rau, G. Coordination in muscle activity during simple movements. Institut voor Perceptie Onderzoek *Annual Progress Report*, 1971, *6*, 73–76.

Wing, A. M., & Kristofferson, A. B. Response delays and the timing of discrete motor responses. *Perception & Psychophysics*, 1973, *14*, 5–12.

Yasuhara, M. Handwriting analyzer and analyses of human handwriting movements. *Japanese Psychological Research*, 1969, *11*, 103–109.

8

Sensorimotor Integration during
Motor Programming

Judith L. Smith

I. Introduction

The concept of sensorimotor integration, a heralded topic of the twentieth century, has been reexamined in light of recent deafferentation studies and recent interpretations of motor behavior data. There is no doubt that movement of some degree of proficiency can be initiated and controlled in the absence of detailed, segmental sensory input. Indeed, the CNS is a marvelously adaptive organ. However, *it is not, nor should it be, conceptualized as an either–or proposition.* During normal movement, sensory integration is available throughout the neuraxis, and it is my purpose in this chapter to explore the neuroanatomical and neurophysiological evidence for sensorimotor integration during motor programming. For the sake of brevity, I have selected to emphasize specific motor programs of the spinal cord and cerebellum concerned with locomotion and specific areas of the primary motor cortex (MI) that control the arm and hand.

II. Sensorimotor Integration at the Spinal Cord

A. Distribution of Primary Sensory Afferents

In direct contradiction to the law of Bell and Magendie (Cranefield, 1974) primary sensory afferents enter the spinal gray via dorsal *and* ventral roots. Approximately 15% of the ventral root (VR) fibers are sensory. Most are un-

173

Information Processing in
Motor Control and Learning

myelinated axons, although a small percentage are myelinated, and, as shown in Figure 1, all VR afferents arise from dorsal ganglion cells (Coggeshall, Coulter, & Willis, 1974; Applebaum, Clifton, Coggeshall, Coulter, Vance, & Willis, 1976). The receptive fields of VR afferents at levels L_7-S_2 in the cat are primarily somatic, located in joint, muscle, and cutaneous tissues (Kato & Tanji, 1971), whereas the unmyelinated VR afferents, tested at S_3-Cx_1, have receptive fields in the pelvic viscera or in the skin and deep tissues at the base of the tail (Clifton, Coggeshall, Vance, & Willis, 1976).

The distribution of primary afferent collaterals in the dorsal horn is extremely complex (see the review by Réthelyi & Szentágothai, 1973). All lamina of the dorsal horn (see Figure 1) are penetrated, and synaptic connections are established with spinothalamic (Trevino, Coulter, & Willis, 1973), spinocerebellar (Oscarsson, 1973), and propriospinal pathways and segmental interneurons (Scheibel & Scheibel, 1968b). Only primary spindle afferents penetrate to make monosynaptic connections with motoneuronal pools (Scheibel & Scheibel, 1968a).

Branches of primary sensory afferents (PSA) that ascend directly into the dorsal column may not reach the medulla to participate in the medial lemniscal system. Many fibers of the fasciculus gracilis, for example, ascend only 1 or 2 segments (the "short system"), whereas other PSA fibers ascend 4 to 12 segments (the "intermediate system") before leaving the dorsal column (Horch, Burgess, & Whitehorn, 1976). Just what neuron populations are influenced by the fibers of these two systems cannot be determined from the data available. However, many PSA fibers supplying proprioceptors of the hindlimb, including muscle spindles, Golgi tendon organs, and joint receptors, participate in the intermediate system (Whitsel, Petrucelli, & Sapiro, 1969; Clark, 1972).

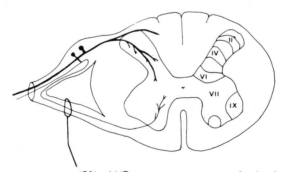

15% of VR axons are sensory and arise in the DRG

12–13% of these sensory fibers in VR are unmyelinated

1–2% of these sensory fibers in VR are myelinated

Figure 1 Ventral root (VR) afferents arise from the dorsal root ganglion (DRG) and enter the gray matter via the ventral root. Dorsal root afferents penetrate all lamina of the dorsal horn.

Spinal and brain stem pathways used to transmit information from hindlimb proprioceptors to the thalamus and sensory cortices are largely undefined, with one exception. Spindle afferents project through Clark's column to nucleus Z in the rostral medulla (Landgren & Silfvenius, 1971). Proprioceptors from the forelimb, however, appear to utilize the more "traditional" dorsal column medial lemniscus pathway (Rosén & Sjölund, 1973).

B. Sensory Control of Interneurons Programming Locomotion

There is compelling evidence for the existence of spinal interneurons that are capable of generating and coordinating flexion and extension of the hindlimbs in an alternate and rhythmic manner (see the reviews by Grillner, 1975; Wetzel & Stuart, 1976). These interneurons, collectively called spinal rhythm generators, can program stepping movements in spinalized, deafferented cats (see Figure 2). Although no supraspinal or spinal afferentation is needed to maintain alternate activity in α and γ motoneurons of flexor and extensor hindlimb muscles (Sjöström & Zangger, 1976), the central generator must be turned on by an injection of L-dopa or Clondine (Grillner, 1973) or by electrical stimulation of the caudal midbrain (see Section III).

The existence of spinal generators does not imply that sensory input is unimportant; information from the periphery is essential if the animal is to compensate for irregularities in the terrain and other environmental and internal states that cannot be predicted by the spinal generators.

For example, when the dorsum of the cat's hindpaw is touched lightly during the swing phase of the step cycle, the entire hindlimb performs a brisk supplementary flexion, as if to clear an unexpected obstacle (Forssberg, Grillner,

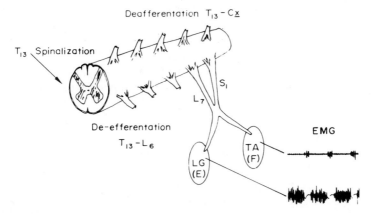

Figure 2 With spinalization (T_{13}) and deafferentation, rhythmic and alternate contractions of an ankle flexor (TA-tibialis anterior) and extensor (LG-lateral gastrocnemius) are initiated and coordinated by "spinal generators."

Rossignol, & Wallén, 1976). The tactile stimulus modifies the spinal generator, such that the flexor burst of the ipsilateral limb is prolonged and the extensor burst of the contralateral limb is prolonged. If, however, the same contact is applied to the paw during the stance phase of the step cycle, there is no flexor response; on the contrary, ipsilateral extensor activity is prolonged as if the cat is attempting to avoid hitting a low-lying obstacle on the walking surface. Thus, cutaneous stimulation applied to the dorsum of the hindpaw during the swing or stance phase yields two functionally opposed reflexes.

Reflex reversals have also been demonstrated for tactile stimulation applied to the plantar surface of the hindpaw (Duysens & Pearson, 1976). With the cat at rest, weak stimulation of the plantar surface evokes an extensor reflex. In decerebrate cats spontaneously walking on a treadmill, the same stimulus applied during the stance phase increases both the amplitude and the duration of ongoing extensor activity, while delaying the extensor burst of the contralateral hindlimb. When applied during the swing phase, this tactile stimulus prolongs ongoing flexor activity and/or shortens the following extensor burst.

These studies demonstrate that preprogrammed bursts used to generate locomotion are greatly modified by sensory stimuli and that traditional spinal reflexes are "plastic." Since cutaneous afferents reach flexor and extensor motoneuron pools through multiple, polysynaptic routes, it is possible that the spinal generators phasically change the transmission of pathways to ensure the best possible match between reflex responses and the current phase of locomotion.

III. Sensorimotor Integration and the Cerebellum

The cerebellum has long been proclaimed as the proprioceptive ganglion (Sherrington, 1906). To date we do not have an accurate sensory map of the cerebellar cortex, and we know very little about the way in which sensory information is processed by the neuronal network. Indeed, the role of the cerebellum in motor control is still uncertain (Grimm & Rusher, 1974; Conrad & Brooks, 1974; Thach, 1975). The mesencephalic walking cat (Shik, Severin, & Orlovsky, 1966), however, offers a nice model, for in this preparation movement is controlled without cerebropontocerebellar influence.

Supported on a treadmill, the mesencephalic cat will locomote when the caudal midbrain is stimulated. With increased stimulation, the cats develop greater forces and speed; often gait changes are seen as the cat progresses from a walk, to a trot, to a gallop (Shik et al., 1966).

During such controlled mesencephalic locomotion, the vestibular nucleus (Orlovsky, 1972a), the red nucleus (Orlovsky, 1972b), and selective reticular nuclei (Orlovsky, 1970a,b) display phasic activity with respect to certain phases of the step cycle. For example, the majority of rubrospinal neurons are maximally active during the swing phase, whereas vestibulospinal and reticulospinal cells are maximally active during the stance phase (Figure 3). When mesencephalic cats are decerebellated, locomotion continues, but the frequency modulation of rubrospinal (Orlovsky, 1972b), vestibulospinal (Orlovsky, 1972a), and reticulospinal (Orlovsky, 1970b) cells is virtually absent or greatly reduced (Figure 3). The cerebellum thus appears to be implicated as the programmer of the brain stem nuclei, which assist the spinal generators during the control of locomotion. Unlike afferent information, which can dramatically alter the temporal patterning of the spinal generator (see section II, 13), stimulation of descending fibers does not alter the temporal pattern generated by the spinal network or activate muscles in the inappropriate phase (Orlovsky, 1972c). However, the magnitude of contraction may be enhanced during stimulation of brain stem nuclei during the appropriate phase of the step cycle. For example, stimulation of the red nucleus during the stance phase influences neither the ankle flexor nor the ankle extensor, whereas a similar stimulus applied during the swing phase markedly enhanced the response of the ankle flexor.

Cerebellar activity during mesencephalic walking is governed primarily by spinal input, although influences directly or indirectly from the midbrain locomotion center and other brain stem nuclei, such as the olive, cannot be ruled out. Two ascending pathways provide sensory information directly to the cerebellum from the lumbosacral cord: the dorsal spinocerebellar tract (DSCT) and the ventral spinocerebellar tract (VSCT). Cells of the DSCT are phasically active during locomotion and exhibit maximal firing during the stance phase (Arshavsky, Berkinblit, Gelfand, Orlovsky, & Fukson, 1972a). With deafferentation of

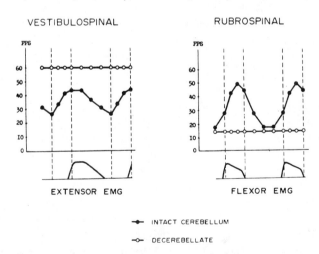

Figure 3   The activity of "average" rubrospinal and vestibulospinal neurons during controlled, mesencephalic locomotion before and after decerebellation. PPS, pulses per second. Adapted from Orlovsky (1972a,b).

the hindlimbs, however, fibers of the DSCT show no modulated activity. Neurons of the VSCT also exhibit rhythmical responses to locomotion (Arshavsky *et al.*, 1972b). However, after deafferentation of the hindlimbs, cells of the VSCT continue to have modulated discharges that are similar to spinal interneurons generating the locomotor rhythm (Arshavsky *et al.*, 1972c). These findings are in keeping with Lundberg's (1971) hypothesis that VSCT transmission to the cerebellum is concerned with the status of spinal interneurons rather than specific afferentation from limbs. The fact that Ia inhibitory neurons and Renshaw cells inhibit some cells of the VSCT gives additional support to the idea that the VSCT relays information about central spinal events (Gustafsson & Lindström, 1973; Lindström & Schomburg, 1973).

It is possible that the VSCT is the analog of the cerebropontocerebellar pathway and is acting as a forward feed system, keeping the cerebellar cortex (Orlovsky, 1972d) and cerebellar nuclei (Orlovsky, 1972e) informed about the state of the spinal generators and the impact of spinal reflexes. The DSCT, conversely, provides detailed sensory information from muscle and joint receptors and is analogous to the spinothalamic and medial lemniscus pathways.

IV. Sensorimotor Integration and the Primary Somatic Motor Area

The precentral gyrus, or the primary somatic motor area (MI), is composed of efferent colonies or zones (Asanuma, 1975). Each cylindrical zone is approximately 1.0–3.0 mm in diameter and both α and γ motoneurons of single muscles are controlled by cortical stimulation (Asanuma & Rosén, 1972). Whether the efferent organization of the precentral gyrus is confined to a strict mosaic arrangement of segregated colonies is controversial (see the discussion in Asanuma, Arnold, & Zarzecki, 1976). Experiments with intracortical microstimulation in the arm area of the MI of baboon (Andersen, Hagan, Phillips, & Powell, 1975) and monkey (Jankowska, Padel, & Tanaka, 1975) show that individual motoneurons receive corticospinal inputs from different areas of the cortex, which are not necessarily continuous; furthermore, there is considerable overlap of cortical areas projecting to specific motoneuronal pools in the ventral horn.

Sensory information converges on the MI from the somatic sensory cortices (Jones & Powell, 1969) and directly from the ventral posteriolateral (VPL) thalamus (Strick, 1975). Rosén and Asanuma (1972) were one of the first to study the afferent inputs to the motor cortex systematically. They found that, in anesthetized monkeys, neurons in a specific efferent zone received proprioceptive inputs from joints or muscles to which that zone projected. Although Rósen and Asanuma (1972) and Wiesendanger (1973) found little evidence for the representation of group I muscle afferents, others (Hore, Preston, Durkovic, & Cheney, 1976; Murphy, Wong, & Kwan, 1975) demonstrated that single cells of MI can encode the information transmitted by muscle spindle primaries (Ia) and Golgi tendon organs (Ib).

Recordings from precentral neurons of conscious monkeys during stereotyped reaching movements and passive manipulations of the arm made it possible to determine what sort of afferent input affected cortical cells associated with particular voluntary movements of the shoulder, elbow, wrist, and digits (Lemon, Hanby, & Porter, 1976). Of 60 MI cells that responded both to active and passive movement of a specific joint, 75% had identical active–passive responses. For example, neurons that were active when the monkey performed shoulder retraction, elbow flexion, or wrist abduction were activated by passively guided movements in the same direction, respectively. Typically, precentral cortical neurons responded to passive movement only in one direction, and passive movement in the opposite direction either had no effect or, in some tonic cortical cells, produced inhibition (Lemon & Porter, 1976). Only 10% of the precentral cells tested responded to tactile stimulation, and the majority of cutaneous receptive fields were located on the ventral surface of the digits. Cortical cells receiving this cutaneous input were generally active during finger flexion only (Lemon et al., 1976).

Of the total 176 movement-related precentral cells studied, approximately 5% were not influenced by passive manipulation of the forelimb, including muscle palpation, tactile stimulation, and passive joint movements (Lemon et al., 1976). Conversely, over 75% of the active–passive couplings were either strongly related or related such that the afferent input field was confined to the area or part of the limb involved in the active movement with which the activity of the cell was correlated. Only about 10% of the movement-related cells received sensory input from a zone anatomically remote from the area involved in the active movement.

The data presented above made it clear that cells of the MI are capable of encoding muscle length, muscle tension, joint movement, and position. Whatever the ultimate role played by this input, it is certain that the motor cortex cells (both pyramidal and intracortical cells) closely monitor the functional state of the limb musculature they control. Rosén and Asanuma (1972) proposed that the pattern of somatic sensory input reaching the motor cortex "appears to be more suited to a role as feedback information, of possible use for modulating the output from individual cortical columns during performance of movements, rather than being involved in the initiation of motor acts [p. 271]."

The cortex, however, is not just a passive receiver of somatic sensory information; corticofugal influences are exerted at all levels of the neuraxis to control the reception of somatic input (for a review, see Towe, 1973). Tsumoto, Nakamura, and Iwama (1975) have described a differential effect of pyramidal cell stimulation upon the transmission of tactile and passive joint information from the thalamus to the cortex. VPL cells responding to cutaneous inputs were inhibited by stimulation of the pyramidal tract, whereas those responding to passive joint movement were facilitated. These findings may help to explain why

Lemon and Porter (1976) found few cells in the MI that responded to cutaneous stimulation in conscious monkeys, and they suggest that the motor cortex is capable of preferentially selecting kinesthetic cues during movement. In fact, Evarts and Tanji (1974) have demonstrated a "gating" effect on sensorimotor control by pyramidal cells during learned movement.

V. Concluding Remarks

The potential for sensorimotor integration during motor programming is tremendous. I have only scratched the surface. We must not get trapped in the game of *either–or*. We must look at the capacities of the sensorimotor system and seek to define the optimal conditions for motor control.

References

Andersen, P., Hagan, P. J., Phillips, C. G., & Powell, T. P. S. Mapping by microstimulation of overlapping projections from area 4 to motor units of the baboon's hand. *Proceedings of the Royal Society of London, Series B,* 1975, *188,* 31–60.

Applebaum, M. L., Clifton, G. L., Coggeshall, R. E., Coulter, J. D., Vance, W. H., & Willis, W. D. Unmyelinated fibres in the sacral 3 and caudal 1 ventral roots in the cat. *Journal of Physiology,* 1976, *256,* 557–572.

Arshavsky, Yu. I., Berkinblit, M. B., Gelfant, I. M., Orlovsky, G. N., & Fukson, O. I. Activity of the neurones of the dorsal spinocerebellar tract during locomotion. *Biophysics,* 1972, *17,* 506–514. (a)

Archavsky, Yu. I., Berkinblit, M. B., Gelfand, I. M., Orlovsky, G. N., & Fukson, O. I. Activity of the neurones of the ventral spinocerebellar tract during locomotion. *Biophysics,* 1972, *17,* 926-941. (b)

Arshavsky, Yu. I., Berkinblit, M. B., Gelfand, I. M., Orlovsky, G. N., & Fukson, O. I. Activity of neurones of the ventral spinocerebellar tract during locomotion of cats with deafferentated hind limbs. *Biophysics,* 1972, *17,* 1169–1176. (c)

Asanuma, H. Recent developments in the study of the columnar arrangement of neurones within the motor cortex. *Physiological Reviews,* 1975, *55,* 143–156.

Asanuma, H., Arnold, A., & Zarzecki, P. Further study on the excitation of pyramidal tract cells by intracortical microstimulation. *Experimental Brain Research,* 1976, *26,* 443–461.

Asanuma, H., & Rosén, I. Topographical organization of cortical efferent zones projecting to distal forelimb muscles in the monkey. *Experimental Brain Research,* 1972, *14,* 243–256.

Clark, F. J. Central projection of sensory fibers from the cat knee joint. *Journal of Neurobiology,* 1972, *3,* 101–110.

Clifton, G. L. Coggeshall, R. E., Vance, W. H., & Willis, W. D. Receptive fields of unmyelinated ventral root afferent fibres in the cat. *Journal of Physiology,* 1976, *256,* 573–600.

Coggeshall, R. E., Coulter, J. D., & Willis, W. D. Unmyelinated axons in the ventral roots of the cat lumbosacral enlargement. *Journal of Comparative Neurology,* 1974, *153,* 39–58.

Conrad, B., & Brooks, V. B. Effects of dentate cooling on rapid alternating arm movements. *Journal of Neurophysiology,* 1974, *37,* 792–804.

Cranefield, D. F. *The way in and the way out: Francois Megendie, Charles Bell and the roots of the spinal nerves.* New York: Futura Publishing Co., 1974.

Duysens, J., & Pearson, K. G. The role of cutaneous afferents from the distal hindlimb in the regulation of the step cycle of thalamic cats. *Experimental Brain Research*, 1976, *24*, 245–255.

Evarts, E. B., & Tanji, J. Gating of motor cortex reflexes by prior instruction. *Brain Research*, 1974, *71*, 479–494.

Forssberg, H., Grillner, S., Rossignol, S., & Wallén, P. Phasic control of reflexes during locomotion in vertebrates. In R. M. Herman, S. Grillner, P. S. G. Stein, & G. S. Stuart (Eds.), *Neural control of locomotion*. New York: Plenum, 1976.

Grillner, S. Locomotion in the spinal cat. In R. B. Stein, K. G. Pearson, R. S. Smith, & J. B. Redford (Eds.), *Control of posture and locomotion*. New York: Plenum, 1973.

Grillner, S. Locomotion in vertebrates: Central mechanisms and reflex interaction. *Physiological Reviews*, 1975, *55*, 247–304.

Grimm, R. J., & Rushmer, D. S. The activity of dentate neurons during an arm movement sequence. *Brain Research*, 1974, *71*, 309–326.

Gustafsson, B., & Lindström, S. Recurrent control from motor axon collaterals of Ia inhibitory pathways to ventral spinocerebellar tract neurones. *Acta Physiologica Scandinavica*, 1973, *89*, 457–481.

Horch, K. W., Burgess, P. R., & Whitehorn, D. Ascending collaterals of cutaneous neurons in the fasciculus gracilis of the cat. *Brain Research*, 1976, *117*, 1–17.

Hore, J., Preston, J. B., Durkovic, R. G., & Cheney, P. D. Responses of cortical neurons (areas 3a and 4) to ramp stretch of handlimb muscles in the baboon. *Journal of Neurophysiology*, 1976, *39*, 484–499.

Jankowska, E., Padel, Y., & Tanaka, R. Projections of pyramidal tract cells to α-motoneurones innervating hind-limb muscles in monkey. *Journal of Physiology, London*, 1975, *249*, 637–667.

Jones, E. G., & Powell, T. P. S. Connections of somatic sensory cortex of the rhesus monkey. I. Ipsilateral cortical connections. *Brain*, 1969, *192*, 477–502.

Kato, M., & Tanji, J. Physiological properties of sensory fibers in the spinal ventral roots in the cat. *Japanese Journal of Physiology*, 1971, *41*, 71–77.

Landgren, S., & Silfvenius, H. Nucleus Z, the medullary relay in the projection path to the cerebral cortex of group I muscle afferents from the cat's hindlimb. *Journal of Physiology, London*, 1971, *218*, 551–571.

Lemon, R. N., & Porter, R. Afferent input to movement-related precentral neurones in conscious monkey. *Proceedings of the Royal Society of London, Series B*, 1976, *194*, 313–340.

Lemon, R. N., Hanby, J. A., & Porter, R. Relationship between the activity of precentral neurones during active and passive movements in conscious monkeys. *Proceedings of the Royal Society of London, Series B*, 1976, *194*, 341–373.

Lindström, S., & Schomburg, E. D. Recurrent inhibition from motor axon collaterals of ventral spinocerebellar tract neurones. *Acta Physiologica Scandinavica*, 1973, *88*, 505–515.

Lundberg, A. Function of the ventral spinocerebellar tract—a new hypothesis. *Experimental Brain Research*, 1971, *12*, 317–330.

Murphy, J. T., Wong, Y. C., & Kwan, H. C. Afferent–efferent linkages in motor cortex for single forelimb muscles. *Journal of Neurophysiology*, 1975, *38*, 990–1014.

Orlovsky, G. N. Work of the reticulospinal neurones during locomotion. Biophysics, 1970, *15*, 761–771. (a)

Orlovsky, G. N. Influence of the cerebellum on the reticulospinal neurones during locomotion. *Biophysics*, 1970, *15*, 928–936. (b)

Orlovsky, G. N. Activity of vestibulospinal neurons during locomotion. *Brain Research*, 1972, *46*, 85–98. (a)

Orlovsky, G. N. Activity of rubrospinal neurons during locomotion. *Brain Research*, 1972, *46*, 99–112. (b)

Orlovsky, G. N. The effect of different descending systems on flexor and extensor activity during locomotion. *Brain Research*, 1972, *40*, 359–372. (c)

Orlovsky, G. N. Work of Purkinje cells during locomotion. *Biophysics*, 1972, *17*, 935–941. (d)

Orlovsky, G. N. Work of the neurones of the cerebellar nuclei during locomotion. *Biophysics*, 1972, *17*, 1177–1185. (e)

Oscarsson, O. Functional organization of spinocerebellar paths. In A. Iggo (Ed.), *Handbook of sensory physiology* (Vol. 2). New York: Springer-Verlag, 1973.

Réthelyi, M., & Szentágothai, J. Distribution and connections of afferent fibres in the spinal cord. In A. Iggo (Ed.), *Handbook of sensory physiology* (Vol. 2). New York: Springer-Verlag, 1973.

Rosén, I., & Asanuma, H. Peripheral afferent inputs to the forelimb area of the monkey motor cortex: Input–output relations. *Experimental Brain Research*, 1972, *14*, 257–273.

Rosén, I., & Sjölund, B. Organization of Group I activated cells in the main and external cuneate nuclei of the cat: Identification of muscle receptors. *Experimental Brain Research*, 1973, *16*, 221–237.

Scheibel, M. E., & Scheibel, A. B. Terminal axonal patterns in cat spinal cord. II. The dorsal horn. *Brain Research*, 1968, *9*, 32–58. (a)

Scheibel, M. E., & Scheibel, A. B. A structural analysis of spinal interneurons and Renshaw cells. In M. A. B. Brazier (Ed.), *The interneuron*. California: University of California Press, 1968. (b)

Sherrington, C. S. *The integrative action of the nervous system*. New Haven: Yale University Press, 1906.

Shik, M. L., Severin, F. V., & Orlovsky, G. N. Control of walking and running by means of electrical stimulation of the mid-brain. *Biophysics*, 1966, *11*, 756–765.

Sjöström, A., & Zangger, P. Muscle spindle control during locomotor movements generated by deafferented spinal cord. *Acta Physiologica Scandinavica*, 1976, *97*, 281–291.

Strick, P. L. Multiple sources of thalamic input to the primate motor cortex. *Brain Research*, 1975, *88*, 372–377.

Thach, W. T. Timing of activity in cerebellar dentate nucleus and cerebral motor cortex during prompt volitional movement. *Brain Research*, 1975, *88*, 233–241.

Towe, A. L. Somatosensory cortex: Descending influences on ascending systems. In A. Iggo (Ed.), *Handbook of sensory physiology* (Vol. 2). New York: Springer-Verlag, 1973.

Trevino, D. L., Coulter, J. D., & Willis, W. D. Location of cells of origin of spinothalamic tract in lumbar enlargement of the monkey. *Journal of Neurophysiology*, 1973, *36*, 750–761.

Tsumoto, T., Nakamura, S., & Iwama, K. Pyramidal tract control over cutaneous and kinesthetic sensory transmission in the cat thalamus. *Experimental Brain Research*, 1975, *22*, 281–294.

Wetzel, M. C., & Stuart, D. G. Ensemble characteristics of cat locomotion and its neural control. *Progress in Neurobiology*, 1976, *7*, 1–98.

Whitsel, B. L., Petrucelli, L. M., & Sapiro, G. Modality representation in the lumbar and cervical fasciculus gracilis of squirrel monkeys. *Brain Research*, 1969, *15*, 67–78.

Wiesendanger, M. Input from muscle and cutaneous nerves of the hand and forearm to neurones of the precentral gyrus of baboons and monkeys. *Journal of Physiology, London*, 1973, *228*, 203–219.

9

Sources of Inaccuracy in Rapid Movement

Richard A. Schmidt
Howard N. Zelaznik
James S. Frank

I. Introduction

Even though the twentieth century has seen a considerable volume of experimental work addressing issues surrounding the control of human motor responding, we have made only modest gains toward understanding the underlying processes responsible for movement. The lawful relationship between even some

Information Processing in
Motor Control and Learning

of the most fundamental characteristics of movement—the movement speed, the length of the movement in space, and the spatial and temporal accuracy demanded—escaped discovery until Fitts (1954) provided what has come to be known as Fitts' law. The law is defined for alternate tapping responses and describes the relationship between the movement amplitude (A), the required movement accuracy (target width, W), and the resulting movement time (MT). Fitts' law has proved to be quite general, and as a result of its success a number of explanations (in terms of underlying processes) have been proposed, perhaps the leading one being the Crossman–Goodeve (Note 1; later described by Keele, 1968) theory involving feedback-based movement corrections. In this chapter, we first describe the Fitts paradigm, indicating some of its empirical support and mentioning some of its limitations as a general method for understanding movement control. Then, we turn to the Crossman–Goodeve theory, pointing out some of its limitations. Finally, we describe an alternative theory that can account for relations among A, W, and MT, including a description of some experiments done by us that provide support for the theory.

II. Fitts' Law

A. The Fitts Paradigm

In 1954, Fitts proposed a relationship among movement time, movement accuracy, and movement length that has stood essentially unmodified for nearly a quarter of a century. In the so-called "Fitts paradigm," the subject is presented with two equal-sized targets of width W, their centers separated by an amplitude A, and the subject's task is to tap a stylus alternately between the two targets as quickly as possible for a short period (e.g., 15 sec). Fitts (1954) proposed that the average time per movement (MT) was related to A and W by

$$MT = a + b \log_2(2A/W) \tag{1}$$

where a and b are constants.

Since Fitts' law (as it came to be called) was introduced, there have been attempts to modify the relation to obtain more accurate predictions of the obtained MTs [see Welford (1968) for a summary of this work], but little or no improvement in the original statement has resulted from these efforts. The relation has been found to hold for movements with great variations in A and W, for movement times ranging from 100 through 900 msec, for movements performed under magnification as well as with direct vision, for the feet as well as the hands (Pew, Note 2), for retarded as well as "normal" individuals [Wade, Newell, and Wallace (Note 3) showed that retarded subjects evidenced a steeper slope than did age-matched "normal" subjects], and for responses in which pegs were to be fit into holes or in which washers were to be placed over pegs rather than the conventional tapping arrangement [see Langolf, Chaffin, and Foulke

(1976) for a review and other examples]. The relation has a great deal of generality—perhaps more than any other in the motor behavior area.

B. Limitations of Fitts' Paradigm

While it is obvious that a great deal has been learned about movement control via Fitts' law, there are a number of features of the paradigm that could be improved. Methodologically, A and W are treated as independent variables, with MT as the single dependent variable. While the investigator can control A rather well, Fitts (1954) and others have recognized that subjects trade off speed for accuracy in such situations; W is objectively fixed by the experimenter, but in a number of cases the subject's "real" W represents the amount of spread of responses about the center of the target, leading to the notion of "*effective* target width" (W_e) as the standard deviation of the subject's movement endpoints. In many situations, W_e cannot be measured because the accuracy is scored dichotomously (see Klapp, 1975), whereas in other cases (Welford, 1968) W_e has been estimated. With the goal of coming to an understanding of movement control in mind, we think that it makes more sense to control experimentally both A and MT (the latter via metronome-paced movements or through previous practice with knowledge of results about movement time), using W_e as the single dependent variable; subjectively, it seems to us that A and MT are determined in advance by the subject, and W_e "results" from these decisions, making W_e a logical choice for a single dependent variable. We have conducted a number of experiments using this technique, and the findings will be discussed shortly.

Second, and perhaps more important, the Fitts task usually involves a "continuous" string of tapping movement (see Klapp [1975] for a different paradigm), with the movement time being estimated by the number of taps completed in a fixed period of time. We think that such a response hides a great deal of the important mechanisms of motor responding. For example, one has no idea about the extent to which corrections are made within each movement, between each consecutive movment, or even between groups of movements. Langolf *et al.* (1976), for example, have eliminated some of these problems by recording the movement trajectories, but the fact remains that the continuous nature of the response appears to hide a number of the underlying control mechanisms present in a single tap. Therefore, we feel that an analysis of the variables studied by Fitts, but with single aiming responses, will provide more fundamental information about movement control.

III. Theories That Account for Fitts' Law

A. The Crossman–Goodeve Theory

Naturally, there have been a number of attempts to provide theoretical explanations for a relation that predicts the observed data so well. Fitts originally proposed that the term $\log_2 (2A/W)$, which he labeled the *index of difficulty*, represented the uncertainty or information content of the movement and that *MT* was linearly related to the amount of information that had to be processed during the movement. Perhaps the most widely accepted alternative explanation of the relation came from Crossman and Goodeve (Note 1) and was re-presented by Keele (1968). Two assumptions are required: (*a*) that the subject detects errors in movement and issues a correction at regular intervals (e.g., every 200 msec) during the tap and (*b*) that the initial movement and any subsequent corrections have a fixed relative accuracy—that is, the variability of the endpoint of any correction is a constant proportion (e.g., from 4 to 7%) of the distance to be moved. The subject is thought to make the decisions about the nature of the initial portion of the movement before it begins; the first response results in a move of within 4–7% of the desired distance. The subject then issues a correction to eliminate the remaining error, this correction having an accuracy of 4–7% as well; *after* the first correction, the subject is $0.07 \times 0.07 = 0.0049 \times 100$, or 0.49%, of the original movement distance away from the center of the target. The subject continues to make corrections until the remaining error is equal to $\frac{1}{2}W$, at which point the last move will achieve the target. Note that the Crossman–Goodeve explanation emphasizes the feedback control in rapid movements, with the limitation in movement speed being defined by the number of 200-msec corrections the subject must make to achieve the target. Using this argument, Keele (1968) has shown that Fitts' law can be derived mathematically. Notice that the major implication of this model is that the limitation in *MT* is the number of 200-msec corrections the subject must make to achieve the target.[1]

B. Limitations of the Crossman–Goodeve Theory

A number of lines of evidence, from widely different paradigms and sources, suggest that subjects may not behave in the way specified by Crossman and Goodeve (Note 1). An important theme in all of these arguments is that, if we can assume that error information *is* stimuli, humans have a very difficult time responding to stimulus information. These arguments have been stated before (see Schmidt, 1975, 1976) and are presented only in brief form here.

Time to generate error. The Crossman–Goodeve theory assumes a correction every 200 msec, with the first coming 200 msec after the initiation of the movement (see Footnote 1). If the first correction appears 200 msec after the movement begins, and the reaction time for the correction is 200 msec, then the error

---

[1] Crossman and Goodeve assumed that corrections occurred at regular intervals, but their model does not specify the exact duration. Keele (1968), as a result of the findings from Keele and Posner (1968) and other data, suggested that the interval should be from 190 to 250 msec, or about the duration of a simple reaction time. For that reason, the value of 200 msec for a simple reaction time is used here.

must have been detected at the moment the movement began. Logically, it would seem that some initial portion of the movement must be carried out before the system could detect that the movement was in error. By our argument, the first correction could not occur until 200 msec after the error *occurred,* perhaps as long as 300 msec after the movement begins.

Corrections are required. The Crossman–Goodeve (Note 1) model holds that corrections are required in a movement, with MT being occupied by the corrections. Langolf (Note 4), however, noted that corrections are seldom evident in microscopic movement [although Langolf *et al.* (1976) found corrections to be somewhat more prevalent], perhaps because the movements were programmed correctly from the beginning. The model does not consider the situation where movements are already correct, that is, require no correction, and we feel that the requirement of corrections in movement is a conceptual weakness of the model.

Hick's law. While it may be possible to make a movement correction with a latency of 200 msec as the theory suggests, this value is based on *simple* reaction time where the number of possible errors to be corrected is minimized at 1. However, we have long known that reaction time increases with the number of stimulus alternatives (Hick, 1952), and if the number of possible ways in which the error can occur (e.g., too high, too fast, too far to the right, etc.) is greater than 1, the 200-msec value for each correction could underestimate the time required.

Psychological refractoriness. The feedback-control argument assumes that the subject makes a series of from one to perhaps five 200-msec corrections that occupy MT. However, we know from studies requiring responses to two consecutive stimuli separated by from 50 to 500 msec that the reaction time to the second of two closely spaced stimuli will be delayed considerably relative to the reaction time to that signal presented alone, perhaps with an *increase* of as much as 300 msec, making a total reaction time for the second signal of 500–600 msec (for a review, see Welford, 1968). Thus, from studies of this so-called "psychological refractory period," it is extremely unlikely that the subject could respond to the second of two closely spaced error signals with a reaction time of 200 msec. Thus, it seems unlikely that the assumption of consecutive 200-msec corrections could realistically be achieved.

Biomechanical evidence. In studies of tapping performance under the Fitts paradigm, Langolf (Note 4; Langolf *et al.,* 1976) has examined the motion trajectories of the limb during attempts to achieve the targets. In general, subjects do not appear to make corrections on every movement (Langolf, Note 4); it is therefore difficult to make the argument that ongoing corrections are characteristic of all tapping responses. In the later investigation, Langolf *et al.* (1976)

showed that subjects sometimes made a single correction, with a latency of 200 msec from the beginning of the movement; there was rarely, if ever, more than this one correction. Langolf *et al.* argued that the Crossman–Goodeve model did not predict the observed data very well.

Summary. There are various lines of indirect evidence, as well as direct evidence from recordings of the movement trajectories, that create considerable concern that the Crossman–Goodeve and Keele models of movement control, at least as it is applied to the Fitts paradigm, may be incorrect. At present, there seems to be no satisfactory model that will account for the Fitts relationship.

IV. An Alternative View: Movement-Output Variability

Nearly all of the attempts to provide an explanation for Fitts' law have been based on the idea that the subject engages in a number of within-movement corrections to achieve the target on each tap (see also Beggs & Howarth, 1972). This closed-loop idea, made popular by those with orientations toward engineering and systems-control theory, is based on a very optimistic view of the subject's capabilities in processing feedback information (see Schmidt, 1975, 1976), placing as it does the limitations in the accuracy of responding in terms of the rapidity and quality of movement corrections. We feel that the motor behaviorists have consistently ignored another, equally likely, possibility for explaining the relations between *A, W,* and *MT*: that the output of the human muscular system is contaminated by "noise" (within-subject variability) and that this variability is perhaps related to the nature of the movement (i.e., to its amplitude and its speed). Before describing the theory, however, it will be helpful to mention some common features of the kinds of movements for which the theory attempts to provide an explanation.

A. Single Aiming Movements

Consider a movement in which the subject holds a stylus with its tip on a starting position, moves it rapidly in the horizontal plane toward a target a few centimeters away, attempting to hit the target with the tip of the stylus. Movement speed is "controlled" by having the subject attempt to move with a particular movement time; this is measured by the interval between the closure of a switch when the subject leaves the starting position until the closure of another switch (in the stylus) on arrival at (or near) the target. In addition, a light accelerometer is attached to the stylus, and its output during the movement is recorded on a polygraph.

In Figure 1 is a record of a "typical" pattern; the instructed movement time was 180 msec, and the subject moved to a target 10 cm away from the starting position. The accelerative portion of the movement is indicated by the downward deflection on the record, and the acceleration ceased when the curve crossed the

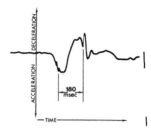

Figure 1 Tracing from an accelerometer attached to a stylus during a 180-msec movement to a target 10 cm away from a starting position.

baseline approximately 90 msec after the movement began. Deceleration then began, indicated by the wave moving upward, and the deceleration was essentially over in another 90 msec when the curve reached the baseline again. The closure of the starting switch caused some vibration in the stylus, seen as small oscillations during the early portion of the acceleration wave; it is perhaps interesting that, although the switch required only approximately 2 mm of movement in order to activate it, there was a considerable amount of acceleration applied (and hence movement produced) over approximately 20–30 msec before the movement time began to be recorded. The arrival of the stylus on (or near) the target is indicated by the large fluctuations (upward then downward) just after the peak of the decelerative phase of the movement. Since the switch in the stylus was closed with contact at the target area, it can be seen that there was considerable deceleration after the end of the measured movement time. It appears from this analysis that the tip of the stylus hit the target surface while it was still moving laterally. Although we do not have records of the path of the movement through space, observation indicates that the hand typically traverses a roughly parabolic course, and strikes the target area at an angle; however, Langolf *et al.* (1976) did measure such trajectories (although in repetitive movements), and their records support our observations. A schematic drawing of the course of this kind of movement is shown in Figure 2. These descriptions will be useful in understanding the theory as it is described in the next sections.

B. The Theory

Central to the present theoretical idea is the notion of the motor program, usually defined as a set of prestructured (i.e., open-loop) muscle commands that, when executed, can carry out movement without involvement from peripheral

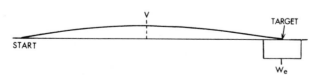

Figure 2 Hypothetical trajectory of a stylus during a rapid movement from a starting position to a target; W_e is the variability achieved in hitting the target over a number of trials.

feedback. [Incidentally, the Crossman-Goodeve (Note 1) and Keele (1968) models also assume that some sort of open-loop mechanism is responsible for control of the movement for the brief periods of time between corrections; the major difference between those theories and the present one is that we assume no within-movement corrections.] Recently, there has been increasing evidence that movement control—especially in rapid (e.g., 200-msec) movements—is carried out "open loop" (i.e., via the motor program), and support has come from both the neurosciences (Brooks, 1974) as well as from the motor-behavior area (Pew, 1974; Schmidt, 1975, 1976). Especially noteworthy are some very recent findings suggesting strongly that the motor program can control movement for far longer than the usual 200-msec estimate, probably for as long as 500–700 msec, and perhaps even for as long as 1300 msec (see Shapiro, 1977, for evidence). The theory assumes that a single tap such as that represented in Figures 1 and 2 are structured in advance; [2] the preprogrammed features include the initiation of agonist contraction, the cessation of agonist contraction, and the initiation of antagonist contraction (and the timing of this change in contraction).

Consider the initial half of the movement associated with acceleration. The area "under" the left half of the force-time curve in Figure 1 is the impulse for acceleration, and it can be thought of as the aggregate of forces applied to the limb in the direction of the target. The velocity of the movement when the accelerative impulse has ceased its action (at point V in Figure 2) can, via physical principles, be shown to be directly proportional to the impulse; doubling the impulse doubles the velocity at the end of acceleration.

$$\text{Impulse} \propto \text{Velocity}_{\text{after accel.}} \tag{2}$$

The next observation is that any factors that cause increased variability (within subjects over trials) in the impulse will be translated into proportional increases in the variability in velocity after acceleration. Thus,

$$\sigma \text{ Impulse} \propto \sigma \text{ Velocity}_{\text{after accel.}} \tag{3}$$

As indicated by the force waves in Figure 1, after this initial acceleration, the antagonists become activated to slow down the movement in order to strike the target. From Figure 2, it appears that, just after the start of the movement, the stylus increases its elevation from the plane of the target, achieving a maximum at about the center of the movement. It seems reasonable to assume that this movement in the vertical dimension, as well as the decrease in elevation as the stylus approaches the target, are programmed in advance together with other aspects of the movement. Since the time during which the movement is dropping

---

[2] Many motor-program theorists would, in fact, argue that a *series* of taps can be preprogrammed (e.g., Pew, 1966, 1974; Schmidt, 1975, 1976).

to the target is determined in advance, a movement with too much horizontal velocity at the approximate midpoint (due to variations in the size of the accelerative impulse—Eq. [3]) will have traveled too far in the horizontal dimension by the time it reaches the plane of the target; conversely, a movement with too little horizontal velocity at the midpoint will fall short of the aimed-for target. This observation, coupled with the reasoning in the previous paragraph, led us to suspect that the variability in the distance traveled in a single-aiming movement was somehow a function of the variabilities in the accelerative impulse. Recognizing that the variability in the total distance traveled is what we (and others dealing with the Fitts paradigm) have termed the effective target width (W_e), one can state the most important relation on which the theory is based: The effective target width (W_e) is directly proportional to the within-subject variability of the velocity after the end of acceleration. This velocity variability is, in turn, directly proportional to the variabilities in the impulse for acceleration. This relation would be hardly surprising to a physicist, but it leads to some important generalizations when we consider the *causes* of variability in the accelerative impulse. That is, if the movement is programmed, factors that increase the variability in the impulse are directly responsible for the size of W_e.

Early in our thinking we suspected that the variability in the force (i.e., the variability in the amplitude of the force/time curve) was directly related to the *amount* of force the subject was to produce. This was interesting, because any factor that would increase the force (e.g., asking the subject to decrease the movement time or to increase the movement distance) would also increase the variability in the impulse, and thus increase the variability in the movement endpoint W_e. For the moment, we will assume that

$$\sigma \text{ Force} \propto \text{Force;} \tag{4}$$

later, we shall describe two experiments that strongly support this assumption.

C. Effect of Movement Amplitude

For a movement with a constant movement time, what is the effect of movement amplitude (A) on the impulse variability and hence on W_e since they are proportional [Eq. (3)]? Consider the hypothetical curves shown in Figure 3. In Movement 2, the amplitude is assumed to be twice that of Movement 1, implying that the velocity at the termination of the accelerative impulse for Movement 2 will have to be twice that for Movement 1. Since the impulses are proportional to the velocity, the impulses for Movement 2 will be twice those for Movement 1, and this relationship is shown in the diagram. The important point is that the increased impulses for Movement 2 come about only because of increased force acting over a constant time (since the movement times are assumed to be the

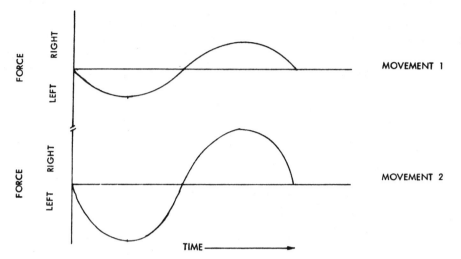

Figure 3   Hypothetical force traces for Movement 1 and Movement 2. Movement times for the two movements are assumed to be equal, but Movement 2 has twice the amplitude of Movement 1.

same for the two responses). Since increased force is associated with increased force variability [Eq. (4)], with constant movement time the effect of doubling movement amplitude (A) is to double the amplitude of the force waves, resulting in a doubled impulse variability. We may write

$$\sigma \text{ Impulse} \propto A. \tag{5}$$

Since we have argued that impulse variability is proportional to W_e, the expectation is that W_e is also proportional to A.

D. Effect of Movement Time

For a movement with a constant amplitude, what is the effect of halving MT? Assume that, in Figure 4, Movement 1 and Movement 2 have the same amplitude, but MT for Movement 1 is 300 msec and for Movement 2 is 150 msec. For now, assume that these movement *times* have no within-subject variability. Since Movement 2 requires twice the velocity as Movement 1, it seems clear that its impulses must be twice those of Movement 1 as well. However, notice that, for Movement 2, there is only one-half the time to develop impulses of twice the size. Thus, the amplitude of the force wave (i.e., the force produced) must be doubled once because the velocity is doubled, and it must be doubled again because there is only one-half the time to apply the force, so that the amplitudes of the force waves are four times as large in Movement 2 as they are in Movement 1. Since the variability in force produced is proportional to the force produced

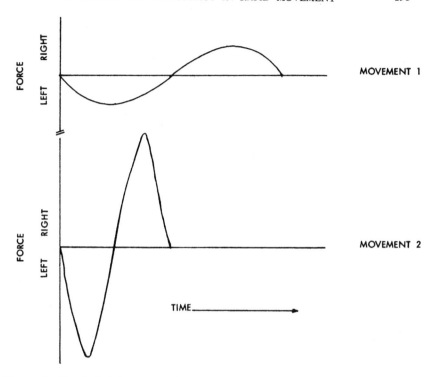

Figure 4   Hypothetical force waves for two movements. Movement 1 has a movement time of 300 msec, while Movement 2 has a movement time of 150 msec.

[Eq. (4)], *assuming no variability in movement time,* the impulse variability is inversely proportional to the square of the movement time, or

$$\sigma \text{ Impulse Amplitude } \propto \frac{1}{MT^2}. \tag{6}$$

However, this is not the entire answer, because the impulse size can be affected not only by changes in the vertical dimension (i.e., by variations in force), but also by variations in the horizontal dimension (i.e., by variations in the time the force is operating). In the preceding paragraph, we assumed (for the sake of clarity) that there was no within-subject variability in MT; this assumption is clearly untenable. If we now assume (again only for clarity) that there is no variability in the level of force produced, what is the effect of MT on the variability of the time during which the impulse is operating? There is evidence (e.g., Michon, 1967) that the longer an interval (like MT) to be "metered," the larger the variability in "metering" it; that is, a time interval and its within-subject variability are nearly directly proportional, or

$$\sigma \text{ Impulse Duration } \propto MT. \tag{7}$$

As with the assumption [Eq. (4)] about force and its variability, we offer Eq. (7) as an assumption here; we will provide evidence strongly supporting this assumption later.

Equation (7) suggests that, as the movement time is lengthened, there is a proportional increase in the variability of the timing of the onsets and offsets of the impulses. Therefore, *assuming a constant force amplitude,* increased variations in the timing of the impulses lead to proportional increases in the variability of the impulse, and we may write

$$\sigma \text{ Impulse} \propto MT. \tag{8}$$

This relation has relevance for understanding variations in W_e, since W_e is proportional to impulse variability [Eq. (3)].

If we now combine Eqs. (6) and (8), the effect of shortening the movement time has two, opposite effects on the impulse variability. Variability in the vertical component of the impulse (force amplitude) varies inversely as the square of the movement time, whereas variability in the horizontal component of the impulse (impulse duration) varies directly with the movement time. Combining these two effects, we see that

$$\sigma \text{ Impulse} \propto MT/MT^2 = 1/MT \tag{9}$$

and that impulse variability is inversely proportional to the movement time.

E. The Composite Model

In the preceding paragraphs, we have argued that impulse variability is the primary determinant of the endpoint variability (W_e) if the response is programmed and that impulse variability is systematically related to fundamental parameters of movement: A and MT. Putting together the information contained in Eqs. (5) and (9), it follows that impulse variability (and hence W_e) is directly proportional to movement amplitude (A) and inversely proportional to the movement time (MT), and we can write

$$W_e = \propto A/MT \tag{10}$$

as the basic statement of the model.

The clear implication of this model is that, as one asks the subject to move faster or farther, the subject does so with greater "noise" in his force- and time-production mechanisms, resulting in greater error in reaching the aimed-for target. The notion of the speed accuracy trade-off, represented by the Fitts equation, fits well into this idea, because it says that when the subject tries to move too quickly, he makes too many errors (which is unacceptable to the experimenter), and the subject slows down as a consequence. Thus, the present theory sees the limitation in the subject's movement time as an indirect result of his inability to be accurate because of variability in the force-production and time-production mechanisms; this is quite different from the Crossman–Goodeve

(Note 1) model, which suggests that the limitation in movement time is the number of corrections the subject must make in arriving at the endpoint.

V. Empirical Support for the Model

A. Experiments 1 and 2

Our first two experiments sought support for the assumption that the variability in force was proportional to the amount of force produced [Eq. (4)]. Subjects were asked to produce a series of brief (150-msec) bursts of force at a rate of one response every 800 msec (controlled by a metronome). The subject's arm was on a fixed lever with the right elbow flexed 90° and either the right hand (Experiment 1) grasping a handle or the right forearm (Experiment 2) resting against a padded plate. A strain gauge was attached so that forces (flexion) produced against the handle or plate were displayed on an oscilloscope (visible to the subject) as well as on a strip-chart recorder. The subject's task was to make the oscilloscope dot "jump" to an indicated line; subjects were instructed to make no corrections within movements, with the burst being programmed and "ballistic." In Experiment 1, each subject practiced five 30-cycle bouts before receiving four 30-cycle test bouts at each of six forces (0.19, 0.38, 0.57, 0.76, 0.95, and 1.14 kg) presented in a randomized order. In Experiment 2, the forces were larger and we provided more initial practice; there were six loads (2.2, 4.3, 6.5, 8.6, 10.8, and 13.9 kg exerted through the plate 25 cm from the elbow), and subjects had ten 50-cycle practice bouts followed by five 30-cycle test bouts, presented in randomized order.

For both experiments we determined the within-subject relationship between the amount of force and the variability in force. In Experiment 1, there was a linear relation between the two measures; the individual correlations ranged from 0.91 to 0.99, with the mean r (computed via Z' transformations) being 0.95. In Experiment 2, the individual within-subject correlations between force and force variability ranged from 0.84 to 0.98, with the average r (again computed via Z' transformation) for six subjects being 0.95. The data (for Experiment 2) averaged across subjects, where average force is plotted against average within-subject variability of force, are plotted in Figure 5, and here the correlation was 0.99. The relationship appeared to be nearly linear; moreover, it can be said that changes in force caused *proportional* changes in force variability since the intercept was nearly zero (0.016 kg). Thus, our initial assumption that force and its variability are proportional appeared to be correct.

B. Experiment 3

In our next experiment, we sought evidence about the relationship between the variability in impulse length and the movement time, since earlier [Eq. (7)] we had assumed that these two variables are related proportionally. In Experi-

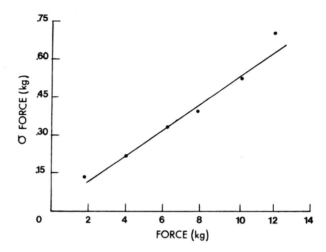

Figure 5   The relation between average force and variability in force (Experiment 2, data averaged across all six subjects).

ment 3, subjects were asked to make a series of oscillating movements of a lever constructed like that described in Experiments 1 and 2. They held a handle attached via a strain gauge to a lever that could rotate in the horizontal plane through 100° via elbow flexion and extension. There were four movement amplitudes (16, 32, 48, and 64°) and four movement times (200, 300, 400, and 500 msec), and each subject performed each of the 16 combinations of amplitude and movement time in a randomized order. Subjects attempted to move to a metronome set at the appropriate times; they tried to move through the appropriate distance, attempting to move as consistently as possible, avoiding within-movement corrections. The movement excursions and force waves produced were recorded simultaneously on strip-chart paper, and the movement excursions were simultaneously displayed via an oscilloscope visible to the subject.

The results strongly supported the assumption that the within-subject variability of the impulse duration and the movement time were linearly related. For individual subjects, the within-subject correlations ranged from 0.85 to 0.96, and the mean *r* (computed via *Z'* transformations) was 0.93. Figure 6 presents the data averaged across subjects, where the average variability in impulse duration is plotted as a function of average movement time, with a single point for each of the 16 combinations of movement time and movement amplitude (each point representing six subjects). The correlation for these data was 0.90. The relation seemed strongly linear; moreover, the movement time and the variability of the impulse duration appeared to be related *proportionally,* since the intercept was nearly zero (−4 msec). (Notice that in Figure 6 the abscissa is "broken" between 0 and 200 msec to save space; the line passes nearly through the origin when the abscissa is extended.)

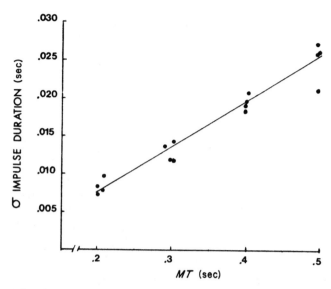

Figure 6   The relation between movement time (*MT*) and the variability in the duration of the impulses. (Experiment 3, data averaged across all six subjects.)

C. Experiment 4

Having provided strong evidence that the two earlier assumptions [Eqs. (4) and (7)], upon which the model presented in Eq. (10) was based, appeared tenable, the final experiment tested the basic prediction of the model: that movement endpoint variability (W_e) is linearly related to the ratio of A and MT. In Experiment 4, four subjects were instructed to make single aiming movements of a hand-held stylus to a target. The subjects began with the tip of the stylus on a starting position and moved horizontally to attempt to hit a dot (3 mm diameter) to the left. All moves were with the preferred hand (i.e., right) at the level of the tabletop, and the subject was positioned so that the target was in line with the midline of the body and in plain view. In keeping with our notion of experimentally manipulating distance and movement time (allowing W_e to be the single dependent variable), movement times were monitored via a millisecond clock, activated when the subject left the starting position and deactivated when a switch in the stylus closed on contact with the target area. Movement time was controlled by instructing he subject as to the desired movement time, and providing knowledge of results during the initial trials in order to train subjects to move at approximately the correct speed.

We studied nine movement conditions, made up of the factorial combination of three movement distances (10, 20, and 30 cm) and three movement times (140, 170, and 200 msec). Each subject performed in all combinations of A and MT, but in a different, randomized order. In each condition, there were 180 trials. The first 40 trials involved KR about movement time; subjects were instructed to move to the target in a movement time that was appropriate for that particular condition. After Trial 40, the remaining 140 trials were performed without KR about movement time, but if the subject deviated by more than 10% of the designated time he was told that he was too fast (or slow). This procedure was employed to encourage the subjects to concentrate on spatial accuracy. We scored only those movements whose movement times were within 10% of the target movement time.

Effective target widths (W_es) along the direction of the movement were measured via an electronic digitizer (Hewlett–Packard 9864A), and the SD of the endpoints were computed with a Hewlett-Packard 9830 lab computer. Errors in dimensions orthogonal to the direction of the movement were ignored in this analysis; that is, errors were scored in relation to an imaginary line through the target which was perpendicular to the movement direction.

Figure 7 shows the W_e scores as a joint function of the A and MT. The mean number of responses (out of the last 140 trials) that met the 10% movement-time criterion ranged from 103 to 127 (overall mean = 115). Both A and MT seemed to produce systematic effects on W_e, with W_e being linearly related to A, and greater MTs resulting in smaller W_es. Both of these effects were significant, with $F(2,6) = 21.37$ for MT, and $F(2,6) = 175.49$ for A, $ps < .01$. An interesting feature of these data is the apparent tendency for the effects of MT and A to be additive, as shown by the nearly parallel curves for the different movement times; this observation was supported by the fact that the effects of A and MT did not interact statistically, $F(4, 12) = .68$, $p > .05$.

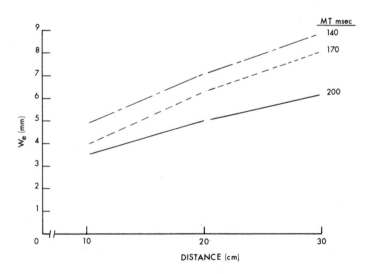

Figure 7 The effect of movement amplitude and movement time on effective target width (W_e). (Experiment 4, data averaged for all four subjects.)

From the point of view of the model, though, the more informative aspect of Experiment 4 was the relation between W_e and the ratio of A and MT. In Figure 8 we have plotted the average A divided by the average MT (for each subject separately, with this mean averaged across the four subjects) against the average W_e. The plot seemed generally linear across a four-fold increase in A/MT, especially when the faster MTs are considered. Using all nine data points, the correlation between A/MT and W_e was 0.97. This initial attempt to show that the model holds for single, rapid aiming responses seemed particularly promising.

VI. Strengths, Limitations, and Future Directions

We have been excited about the possibilities provided by the present model for a number of reasons. First, it is derived from physical principles that have been well understood for centuries; there has been no need to argue from questionable assumptions as is often the case with theories in our field. Second, the assumptions we were forced to make early in the project—namely (a) that force and the variability in force were proportional and (b) that movement time and the variability in the impulse length were proportional—were strongly supported in Experiments 1, 2, and 3. Finally our initial attempts to predict W_e from the ratio of A and MT according to the model resulted in a reasonably strong linear relationship. Our enthusiasm about these initial findings had us believing that

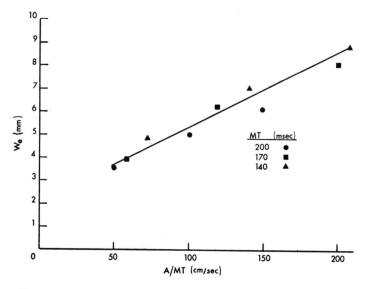

Figure 8 The relation between effective target width (W_e) and the ratio of the movement amplitude (A) and the movement time (MT). (Experiment 4, data averaged for all four subjects.)

Equation 10 describes the relationship among some of the most fundamental aspects of movement control—the movement speed, the movement distance, and the movement accuracy.

But when the euphoric state subsided, we saw that there are a number of problems and unanswered questions that do not permit such enthusiasm just yet. First, the model predicts that the function relating A/MT to W_e should pass through the origin—that is, that W_e and A/MT should be proportional. An examination of Figure 8 shows that the relation is clearly not a proportional one, and that a constant of 2.08 mm is needed in order to fit the points with a linear equation (i.e., $W_e = 2.08 + 0.33 \ (A/MT)$). One possibility is that errors in measurement (scoring, etc.) for all of the data points increased the measured W_e by a constant amount. We attempted to assess the magnitude of the errors associated with recording the data points, positioning the paper on the digitizer, etc., and the value of this error in measurement was approximately .6 mm, considerably less than the 2.08 mm shown in the intercept for Figure 8. Thus, while some of the deviation from proportionality can perhaps be accounted for by errors in recording and the like, it seems clear that all of the deviation cannot. Another possibility is that the relation between A/MT and W_e breaks down when the velocity is very low (i.e., when A/MT is very close to zero). Karl Newell has suggested in a personal communication (Newell, Note 5) that the accurate recruitment of motor units for very small impulses is particularly difficult for the subject, and that this is accentuated by tremor and other sources of noise in the motor system. Whatever the reason, the departure from proportionality is a problem in the present model, and research is currently under way to investigate it. [For a report of further work on these issues, see Schmidt, Zelaznik, Hawkins, Frank, and Quinn (Note 6).]

Another aspect of Experiment 4 that deserves comment is the apparent additivity of the effects of A and MT on W_e. It could be argued that the lack of statistical interaction between A and MT was caused by low power associated with the use of only four subjects. While this is certainly possible, the curves in Figure 7 appeared to be relatively stable, suggesting a minimum of error variability. Also, there was almost no tendency for the curves to converge as A increased, with the curves appearing to be remarkably parallel. The model predicts that the effects of A and the effects of MT should cause particular changes in W_e because they each produce specific changes in the variability of the velocity of the response at the end of acceleration. When, in Eq. (10), we combined these separate effects to form the composite model, the implication was clearly that these effects sum in direct proportion to the amount of change in each. We, therefore, regard the additivity of the A and MT effects as providing an addition at line of support for the model.

Finally, what are the boundary conditions surrounding the model, especially those with respect to movement time? In Figure 8, there is the suggestion that the slope of the curve for the 200-msec movements (filled circles) appears to be somewhat lower than for the remainder of the movements (140 and 170 msec). It is possible that this is simply "noise" in the data, of course; but if this difference is reliable, it could perhaps indicate that subjects were beginning to use visual feedback to correct the movements in progress when the movement times were 200 msec, with more rapid movements being performed without visual corrections. Keele and Posner (1968) found that the time required to process visual feedback in movements very much like those in Experiment 4 was from 190–250 msec, adding some support to this interpretation. It may be the case that 200 msec represents a movement-time boundary condition for the model, above which corrections can be applied to reduce W_e below the predicted value determined by the ratio of A and MT. With movement times greater than 200 msec, the subject could execute a violent initial impulse (with a great deal of variability in the resulting velocity), assess the errors that will be produced, and initiate another motor program to correct for the impending error. Taken to its logical conclusion, when the movement time is very long (e.g., 1000 msec), with a 20-cm movement, the nature of the noise in the initial impulse is nearly irrelevant for the accurate arrival at the target, since ample time is available for corrections; the slope between A/MT and W_e in this case should be nearly zero, and W_es would be quite small. It therefore seems clear that there will be some MT above which the relation between A/MT and W_e will no longer hold, and the lower boundary of this change might be 200 msec.

Does this imply that the relevance of the model presented here is limited to movements with durations less than 200 msec? We do not think so. A working hypothesis at this stage is that the present model breaks down when movement times are long only if the subject is monitoring endpoint accuracy. Presumably, if such movements are not monitored, they must be governed by a program whose execution time might be far longer than 200 msec (see Shapiro, 1977, for evidence of 700-msec movements that seem to be programmed). The law defining the accuracy of such programs could be approximated by the expression described here—the accuracy is proportional to the average velocity. When we stop to consider that the overwhelming majority of the movements we make in daily life are not monitored in a way similar to attempting to hit a target with a stylus (e.g., leg movements in walking, or movements in parts of the body that are not primarily responsible for accuracy), the model would seem to have a great deal of potential applicability. For that class of movements that are visually guided (or guided by some other feedback channel), it is reasonable that the best description of the relation among A, MT, and W_e might be the Fitts equation, judging from the robustness of this formulation in past research using this kind of movement.

To the extent that the foregoing is correct, it would seem that a logical research goal would be to combine the present model, which seems to describe the accuracy of programmed movements, with other models (such as Fitts') that seem to provide a description of feedback-guided movements. Such a model would provide a much needed description of movements over the entire range of movement times.

Acknowledgments

Thanks are due to E. R. F. W. Crossman, S. W. Keele, S. T. Klapp, and A. T. Welford for helpful comments on an earlier draft of this paper.

Reference Notes

1. Crossman, E. R. F. W., & Goodeve, P. J. Feedback control of hand movements and Fitts' law. *Proceedings of the Experimental Society.* Oxford, England, 1963. Unpublished.
2. Pew, R. W. Personal communication, April, 1977.
3. Wade, M. G., Newell, K. M., & Wallace, S. A. *Decision time and movement time as a function of response complexity in retarded persons.* Unpublished manuscript, Institute for Child Behavior and Development, University of Illinois at Urbana-Champaign, 1977.
4. Langolf, G. D. *Human motor performance in precise microscopic work.* Unpublished Ph.D dissertation, University of Michigan, 1973.
5. Newell, K. M. Personal communication, March, 1978.
6. Schmidt, R. A., Zelaznik, H. N., Hawkins, B. M., Frank, J. S., & Quinn, J. T., Jr. *Motor output variability: A theory for the accuracy of programmed motor acts.* Manuscript under review, May, 1978.

References

Beggs, W. D. A., & Howarth, C. I. The accuracy of aiming at a target—some further evidence for intermittant control. *Acta Psychologica,* 1972, *36,* 171–177.
Brooks, V. B. Some examples of programmed limb movements. *Brain Research,* 1974, *71,* 299–308.
Fitts, P. M. The information capacity of the human motor system in controlling the amplitude of movement. *Journal of Experimental Psychology,* 1954, *47,* 381–391.
Hick, W. E. On the rate of gain of information. *Quarterly Journal of Experimental Psychology,* 1952, *4,* 11–26.
Keele, S. W. Movement control in skilled motor performance. *Psychological Bulletin,* 1968, *70,* 387–403.
Keele, S. W., & Posner, M. I. Processing of feedback in rapid movements. *Journal of Experimental Psychology,* 1968, *77,* 155–158.
Klapp, S. T. Feedback versus motor programming in the control of aimed movements. *Journal of Experimental Psychology: Human Perception and Performance,* 1975, *104,* 147–153.
Langolf, G. D., Chaffin, D. B., & Foulke, J. A. An investigation of Fitts' law using a wide range of movement amplitudes. *Journal of Motor Behavior,* 1976, *8,* 113–128.
Michon, J. A. *Timing in temporal tracking.* Soesterberg, The Netherlands: Institute for Perception RVO–TNO, 1967.

Pew, R. W. Acquisition of hierarchical control over the temporal organization of a skill. *Journal of Experimental Psychology*, 1966, *71*, 764–771.

Pew, R. W. Human perceptual-motor performance. In B. H. Kantowitz (Ed.), *Human information processing: Tutorials in performance and cognition.* New York: Erlbaum, 1974.

Schmidt, R. A. A schema theory of discrete motor skill learning. *Psychological Review*, 1975, *82*, 225–260.

Schmidt, R. A. Control processes in motor skills. *Exercise and Sport Sciences Reviews*, 1976, *4*, 229–261.

Shapiro, D. C. A preliminary attempt to determine the duration of a motor program. In D. M. Landers & R. W. Christina (Eds.), *Psychology of motor behavior and sport* (Vol. 1). Urbana, Illinois: Human Kinetics, 1977.

Welford, A. T. *Fundamentals of skill.* London: Methuen, 1968.

10

Testing Tapping Time-Sharing: Attention Demands of Movement Amplitude and Target Width

Barry H. Kantowitz
James L. Knight, Jr.

I. Introduction

This chapter is concerned primarily with the attentional demands of a simple voluntary positioning movement. This topic closely fits the theme of this volume since we try to show how an understanding of motor control and performance can be aided by an information-processing approach. To set the stage for the present experiment, we first review four topics that together offer a framework for this research: aiming and motor control, information processing and aiming, previous efforts on tapping time-sharing, and the specific rationale for the present experiment. After presenting the results and other details, we conclude with a discussion of general issues in the time-sharing of motor skills.

Information Processing in
Motor Control and Learning

II. Aiming and Motor Control

The study of voluntary positioning movements is a venerable topic in experimental psychology with antecedents as early as the nineteenth century (Woodworth, 1899). While the decade 1968–1978 has seen many psychologists turn away from the study of skills and human performance (see Kantowitz, 1975) in favor of more cognitive and mentalistic endeavours such as psycholinguistics, there has been a resurgence of interest in skill behavior (Stelmach, 1976) due to the development of information-processing techniques relevant to motor control (Kantowitz, 1974a, especially Chapters 1–3) and to the researchers in physical education and movement science who have eagerly applied these techniques to issues in motor behavior. It appears that this coalition of psychologists and movement scientists may restore the field to the central position it held at the beginning of the twentieth century.

A simple positioning movement requires an individual, sometimes called a subject (psychology jargon) or an operator (engineering jargon), to relocate a pointer such as a stylus or a finger by executing a spatial movement to reach a well-defined target position. The experimenter who induces such a voluntary movement is interested primarily in the speed and accuracy with which the pointer gets from here to there. How the pointer gets to the target is of considerably less interest and it is the rare experimenter who places any constraints upon the path of the movement (e.g., Kvålseth, 1973). This differs substantially from research on tracking, where the subject is instructed to keep to the path at all costs. Such simple positioning movements are part of our everyday actions and except for engineering psychologists and motor skill researchers few people devote much thought to the problems involved in picking up a pencil or actuating an electrical switch.

In 1899, Woodworth conceived of a simple positioning movement as consisting of two components, and his distinction is still valid and frequently used. He termed the lift-off or start of the movement *initial impulse* and the terminal portion *current control*. This latter term implied that feedback information was used to guide the movement, thus influencing its accuracy. This early concept of sensory feedback or retroflex (Troland, 1928) remains one of the key ideas that govern theoretical explanations of motor control.

Since there is no strong path constraint in the typical aiming task, one common conception (Keele, 1968; Pew, 1974; Crossman & Goodeve, Note 1) is based upon the idea that the subject uses feedback information to make corrective movement based not on his deviation from some preselected path (as would, for example, an airplane pilot being told he is currently 50 ft above the glidepath), but on the relative positions of the pointer and the target or goal. When this is put mathematically (in a first-order difference equation), movement time (MT) can be shown to be a linear function of an index of difficulty (ID) defined by Fitts

(1954) as $\log_2(2A/W)$, where A is the distance to be moved (amplitude of movement) and W is the target width. This linear function has been widely replicated, provides a very good fit to data, and is often celebrated as Fitts' law. The reciprocal of the slope of the Fitts' law function is frequently interpreted as a rate of gain of information or channel capacity for the human central processor in charge of movement generation. Fitts and Peterson (1964) compared discrete positioning movements to the continuous back-and-forth movements required by Fitts (1954) and attributed the lower slope of the discrete Fitts' law function to additional feedback-monitoring requirements imposed by the continuous task. There was a slight artifact in that this comparison was biased because the continuous tapping task of Fitts (1954) included time spent in contact with the targets as part of MT, but when this is removed (Megaw, 1975) the conclusion remains unchanged.

Although terminology has changed, current views about simple positioning movements bear a strong resemblance to the position stated by Woodworth (1899). A ballistic or open-loop initial movement phase is followed by a closed-loop phase in which the processing of feedback information controls pointer position until the target is reached. The open-loop portion of movement is quite often said to be under the control of a *motor program* (Keele & Summers, 1976). This attractive analogy is borrowed, as are many of the concepts in the psychology of information processing, from computer programming. A motor program is a higher-level theoretical concept inferred from behavior and even less observable than an operating computer program. While it is difficult to find an extremely precise definition of the concept, it is generally agreed that a motor program consists of some central representation of a series of sequential actions or commands performed as a molar unit without benefit of feedback; that is, later segments of the program are performed with no reference to peripheral feedback that may arise from execution of earlier program segments. Since the most compelling argument in favor of motor programs in humans operates by default— How else could a skilled performer (such as a pianist or a typist) do it so fast? —some researchers are skeptical about the utility of this concept (Adams, 1976; Pew, 1974). While we introduce the concept because it is necessary to understand skill research, if not also skill behavior, we refuse to take sides in this debate and maintain an agnostic position, since, as we shall explain, our results can be accommodated with or without motor programs.

However, once motor programs are allowed, even if only for the sake of argument, the possibility of preprogramming emerges (Glencross, 1973; Klapp, 1975). By linking analogies, Glencross likens the organization of the elements of a movement to a computer language assembler or compiler. (This analogy is of course recursive since an assembler or compiler is itself a computer program.) As the complexity of a prospective movement increases, so does the time needed to select and assemble (or compile) the requisite elements of a motor program.

Klapp (1975) has used this concept to explain the results of an experiment similar to that of Fitts and Peterson (1964), except with far shorter movement amplitudes. For these short programmed movements, MT and reaction time (RT—the time between onset of a signal indicating which of two targets was the goal and lift-off of the pointer) increased as target width decreased, but only MT increased with increasing movement amplitude. Klapp interpreted the increase in RT as added programming time needed for the more precise, and therefore more complex, movement. However, if this explanation is accepted, the increase in MT is embarrassing. Since the short movement is programmed and not dependent on feedback processing, as are longer movements, Fitts' law does not apply, and there is no obvious reason for an increase in MT. Indeed, since the greater complexity of the response has already been accounted for by increased assembly time, we might expect MT to remain constant. While Klapp (1975) did not directly address this problem, perhaps he might have explained it quite simply by noting that, by definition, more complex movements require greater MT. This would also explain why MT increased when amplitude increased, even though the amplitude was still short enough to qualify as a programmed movement. However, we then have the problem of RT not increasing even though movement complexity did, as evidenced by increased MT. This confusion becomes even greater when we realize that targets were placed symmetrically about the home (starting) position. A "smart" assembler would have the movement program completely assembled except for a parameter indicating direction of motion. Since the targets were symmetric, the movements in either direction appear to be equally complex. Furthermore, Fitts and Radford (1966) found that allowing unlimited preparation time did not alter MT. Finally, RT and MT were not operationally independent in Klapp's experiment. The subject could trade off MT for RT by simply lifting off the pointer before he was completely prepared to move and then waiting briefly before executing a movement. This would decrease RT at the expense of MT and might explain the finding of increased MT and constant RT. Believing by fiat that RT and MT measure different mental operations in a discrete Fitts' law task can be dangerous when only main effects are considered. This assumption is far more testable when patterns of interaction and additivity, rather than main effects, are sought (Kantowitz, 1969). Therefore, although we are on the fence about motor programs, we are skeptical about assembling and compiling them. Even the best analogy can be carried overboard.

III. Aiming and Information Processing: Attention Demands of Movement

If the preceding two-phase division of a simple aiming movement is correct, we would expect that a movement segment controlled by a motor program or initial impulse would not require attention (Bahrick & Shelley, 1958), and, indeed, it has occasionally been suggested that devoting attention to such a movement would impair its execution (Bliss, 1892–1893; Posner & Keele, 1969). However, movement segments controlled by the processing of feedback information should require attention. Attention can be a complicated concept in psychology, with multiple meanings (see Kantowitz, 1974b) that exceed the scope of this chapter. Here we shall limit our use of the term to a double-stimulation or multiple-task situation, in which a deficit on secondary task performance indicates an attentional demand of a primary task. In this section, we will discuss techniques that have been used to assess the attentional requirements of aimed movements. Since time or lag has been occasionally used as an index of attention (Broadbent, 1965), the reader must be careful not to confuse the distinction between time/accuracy requirements and attentional demands (Kerr, 1973). In turn, we shall be careful not to use RT per se as an indicant of attention and will not claim that operations requiring greater time necessarily also demand more attention. Instead, we shall limit our discussion to instances where attention is measured by imposing a secondary task to be performed with a primary aiming movement.

A. Probe Task

When the secondary task is a discrete reaction-time task, most often with a motor response component of limited movement amplitude and precision, such as a keypress, it is called a *probe* in the terminology of human information processing. The logic behind the probe task and some of the methodological cautions associated with it have been discussed by Kantowitz (1974b, pp. 123–124). Increases in probe RT relative to a control condition in which only the probe task is performed are interpreted as indicating attentional demands of the primary task. Under certain conditions this interpretation is likely to be valid.

Posner and Keele (1969) used a simple RT probe and found probe RT to be greater for a small target than for a large target. Both targets showed elevated RT relative to a single-stimulation control condition. An advantage of the probe technique is that, by varying the presentation time of the probe, it can sweep out attentional demands over different portions of the movement. Posner and Keele found a U-shaped function with elevated RT at the start and termination of a simple wrist rotation. A similar study also performed at the University of Oregon by Ells (1973) improved considerably on the Posner–Keele study by using a two-choice probe and a greater number of experimental conditions. Again, probe RT was greater for a narrow than for a wide target and less for a control condition. However, contrary to earlier results, probe RT in two experiments consistently decreased as the pointer approached the target. Neither of these two findings fits well with the two-phase model of simple aiming that predicts monotonically increased probe RT as the target is approached, and sensory feedback must be monitored. Indeed, the contradictory results of the two studies might even suggest that using a probe to measure attention is more complex than might appear at first.

This complexity was demonstrated by Salmoni, Sullivan, and Starkes (1976) in ways intended and unintended. They noted that an important procedural difference between the Posner–Keele and Ells studies was probe probability, which was 0.66 in the earlier study and 1.0 in the Ells study. When the probe is considered as a case of double stimulation, S_2 probability would be expected to have an effect upon performance (Kantowitz, 1974b). They therefore repeated a similar experiment with probe probabilities of 0.33, 0.66, and 1.0. When probe RT was plotted as a function of probe position, U-shaped functions were obtained for the first two conditions, whereas a monotonically decreasing function was found when the probe was presented continuously. This neatly resolved the discrepancy as a methodological artifact. Unfortunately, Salmoni et al. neglected to include a control condition with a block of trials in which no probe was ever presented, an especially relevant control condition considering that one group of subjects always received the probe stimulus ($p = 1.0$). Indeed, such a blocked single-stimulation control condition is desirable even for conditions with probabilistic probes (Kantowitz, 1974b) since is it logically possible that performance on the no-probe control trials might vary as a function of no-probe probability. Indeed, if only for reasons of symmetry, let alone models of double stimulation, we might reasonably expect that, if probe probability has an effect on probe RT, then perhaps nonprobe probability would affect the primary task. A blocked single-stimulation condition would remove any doubts on this score. Indeed, Salmoni et al. did not present a comparison of MT data for probe and no-probe trials, so the reader cannot determine if the basic assumption of the probe paradigm, that the probe does not affect attention allocation to the primary task, was satisfied.

Salmoni et al. conclude that all probe researchers should standardize upon a probe probability of 0.667. The kindest remark we can offer about this suggestion is that it is naive. It completely ignores any theoretical implications of the probe technique and, if adopted, would produce an extremely limited view of attention that could potentially be shattered by any upstart researcher who used a probe probability of 0.443. While we are sympathetic and well aware of the problem Salmoni et al. are trying to solve, tunnel vision or blinders are not the best answers. We prefer to attempt to understand the theoretical implications of a probe methodology, even though this is complex. There are several alternative solutions, such as using payoff matrices to control division of attention between primary and secondary tasks and examining micro- and macroperformance operating characteristics (Kantowitz & Knight, 1976b), and the choice among them cannot be made without an appreciation of the theoretical implication of each technique. There is no magic panacea for measuring attention that eliminates the need for thought.

By now the point we are trying to make should be clear. Probe methodology is not without many pitfalls. To use this technique requires that several assumptions be validated. This in turn requires an adequate experimental design with perhaps redundant control conditions. We deliberately use the word "perhaps" because unless these "extra" blocked control conditions (among others) are tested, one can never know that they are unnecessary. Having one control condition too many is far better than having one too few. These methodological considerations have been discussed at great length by Kerr (1973) and by Kantowitz (1974b, 1978) and we urge researchers to take these points into account.

IV. Previous Research concerning Tapping Time-Sharing

We will briefly discuss four published experiments where a primary Fitts' law tapping task was combined with a secondary task. The earliest experiment (Kantowitz, 1969) was quite similar to that of Fitts and Peterson (1964) except that a second stimulus (S_2) followed the stimulus indicating that movement to the left or right target was demanded. The interstimulus interval (ISI) between these two stimuli was quite short so that S_2 occurred before the pointer could be lifted. No response was demanded by S_2 so the paradigm can be schematized as S_1-R_1,S_2. Furthermore, since S_2 was always the only remaining stimulus light it conveyed no information once S_1 had occurred. The rationale for this procedure is beyond the scope of this chapter (but see Kantowitz, 1974b), but it was related to models of double stimulation and psychological refractoriness. The results are shown in Figure 1. While Fitts' law clearly holds, the intercept varies systematically with ISI. Movement time increased as S_2 approached S_1—the signal to move left or right. Since S_2 occurred before movement started, it is difficult to explain this increment in MT as being associated with processing of sensory feedback arising from motion. As was noted by Kantowitz (1969), these data reject the conclusion of Fitts and Peterson that RT and MT are independent and reflect the action of different mental operations, although this view of the discrete tapping task is still widely maintained (e.g., Ells, 1973; Klapp, 1975). Instead, these data suggested that a molar response selection process could be modified by the output of earlier processing stages resulting in decrements in response execution. Indeed, Kantowitz (1969) speculated that the ISI independent variable introduced noise into the input of a motor control stage. This definition of a stage differs from that of Sternberg (1969) since it allows an independent variable to affect the output as well as the duration of processing stages.

This research suggested that processing associated with S_2 interfered with movement execution, perhaps by removing necessary capacity from the processing stage(s) controlling response execution. While this could have been tested further by requiring an overt response to S_2, such a paradigm would have had the drawbacks discussed earlier (see Section III,A). Indeed, a probe methodology might be particularly inappropriate if, as was suspected, capacity could be reallocated among processing stages.

In light of this, a time-sharing paradigm was selected for the remaining experi-

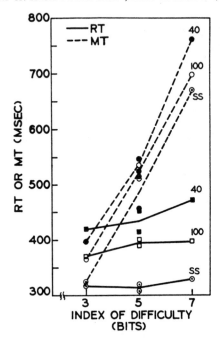

Figure 1   Mean latencies as a function of ID. SS, single-stimulation control condition; 40, 40-msec interstimulus interval double-stimulation condition; 100, 100-msec interval [Data from Kantowitz (1969). Copyright 1969 by the American Psychological Association. Reprinted by permission.]

ments. Kantowitz and Knight (1974) combined a secondary digit-naming task with the tapping task. Tapping was continuous and paced at a rate of 2 taps/sec. While this procedure is the inverse of the original Fitts (1954) task where tapping was self-paced, Bainbridge and Sanders (1972) have shown Fitts' law to be equally applicable to this paced procedure. Naming was unpaced so that the number of emitted digits was the dependent variable for the secondary task. The self-paced continuous secondary task allowed subjects to adjust secondary load over automatic and attention-demanding segments of the primary movement task. An important methodological feature of this experiment, not always seen in studies of time-sharing, was to incorporate more than one level of task difficulty, in addition to single-stimulation control conditions of tapping only and naming only, for both primary *and* secondary tasks. The need for this was spelled out by Kantowitz and Knight (1976a, Figures 1 and 2) and their argument will not be repeated here. For our purposes, we merely note that their results stressed processing demands of a response execution and control stage that required attention. Two experiments by Kantowitz and Knight (1976a) replicated and extended the generality of these findings, leading to the model shown in Figure 2, which

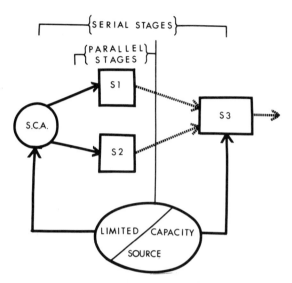

Figure 2 The hybrid model of Kantowitz and Knight (1976a). Solid lines represent capacity allocation to stages, whereas dotted lines represent information flow between stages. The information flow inputs to stages 1 and 2 (S1 and S2) have been deleted to improve the clarity of the diagram. A limited-capacity source dynamically feeds both S3 and a static-capacity allocator (S.C.A.), which partitions capacity between S1 and S2. S1 and S2 operate in parallel and S3 operates in serial with both preceding stages. Each stage can potentially be broken down into smaller stages depending on the level of analysis. For example, S3 is a molar representation of response selection, execution, and control processes. [From Kantowitz and Knight (1976a). Copyright 1976 by North-Holland Publishing Co. Reprinted by permission.]

is an extension of an earlier response-conflict model (Kantowitz, 1974b). Rather than giving the stages such fanciful names as "stimulus–response translator," "pattern normalizer," and "memory scanner," as is often done, we have modestly labeled them S1 (Stage 1) and so forth to help us refrain from believing too deeply in our analogies. In information-processing flow diagrams of this type, stages are named by fiat according to the investigator's belief about what an independent variable really controls. Hence, the safest procedure is merely to label the stages with the name of the independent variable, as was done, for example, by Kantowitz (1969). However, few researchers can resist the temptation to make larger statements, thereby increasing the generality of their models. Since these early theoretical statements often lack the support of converging operations that help define processing stages, there is a danger that "meaningful" stage names may be only reifications (Kantowitz & Roediger, 1978, Chapter 1), and so humility seems the best course.

S1 is an early stage that processes tapping information, and S2 deals with naming digits. Both stages feed into a bottleneck, S3, that handles response organization and execution; a more detailed portrait of S3 was given by Kantowitz (1974b, Figure 4). Kantowitz and Knight (1976a) explain how this model accommodates patterns of interaction and additivity when tapping and digit naming are time-shared. The next study focuses on capacity demands of S3 when movement amplitude and target width are orthogonally manipulated.

V. Attention Demands of Movement Amplitude and Target Width

The studies discussed earlier that evaluated attention demands of movement (Posner & Keele, 1969; Ells, 1973) concluded that narrow targets required more attention that wide targets. Fitts' law states that the information-processing demands reflected in movement time depend on both movement amplitude and target width. Since the earlier studies did not investigate changes in movement amplitude, although Posner and Keele did suggest, based upon memory research, that large movements might not require attention, three logical possibilities remain: Target width controls attention demands, movement amplitude controls attention demands, and Fitts' index of difficulty controls attention demands. If the last possibility holds, then the first two are trivial since a change in either target width or movement amplitude will cause a change in index of difficulty. The two-phase model of aiming discussed earlier (see Section II) would clearly imply that narrower targets require greater attention since more feedback information must be processed. It also implies that, as movement amplitude is decreased, a larger proportion of the total movement is devoted to current control so that attention demands should increase. Since the two-phase model does not specify detailed trade-offs between the phases, it is mute on the possibility that the Fitts' ID acounts for attention demands of both movement amplitude and target width.

The logic of the present experiment is simple. A dual-task methodology is used to assess attention demands of movement in preference to the probe methodology discussed in Section III,A. As Table I shows, ID is held constant at 4 or 6 bits while either movement amplitude or target width is varied. This will allow us to separate and unconfound effects of amplitude, width, and ID.

A. Method

1. Subjects

Twenty right-handed males participated as partial fulfillment of an introductory psychology course requirement at Purdue University.

2. Apparatus

Event timing and data recording were controlled by an Automated Data Systems 1800E minicomputer with a crystal timebase accurate to 0.1 msec. The tapping apparatus was an improved version of that used by Kantowitz and

Knight (1974). Symmetric target pairs were etched on heavy-duty printed circuit stock. This enabled targets to be rapidly and accurately changed by plugging in the appropriate circuit board. Targets were 10 cm deep with the distances between target centers (A) and target widths (W) specified in Table I. Two cylindrical pacing lights 27 cm long were placed behind the targets, as shown in Figure 3. A light (28 g), pencil-like stylus, connected by a thin wire to the computer, was used by subjects to tap between target plates in time with the pacing lights, which cycled at a rate of 2 taps/sec. Target hits, undershoot and overshoot errors were recorded by the computer.

Digits were visually displayed on a small (1 × 1 cm) L.E.D. cell mounted equidistant between the two targets so that they were placed symmetrically on either side of it. The subject was seated with the midline of his body aligned with the L.E.D. cell. The verbal responses made to the digits were sensed by a microphone and voice-actuated relay interfaced with the computer. This voice-relay system could respond at rates of up to 10 Hz. Activation of the voice-relay system resulted in the immediate presentation of the next visual digit.

3. Design

Each of the 20 subjects participated in two experimental sessions on consecutive days. Each session consisted of 21 trials. During each 60-sec trial subjects performed either experimenter-paced continuous tapping, self-paced digit naming, or both simultaneously.

Target pairs had an index of difficulty (ID) of either 4 or 6 bits. Since tapping

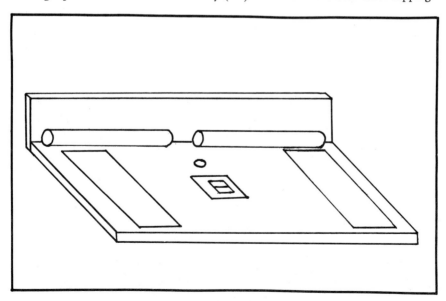

Figure 3 The experimental apparatus.

was performed at a rate of 2 taps/sec, perfect performance would generate either 8 or 12 bits/sec of transmitted information. As Table I shows, six target pairs were used in each experimental session. These were combined with two levels of the digit-naming task: Name the digit (N) or subtract the digit from 9 $(9 - N)$. Kantowitz and Knight (1974, 1976a) found these manipulations of stimulus–response complexity to differ in performance. This produced 12 dual-task trials (6 sets of targets $\times$ 2 levels of naming). Another 8 trials were allocated to performance of tapping or naming alone (6 tapping + 2 naming). These 20 trial types were arranged according to a 20 $\times$ 20 digram-balanced Latin square with one subject assigned randomly to each row. In the second experimental session, the 20 trial types were administered in the reverse order used for the first session. In addition, each session began with one practice trial requiring time-sharing between tapping (Table I, target plates C6) and $9 - N$.

As Table I shows, the two ID values were achieved with different combinations of A and W. In the varied width(VW) session, three values of A were selected and, for each of these values of A, two values of W were chosen to achieve the desired IDs. Thus, the effects of changing target width could be observed at three levels of movement amplitude. For the varied amplitude (VA) session, A and W changed roles relative to Session VW. Note that some target sets (A6, B6,

Table I
Target Dimensions and Codes Used in Sessions VW and VA

Movement amplitude, A (cm) (center-to-center target separation)	Session VW			
	ID bits [a]		ID bits [b]	
	4	6	4	6
10.2	1.25	0.35	C4	A6
20.5	2.50	0.70	D4	B6
41.0	5.00	1.25	E4	C6

Target width, W (cm)	Session VA			
	ID bits [c]		ID bits [d]	
	4	6	4	6
0.35	2.7	10.2	A4	A6
0.70	5.2	20.5	B4	B6
1.25	10.2	41.0	C4	C6

[a] The entries are target widths, W, in centimeters.
[b] The entries are target codes (e.g., for target set C4, $A = 10.2$ cm and $W = 1.25$ cm).
[c] The entries are movement amplitudes, A, in centimeters.
[d] The entries are target codes (e.g., for target set A4, $W = 0.35$ cm and $A = 2.7$ cm).

C4, and C6) were used in both Sessions VA and VW. This permits a control comparison between sessions. Ten subjects experienced Session VA first, whereas the remaining 10 had the opposite order (VW–VA).

4. Procedure

Subjects were tested individually. At the start of each 60-sec trial, they were told either to name digits, to tap, or to do both together. Digit series, when presented, consisted of the digits 1–8 presented in random order. The pacing lights alternated at the 2/sec rate even when only digit naming was required in order to make all conditions as comparable as possible. Digit responses were manually recorded by the experimenter so that their accuracy could be determined. (Our minicomputer cannot yet recognize spoken digits.) Instructions emphasized the importance of accurate and well-timed tapping and further indicated that digit-task performance was less important in dual-task conditions. About 2 min of rest was provided between successive trials.

B. Results

1. Digit-Naming Performance

Table II shows the mean number of correct digit responses (CDR) emitted during the various 60-sec trial types. As expected, the N transformation produced more correct responses (mean $= 59.9$) than did the $9 - N$ transformation (41.5), $F(1, 19) = 24.81$, $p < 0.001$, $MS_e = 1113$. Also as expected, fewer correct digit responses were emitted in dual-task conditions with the 6-bit target (43.0 CDR) than with the 4-bit target (49.8 CDR), $F(1, 19) = 48$, $p < 0.001$, $MS_e = 115$.

Now we come to the main purpose of this experiment: Did secondary digit-naming performance depend upon the manner in which ID was manipulated, that is, by changes in amplitude and width separately, or can ID account for secondary task performance by itself? Rephrasing this, are there attention demands of changing movement amplitude or target width beyond those that can be accommodated by the concomitant alteration of ID that necessarily accompanies variation in A or W? Happily, Table II is quite clear on this point, revealing that the manner in which ID was changed was unimportant. When amplitude was varied (Session VA) the 6-bit ID produced 49.4 CDR, as compared with 50.2 CDR when width was varied (Session VW). Similarly, the corresponding mean CDRs for the 4-bit ID were 42.5 (VW) and 43.6 (VA). The effect of target condition—the leftmost independent variable listed in Table II, that is, target width for Session VA and movement amplitude for Session VW—was not statistically significant, $F(8,152) = 1.16$, $p > 0.1$, $MS_e = 62.2$. This is consistent with the claim that movement amplitude and target width can be traded to produce equivalent effects upon secondary task performance. Fitts (1954) first

Table II
Number of Correct Digit Responses

	Session VA digit transformation							
	N			$9 - N$			Corresponding amplitudes (cm)	
Target width (cm)	Target ID			Target ID				
	4 bits	6 bits	$\bar{X}$	4 bits	6 bits	$\bar{X}$	4 bits	6 bits
0.34	56.6	50.9	53.8	38.5	36.9	37.7	2.7*	10.2†
0.7	61.2	46.7	60.0	40.1	37.3	38.7	5.2	20.5‡
1.25	57.1	48.0	52.6	43.1	35.0	39.1	10.2	41§
	No tapping, 92.7			No tapping, 58.8				

	Session VW digit transformation							
	N			$9 - N$			Corresponding target widths (cm)	
Movement amplitude (cm)	Target ID			Target ID				
	4 bits	6 bits	$\bar{X}$	4 bits	6 bits	$\bar{X}$	4 bits	6 bits
10.2	55.3	51.0	53.2	42.3	35.5	38.9	1.25*	0.35†
20.5	58.7	51.4	55.1	41.9	38.2	40.1	2.5	0.7‡
41	63.3	48.2	55.8	39.9	37.7	38.8	5.0	1.25§
	No tapping, 97.1			No tapping, 56.4				

Note. The symbols next to certain values indicate the same target.

demonstrated this trade-off between A and W for the time required to generate a movement. The present results extend this trade-off to time-shared performance of a secondary digit-naming task. As long as ID is constant, different combinations of A and W produce the same effect upon time-sharing. In particular, the data of Table II fail to reveal either a consistent change in the effect of target width as movement amplitude varies (such that target width fails to compensate properly for changes in amplitude) or a consistent change in the effect of movement amplitude as target width varies (such that amplitude fails to compensate properly for changes in width). This is indeed a parsimonious outcome, with implications to be explored in Section V,C.

Although less important for present considerations, we duly note that comparing single- and dual-task conditions in Table II reveals a significant interaction between digit-transformation complexity and tapping condition (4 bits, 6 bits, no tapping), $F(12,228) = 11.03$, $p < 0.001$, $MS_e = 78.6$, replicating the previous findings of Kantowitz and Knight (1974, 1976a). When tapping is added to the easier N digit transformation, the resulting performance decrement is much worse than when tapping is added to the more complex $9 - N$ transformation. This was taken as support for the importance of response processes as a primary locus of intertask interference, as shown in box S3 of Figure 2. However, when only dual-task conditions are analyzed, this same interaction remained, $F(1,19) = 8.42$,

$p < 0.01$, $MS_e = 93.3$, although greatly reduced in magnitude, contrary to the earlier results of Knight and Kantowitz (1974, 1976a). This apparent discrepancy poses no special problem for the model of Figure 2 when we realize that the present tapping tasks were considerably more difficult than those used earlier: IDs of 1.96 and 5.0 bits in the prior studies versus 4.0 and 6.0 in the present study. Since Figure 2 is a limited-capacity model, it is not surprising that, as the rate of transmitted information demanded by the primary task becomes high (12 bits/sec), the results of even dual-task comparisons should start to approximate the single- versus dual-task interaction that defines a limited-capacity model. Since more digits are emitted for the N naming task, it places a greater load (than $9 - N$) on S3 and thus suffers proportionately more in dual-task conditions.

Analysis of incorrect digit responses showed more errors for the $9 - N$ transformation (mean $= 2.29$/trial) than for the N transformation (0.46), $F(1,19) = 21.2$, $p < 0.001$, $MS_e = 22.1$. Of greater importance was the finding that incorrect digit responses were not affected by tapping task difficulty (means of 1.46, 1.42, and 1.54 for 4 bits, 6 bits, and no tapping, respectively), $F(12,228) = 1.29$, $p > 0.1$, $MS_e = 1.87$. Thus, while tapping difficulty affected the number of emitted responses, it did not control their accuracy. Again, this replicates earlier findings implicating a response bottleneck (S3 in Figure 2), rather than arithmetic processing (S2), as the locus of intertask interference.

2. Tapping Task Performance

A great advantage of the Fitts tapping task is that a rational procedure for equating task conditions with varying error rates exists. This is especially useful when high rates of transmitted information are demanded from unpracticed subjects. Many other motor tasks either have no rational method for handling varying error rates or require a very specific model before such corrections can be applied. The tapping task, however, requires only that the shape of the hit plus error distribution be known. (The earlier Kantowitz–Knight tapping studies used easier targets and therefore did not need to report this correction.)

Since target undershoot and overshoot errors were appreciable, 6% for the 4-bit ID and 22% for the 6-bit ID, effective target widths were calculated using the correction suggested by Crossman (cited in Welford, 1968). This procedure assumes that hits and errors are normally distributed about the center of the targets and uses the area under the normal curve to find a corrected target width, W', which is then inserted into the ID calculation to obtain an effective ID'. If there are many errors, the target is functionally wider and the effective ID' is lower than the nominal ID. Corrections were, of course, calculated separately for each subject and each condition. In addition, left and right targets were corrected separately. No correction to amplitude was used due to the symmetrical nature about target centers of the movement distributions.

The results are listed in Table III. As expected, more information was transmitted for the 6-bit targets (520 bits/trial) than for the 4-bit targets (429 bits/trial), $F(1, 19) = 124$, $p < 0.001$, $MS_e = 6118$. Slightly more information was transmitted in session VW (486 bits) than in session VA (468 bits), $F(1, 19) = 11.8$, $p < 0.01$, $MS_e = 4129$. However, a significant interaction between Session and ID, $F(1, 19) = 15.85$, $p < 0.001$, $MS_e = 2734$, shows this difference to be entirely due to the 4-bit ID with means of 406 bits (VA) and 451 bits (VW). Performance was identical for the 6-bit target: 520 bits (VA) and 521 bits (VW).

Contrary to the results for digit-naming, ID was not sufficient to account for effects of variation in movement amplitude or target width. Different amounts of information were transmitted in the three tapping conditions within each session (i.e., the three amplitudes within VW and the three widths within VA), $F(8, 152) = 21.56$, $p < 0.001$, $MS_e = 1090$. This may seem startling, since it held even for the tapping-only conditions, but actually replicates the results of Fitts (1954) quite well. In his seminal article Fitts (1954, Table 3, p. 388) used an index of performance I_p, essentially equivalent to transmitted information, to assess performance at various combinations of amplitude and width. For fixed ID values of 3, 4, 5, and 6 bits/movement, I_p increased slightly as both movement amplitude and target width increased in a compensatory manner. This result also

Table III
Information Transmitted in Tapping Task during Each 60-sec Trial

	Session VA					
	No-digit task		N		$9 - N$	
Target width	Target ID		Target ID		Target ID	
(cm)	4	6	4	6	4	6
0.35	437	554*	371	467	364	467
0.70	451	563†	360	497	358	471
1.25	487‡	603§	409	527	419	530

	Session VW					
	No-digit task		N		$9 - N$	
Movement	Target ID		Target ID		Target ID	
amplitude (cm)	4	6	4	6	4	6
10.2	472	528*	431	469	419	454
20.5	467	580†	460	497	439	492
41.0	469‡	605§	449	530	455	539

Note. Table entries are in bits. Target widths have been corrected based on under- and overshoot data as discussed in the text. The symbols next to certain values indicate the same target and apply to double-stimulation conditions. Target ID is nominal bits.

held for ID values of 7 and 8 bits until movement amplitude exceeded 8 in.: Beyond this, I_p fell. The present results (Table III) show a greater effect of changing amplitude and width within the more difficult 6-bit tapping condition than within the 4-bit ID. This too replicates the data of Fitts (1954, Table 3), where changing amplitude and width produced a 3.18-bit performance variation (over an amplitude range of 1 to 4 in.) in a 6-bit ID task, whereas a similar change in amplitude produced only a 1.83-bit change in a 5-bit task.

Table IV shows the interaction between tapping difficulty and digit-naming complexity. When all data are analyzed, this interaction is significant, $F(2,38) = 5.41$, $p < 0.01$, $MS_e = 1123$, replicating the findings of Kantowitz and Knight (1974, 1976a). When only double-stimulation data are analyzed (no-digit task condition deleted), this interaction vanishes, $F(1,19) < 1.0$, $MS_e = 1060$, again replicating earlier results. This consistency is slightly marred by a significant three-way interaction with Session because the 4-bit ID target for Session VW declined less steeply than the other three combinations of Session and ID, $F(2,38) = 7.24$, $p < 0.01$, $MS_e = 773$. We do not believe that this oddity is important and report it only to be complete. Kantowitz and Knight (1976a) interpreted the single- versus double-stimulation interaction as supporting the limited-capacity bottleneck in Figure 2 and the double-stimulation additivity as supporting the parallel stages of Figure 2.

C. Discussion

These results show rather clearly that, at least for the range of conditions tested in this study, Fitts' ID is a better predictor of the attention demands of movement than of the number of movements that can be completed in a fixed time. Since Bainbridge and Sanders (1972) have shown that Fitts' law applied equally well to the present paced movement, this conclusion can be extended by stating that the ID is a better predictor of attention than of movement time.

Is this an astonishing conclusion? At the time of Fitts' original work, the distinction between the time required for an action and the attention demands of

Table IV
Mean Transmitted Information as a Function of
Target ID and Digit-Naming Complexity

ID	Digit transformation		
	No-digit task	N	$9 - N$
4	464	413	409
6	572	497	492

Note. These data are taken from Table III and are listed again for the sake of clarity, good cheer, and dramatic impact.

that action was either vague or entirely absent. Now, of course, this distinction has been so stressed (e.g., Broadbent, 1965; Kerr, 1973) that its novelty has worn off, making it difficult for us to appreciate the conceptual difficulties of earlier times when time and attention were practically synonomous issues. The analogy to Shannon's limited channel that Fitts (1954) used was imprecise at best. Indeed, feedback considerations offer a more satisfying explanation of Fitts' law than his original analogy (Keele, 1968, among others), when movement time is at issue. It may well have been that the more basic analogy is to attentional mechanisms and that Fitts was ahead of his time and created his analogy by thinking of attention. Certainly a channel limited by a rate of flow of information is more akin to modern conceptions of attention than of time itself. Thus the parsimonius way in which Fitts' ID accounts for attentional effects is not only gratifying, but perhaps not inconsistent with his original analogy and conception.

What, then, of Fitts' ID as an explanation of movement time? Psychologists have been impressed by the high correlations between data and Fitts' law. How-

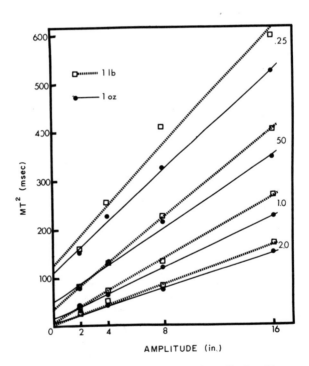

Figure 4 Movement time squared as a function of amplitude with target width as a parameter ranging from 0.25 to 2.0 in. Data are from Fitts (1954). Dashed lines represent a heavy stylus and solid lines a light stylus. Lines are fitted by the method of least squares. The prediction of the bang-bang model fits the data of Fitts (1954) quite well. [From Kantowitz & Herman, Note 1.]

ever, this is not a sufficient criterion for accepting a model of behavior, as opposed to mathematical curve fitting. Other models yield fits to data that are equally or even more impressive than that of Fitts' law. For example, Kantowitz and Herman (Note 2), investigating a bang–bang (sometimes called an on–off or maximum effort controller) model—a nonlinear servomechanism that in this application accelerates with maximum capability until halfway to the target and then decelerates with maximum capability—predicted MT^2 to be a linear function of movement amplitude and created the family of curves shown in Figure 4. Correlation coefficients were quite high, ranging from 0.987 to 0.999 with a median of 0.998. We do not wish to digress into calculating χ^2 to see which model fits best. Our point is only that psychologists have been uncritical in accepting the basic analogy behind Fitts' law because of its fit to data uncompared to other models.

While Fitts' law is an excellent predictor of MT, it is not a theoretical explanation of movement control. Furthermore, Langolf, Chaffin, and Foulke (1976) have shown that no linear control model, including the feedback-processing model proposed by Crossman and Goodeve (Note 1) and Keele (1968), can explain the details of movement in a Fitts' law task. It is clear that for any fine-grained explanation of movement we shall have to turn to nonlinear models, such as the bang–bang servomechanism mentioned in the preceding paragraph. Even so, the Fitts ID will not be forgotten: It will remain as an index of attention.

VI. Conclusions

In this concluding section, we briefly return to more general issues in motor performance and the implications of our results for models of voluntary aiming movements. The modal two-phase model with initial impulse followed by current control is at best only weakly supported by the present results. In particular, it was not clear that the initial impulse portion of the movement did not require attention. Provided that ID was held constant, lesser movement amplitudes did not require greater amounts of attention as measured by decrements in a time-shared secondary task.

Furthermore, the data of Kantowitz (1969) shown in Figure 1 also argue against the initial impulse stage being automatic. The occurrence of a second stimulus that was presented before movement began nevertheless caused a reliable increase in MT. Similar findings of Megaw (1974) show that S_2 as well as error correction procedures can affect early stages of movement. All of these data suggest that voluntary *aiming* movements are not automated.

How does this conclusion affect the concept of a motor program? Megaw (1974), while recognizing that his results showed that what was considered open-loop movement could be modified, nevertheless tried to argue for motor programs. He suggested that the response was modified "by up-dating a motor program [p. 438]" and went on to postulate hierarchical levels of motor programs within motor programs within motor programs.

If theorists are willing to accept the ongoing modification of parts of motor programs (subroutines?), then our results can be accommodated within this framework. However, under a strict definition of a motor program, no part of which can be modified while it is in operation, our results do not support this concept. Kerr (1975) tested attention demands of a movement to a stop (thus not an aiming movement, which requires a well-defined target) and was astonished to find that attention was demanded, even though previous research had shown movement to a stop to be automated. She suggested that the motor program concept was valid only for a restricted range of movements, although this range was not specified. However, since her task required movement to be guided along a constrained path, it was really a tracking task and should require attention. The earlier studies (Posner & Keele, 1969; Ells 1973) used mechanical arrangements (levers or knobs) that prevented the subjects from straying from the path as they approached the stop and so were neither tracking tasks nor aiming tasks. The strict motor program concept may be valid only for movement that cannot be classified as aiming or tracking. Even then, the concept has difficulties. Glencross (1976) examined a non-aiming movement (horizontal arm sweep with no target) and aiming movements with three targets of different sizes. This was a single-stimulation study with no direct measures of attention. He expected that movements requiring greater precision would lead to motor programs of greater complexity, which would result in increased RT. However, the results of three experiments failed to support this hypothesis. While the results of the three aiming conditions are entirely consistent with present data and interpretation, it is surprising that even the non-aimed movement did not reveal increased RT. While this could most parsimoniously be explained by rejecting the motor program concept entirely, it is also possible that complexity of movement (Glencross, 1973) is not related to movement parameters such as amplitude and width.

So far our discussion of motor programs has accepted the operational definition of an automatic process suggested by Bahrick and Shelley (1958): Automatization releases attention or capacity so that it is available for performing a secondary task. It is only fair to note that the concept of a motor program could avoid some of the difficulties sketched here if automatization were redefined so that it did not imply a release of attention. Pew (1974) has doubted that the operational definition of Bahrick and Shelley is of wide generality and Glencross (personal communication) has suggested that execution of a motor program requires capacity as a resource. The price in theoretical parsimony that must be paid for this redefinition may be high since it no longer allows the first phase of movement control (initial impulse) to be easily distinguished on the basis of capacity demands from the second, feedback-utilization (current control) phase of movement control. While our data are consistent with the view that the first phase demands capacity, this does not prove that motor programs demand capacity since there is no converging operation to show that a motor program was necessarily used to control the initial impulse phase of movement. In fact, such a redefinition of automatization makes it extremely difficult to reject the motor program construct at all and so decreases the value of the concept. Indeed, Schmidt (1975) has stated that no experiments with humans have been performed that demonstrate either that feedback is present and not used or that movement can occur without feedback, as demanded by the motor program construct. Allowing motor programs to demand capacity makes the construct even more immune to experimental test, especially since present methodologies are not well-suited for distinguishing between a motor program that demands just a little bit of capacity while it is running and a feedback-controlled process that demands just a little more capacity.

Where do we go from here? Although time-sharing paradigms are in some ways methodologically simpler than probe paradigms, they cannot sweep out time patterns of attention throughout a movement when analyzed as we have done here. To obtain a fine-grained picture, we have also recorded interresponse time data for primary and secondary tasks. These are being analyzed by assorted spectral techniques in the hope of revealing more about the detailed relationships between time-shared tasks. For example, we can tell you that digits are emitted near the middle of a movement between targets (actually slightly closer to the initiation than termination of a movement). This might be reasonable if attention demands of movement are minimal in this region with almost a ballistic motion. Limitations of space make this a discussion for another time.

Acknowledgments

This research was supported by Grant MH 26302 from the National Institute of Mental Health. This research was carried out at Purdue University and this report was written while the first author was on sabbatical leave at the Norwegian Institute of Technology. We thank D. J. Glencross and T. O. Kvålseth for commenting on the manuscript.

Reference Notes

1. Crossman, E. R. F. W., & Goodeve, P. J. *Feedback control of hand movement and Fitts' Law.* Communication to the Experimental Society, July 1963.
2. Kantowitz, B. H., & Herman, L. M. *Effects of increasing feedback processing requirements on motor system capacity and on Fitts' law.* Paper presented to the Midwestern Psychological Association, Chicago, 1967.

References

Adams, J. A. Issues for a closed-loop theory of motor learning. In G. E. Stelmach (Ed.), *Motor control: Issues and trends.* New York: Academic Press, 1976.

Bahrick, H. P., & Shelley C. Time-sharing as an index of automatization. *Journal of Experimental Psychology,* 1958, *56,* 288–293.

Bainbridge, L., & Saunders, M. The generality of Fitts' law. *Journal of Experimental Psychology,* 1972, *96,* 130–133.

Bliss, C. B. Investigations in reaction time and attention. *Studies from the Yale Psychological Laboratory,* 1892–1893, *1,* 1–55.

Broadbent, D. E. Application of information theory and decision theory to human perception and reaction. In N. Wiener & J. P. Schade (Eds.), *Cybernetics of the nervous system.* Amsterdam: Elsevier, 1965.

Ells, J. G. Analysis of temporal and attentional aspects of movement. *Journal of Experimental Psychology,* 1973, *99,* 10–21.

Fitts, P. M. The information capacity of the human motor system in controlling the amplitude of movement. *Journal of Experimental Psychology,* 1954, *47,* 381–391.

Fitts, P. M. & Peterson, J. R. Information capacity of discrete motor response. *Journal of Experimental Psychology,* 1964, *67,* 103–112.

Fitts, P. M., & Radford, B. K. Information capacity of discrete motor responses under different cognitive sets. *Journal of Experimental Psychology,* 1966, *11,* 475–482.

Glencross, D. J. Response complexity and the latency of different movement patterns. *Journal of Motor Behavior,* 1973, *5,* 95–104.

Glencross, D. J. The latency of aiming movements. *Journal of Motor Behavior,* 1976, *8,* 27–34.

Kantowitz, B. H. Double stimulation with varying response information. *Journal of Experimental Psychology,* 1969, *82,* 347–352.

Kantowitz, B. H. (Ed.). *Human information processing: Tutorials in performance and cognition.* Hillsdale, New Jersey: Erlbaum, 1974. (a)

Kantowitz, B. H. Double stimulation. In B. H. Kantowitz (Ed.), *Human information processing: Tutorials in performance and cognition.* Hillsdale, New Jersey: Erlbaum, 1974. (b)

Kantowitz, B. H. On the beaten track. *Contemporary Psychology,* 1975, *20,* 731–733.

Kantowitz, B. H. Channels and stages in human information processing: A limited review. *Cognitive Psychology,* 1978, in press.

Kantowitz, B. H., & Knight, J. L. Testing tapping timesharing. *Journal of Experimental Psychology,* 1974, *103,* 331–336.

Kantowitz, B. H., & Knight, J. L., Testing tapping timesharing. II. Auditory secondary task. *Acta Psychologica,* 1976, *40,* 343–362. (a)

Kantowitz, B. H., & Knight, J. L. On experimenter-limited processes. *Psychological Review,* 1976, *83,* 502–507. (b)

Kantowitz, B. H., & Roediger, H. L. *Experimental psychology: Understanding psychological research.* Chicago: Rand McNally, 1978.

Keele, S. W. Movement control in skilled motor performance. *Psychological Bulletin,* 1968, *70,* 387–403.

Keele, S. W., & Summers, J. J. The structure of motor programs. In G. E. Stelmach (Ed.), *Motor control: Issues and trends.* New York: Academic Press, 1976.

Kerr, B. Processing demands during mental operations. *Memory and Cognition,* 1973, *1,* 401–412.

Kerr, B. Processing demands during movement. *Journal of Motor Behavior,* 1975, *7,* 15–27.

Klapp, S. T. Feedback versus motor prorgamming in the control of aimed movements. *Journal of Experimental Psychology: Human Perception and Performance,* 1975, *104,* 147–153.

Kvålseth, T. O. Fitts' law for manipulative temporal motor responses with and without path constraints. *Perceptual and Motor Skills*, 1973, *37*, 427–431.

Langolf, G. D., Chaffin, D. B., & Foulke, J. A. An investigation of Fitts' law using a wide range of movement amplitudes. *Journal of Motor Behavior*, 1976, *8*, 113–128.

Megaw, E. D. Possible modification to a rapid on-going programmed manual response. *Brain Research*, 1974, *71*, 425–441.

Megaw, E. D. Fitts tapping revisited. *Journal of Human Movement Studies*, 1975, *1*, 163–171.

Pew, R. W. Human perceptual motor performance. In B. H. Kantowitz, (Ed.), *Human information processing: Tutorials in performance and cognition*. Hillsdale, New Jersey: Erlbaum, 1974.

Posner, M. I., & Keele, S. W. Attention demands of movements. In *Proceedings of the XVII'th Congress of Applied Psychology*. Amsterdam: Zeitlinger, 1969.

Salmoni, A. W., Sullivan, S. J., & Starkes, J. L. The attention demands of movements: A critique of the probe technique. *Journal of Motor Behavior*, 1976, *8*, 161–169.

Schmidt, R. A. A schema theory of discrete motor skill learning. *Psychological Review*, 1975, *82*, 225–260.

Stelmach, G. E. (Ed.). *Motor control: Issues and trends*. New York: Academic Press, 1976.

Sternberg, S. The discovery of processing stages: Extensions of Donders' method. *Acta Psychologica*, 1969, *30*, 276–315.

Troland, L. T. *The fundamentals of human motivation*. New York: Van Nostrand, 1928.

Welford, A. T. *Fundamentals of skill*. London: Methuen, 1968.

Woodworth, R. S. The accuracy of voluntary movement. *Psychological Review Monograph*, 1899, *3*, 1–114.

11

Theoretical Issues for
Knowledge of Results

Jack A. Adams

I. Introduction

History has lessons for us, we are told, and so it should attract us all. A benefit of history is the satisfaction of knowing our roots and basking in a lineage of important people and ideas. A benefit is perspective in seeing the ebb and flow of ideas. Another benefit is seeing what has endured from the past, what we have cast off, and what we have changed or keep trying to change. Without historical perspective, the enduring elements seem so natural and right that we never think of challenging them, the cast-off elements are forgotten, and the elements being changed appear as part of the modern flux and seem new to us. My topic is knowledge of results, or KR as we handily say, and I will base this discussion of human reinforcement on the work of Edward L. Thorndike (1874–1949). He gave us a strong push down the motor learning road, and it is instructive to look at this part of psychology's history, see the legacies, and ask what they mean for us today.

Information Processing in
Motor Control and Learning

II. Thorndike and His Ideas

Man has had an intuitive understanding of reward and punishment since his beginning, but it is only in the experimental era of psychology that we have subjected reward and punishment in instrumental learning to close scrutiny. Systematic thought on instrumental learning began with the animal research of Thorndike (1898). A dimension of Thorndike's early animal work was scientific objectivism as he reacted against the practice of his day that imputed human conscious processes, like reasoning, to animals, and in a few years this objectivism was complemented by the superobjectivism of John B. Watson (1913) and his behaviorism. Watson was more interested in Pavlovian conditioning than in the instrumental learning that fascinated Thorndike, and Thorndike was not an evangelist for behaviorism like Watson, but the two were allies in rejecting the mentalism of the past and in asserting objectivism in psychology. These two major figures in our history gave American psychology a strong interest in learning, and their mutual concern with objectivism got learning off to a hard-headed start.

Thorndike's (1898) doctoral dissertation is famous, and it is worth reading today. There were various studies in it, but typical and influential ones were with a puzzle box. He placed a cat on the inside of a slatted box from which it could see outside. Food was put on the outside, and the pull of a wire loop on the inside opened the door and made the food available as reward. The solution times were long on the early trials, but as the rewarded trials continued the response times became shorter and shorter until the response was swift and sure. This approach to learning was objective, quantitative, and reliable; it met basic criteria of science.

Thorndike's interest in animal research lasted only a few years, but during that time the mysteries of adaptation through instrumental learning became clear to him. Out of all of the responses that can be made in a situation, how does an organism adjust? How are adaptive responses strengthened and maladaptive responses weakened? The answer was selective learning and the law of effect. Selective learning is what Thorndike (1913) called "multiple response to the same external situation [p. 12]." An early statement (Thorndike, 1907) of the law of effect was

> . . . that any act which in a given situation produces satisfaction becomes associated with that situation, so that when the situation recurs the act is more likely than before to recur also. Conversely, any act which in a given situation produces discomfort becomes dissociated from that situation, so that when the situation recurs the act is less likely than before to recur [p. 203].

The aftereffects of a response class affect the probability of future responses in the situation; they select one response class out of many in the situation and change it. Thorndike advocated associationism, not between ideas, as in an earlier day, but between stimulus and response, and a hedonism with the emphasis on pleasure and pain.

Notice in the law of effect that reward strengthens and punishment weakens. When Thorndike shifted away from animal learning and toward human learning, he began to trade in symbolic reward and punishment. Here he found little in the way of opposing effects of reward and punishment. He would use "right" as reward and "wrong" as punishment, and while "right" increased the probability of response occurrence, "wrong" had variable, inconsistent effects. Increasingly, Thorndike began to appreciate that reward and punishment were not neatly opposite in their effects. He came to believe that reward strengthens a response, but that punishment causes a shift to some other behavior rather than a weakening of the response (Thorndike, 1932, p. 277). Reward is the key agent for changing behavior; punishment is different, less reliable, and probably more complex.

There were other implications that flowed from Thorndike's thinking and research. One was the assertion of what we would now call a behavioristic account of learning. The change in behavior that is learning was due to a "connection," or a "bond," or a "habit" between stimulus and response. Learning was not a change in ideas, images, consciousness, or any other cognitive property of the mind. Conscious awareness was unnecessary for learning. The reward was not information that the subject consciously processed but an automatic agent that strengthened the connection. Thorndike (1935) said that "a person may increase the probability that certain situations will evoke certain responses without knowing at the time that he is doing so or afterward that he has done so [p. 62]." Similarly, Thorndike (1935) said that reward will strengthen the connection "regardless of the learner's knowledge about the tendency or ability to identify, describe, or control it [p. 63]."

A second implication was that mind is not a conscious, reflective, cognitive entity but a network of stimulus–response associations. Association was the law of mind, whether animal or human. The human did not have emergent mental powers like consciousness, only the power of more associations than lower animals. Thorndike (1913) said that "learning is connecting, and man is the greater learner primarily because he forms so many connections [p. 54]."

III. The Thorndike Legacies

I see four legacies of Thorndike to motor learning and knowledge of results (KR). We accept some of them today without thinking. Others we have challenged. Let me indicate the legacies and some of their ramifications.

A. Punishment Is Hardly Used in the Shaping of Motor Behavior

For Thorndike, reward was a reliable way of effecting a human response and punishment was not; punishment was uncertain and indeterminate in its effects. We run true in motor learning to this sentiment of Thorndike by not using punishment, and we hardly ever think about it. For us, KR connotes harmless but informative statements, such as "10 in. high" or "right." Sometimes we use mild reproof like "wrong," which certainly is informative but hardly punishing as Thorndike believed.

We are not the only ones concerned with human learning who have sidestepped punishment. For a long time, behavior modification, at the urging of B. F. Skinner (1971), shied from punishment because Thorndike influenced it as much as he did motor learning, but in recent years behavior modifiers have been giving more attention to punishment because it can produce a lot of behavior change for the input. Today, more and more, behavior modifiers are taking their hint from animal learning that has shown us that learning based on punishment and fear can be very efficient. I suggest that we should take the hint also and ask what is in aversive KR for the shaping of human motor behavior. Obviously I am not talking about gentle reproof like "wrong," but physical discomfort and the fear based on it.

A search of the KR literature for examples of physically aversive KR and its effects on motor behavior is almost in vain. An exception is a series of experiments by R. B. Payne (Payne, 1970; Payne & Artley, 1972; Payne & Richardson, 1972, 1974; Payne & Dunman, 1974). Prior to motor learning trials, Payne created an aversive KR event by pairing electric shock and the stimulus to be used as the signal for off-target behavior in the tracking task that was to be learned. Performance in the tracking task showed substantial benefits of the aversive KR, and the benefits remained when the aversive KR was withdrawn. Payne was capitalizing on the mild fear of the aversive KR event that was cultivated in the pretraining series. Being off target was made uncomfortable, and the discomfort was minimized by being on target.

Aversive KR can be an entirely new theoretical enterprise for motor learning. Previously, we have thought of KR as an agent for habit, or a source of information, but aversive KR is a matter of secondary motivation and what it means for the regulation of movement. Payne has shown us that the consequences of punishment can shape the pattern of movement in durable ways, and theoretically the explanation may be the same as for fearful animals turning wheels, running alleys, and jumping hurdles. It would be a scientific economy if this were so.

B. The Knowledge of Results Is Delivered Once at the End of the Response Being Trained

No matter what moves they made, or with what speed, Thorndike's cats were not rewarded until they successfully solved the problem of opening the door to the puzzle box and getting outside, and the reinforcement was a single event at the end of the sequence. This tradition of reward for *acts* rather than *movements* (Spence, 1956, p. 43) is widely accepted in the psychology of learning, and Thorndike handed it to us. Spence (1956) said that "differences in the detailed movements or patterns of muscular activity from one occurrence to another are ignored, and all instances that produce the same environmental change are treated as a single response class [p. 42]." If a rat reaches the goal box or presses the bar in the Skinner box, it gets a reward; otherwise it does not, and we do not care what movements are involved in getting there. Any motor learning task that delivers a single KR event after the goal has been attempted is an example of the same thing. Little concern is shown for skill in executing the act, although the approach sequence to the goal will undergo change as the behavior adjusts in the process of learning to attain the goal. Notwithstanding, it is the goal attainment that interests us in our laboratory research on KR, not movement patterns in reaching the goal.

The price that we have paid for following this tradition is that we know little about training precise movement sequences in reaching a precise endpoint. If we were training Chopin's Minute Waltz we would reward the pianist for finishing in 60 seconds and not care what notes were used in getting there. A competition diver must not only hit the water at a certain point, he must also make very specific moves along the board and through the air, and we know nothing in a systematic scientific way about applying KR events for time and position throughout the sequence to shape the behavior into a precision dive. Athletic coaches, not knowing about Thorndike or our research on KR, have been doing this sort of thing for a long time and with some success. The basis of their success is intuition and the accumulated wisdom of physical education, and this can carry a coach a distance, but his is an art, not a science. A beauty of science is that it pushes beyond the accumulated wisdom that is intuition into an undreamed of world of subtlety.

It is time that we begin thinking about scenarios of multiple KR events that will train long movement sequences in attaining goals. Without this knowledge, there will continue to be a reliance on accumulated wisdom and intuition, and we will continue to have a lot of variability in reaching task goals. We can dignify this variability with such labels as "the subject's strategy in reaching the goal" if we wish. Today, subjects have different behavioral strategies in reaching a goal, and one way of seeing these strategies is that we have not bothered to shape the movement sequence in a specific way, so subjects reach task goals in any way they please. When we come to understand KR scenarios for the entire sequence, these idiosyncratic strategies will disappear because the behavioral pattern to the goal, and goal attainment, will come under close control. Scientists concerned with the training of motor behavior may then have something to say to athletic coaches. Perhaps piano teachers will inquire about ways of teaching the "Minute Waltz."

C. Learning Is Explained as the Strengthening of "Habits," "Bonds," or "Connections"

That KR affects the probability of response is an empirical fact but that it automatically affects a noncognitive habit state is theory, and this is part of the Thorndike legacy that we have rejected. The rejection has taken two forms. One is that we assert the cognitive character of learning where KR is information that is actively, consciously if you wish, processed; the KR has a directive function for subsequent responses. The other is that KR has a motivational role, an energizing function for subsequent responses, in addition to the learning, or directive, function. First, let me discuss the information view of KR.

Introspect while you learn a motor task, or talk to a few subjects who have learned one, and be convinced that there is a lot of mental activity that accompanies the motor activity. The functionalist psychologists about the turn of the century, like Angell (1904) and James (1890), believed this because they wrote about the importance of conscious processes in learning and how conscious factors eventually dropped out as the learning progressed and became "automatic." Then, in the 1930s and 1940s, the cognitive learning theory of Tolman (1932, 1948, 1958), as a minor threat to reigning behaviorism, gave rebirth to a cognitive viewpoint of learning. Tolman did not give consciousness a central role in his theorizing; he believed that conscious awareness could accompany learning but he saw no necessity for it (Tolman, 1958, pp. 109–112). However, he did believe that learning was perceptual where we learned what goes with what and what leads to where in the situation. In working out these perceptual relations we entertain and test hypotheses; learning is a problem-solving situation. Learning, for Tolman, certainly was not the association of responses to stimuli. In time, Tolman's cognitive influence faded, and it was not until the 1960s that the cognitive viewpoint reappeared, and it is still with us, not as a specific theory like Tolman's, but as a broad conceptual frame of reference.

With this history of cognitive learning in the background, and with the cognitively oriented research on natural language mediation in verbal learning that W. E. Montague and I carried out (for a review, see Montague, 1972), which convinced me that an account of human learning that omits thinking is a dead end, I proposed a closed-loop theory of motor learning in 1971 that had an informational view of KR (Adams, 1971). Learning, I said, is problem solving, and KR is information about error that tells the subject how well he is succeeding in the problem-solving task. The KR as information is actively processed in the post-KR interval, and the subject forms a hypothesis about how to improve his performance on the next trial. This hypothesis behavior eventually drops out, in good functionalist fashion, when a high level of proficiency is attained. Schendel and Newell (1976), and Newell (1977) in a review of KR and motor learning, say that the evidence tilts toward the information view but that it is not always decisive.

The motivational view of KR, as another dimension of rejecting Thorndike's noncognitive view, has two aspects. One aspect implies that organisms are error-reducing systems. Whenever error is perceived the subject is motivated to eliminate the error. Error is an intrinsic source of motivation, almost like hunger or thirst, although I would pause before I would call it primary motivation. Thus, KR, which is error information and a basis of human learning, produces the motivational charge to eliminate itself. I tend to believe this viewpoint, although it has not received much research attention. Elsewhere (Adams & Bray, 1970, p. 396; Adams, 1971, p. 128) I have discussed that it is also believed by the Russians (Sokolov, 1969; Anokhin, 1969), whose orientation is physiology and Pavlovian conditioning, by Miller (1959, pp. 248–252), whose interest is animal motivation, and by Festinger (1957), whose area is social psychology.

The other aspect says that there are tasks in which KR affects motivation alone. This is an argument to which I once succumbed (Adams, 1969) and to which Locke and his associates have given considerable attention (Locke, 1968; Locke, Cartledge, & Koeppel, 1968). The gist of the argument is that there are tasks so simple that no learning is required or that there are fully learned tasks for which no further learning is possible. Squeezing a dynamometer is an example. Reaction time is another example. A repetitive industrial task being performed by an experienced worker is still another example. Because KR will enhance performance on tasks such as these, and because learning is not considered possible, the effects are assumed to be motivational.

Consider an example where the motivational argument is made from a goal-setting situation in industry. A worker has a stable level of production in his job and then the supervisor sets a higher work goal. Each day the supervisor reports his production to him. In time the worker attains the new goal, and some psychologists will say that the new goal has raised his motivation and increased his production. This paradigm is also represented in athletic competition where athletes compete against championship records or in self-improvement programs where the subject competes against himself. It is from this goal-setting paradigm that the evidence about KR as a motivational agent primarily comes.

Separating the goal-setting situation from the learning situation is a problem that I see. It is typical of goal-setting situations to report *performance score* to the subject, not error, so it seems that the subject is striving to improve his performance and reach the goal. The assumption is that the goal mediates performance, and there is an intuitive reasonableness about the assumption when we watch striving workers and competing athletes. However, certainly the subject must covertly calculate the difference between his performance score and the goal, which is error, and so he is an error reducer in the goal-setting situation just as in the learning situation. It is error, not the goal, that is mediating performance. If this is so, then the operations for the goal-setting situation, which is explained by motivation, and the learning situation are the same, which is conceptually clumsy because learning and motivation, as two distinct theoretical states, are defined by the same operations. As implied in the next paragraph, there are ways of distinguishing the learning and motivation points of view.

Another problem for the motivational view of KR is that advocates pass intuitive judgment on what is a learning task and what is not; they may not have ruled out learning effects in their studies of KR and motivation like they think they have. Who is to say that we cannot learn better ways of squeezing a dynamometer? We might learn to recognize the proprioceptive feedback associated with a harder squeeze, for example. Learning to respond faster may be the selection of a movement already in the behavioral repertoire, not motivation (selective learning has been an established type of learning since Thorndike). Dynamometer and reaction time studies, which show beneficial effects of KR, have been interpreted in behalf of motivation (Adams, 1969; Newell, 1977), but there are features of these data that suggest a directive, or learning, function for KR instead. A dynamometer study by Manzer (1935) showed that the performance advantages of KR persisted when KR was withdrawn. One of my vigilance studies (Adams & Humes, 1963) had the same finding. Reaction time was the performance measure. The subject received KR as deviation from his own best previous performance. Performance benefited from KR, and the benefit remained when KR was withdrawn. That performance advantages of KR remain when KR is withdrawn is what we would expect if KR is serving in its learning role. If KR has a motivational charge, should not the withdrawal of KR cause a decrease of motivation that would be reflected in a decrease in performance?

So, Schendel and Newell (1976) and Newell (1977) believe that the informational view of KR must be strengthened with more and better research if it is to flourish, and I believe that the motivational view has problems. We all have rejected Thorndike's habit view, and I think that it will remain rejected, but we have not worked hard enough to secure its theoretical successor.

D. The Reinforcement Is an Objective External Event
Delivered after the Response

This was a cherished principle of Thorndike's, and we do not dare reject it because it is empirical fact. We can, however, ask if there is more to it, and that is what I have done in my arguments for subjective reinforcement (Adams & Bray, 1970; Adams, 1967, 1968, 1971, 1976). The reasoning goes like this: We have the power to judge, with accuracy, the degree of error in our own behavior. This is true for both verbal and motor responses (e.g., Adams & Bray, 1970; Adams & Goetz, 1973; Newell, 1974). If KR, as an objective source of error, is an unquestionable basis of learning, then why cannot a subjective source of error be the same? Why should one source of error be different from another? I have argued that they are the same. The subject should not care where he gets his error information. The fascinating implication is that, after some learning with KR has occurred, and the power to appraise our own error subjectively is developed, we should be able to learn without KR because the error information for response correction is now available from within us. As appealing as this logic is, it has been criticized as theory (Schmidt, 1975), and there is no decisive evidence for it. The canons of rational science would say that there are no better grounds for abandoning an idea, but I am not ready for rationality yet. In clinging to this idea I am haunted by all of the learning without KR that goes on in the everyday world.

An ambitious young basketball player can teach himself how to shoot baskets by nailing a hoop to the side of the barn and practicing by himself. He can see the degree of his error, adjust his behavior to reduce it, and learn. You might say that seeing the error is conceptually no different from having the coach report it to you; the world has many kinds of KR. Perhaps this is true, but it is also true that the player has internalized the visual standard for a correct shot, and the comparison of visual feedback with the standard of correctness is his perception of error. The error perception is subjective, and knowledge of it is subjective reinforcement. Here the perceptual learning of the standard of correctness was undoubtedly easy and occurred a long time ago. It is the movements, made to the perceived visual error, that are difficult and it is with them that the self-learning occurs.

I am suggesting that if the standard of correctness for a feedback loop is learned early it can be used as a source of error information for subsequent learning in the other feedback loops. Vision is an influential and accessible feedback channel that could be used to test this idea, as in my basketball example, but in principle any feedback channel could be learned early and be the basis of subjective reinforcement. Evidence for this idea was reported by Newell (1976), and Zelaznik and Spring (1976). In both of these studies the subjects heard the auditory cues of a partner learning a ballistic movement task. Unmistakable learning was observed in the no-KR trials on the task that followed the listening. Notice that the primary treatment in these experiments on motor learning is perceptual learning operations, in which experience with stimuli refines appreciation of their properties (Gibson, 1969). This is where a theoretical emphasis on feedback stimuli and learning about them will lead you. It has been my stance that body motion and perceptual learning are linked by common principles (Adams, 1971, p. 124).

Obviously there are various kinds of tasks that should not show subjective reinforcement. If the task does not have a feedback channel that can be learned early then there cannot be subjective reinforcement. I cannot see a student dancer making much progress in teaching himself ballet. There does not appear to be a feedback channel where the standard of correctness can be learned early. Nor should there be subjective reinforcement when the visual and the motor sides of the task are learned at about the same rate. By the time the visual standard is learned the motor requirements are mostly learned also, and little further self-learning is possible. The laboratory learning of the commonplace and easy self-paced linear positioning task under visual conditions is probably of this sort, and if this analysis is correct it is not surprising that we have not found evidence for subjective reinforcement in our laboratories.

My interest in subjective reinforcement is not a disavowal of KR from an external source. That an objective event after the response can affect probability of response is an unassailable truth. The KR is necessary in the early stages of learning when the standards of correctness for the regulating stimuli are not known. The KR administrator knows the standards of correctness and the error in meeting them, and he provides the information until the subject acquires the standards of correctness for himself on one or more feedback channels.

E. Conclusion

These, then, are the four legacies of Edward Thorndike. Two of them we accept without thinking: the one that causes us to shy from punishment operations, and the one that has us reward the success of the act, ignoring the details of the movement sequence. I have suggested that we cast these restrictive legacies aside. The other two legacies on why KR affects behavior as it does, and the need for objective KR, have been challenged. We have new ideas on these matters, we are trying to refine them, we are arguing about them, and we are doing experiments on them. We are moving slowly on these new ideas, however. Maybe the new ideas are wrong, but maybe the power of the Thorndike tradition makes it difficult for us to adopt new ways of thinking. I submit that a scientist who can hold our minds so firmly for so long deserves respect.

References

Adams, J. A. *Human memory*. New York: McGraw-Hill, 1967.

Adams, J. A. Response feedback and learning. *Psychological Bulletin*, 1968, *70*, 486–504.

Adams, J. A. Acquisition of motor responses. In M. R. Marx (Ed.), *Learning: Processes*. Toronto: Macmillan, 1969.

Adams, J. A. A closed-loop theory of motor learning. *Journal of Motor Behavior*, 1971, *3*, 111–149.

Adams, J. A. *Learning and memory: An introduction*. Homewood, Illinois: Dorsey, 1976.

Adams, J. A., & Bray, N. W. A closed-loop theory of paired-associate verbal learning. *Psychological Review*, 1970, *77*, 385–405.

Adams, J. A., & Goetz, E. T. Feedback and practice as variables in error detection and correction. *Journal of Motor Behavior*, 1973, *5*, 217–224.

Adams, J. A., & Humes, J. M. Monitoring of complex visual displays. IV. Training for vigilance. *Human Factors*, 1963, *5*, 147–153.

Angell, J. R. *Psychology*. New York: Holt, 1904.

Anokhin, P. K. Cybernetics and the integrative activity of the brain. In M. Cole & I. Maltzman (Eds.), *A handbook of contemporary Soviet psychology*. New York: Basic Books, 1969.

Festinger, L. *A theory of cognitive dissonance*. Stanford: Stanford University Press, 1957.

Gibson, E. J. *Principles of perceptual learning and development*. New York: Appleton-Century-Crofts, 1969.

James, W. *The principles of psychology* (Vol. 1). New York: Holt, 1890.

Locke, E. A. Toward a theory of task motivation and incentives. *Organizational Behavior and Human Performance*, 1968, *3*, 157–189.

Locke, E. A., Cartledge, N., & Koeppel, J. Motivational effects of knowledge of results: A goal-setting phenomenon? *Psychological Bulletin*, 1968, *70*, 474–486.

Manzer, C. W. The effect of knowledge of output on muscular work. *Journal of Experimental Psychology*, 1935, *18*, 80–96.

Miller, N. E. Liberalization of basic S–R concepts: Extensions to conflict behavior, motivation, and social learning. In S. Koch (Ed.), *Psychology: A study of a science* (Vol. 2). New York: McGraw-Hill, 1959.

Montague, W. E. Elaborative strategies in verbal learning and memory. In G. H. Bower (Ed.), *The psychology of learning and motivation* (Vol. 6). New York: Academic Press, 1972.

Newell, K. M. Knowledge of results and motor learning. *Journal of Motor Behavior*, 1974, *6*, 235–244.

Newell, K. M. Motor learning without knowledge of results through the development of a response recognition mechanism. *Journal of Motor Behavior*, 1976, *8*, 209–217.

Newell, K. M. Knowledge of results and motor learning. In J. Keogh & R. S. Hutton (Eds.), *Exercise and sport sciences reviews* (Vol. 4). Santa Barbara, California: Journal Publishing Affiliates, 1977.

Payne, R. B. Functional properties of supplementary feedback stimuli. *Journal of Motor Behavior*, 1970, *2*, 37–43.

Payne, R. B., & Artley, C. W. Facilitation of psychomotor learning by classically differentiated supplementary feedback cues. *Journal of Motor Behavior*, 1972, *4*, 47–55.

Payne, R. B., & Dunman, L. S. Effects of classical predifferentiation on the functional properties of supplementary feedback cues. *Journal of Motor Behavior*, 1974, *6*, 47–52.

Payne, R. B., & Richardson, E. T. Effects of classically differentiated supplementary feedback cues on tracking skill. *Journal of Motor Behavior*, 1972, *4*, 257–261.

Payne, R. B., & Richardson, E. T. Control of supplementary feedback cue properties by differentiation and extinction procedures. *Bulletin of the Psychonomic Society*, 1974, *4*, 100–102.

Schendel, J. D., & Newell, K. M. On processing the information from knowledge of results. *Journal of Motor Behavior*, 1976, *8*, 251–256.

Schmidt, R. A. A schema theory of discrete motor skill learning. *Psychological Review*, 1975, *82*, 225–260.

Skinner, B. F. *Beyond freedom and dignity*. New York: Knopf, 1971.

Sokolov, E. N. The modeling properties of the nervous system. In M. Cole & I. Maltzman (Eds.), *A handbook of contemporary Soviet psychology*. New York: Basic Books, 1969.

Spence, K. W. *Behavior theory and conditioning*. New Haven: Yale University Press, 1956.

Thorndike, E. L. Animal intelligence: An experimental study of the associative processes in animals. *Psychological Review*, 1898, *2*, (4), (Monograph Supplement, Whole No. 8).

Thorndike, E. L. *The elements of psychology* (2nd ed.). New York: Seiler, 1907.

Thorndike, E. L. *Educational psychology: The psychology of learning* (Vol. 2). New York: Teachers College Press, 1913.

Thorndike, E. L. *The fundamentals of learning.* New York: Teachers College Press, 1932.

Thorndike, E. L. *The psychology of wants, interests, and attitudes.* New York: Appleton-Century, 1935.

Tolman, E. C. *Purposive behavior in animals and men.* New York: Century, 1932.

Tolman, E. C. Cognitive maps in rats and men. *Psychological Review,* 1948, *55,* 189–208.

Tolman, E. C. *Behavior and psychological man.* Berkeley: University of California Press, 1958.

Watson, J. B. Psychology as the behaviorist views it. *Psychological Review,* 1913, *20,* 158–177.

Zelaznik, H., & Spring, J. Feedback in response recognition and production. *Journal of Motor Behavior,* 1976, *8,* 309–312.

12

Perceptual Organization in Motor Learning[1]

Gordon L. Diewert
George E. Stelmach

I. Introduction

Organization is a topic that has received much discussion but very little substantive or systematic investigation in the motor learning area. Organization has been extensively examined by verbal psychologists such as Tulving, Mandler, and

[1] This research was supported by Research Grants NE–G–00–3–009 from the National Institute of Education, 160345 from the Research Committee of the Graduate School of the University of Wisconsin, and by a Royalty Fund Award from the Center of Cognitive Learning and Development at the University of Wisconsin to George E. Stelmach.

Information Processing in
Motor Control and Learning

Bousfield, but researchers in the motor area have yet to make similar progress. It is to both this theoretical and investigative void with respect to motor organization that this chapter is addressed.

Most psychomotor research has been almost entirely stimulus–response and feedback oriented (see Gentile & Nacson, 1976) and, in most instances, the research relevant to organizational theory has dealt primarily with response or output organization. Contemporary work on motor programs (Keele, 1973; Schmidt, 1975) and schema formation (Pew, 1974; Schmidt, 1975) has failed to address the effects of organization prior to movement execution. Concurrently, the theoretical emphasis has been on a feedback-based learning process where the learner plays a passive role. The historical emphasis in motor learning has been on the secondary consequences of movement and there has been little discussion of a cognitive or dynamic view of motor learning. Conversely, we propose that learning is dynamic and that the learner, in fact, can add much to a learning process based on feedback through his or her *perceptions* of the environment and development of strategies, plans, etc. Perception is so crucial to the human organism that it is imperative not to limit research on organization to the output side of an information-processing system but also to consider the establishment of memory representation that must precede movement execution. It is therefore proposed that the organizational processes that aid in memory representation be termed *perceptual organization*.

In light of the present use of the term organization, it is crucial to explain the more limiting term of perceptual organization. This clarification can be made by use of any of the contemporary stage models of movement information flow (e.g., Pew, 1974; Welford, 1977). Information in such a model can be conceptualized as moving serially or in parallel from perception to other stages such as response organization. Since perception precedes all other processes in sequence, it makes theoretical and pragmatic sense to deal with perceptual organization before other processes further along in the sequence can be clearly understood. Since response depends on perception or "perception is tied to action," output or response organization would be a function of any organizational benefits in the perceptual or memory mode. Therefore, and as mentioned before, it can be concluded that perceptual organization research is a current requirement or even a prerequisite to examination of response organization. This is not to say, however, that perception and response are strictly separate. We only wish to focus our review on the processes establishing memory representation, not those that produce movement in relation to those representations.

II. Definitions of Organization

Tulving (1968) defined organization in the following way: "The definition of the concept is implicit or confined to a single operational criterion, i.e., output consistency or negative part–whole transfer. . . . This is seen in outputs not common to the input [p. 15]." Mandler (1967a) said that a set of objects or events is organized when a consistent relation among the members of the set can be specified and, specifically, when membership of objects or events in subsets is stable and identifiable. Mandler further stated that organization has occurred when relations have been established and partitioned into subsets. Another definition was offered by Bower (1970): "Organization is a cognitive process and these processes group and relate and are the basis of learning [p. 19]."

These definitions are representative of how verbal psychologists conceptualize organization. It should be noted that the concepts differ very little in meaning and differ most in scope. What is needed, however, is an operational definition that will facilitate the examination of perceptual–motor organization. Therefore, perceptual–motor organization will be defined, in lieu of extensive research and based in part on verbal theories, as a cognitive process that assimiliates memory representation into a close, meaningful relationship resulting in a more stable memory structure than a single less associated representation. This view of organization leads to the formulation of three hypotheses. First, since a more stable memory implies better access to memory "traces," an increase in organization should be accompanied by improved performances (e.g., Tulving, 1962). Second, the relationships are stable over time and, therefore, any structure or organization should be observable at recall or reproduction. This hypothesis is in accordance with the evidence that subjects often impose a structure or organization on to-be-remembered items. Third, even in the absence of improved performance, organization may occur in that structure and need not always be linked to measurable performance change.

III. The Role of Oganization

The question that comes to mind at this point concerns the necessity of or the role of perceptual organizaiton. It is well known and accepted that man is a limited information processor (e.g., Broadbent, 1958) with respect to both the absolute amount of information that can be processed and processing over time. Furthermore, it is thought that perceptual organization (often referred to by others as chunking or coding) is necessary, if not essential, to allow processing of stimuli of even minimal complexity and load. In this way, structure or organization presented to or determined by the subject permits processing of large amounts of information and possibly better processing of smaller amounts of information within the bounds of the limited capacity model.

The following section provides a brief historical sketch of organization research relevant to the present topic of perceptual organization. This will be followed by discussions of how organization may be measured, how it can be presented, and how it has been examined within the context of motor behavior.

IV. History of Organizational Research

While more thorough historical discourses are available (Crowder, 1976; Bower, 1970; Mandler, 1967a; Tulving & Donaldson, 1972), it is enlightening to have a general knowledge of the evolutionary form of nonmotor (verbal) organization research.

Many researchers have pointed out the shift of emphasis in psychological research. For example, Broadbent (1971), Miller, Galanter, and Pribram (1960), and Postman (1972) have all addressed themselves to the progression of psychological theory and methodology from stimulus–response bond and habit strength concepts to contemporary cognitive and process-oriented theories of organization (Miller, 1956a; Tulving, 1962), coding (Melton & Martin, 1972), and schema formation (Schmidt, 1975). Just as psychology in general had adopted an active, organizational focus, so had the specific area of verbal psychology. Associationistic theory has as its basic premise that man is a passive transmitter of information and that stimulus-response bonds and, ultimately, organization are established by repeated exposure. The crucial point is that man is a passive processor in the sense that the person does not actively impose or contribute to the learning process. This approach would take the view that organization depends on association. The organizational view of memory and learning has its roots in Gestalt psychology, specifically, the principles of organization and perceptual grouping. Advocates of Gestalt psychology emphasized how memory traces changed over time with respect to neural interaction and organization. Four basic tenets of the Gestalt view will be listed for insight as to how perceptual–motor organization may function. First, organization depends largely on initial perception of events. Second, the form of organization is correlated to the commonalities of the component units or events. This implies that an optimal or natural organization exists for all situations or any given situation. Third and fourth, the availability of past experiences for recall depends on memory strength and accessability of memory representations for recall depends on commonality between memory units and current stimuli. Although all four points have relevance to perceptual–motor organization, the present emphasis will be on grouping, perception, and optimal organization. Furthermore, with respect to the theoretical orientation of organizational psychology, it is thought that man can develop rules and plans for perception and storage in memory and can actively construct, reconstruct, and alter memory. An advocate of this approach might state that associations occur because of organization, not as an antecedent of organization.

Paralleling the shift from association-based to organization-based memory is a shift from serial and paired associate learning to free recall methodology. Although these methodologies differ theoretically, they have all been employed, at least to some extent, to investigate verbal organiaztion. Since the free recall paradigm has been the most productive and enlightening, the paragraphs to follow will only briefly describe paired associate and serial learning paradigms, whereas free recall theory and design will be discussed at length.

A. Serial and Paired Associated Learning

In serial learning the subject is presented with a serial list of items and is then asked to recall those items in the same order (see the reviews in Bower, 1970; Mandler, 1967a,b; McGeoch & Irion, 1952). Since this procedure is characterized by both input and output inflexibility it is not clear how the subject is organizing. Therefore, it would be impossible to examine how the subject organizes except by inference from recall performance. However, "performance structure," such as parts of a serial list being recalled relatively better than other parts, or even overall consistency may allow indirect speculation as to the nature of possible perceptual organization constellations. Alternately, experimenter-presented organization (EPO) could be directly examined by presenting lists of varying serial organizations or structures and then observing performance differences.

For paired associate learning, the usual methodology involves presentation of word pairs. Then the subject is presented with one word of a pair and he or she is asked to recall the other word of the pair. This procedure has been used more frequently by contemporary researchers (e.g., Battig, 1966; Crowder, 1976; Glanzer, 1962; Segal & Mandler, 1967; Underwood & Schulz, 1960; see reviews in Bower, 1970; Mandler, 1967a) to investigate organization. Interest has been directed at the organizational processes needed for grouping, clustering, and mnemonic links to determine the differential accessability of the words within a pair and to determine the structure of the pairs themselves in memory. Just as was noted for serial learning, however, structure and inflexibility are present at both input and recall, limiting application to EPO-type questions. Again, inference about subject-discovered organization (SDO) must predominantly rely on the indirect evidence of performance measures.

Both serial and paired associate paradigms present at least two major problems to the investigation of organization. First, as mentioned above, without freedom to recall in the order the subject finds to be optimal, the results are confounded with respect to EPO and SDO. Only performance change can be measured in this paradigm. Second, although this point was not explicitly made before, structure imposed by the experimenter at input, such as a serial list and/or word pair followed by a similarly structured recall order, will mask any SDO effects. Nevertheless, later work has lead to an experimental procedure, termed free recall, that attempts to circumvent these problems.

B. Free Recall

Free recall paradigms usually involve random presentation of test items after which the subject recalls or reproduces, in any order, as many of the items as he or she can remember. This procedure has become popular since researchers have been able to examine how the subject's organization correlates with performance; in fact, even if exact free recall procedures are not employed, free recall theory prevails.

This paradigm has been pioneered by Tulving (1962, 1964, 1965, 1966) based on the work and theoretical developments of Bousfield (1953), Cofer (1959), and Miller (1956a,b). A series of experiments by Tulving exemplifies a logical approach to measuring organization, to investigating the organization versus repetition issue, and to determining how organization and performance covary; it is of particular interest that Tulving makes use of paired and serial tasks when appropriate even though free recall thoughts and theories predominate his thinking.

The classic study on organization was undertaken by Endel Tulving at the University of Toronto in the early 1960s (Tulving, 1962). To determine the way in which subjects grouped or related words at recall, he developed a measure of subjective organization (SO). SO is derived in such a way that, as consistency of recall order from trial to trial is maintained, SO increases. The subject's task in the course of experimentation was to attempt to recall as many words as possible from a random list of 16 unrelated words presented in a free recall experiment on each of 16 trials. As would be expected, performance improved from five to six correct to close to perfection after 16 trials. The interesting finding, however, was that, even though the subjects were free to recall in any order and presentation order varied randomly from trial to trial, subjects tended to establish and maintain similar recall orders. Furthermore, SO increased significantly over the 16 trials. Tulving concluded that, since organization and performance were correlated, it is not unreasonable to posit that SO *causes* improved performance.

One must be cautious, however, in proposing a causal relationship between organization and performance since a significant correlation does not necessarily denote causation. Studies by Dallett (1964) and Tulving (1965) apply directly to this question of causality. In a first experiment, Tulving (1965) presented two groups of subjects in a free recall experiment with lists of words characterized by either high organization or low organization, respectively. These lists were derived from Tulving's (1962) experiment and SO was used as a criterion for levels of organization. The high-organization group learned the words much faster and more faithfully retained the input order. The low-organization group took much longer to learn the words and, not surprisingly, attempted to adopt the order presented to the other group even though they had never been exposed to that order. A second experiment in the same study found evidence based on converging operation using a serial anticipation (serial learning) task. Subjects in the high-organization group learned much faster. Clearly then, the relationship between organization and performance is causal since manipulation of organization directly affected performance.

Tulving (1966) provided evidence on how organization and performance interact with repetition. Two experimental groups were given the task of reading 22 pairs of items in six continuous trials. One group read the words that were to be memorized later while the control group was presented with words unrelated to those that they would later memorize. Since the two groups did not differ in later attempts at recall and memorization, Tulving suggested that repetition alone is not the crucial factor in memory storage. In a follow-up experiment from the same study, Tulving found that learning part of a list of words before learning the whole list retards learning of the whole list, whereas prior learning of irrelevant words had no effect on learning in a control group. One explanation of this finding is that the organization developed from the partial list is not appropriate to the whole list; therefore, to learn the whole list the subject must reorganize units already in memory. Again, the structure or organization of practice appears to be the crucial factor superseding unstructured practice or repetition.

In summary, it appears that organizational research is becoming dominated by free recall theory and experimentation, whereas serial and paired associate learning is receiving decreasing interest but it still of use in certain situations. The question remains, however, as to which procedure or procedures are best for investigation of perceptual–motor organization. Even though movements are serial or even "paired" by nature of their use in execution of movement, any preconceived experimental procedure, other than totally random or subject controlled, superimposes a structure when that specific structure may not be optimal or even desired in the free recall situation. If the experimenter wishes to work within this framework, he must be aware of this problem and be prepared to deal with it adequately, especially if he chooses to work with structured inputs. Therefore, perceptual–motor research faces the dilemma of choosing a procedure based on verbal work, where free recall theory is probably best, or implementing totally new procedures along with verbal paradigms. The best strategy appears to be the latter since the skilled researcher can prevent many problems of verbal research while instituting procedures appropriate to motor behaivor. In any case, whatever research tack is undertaken, measurement of organization will be a crucial topic.

V. Measurement of Organization

Essential to this review and to future research is an understanding of how organization has been or could be measured. Based on general experimental procedures, an unstructured input can be presented and then recall or reproduction structure and/or performance measured; in this situation we are dealing with subject-discovered organization (SDO). Alternately, a structured input can be presented and then reproduction structure and/or performance measured; here we are dealing with experimenter-presented organization (EPO). From these basic conditions, various measures of organization have been formulated. Other than qualitative measures of grouping or relating, or even simple observation of consistent patterns and direct performance measures, various ingenious measures of organization are available.

A. Intertrial Repetition and Clustering

Clustering measures were proposed by Bousfield (1953) and he defined them as the sequential occurrence in free recall paradigms of two items belonging to a category present in the stimulus list. The number of repetitions in a cluster is therefore one less than the number of items in the cluster.

Intertrial repetition is a term proposed by Bousfield and, since it is very similar to Tulving's (1962) subjective measure, its description will be incorporated into the following paragraph. Exact descriptions of intertrial repetition and subjective organization can be found in an excellent paper by Bousfield and Bousfield (1966).

Subjective organization (SO) (Tulving, 1962, 1968) is a measure based on the constancies in response orderings that develop in a series of free recall trials when the order of presentation is changed from trial to trial. It is a measure based on information theory that reflects noise in an information transmission situation, that is, information or structure present at recall that was not present at input. In essence, it is an index based on a ratio of obtained organization relative to the total possible organization. Both SO and intertrial repetition reflect consistency or organization imposed on the input information by the subject, constrained by the amount of structure that is inherently present in the input at the time of presentation.

There are some problems, however, with these measures. Even though performance approaches perfection, the measures of organization rarely surpass 50% (Postman, Burns, & Hasher, 1970). This implies that organization as indexed by output organization may play a modest role in performance or that the measures used are only partial indexes of the degree of organization. As Postman (1971) pointed out, organization may not be directly reflected in output consistency and only in certain limited situations, such as sequential recall tasks, may organization be properly reflected. Stated another way, the very way in which the subject recalls the items, one at a time, limits us to the type of organization measure that can be implemented. For example, SO and intertrial repetition do not reflect clustering in a "spatial" sense because recall is always sequential.

Another problem is that, even though performance is often correlated to SO and intertrial repetition, by use of instructions the measures of organization can be increased without at the same time effecting increases in performance (Mayhew, 1967; Puff, 1970). It appears that the experimenter's instructions can affect the degree to which organization can account for performance change.

B. Transfer

Tests of transfer provide an alternate experimental avenue to assess the functional significance of subjective organization with respect to the nature and form of the memory structure. Although transfer can be examined in light of both subjective groupings and associations (Postman, 1972), only subjective groupings will be considered here. Postman (1972) further stated the following.

Studies of transfer between successive free recall tasks bring into focus the assumption that speed of learning depends on the particular structure that has been imposed on the materials during acquisition. To sharpen the prediction, it becomes useful to add the further assumption that for each subject learning a given list of items there is an optimal organization that will serve to maximize his performance. Prior practice that established groupings inconsistent with the optimal structure should, therefore, be a source of interference. One important implication of this hypothesis is that there should be negative transfer from part-list to whole-list learning when the items are drawn from a pool of unrelated words: The higher order units established during part-learning should be less than optimal for the mastery of the total list [p. 26].

Even though transfer effects have been found (Bower & Lesgold, 1969; Tulving, 1966), there are alternate explanations of some merit. Roberts (1969) suggested that the deficit in performance may be produced by the subject's failure to give an adequate amount of attention to all items during both input and output. Tulving and Osler (1967) argued that the deficit may be due to failure to discriminate between recent items and the remainder of the material. Nonetheless, transfer studies appear to reveal much about organization; in fact, researchers have begun to look at positive transfer as a new approach to the investigation of organization (see Bower, 1970; Tulving, 1968).

C. Measurement of Perceptual–Motor Organization

How could organization of movement information be measured? If random movements are presented for recall, a measure of organization such as SO could be used on the order of reproduction. Measures based on extensive new research could be developed that are sensitive to nonsequential structures and appropriate to motor organization. Alternately, for structured inputs, both consistency and performance may be indicative of organization, but only where the structure is present and not immediately apparent, such as in a list of words containing items from only four categories (e.g., Bousfield, 1953). Otherwise, only the effects of EPO can be considered. In any event, when linear positioning tasks are employed, qualitative description of trial to trial reproduction order appears to be complete and sufficient due to the simplicity of the task.

With respect to transfer interference, this appears to be a promising procedure. Just as researchers use capacity and structural interference to determine storage codes (Diewert, 1975), interference could also be used to examine the memory structure when the experimental procedures prohibit measurement of output consistency, such as is the case when the reproduction order is fixed by the experimenter. One approach may be to interpolate movements ordered in various ways between presentation and reproduction of movements. It should be expected that a constellation of movements most similar to how the subject is organizing will maximally disrupt performance and/or learning (see Melton & Martin, 1972). Therefore, it seems best to use a multifaceted approach based on both structured and unstructured inputs depending on the question of interest. Structured inputs appear to be indicative of EPO, whereas unstructured inputs tell us more about the role the subject plays in manipulation and perception of input information.

VI. Experimenter-Presented and Subject-Discovered Organization

Postman (1972), based on the increasing criticism of experiments that present subjects with organized instead of random information, suggested that a separation of environmental or EPO and SDO is necessary. An EPO experiment usually consists of a lists of words to be recalled that has an organization structure. An example of this procedure is found in the classic study by Bousfield (1953). He presented subjects with a list of words that had four obvious categories for classification. In recall, it was found that the resulting organization (clustering) was above a chance level. Bousfield concluded that the clustering was evidence for the operation of organization; however, as Bousfield himself mentioned, there are some alternate explanations that link the clustering to an association-based mechanism called *habit strength*. In this respect, Postman (1972) criticized this type of study based on the premise that an explanation of the findings need not include subjective organization-based mechanisms. This critique is based on the fact that clustering tendencies can be explained by processes such as response contiguity and information reduction. Moreover, it is implicit that the subject using EPO does not have to select his own organizational plan. He need only observe what organization is present, store it, and transmit the structure to recall to facilitate performance. Therefore, EPO experiments only allow inference to how organization can be used but not to how it can be formed.

Conversely, SDO experiments employ theory and methodology which seem best to investigate the actual organizational process in that the subjects are influenced as little as possible by list structure or method of presentation. Tulving (1962) revealed this approach clearly in a free recall experiment that was discussed earlier. The experiment was similar to Bousfield's (1953) except that the words in the list presented for recall were unrelated; that is, there was no obvious, inherent structure. The results indicated that the subjects were clustering identical words in the same way for each trial. In this type of experiment, it is clear that the subject has to rely on his own organization that can be used with the list of words, not on an experimenter-presented plan. This study found, as did Bousfield's (1953), that, as performance (percentage correct) increased, there was a concomitant increase in SO, indicating that organization, as measured by clustering or redundancy, is an important process in memory. Furthermore, even though

EPO was avoided as much as possible, the subject was still able to organize, which strongly supports using unstructured inputs to determine the organizational ability of subjects.

Postman (1972) summed up the difference between EPO and SDO as follows: "When a known structure is imposed on the input by the experimenter and is reflected in the output, it becomes far less clear what inferences can be legitimately drawn about the role of organizational processes [p. 35]." In addition, as mentioned before and repeated for emphasis here, Postman believes that, along with learning by association, the improved recall and clustering in EPO experiments could be brought about by response contiguity or "learning by rote"; for example, the input structure is transmitted to storage and is then recalled with a minimum of cognitive processing required by the subject.

At this point it appears that the unstructured, free recall paradigm is best for the investigation of verbal organization. However, the criticism of EPO designs arises in verbal research and therefore may not have the same problems in motor behavior. Perhaps the dilemma can be resolved by considering two possible questions that an experimenter may ask:

1. What effect does organization have?
2. How does a subject organize?

If a researcher seeks to answer the first question, the best strategy may be to structure the environment and examine performance. With respect to the second question, the preceding discussions support using SDO designs. At least SDO designs as defined are of merit because the subject must impose his or her own preference for organization. This is illustrated by Tulving (1962), who reported that even though subjects tended to organize in a similar manner, the SO measures indicated that organization had intrasubject properties; that is, each subject had some form of unique classification.

Verbal research clearly favors SDO experiments. However, the motor area does not have a research base on which to justifiably favor either EPO or SDO. This being the case, future research in motor learning should use whatever approach is best suited to answer the question of interest.

VII. Research in Motor Learning Relevant to Perceptual–Motor Organization

As mentioned in Section I, very little work has been done on perceptual–motor organization and the research that has been conducted has stressed organization for movement execution. Nevertheless, there is some research that bears directly on this topic. Although there are numerous studies of peripheral interest, the preliminary work conducted by Marteniuk (1973) and Roy and Diewert (1975) plus the extensive work done at the Motor Behavior Laboratory at the University of Wisconsin (Stelmach, 1977; Stelmach & Kelso, 1977; Stelmach & McCracken, Note 1) supported the notion that premovement organization or strategy formation is a potent independent variable. Almost without exception, a self-terminated movement or a movement whose relationship to other movements is known is reproduced better than movements lacking premovement organization. A review of these preselected versus constrained versus passive movement studies can be found in Stelmach and Kelso (1977).

Nacson, Jaeger, and Gentile (1972), as well as Shea (1977), found that verbal labels or knowledge of movement relationships given to subjects resulted in improved reproduction performance as well as differential performance patterns. These results indicated that movement reproduction depends on more than movement-generated feedback, as suggested by Adams (1976).

The foregoing studies discussed suggest a dynamic role for the subject as indicated by an ability to supplement feedback by higher-order strategies and organizational mechanisms. In light of the contemporary dichotomy of stimulus–response and organizational psychology, the organizational or cognitive view has support. Therefore, the research section to follow will begin to examine the feedback versus organization issue and its replicability and generality to motor learning.

VIII. Perceptual Organization: Experimenter-Presented and Subject-Discovered Organization

A. Experimenter-Presented Organization

The experiment by Nacson (1973) suggested that the learning of movement information is not merely a function of repetition or feedback. Nacson provided evidence that the order of movement presentation or organization facilitated learning and retention since performance during both knowledge of results (KR) trials and KR withdrawal trials was better than movements that were presented randomly. The interpretation presented by Nacson and by Gentile and Nacson (1976) centered around active organization of movement information based on recognition of the number of movements and equal interval sizes between movement endpoints.

An attempt was made to replicate the Nacson (1973) findings. Three experimental groups ($n = 6$; all between-subject groups reported in this paper, except where otherwise noted, were of this size) were presented with movements of lengths of 10, 20, 30, 40, and 50 cm on a linear positioning apparatus. The sequential group (sequential–sequential) received the order 10–20–30–40–50, the long–short group received the order 50–10–40–20–30, and the random group (random–random) received a different order in every trial block.

Each trial block consisted of reproduction attempts in the order specified by the experimental group. Any one trial within a block consisted of the blindfolded subject moving the positioning handle to a stop placed at the appropriate position followed by a reproduction attempt with the stop removed. In all instances, the experimenter returned the positioning handle to the start position. After each block of five trials, each movement had been presented an equal number of times. All subjects received a total of 10 trial blocks; during the first 6 blocks or the learning phase, verbal KR to the nearest millimeter was given. The remaining 4 blocks, or withdrawal phase, consisted of trials where KR was not given. During the KR phase, subjects were instructed to reduce errors as much as possible; for the withdrawal phase, subjects were requested to attempt to keep reducing error in reference to what they had learned during the KR trials.

Replication of the Nacson (1973) results would be revealed by a difference between experimental groups and/or an interaction with trials. Although there were significant effects in absolute error (AE) and constant error (CE), these were related only to reduction in error over learning trials and differential CE effects for each movement length. Neither of the effects necessary to support Nacson was found. One explanation may be the present use of a linear slide; Nacson employed a curvilinear apparatus which may have somehow facilitated organization. Alternately, since the Nacson study was never reported in full, it is possible that the failure to replicate was a function of experimental instructions.

Organized movement sequences may improve performance and learning only if, as Nacson himself implies (see Gentile & Nacson, 1976), subjects are aware of the organization. During debriefing in the experiment just discussed, three of six subjects in the sequential–sequential and long–short groups noticed the presentation orders, whereas not one subject knew that the movements were equidistant. These reports suggested that one way to ensure maximum benefit of EPO is to direct the subjects, through instructions, to attempt to determine the movement sequences and lengths. Therefore, this experiment attempted to ascertain if the effects of EPO are realized when the subject actively seeks to determine and use the structure and order presented.

The procedures were the same as described earlier except that the long–short group was not tested since organization effects were minimal. The number of KR trial blocks was increased to 10 and the number of withdrawal blocks to 6. Before the experiment began and after every 2 trial blocks, the subjects were reminded to attempt to determine if a consistent order of presentation was used and to try to ascertain the endpoint interval sizes. It is important to note that each group received identical instructions.

For the learning phase in AE, there were significant differences between Groups, Movements, and Trials as well as a three-way interaction ($p < 0.01$). The Groups × Trials interaction is presented in Figure 1; the Movements effect was characterized by largest error at 30 cm. In CE, the effects were due to larger positive bias at 30 cm, especially for the random–random group.

All effects in withdrawal for AE were significant ($p < 0.005$) except the

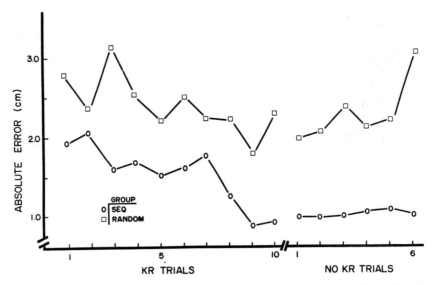

Figure 1 Absolute error as a function of KR trials (learning phase) and no KR trials (withdrawal phase) for both sequential–sequential (SEQ) and random–random (RANDOM) groups.

Movements × Trials interaction. As before, error increased and then decreased as movement length increased. The Groups × Trials interaction is also presented in Figure 1. For CE, the effects were primarily due to positive bias for the 30-cm movement.

Examination of the results supported the speculation concerning the role of instructions and/or direction of attention in perceptual–motor organization. The sequential–sequential group was markedly superior in both the learning and withdrawal phases. In fact, the AE scores in the withdrawal phase remained remarkably steady for the six trial blocks tested. Furthermore, all subjects in the sequential–sequential group immediately discovered the order and all but one subject stated that interval sizes were equal by Trial 10. Therefore, the Nacson (1973) results were replicated only when specific instructions to use the EPO were given.

The previous experiment clearly demonstrated that the structure or organization of practice is a potent factor in motor learning. However, it is important to know if performance on any one movement is maintained outside of the sequential presentation order. If performance is tied to the position in a sequence, then the organization examined here lacks generality and implies that an intact and rigid memory constellation has been established. On the other hand, if performance is not affected by removal of the structure, EPO is a potent process facilitating individual memory representation. If this is the case, the implication for generality and application of memory units into a new context is clear. The next experiment attempted to answer this question by having subjects learn under the sequential–sequential conditions and then switch to random orders in the withdrawal phase and similarly learn under random orders and switch to sequential–sequential conditions in withdrawal. The procedures and number of trials presented were the same as those used in the previous experiment. The four experimental groups were labeled sequential–random (S–R) and random–sequential (R–S), depending on the position of organized trials. The sequential–sequential (S–S) and random–random (R–R) groups were also retested.

For the learning phase in AE, the Groups, Movements, and Trials effects were significant ($p < 0.001$). The Trials effect was caused by decreasing error and the Movement effect was caused by error increasing with the length of the movement tested. Figure 2 clearly displays the Group differences. First, note that sequential–sequential and random–random groups are convincing replications of the data presented in Figure 1. Specifically, note that the learning phases of the sequential–sequential and random–random groups match the learning phases of the same groups in the preceding experiment.

In the withdrawal phase for AE, the Groups, Movements, Groups × Movements, and Groups × Trials interactions were significant ($p < 0.001$). Similar to the learning phase, effects involving the Movement factor were characterized by a positive correlation between length and error. The Groups effects,

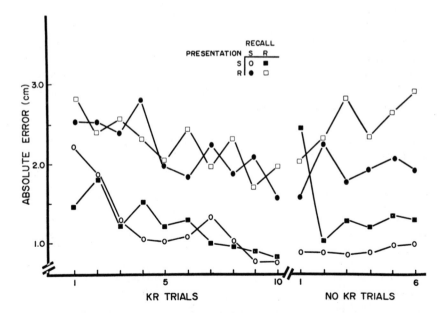

Figure 2 Absolute error as a function of KR trials (learning phase) and no KR trials (withdrawal phase) for the S–S, R–R, R–S, and S–R groups (S, sequential; R, random).

however, tell most about the organizational effects. The sequential–sequential group is again superior and differs from the sequential–random group only for Trial 1. The random–random group is again the worst with the random–sequential group placed between the sequential–sequential and sequential–random groups and the random–random group.

The CE effects mirrored the AE data except for a "bowed" trend characterized by least bias at both short and long movements. In most instances, CE was near zero and positively biased.

Figure 2 clearly indicates that the sequential–sequential group does not differ from the sequential–random group in withdrawal. Therefore, it can be concluded that perceptual–motor organization effects are not limited to structured situations. Movement components learned under an organized regimen can be performed as well in a novel situation, that is, a random order. A memory of nonrigid structure and of strong representation is therefore indicated. The efficacy of perceptual organization is further supported by the superiority of the random–sequential group over the random–random group in withdrawal. Since the only difference between the two groups is the sequential reproduction in withdrawal, the difference should be attributed to organization. Note, however, the first withdrawal trial for the sequential–random group. This point differs from the sequential–sequential first trial point. After consultation with each subject, it is suggested that it took one trial for subjects to "refocus" their perception and organization of the task. Furthermore, with respect to sequences and interval sizes, all subjects in the sequential–sequential and sequential–random groups immediately or by Trial 5 noticed the sequential order in the appropriate phase and all subjects were sure of equal interval sizes by Trial 2 in the appropriate phase. It also is interesting to note that few subjects in the random–random and random–sequential groups noted the organization. Only when organization was presented in the withdrawal phase for the random–sequential subjects was it detected. In summary, organization presented by the experimenter to the subject (EPO) is a potent variable in motor learning, supporting a cognitive view of motor learning.

B. Subject-Discovered Organization

With some evidence that EPO is beneficial in motor behavior, it seemed fruitful to turn to a free recall situation for movement information. Two relevant theoretical questions come to mind:

1. Does reproduction performance improve with subjective organization?
2. Do subjects develop a consistent reproduction order?

To gain some insight into the application of the free recall paradigm to motor learning, four additional trials were given to the subjects in the four experimental groups of the experiment just discussed. Subjects were requested to show the experimenter each of the five movements, one at a time, in an order that would allow maximum accuracy. These reproduction movements were further constrained by the requirement that reproduction be in blocks of five, each block consisting of one reproduction of each movement.

With respect to AE, there were significant effects for Groups, Movements, and the Movements × Trials interaction ($p < 0.01$). Again Movements effects were related to error increasing as a function of length, especially in the random-sequential group. CE effects were related to increased positive bias as a function of length.

The results presented in Figure 3 support the memory strength and flexibility notions presented earlier. That is, switching to a new experimental situation has little effect on performance when a strong memory representation is established through learning in an organized manner. With respect to how subjects organize, all free reproduction attempts were done in a sequential manner. This is not surprising, however, since the subjects in the sequential–sequential, sequential–random, and random–sequential groups had experience with the sequential reproduction pattern. What is surprising is the fact that subjects in the random-

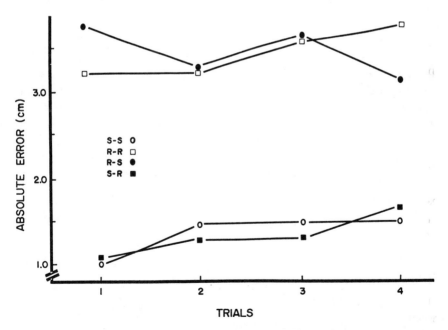

Figure 3 Absolute error as a function of the S–S, R–R, R–S, and S–R groups in free recall (S, sequential; R, random).

random group, when "free" to reproduce how they wish, chose a sequential pattern. The finding that in free recall the groups that learned under sequential sequences performed better than groups that learned under random conditions suggests that input order is a crucial variable in motor learning. However, since both groups recalled with identical orders indicates that subjects organize their movements sequentially regardless of input order.

The free recall findings just discussed provided some evidence for movement information with respect to free recall performance. More realistically, however, movements should be learned under conditions most conducive to SDO that do not bias reproduction order. This could be achieved by presenting the movements in random blocks of five with each block followed by the subject reproducing the movements in any order he or she wishes. This procedure would be strictly analogous to that used by Tulving (1968) in his free recall experiments. Two important questions can be answered by testing two groups, one with KR and one without KR: First, is KR unnecessary when a subject is allowed to organize in a free situation? Second, can subjects develop a consistent reproduction strategy?

Movements were presented in 10 random blocks of five movements each; all movements were made to a stop from the starting position. After each block of five movements was presented, the subject was asked to reproduce each of the five movements presented by the experimenter in any order desired by the subject. Each reproduction attempt was also made from the starting position. It should be clearly pointed out that no reproduction attempts were made until all five movements were presented, resulting in the following repeating sequence: five presentations–five reproduction attempts. As in the EPO experiments, the instructions stressed reduction of error and further stressed establishment of a consistent reproduction order that would permit such error reductions. When KR was an independent variable, it was given after *each* reproduction attempt.

For both the KR group and the no-KR group the Trials effect was significant in AE ($p < 0.05$). For CE, the no-KR group was characterized by large error at 50 cm. No other effects were significant and even at a liberal probability level the Groups effect did not differ (Figure 4).

There is clear evidence that learning has occurred without KR, specifically, without verbal KR given to the nearest millimeter. The fact that the KR and no-KR groups did not differ suggests that KR is unnecessary when the subject is free to reproduce in his own way. Organization therefore is cast as a potent process even in unstructured situations.

With respect to reproduction order, the subjects in the no-KR group all established a linear reproduction order. Four of six subjects reproduced in a strictly linear manner (1–2–3–4–5), whereas the other two subjects also reproduced linearly in an order such as 5–4–3–1–2. In the KR group, five of six subjects reprooduced in the strictly linear manner, whereas the other subject reproduced in

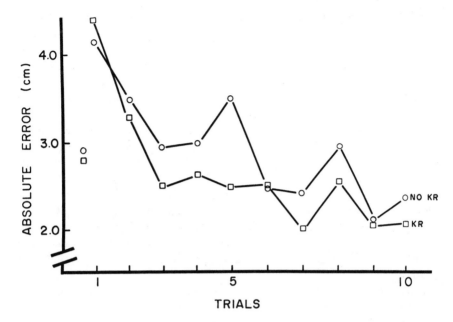

Figure 4 Absolute error as a function of trials for both KR and no-KR groups in free recall.

the order 1–2–3–5–4. Therefore, under the constraints of the task, it appears that subjects can organize in a free recall situation, reduce error independently of verbal KR, and prefer to do so using a linear reproduction strategy.

The finding of learning without KR is to some extent surprising and suggests that SO can replace KR in certain situations. However, such a finding bears replication to differentiate further, both theoretically and pragmatically, the interactive roles of KR and SO. It is possible that by systematically modifying and preventing SO the contribution of perceptual–motor organization can be isolated more exactly.

Three experimental groups ($n = 10$) were tested. The first group was a replication of the experiment just described: SO—half the subjects received KR and half did not. The second group was asked to reproduce movements from shortest to longest. This group was labeled EPO and again half the subjects received KR. Finally, a group termed forced random (FR) was required to reproduce in the random presentation order used each time regardless of the presence or absence of KR. All other procedures were identical to those reported earlier except that an additional six trial blocks were given where, in the case of the KR conditions, KR was withdrawn. The first 10 trials were termed Phase 1 and the remaining 6 trials, where neither group received KR, were labeled Phase 2.

The CE data tend to support the AE data in all instances and, since no particular patterns of bias were apparent, only AE data will be discussed. The Groups, Movements, Trials, and Groups × KR Level × Trials interaction were all highly significant ($p < 0.025$) in Phase 1. From Figures 5 and 6 it can be seen that, when organization was available, KR was again found to be unnecessary for learning to take place. This must be the case since learning occurred in the SO and EPO groups even when an external error report was not given. In addition, since learning is not nearly as proficient when organization is prevented and KR is present, as is the case in the FR group, organization is left as the only variable that could be causing the learning effect in both this and the previous experiment. With respect to the Movement effect, the trend for increasing error with length was again noted.

The Phase 2 data were highly supportive of the role of organization in motor learning. A significant Groups effect ($p < 0.001$) demonstrated that SO allows more accurate performance than EPO, and both organized groups were better than the FR group. The fact that error varies as a function of level or organization is strong converging evidence that organization, not KR, was the important variable in operation.

Again Movements effects were caused by the increasing error associated with length. However, the most interesting finding revolves around the main effect of KR Level ($p < 0.005$), where it was noted that, in Phase 2, performance based on previous trials without KR was best. When this fact is considered, along with the

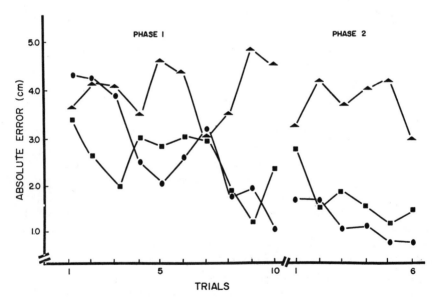

Figure 5   Absolute error as a function of trials in Phases 1 and 2 for the no-KR groups in free recall (●, SO; ■, EPO; ▲, FR).

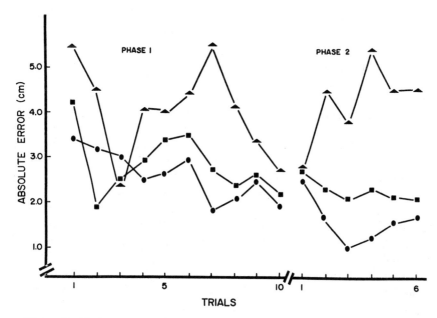

Figure 6 Absolute error as a function of trials in Phases 1 and 2 for the KR groups in free recall (●, SO; ■, EPO; ▲, FR).

significant interaction of Groups × Trials ($p < 0.025$) plotted in Figures 5 and 6, the resilience of the organized memory representation is obvious.

In summary, just as was the case for EPO, SO is a strong variable for motor learning. However, now it appears that performance is best in a situation where the subject initiates the organization even though the organization is almost exactly the same. This statement can be made since the SO groups, almost without exception, chose to reproduce in a sequential manner. Finally, and perhaps most important, it appears that in certain situations learning can occur (based on organization) without KR and without the necessity for previous trials where KR was given.

This type of finding casts doubts on the theoretical role typically given KR in establishing memory representation (Adams, 1976). As can be seen in the data, KR in its classical sense is not needed for motor learning.

IX. Summary and Future Directions

With respect to the theoretical questions related to perceptual organization, various important conclusions are possible. First, experimenter-presented organization is an important factor in motor learning only when the subject is able to seek and to utilize organization actively; the mere presentation of organization is not sufficient. This suggests that the experimenter must carefully instruct subjects to realize the full benefits of organization on memory representation; what the subject is perceiving and processing is not necessarily what is in fact occurring.

No less important is the fact that individual memory representations, built up through presentation of organized stimuli, are not locked to that organization. In other words, reproduction of individual movements under KR withdrawal conditions did not depend on the learned organizational sequence. Therefore, the conclusion is possible that the effects of perceptual organization are generalizable to new or altered experimental situations and, taking the results one step further, perhaps to novel everyday movement situations.

Free recall paradigms tell us much about the learning process for movement. Subjects quickly established an optimal reproduction order and, more important, learning occurred independently of the presence or absence of verbal KR. In fact, the results strongly supported the dynamic role of the subject for learning of movement.

The future holds much promise beyond the results presented here. More work is needed to further define and differentiate the effects of subject-discovered and experimenter-presented organization. More specific work is needed on the relationship between perceptual–motor organization and recall, recognition, and retrieval as well as long- and short-term memory. Of course, other researchers will consider how perceptual organization relates to more "ecologically valid" movements such as those made in two- and three-dimensions, those that are time and/or speed stressed, and those made with and without the presence of efference. Research is also needed to determine how perceptual organization changes with development and how learning based on organization may be facilitated at different age levels.

Perceptual organization also may be found to directly affect movement organization for response execution. However, a word of caution is in order. Research must be extensive and systematic, not haphazard, as it has been in the past. More important, researchers in motor learning must not blindly adopt verbal theories and methodologies. Instead, we should borrow from verbal theory as an impetus for our own work only when necessary. We should also strive to retain the uniqueness of the motor system and not allow it to be masked by these verbal theories.

In conclusion, the present series of experiments have provided a much needed start toward establishing the importance of organizational processes in motor behavior. The most striking conclusion is that memory representation of movement can be enhanced by perceptual organization which is a set-back for those closed-loop theorists who have advocated that movement memory representation is dependent entirely on feedback and practice. While the findings are much too preliminary to begin theorizing about the mechanisms involved, they do stress the importance of cognitive activity in motor behavior and open the door for new and different types of experimenters. As theories and models of motor learning, specifically of perceptual motor organization, are established, this knowledge should have direct application to the teaching and rehabilitation of motor skills. As such, organization research should produce theoretical and practical benefits for all aspects of motor behavior.

Reference Notes

1. Stelmach, G. E., & McCracken, H. D. *Storage codes for movement information.* Paper presented at the Attention and Performance VII Symposium, Marseille, France, August, 1976.

References

Adams, J. A. Issues for a closed-loop theory of motor learning. In G. E. Stelmach (Ed.), *Motor control: Issues and trends.* New York: Academic Press, 1976.

Battig, W. F. Evidence for coding processes in "rote" paired associate learning. *Journal of Verbal Learning and Verbal Behavior,* 1966, *5,* 177–181.

Bousfield, W. A. The occurrence of clustering in the recall of randomly arranged associates. *Journal of General Psychology,* 1953, *49,* 229–240.

Bousfield, A. K., & Bousfield, W. A. Measurement of clustering and of sequential constancies in repeated free recall. *Psychological Reports,* 1966, *19,* 935–942.

Bower, G. H. Organizational factors in memory. *Cognitive Psychology,* 1970, *1,* 18–46.

Bower, G. H., & Lesgold, A. M. Organization as a determinant of part to whole transfer in free recall. *Journal of Verbal Learning and Verbal Behavior,* 1969, *8,* 501–506.

Broadbent, D. E. *Perception and communication.* London: Pergamon, 1958.

Broadbent, D. E. Cognitive psychology: Introduction. *British Medical Bulletin,* 1971, *27,* 191–194.

Cofer, C. N. A study of clustering in free recall based on synonyms. *Journal of General Psychology,* 1959, *60,* 3–10.

Crowder, R. G. *Principles of learning and memory.* Hillsdale, New Jersey: Erlbaum, 1976.

Dallett, K. M. Number of categories and category information in free recall. *Journal of Experimental Psychology,* 1964, *68,* 1–12.

Diewert, G. L. Retention and coding in motor short-term memory: A comparison of storage codes for distance and location information. *Journal of Motor Behavior,* 1975, *7,* 183–190.

Gentile, A. M., & Nacson, J. Organizational processes in motor control. In J. Keogh & R. S. Hutton (Eds.), *Exercise and sport sciences reviews* (Vol. 4). Santa Barbara, California: Journal Publishing Affiliates, 1976.

Glanzer, M. Grammatical category: A rote learning and word association analysis. *Journal of Verbal Learning and Verbal Behavior,* 1962, *1,* 31–41.

Keele, S. W. *Attention and human performance.* Pacific Palisades, California: Goodyear, 1973.

Mandler, G. Organization and memory. In K. W. Spence & J. T. Spence (Eds.), *The psychology of learning and motivation* (Vol. 1). New York: Academic Press, 1967. (a)

Mandler, G. Verbal learning. *New directions in psychology: III.* New York: Holt, 1967. (b)

Marteniuk, R. G. Retention characteristics of motor short-term memory cues. *Journal of Motor Behavior,* 1973, *5,* 249–259.

Mayhew, A. J. Interlist changes in subjective organization during free recall learning. *Journal of Experimental Psychology*, 1967, *74*, 425–430.

McGeoch, J. A., & Irion, A. L. *The psychology of human learning*. New York: McKay, 1952.

Melton, A. W., & Martin, E. *Coding processes in human memory*. New York: Wiley, 1972.

Miller, G. A. The magical number seven, plus or minus two: Some limits on our capacity for processing information. *Psychological Review*, 1956, *63*, 81–97. (a)

Miller, G. A. Information and memory. *Scientific American*, 1956, *195*, 42–46. (b)

Miller, G. A., Galanter, E., & Pribram, K. H. *Plans and the structure of behavior*. New York: Holt, 1960.

Nacson, J. Organization of practice and acquisition of a simple motor task. In *Proceedings of the First Canadian Congress for the Multidisciplinary Study of Sport and Physical Activity*. Montreal, 1973.

Nacson, J., Jaeger, M., & Gentile, A. Encoding processes in short-term motor memory. In I. D. Williams & L. M. Wankel (Eds.), *Proceedings of the Fourth Canadian Psychomotor Learning and Sports Psychology Symposium*. Ottawa, Canada: Department of National Health and Welfare, 1972.

Pew, R. W. Human perceptual-motor performance. In B. H. Kantowitz (Ed.), *Human information processing: Tutorials in performance and cognition*. New York: Erlbaum, 1974.

Postman, L. Organization and interference. *Psychological Review*, 1971, *78*, 290–302.

Postman, L. A pragmatic view of organization theory. In E. Tulving & W. Donaldson (Eds.), *Organization of memory*. New York: Academic Press, 1972.

Postman, L., Burns, S., & Hasher, L. Studies of learning to learn. X. Nonspecific transfer effects in free recall learning. *Journal of Verbal Learning and Verbal Behavior*, 1970, *9*, 707–715.

Puff, C. R. Free recall with instructional manipulation of sequential ordering of output. *Journal of Experimental Psychology*, 1970, *84*, 540–542.

Roberts, W. A. The priority of recall of new items in transfer from part list learning to whole list learning. *Journal of Verbal Learning and Verbal Behavior*, 1969, *8*, 645–652.

Roy, E. A., & Diewert, G. L. Encoding kinesthetic extent information. *Perception and Psychophysics*, 1975, *17*, 559–564.

Schmidt, R. A. A schema theory of discrete motor skill learning. *Psychological Review*, 1975, *82*, 225–260.

Segal, M. A., & Mandler, G. Directionality and organizational processes in paired associate learning. *Journal of Experimental Psychology*, 1967, *74*, 305–312.

Shea, J. B. Effects of labelling on motor short-term memory. *Journal of Experimental Psychology: Human Learning and Memory*, 1977, *3*, 92–99.

Stelmach, G. E. Prior organization in motor control. *Journal of Human Movement Studies*, 1977, *3*, 157–168.

Stelmach, G. E., & Kelso, J. A. S. Memory processes in motor control. In S. Dornic (Ed.), *Attention and Performance VI*. Hillsdale, New Jersey: Erlbaum, 1977.

Tulving, E. Subjective organization in free recall of "unrelated" words. *Psychological Review*, 1962, *69*, 344–354.

Tulving, E. Intratrial and intertrial retention: Notes toward a theory of free recall verbal learning. *Psychological Review*, 1964, *71*, 219–237.

Tulving, E. The effect of order of presentation on learning of "unrelated" words. *Psychonomic Science*, 1965, *3*, 337–338.

Tulving, E. Subjective organization and effects of repetition in multitrial free recall learning. *Journal of Verbal Learning and Verbal Behavior*, 1966, *5*, 193–197.

Tulving, E. Theoretical issues in free recall. In T. R. Dixon & D. L. Horton (Eds.), *Verbal behavior and general behavior theory*. Englewood Cliffs, New Jersey: Prentice-Hall, 1968.

Tulving, E., & Donaldson, W. *Organization of memory*. New York: Academic Press, 1972.

Tulving, E., & Osler, S. Transfer effects in whole./part free recall learning. *Canadian Journal of Psychology*, 1967, *21*, 253–262.

Underwood, B. J., & Schulz, R. W. *Meaningfulness and verbal learning*. Philadelphia: Lippincott, 1960.

Welford, A. T. Motor performance. In J. E. Birren & K. W. Schaie (Eds.), *Handbook of the psychology of aging*. New York: Van Nostrand, 1977.

13

The Role of Eye
and Head Positions in
Slow Movement Execution[1]

Ronald G. Marteniuk

I. Introduction

"Ecological validity" is a term that is used to describe theories that have relevance for some class of events in the everyday world. As Neisser (1976) points out, theories that lack ecological validity will be abandoned sooner or later. To him, theory and application to real-life situations go hand in hand in that an experimental finding may shed some light on a real-life problem and observations made in the real world may suggest new hypotheses.

The purpose of this chapter is to question the ecological validity of a large body of work in the motor behavior literature concerned with studying the accuracy with which subjects can position their arms and hands in slow, movement positioning tasks. While much of this work has been concerned with the

---

[1] The three experiments reported in this chapter were completed through funds from a National Research Council of Canada grant to the author.

Information Processing in
Motor Control and Learning

topic of motor short-term memory, the intent of this chapter will be to generalize the resulting implications to all experimental paradigms that use the accuracy of slow positioning movements as a dependent variable. In essence, it will be shown that for movements of this kind subjects utilize a spatial reference system that has been developed over years of experience in reaching for objects in their immediate environment. At the base of this spatial reference system is the relationship among the positions of the eyes, hands, and limbs. By taking into account the natural influence that such a system has on slow movement positioning tasks, the results of laboratory work will be more ecologically valid in that such results can be interpreted in terms of a system that human beings naturally develop over many years of interaction with their environment.

It is important to note at this point that this chapter is delimited to the study of slow, graded positioning movements. This delimitation is necessary because of the basic differences in the underlying control processes of slow, graded movements versus those that are programmed in nature. If, for a given task, the emphasis is on producing a movement where the sequencing and phasing of its various components must be produced as rapidly and consistently as possible, the performer will probably attempt to acquire and use a motor program. Here, the emphasis is on structuring the necessary details of the desired movement before execution and then executing the entire movement without reference to feedback. Evidence for this type of programmed control has been presented by Brooks (1974), Marteniuk and Sullivan (1976), Schmidt (1975, 1976) and Shapiro (1977).

Situations where slow, graded movements are used differ from those that require programmed movements. In situations where there is no time stress (i.e., the movement can be executed in a slow, graded manner) and where there is a necessity for a large degree of terminal accuracy, control is probably of a closed-loop mode. Unlike the programmed movements, there is no necessity for the performer to completely prestructure the movement within the central nervous system before execution begins. Rather, there is only a necessity to begin movement in the approximate direction of the desired end location and then rely on movement corrections, based on feedback regarding the discrepancy between the current position of the moving limb and the desired end location, to guide the limb to its terminal position.

Evidence for this type of closed-loop movement control comes from the work of Brooks (1974). Using monkeys as subjects he found that, for task situations either that were new to the monkeys or where there was considerable uncertainty of the task demands, the monkeys used what Brooks defined as "discontinuous" movements. These movements, made over an extent of 90° for arm flexion or extension, demonstrated several velocity peaks between successive brief pauses where the velocity was zero and the acceleration functions crossed the zero line. Brooks (1974) concluded that these kinematic records indicated that the movements were made in a number of steps, with each step resembling a small motor program where conscious utilization of feedback occurred after each step.

While this discussion serves to highlight differences between slow, graded movements and programmed movements, these movements do have at least one common characteristic. Lashley (1951) suggested that a space coordinate system must underlie every gross movement of the body or limbs, in that these movements are made with reference to this system. While both rapid and slow movements probably rely on this system, the view here is that they rely on it in different ways. For rapid movements, the spatial coordinate system may serve initially to map out the space requirements of the skill, but after this a fairly complex movement planning, initiation, and execution sequence must be accomplished. These latter operations, of course, would be involved in determining and controlling the kinematic and kinetic parameters of the movement. Thus, rapid movements are seen to be a function of both the spatial coordinate system and the motor system. For slow movements, on the other hand, the emphasis shifts to more of an almost total reliance on the spatial coordinate system. The motor component for slow, positioning movements is seen here as being relatively simple in nature where a limb has to be propelled for a series of very short distances; after each movement, feedback arising from the movement is compared to the spatial coordinate system to determine its location in reference to the desired end location. In essence, there is no need to preprogram slow movements; rather, the emphasis becomes more of recognizing when a limb is in a desired spatial location. For this reason, slow, positioning movements can be seen to be more a function of the perceptual end of performance and programmed movements can be seen to be more related to the effector end.

II. Evidence that Slow Movement Execution Relies More on Perceptual Processes Than on Effector Processes

This section will be devoted to examining the contention that slow, positioning movements rely quite heavily on a space coordinate system and hence can be described as relying relatively more on perceptual processes than on effector processes. This point is quite important because it not only has implications for future research but it ties in much of the work on positioning movements (e.g., in the motor short-term memory area) to a much broader area of inquiry, namely, visually guided reaching. This area, in turn, is closely related to basic developmental and learning processes in children. What I will demonstrate is the possibility that slow, positioning movements in college-age subjects are at least partially dependent on processes that were developed through the learning of visually guided reaching. This would place much of the present work in the study of slow positioning movements into a more natural, real-life situation and hence serve to increase the ecological validity of a large amount of laboratory work by interpreting the results of such work in terms of a process people use in everyday life.

The phenomenon in the developmental area of specific interest here concerns what Hein (1974) termed a *body-centered map of visual space*. He maintained that, when an individual has the capacity for visually guided locomotion, utilization of a body-centered map of visual space is implied. He believed that the limbs of an individual are given visual positions by the coordinates of this map. In addition, the body-centered map of visual space is formed from visual feedback of a limb being correlated or integrated with active movement of the same limb. This latter contention was supported by work with kittens deprived of vision of one forelimb from birth to 4–12 weeks of age (Hein, 1974) and by work with monkeys (Held & Bauer, 1974) for which both forelimbs were obscured from vision from birth to 1 month of age. These animals, upon being tested for visually guided reaching with the forelimb, were unable to localize targets that were easily reached by control animals. However, after the experimental animals were allowed full sight of their forelimbs and were given experiences in visually guided reaching, they soon reached normal competency. This indicates adaptability of the body-centered map of visual space and indicates that its recalibration is probably due to the correlation of vision of the limb and active movement of that limb.

The idea of a body-centered map of visual space is closely tied to Lashley's (1951) concept of a space coordinate system. As mentioned previously, Lashley proposed that all gross movements are made with reference to this space system. Moreover, this system is continually undergoing modification through the perceptions from vision, audition, and proprioception. Such a system could thus be used to localize a target or object in the environment since it has a definite relation to the position of the body.

At the base of the space coordinate system must be an integrated store of information similar to that described by Marteniuk (1976), where perceptions from vision, audition, and proprioception are intercalibrated. Once formed, such a system could then serve to spatially code a visual object (i.e., give it coordinates in the spatial coordinate system). Once the object is spatially coded, and since the position of the reaching limb is also part of this spatial reference system, the individual can then carry out the movement required to reduce the discrepancy between the current position of the reaching limb and the location of the object. Since constant reference is made to the spatial map, a closed-loop mode of control is adopted, resulting in a series of small steplike movements, until the object is within grasping distance.

An important part of the above description of the positioning response is the initial spatial coding of the visual object. Gazzaniga (1969), Paillard (1971), and Paillard and Beaubaton (1976) provide evidence (behavioral and physiological) suggesting that proprioceptive reafferents from the positions of the eyes and the head play a central role in the spatial coding of visual information. In essence, it is postulated that the orientation of the eyes and head toward a target or object in space serves to spatially code the object into the spatial reference system. In support of this contention, Paillard (1971) cited evidence that the pointing accuracy of human subjects was impaired by an experimenter-imposed misalignment between the direction of the gaze of the subject and the position of the target. In this case a visually *directed* pointing task (as opposed to visually guided pointing) was used where subjects could not see their arms while pointing.

Results from a study by Cohen (1961) also pointed directly to the neck muscles as the main mechanism for spatially coding visual cues. Proprioceptive information from the extraocular muscles, ciliary muscles of accommodation, and neck muscles was abolished singly and in combination in monkeys and the effects on the orientation and motor coordination of the animals were observed. Although minor effects were obtained from abolishing information from the eye muscles, these were insignificant when compared to the effects of eliminating information from the neck muscles. Of special interest was the inability of the animals to reach accurately in space to a point upon which they had fixed their eyes. Visually guided reaching was almost totally eliminated. As Cohen (1961) mentioned, however, his results do not necessarily rule out the possibility of the importance of the eye muscles in spatially coding visual cues. It may have been that, in his experiment, other orientating mechanisms left intact could have compensated for the loss of the information from the eye muscles.

Up to now in the discussion of factors underlying the execution of slow, graded movements the following points have been made.

1. Slow movements of long duration are discontinuous in nature; that is, they are executed in a steplike fashion. This steplike approach to the target probably indicates that the processes of movement organization, initiation, and execution are relatively trivial in nature and consist of small motor programs that propel the limb for short periods of time. After each step, feedback is used to compare the present position of the limb to the desired position. Because of these characteristics, accuracy of slow movement is more dependent on perceptual processes than on effector processes.

2. A spatial reference system (analogous to an integrated store of visual, auditory, and proprioceptive information) underlies visually guided reaching. The coordinates of the target as well as those of the reaching limb all have representation in this system.

3. Proprioceptive information from the orientation of the eyes and head (neck muscles) may serve a central role in the orientation of the spatial reference system. The correct orientation of the eyes and head toward the desired target in

space may be a necessary prerequisite for the accurate coding of the target as well as the accurate mapping of the current position of the limbs on the spatial reference system. In this way, the position of the eyes and head may be critical for the coding of spatial cues relevant to accurate slow positioning.

III. Experimental Support for the Role of Eye and Head Positions

This section focuses on the issue of whether the positions of the eyes and head have any role (*a*) in localizing a target in space through the use of slow, graded movements and (*b*) in coding movement cues for the reproduction of slow movements. Three experiments were conducted that used a two-dimensional slow positioning task (Marteniuk & Sullivan, Note 1). The use of a two-dimensional task allows subjects a more natural method not only for localizing a target but also for attempting to reproduce criterion movements. Another advantage of this type of task is that it allows the study of errors in both movement amplitude and direction. The utility of a two-dimensional task in making references about basic human performance and learning mechanisms is demonstrated in works by Foley and Held (1972) and Tooley (Note 2).

The two-dimensional task used for the present experiments essentially involved subjects sliding a cursor on a tabletop. The cursor, which slid freely on the arborite top of the table, was part of a digitizer that spontaneously displayed the *x,y* coordinates of the cursor. Knowing the coordinates of the starting position of the cursor, the coordinates of the *desired* end location of the movement, and the coordinates of the subject-produced end location gave information capable of being used to calculate an amplitude error (subject-produced amplitude errors greater than the criterion value were arbitrarily given positive signs and those of lesser amplitude were given negative signs) and a directional error (angles to the right of the criterion angle were arbitrarily given a positive sign and those to the left were given a negative sign). For all three experiments only constant error (an average of the algebraic errors) and absolute error (the average of the absolute errors) were calculated. Variable error was not included because no single movement was given twice in any of the experiments; thus, any variability over movements, within a given subject, would not be an accurate measure of within-subject variability.

A. Experiment 1

The first experiment was designed to investigate whether locating a target in space and reproducing movement were a function of head position (neck muscles being primarily responsible) and the visual system (eye position and related efferent and proprioceptive information) or just a function of the visual system. The literature reviewed in Sections I and II suggests the prediction that the orientation of the head in the direction of the target would serve to help to spatially code the location of the target and at the same time specify the spatial relationship between the localizing limb and the target. On the other hand, Turvey (1977) makes a case for the visual system being the prime trigger for movement organization and initiation. His notion is that visual perceiving and acting are dual representations of common neural events and thus the fixation of the eyes on the target would be the prime prerequisite to successful localization of the target. This would especially be true for the directional component of the localization movement, with amplitude perhaps being more dependent on depth perception rather than eye position.

Twenty subjects were randomly assigned to one of two conditions: head fixed and head free. Subjects in the head-fixed group were seated in front of the table on which movements were to be made. Their heads were immobilized by means of a chin rest so that only their eyes were free to orientate visually toward the visually presented target. The head-free group was seated in an identical manner but without the constraint of the head rest and the subjects were instructed to orientate their eyes and head to the visually presented target. The tabletop or working space was arbitrarily divided into three sections. The middle section, Section 2, was the middle third of the tabletop and represented a width of approximately the distance between the subjects' shoulders. The subject was seated so that his midline was in the center of this section. Section 1 was the section of the table to the left of Section 2 and Section 3 was to the right of Section 2. Target locations were placed within each of these sections so that no order was apparent to the subject and so that all targets could be easily reached.

Targets were presented visually by the experimenter using a pointer to indicate a location in one of the three sections. This pointer was held in place for 2 sec so that subjects could orientate their eyes to it (head fixed) or their eyes and head (head free). The experimenter then removed the pointer, and the subject, maintaining the orientation previously attained, was instructed to move the cursor to where he thought the target had been. Once at the desired location, the subject maintained this location for 2 sec and then released the cursor while the experimenter returned it to the starting position just in front of the center of the subject's body. Subjects in the head-fixed condition were then instructed to orientate their eyes to a mark on the wall directly in front of them and then close their eyes, whereas the subjects in the head-free condition were told to maintain their heads and eyes in the direction of the end location of their movement but to close their eyes. Subjects then had to grasp the cursor and *reproduce* the end location of the movement they had just made. Thus, error of movement reproduction was the difference between the end location of the movement the subject made in attempting to localize the target (i.e., regardless of its accuracy) and his attempt at reproducing that end location. This reproduction movement was made either immediately (0-sec retention interval) or after sitting quietly (resting) for 30 sec. All subjects were given 30 trials: 10 per table section and within each section 5 per retention condition.

Significant effects are presented in Tables I and II. Bias is the average of the algebraic errors, whereas variability represents the mean absolute errors. Only directional error is reported because no systematic effects were found for amplitude errors. Bias in the present context can be thought of as representing any constant effects in localization and in movement reproduction ability that are attributable to perception of the target location or movement end location, respectively. Absolute error, or variability around the target, can be thought of as being due to variability in the movement control system (Foley & Held, 1972).

The results on localization of the target (Table I) indicated a significant ($p < 0.05$) position of the head and eyes $\times$ working section interaction, which was caused by subjects in the head-fixed group significantly biasing their movements by localizing to the left of the target in Section 1 and to the right of the target in Section 3, whereas the head-free group had relatively small directional errors in each of the three sections. In variability of localization only the main effect of head position proved to be significant ($p < 0.05$). For bias in reproduction of the localizing movement (Table II), the same interaction of head position $\times$ sections was significant ($p < 0.05$), the only difference being that the head-free group demonstrated a "central tendency" effect over the three sections. That is, errors in direction were made toward the center of the working space. Finally, in terms of variability, the retention interval effect, while significant ($p < 0.05$), proved to be independent of head position and section of working space.

Table I
Effects of Positions of Eyes and Head (Fixed or Free) on the Ability to Localize a Target

Head position	Bias (constant directional error in degrees)		
	Section 1	Section 2	Section 3
Head free	0.88	0.90	0.57
Head fixed	−2.74	1.68	2.12
	Variability (absolute directional error in degrees)		
Head free	2.44		
Head fixed	4.79		

Table II
Effects of Positions of Eyes and Head (Fixed or Free) on the Abiltty to Reproduce Movement

	Bias (constant directional error in degrees)		
	Section 1	Section 2	Section 3
Head free	3.02	0.89	− 2.39
Head fixed	− 3.07	3.45	1.33
Retention interval (sec)	Variability (absolute directional error in degrees)		
0	4.27		
30	6.05		

The above results indicate that, at the very least, the head and eyes must be oriented toward the target location for accurate localization to occur. Visual information in terms of eye·position is not sufficient for accurate localization of a target in space. Furthermore, even when subjects have the effector and proprioceptive information available from moving their limb to a location in space, the positioning of the head and eyes has a significant influence on movement reproduction ability. These results lead to support of the contention that head *and* eye positions may be central to the initial perception of the spatial requirements of a task as well as to the coding of movement information received from active movement. This leads to support of the notion of a spatial reference system underlying slow positioning movements with head and eye positions not only being the central aspect of this reference system but also serving as a method by which the limbs of the body as well as targets in space are given spatial coordinates. The fact that the retention condition did not interact with the head position condition also leads to the idea that the spatial reference system is relatively stable for at least up to 30 sec.

The results of Experiment 1 also argue against the point of view espoused by Turvey (1977) that the position of the eyes alone and the resulting visual perception play a central role in reflexively tuning the segments of the limbs required for the movement that, in turn, facilitates the movement of the limbs as they reach for an object in the individual's immediate environment. However, what the present results do not rule out is the possibility, also pointed out by Turvey (1977), that the positions of the eyes and head act as a functional tuning link for the limbs and thus produce the needed parameters for the execution of the desired movement. It may be, for instance, that, in the head-fixed condition, the position of the head reflexively tuned the limbs for a movement in the direction in which the head was oriented and, thus, this tuning may have interfered with the accurate localization and reproduction of movements away from the direction in which the head was oriented.

It may be that this reflexive tuning of the limbs of the body can be used to explain the "overcompensation" effect apparent in the constant errors of the head-fixed conditions in Tables I and II. The directions of the errors, compensating to the left of the target in Section 1 and to the right of the target in Section 3, were not expected. In fact, it was expected that the errors would tend toward the direction of the head and eyes, which would have produced constant errors similar to those of the head-free group in Table II. That such was not the case indicates the strong effect that positions of the eyes and head have on localizing targets and reproducing movements.

Another possible explanation for the overcompensation effect implicates an illusion as causing the bias in target localization. It may be that the proprioceptive feedback from the positions of the head and eyes in the head-fixed condition resulted in a miscalibration of the central frame of reference for the spatial reference system. Normally, as explained previously in Section II, the proprioceptive reafferents from the positions of the eyes and head play a central role in the spatial coding of visual information. When the normal congruency between positions of the eyes and head and the desired direction of movement is disrupted, however, the resulting proprioceptive reafferents may result in a miscoding of the proper location of visual targets in space. The resulting illusion then manifests itself as directional bias when subjects attempt to localize objects in their immediate environment.

The question of whether the overcompensation effect is due to a pretuning of inappropriate neural pathways or to an illusion will be dealt with in Section III,C (Experiment 3).

B. Experiment 2

This experiment was designed to test further the importance of head and eye orientation in target localization and movement reproduction. In Experiment 1, it could be argued that the coding of a visual target in the head-fixed condition was actually interfered with by the awkward position the eyes had to assume when fixing on targets in Sections 1 and 3 of the working space. Therefore, in this study the presentation of the visual target was identical for the two conditions in which the positions of the eyes and head were varied.

A second purpose of this experiment was to examine the stability, over time, of the localization accuracy of a target and, in particular, to determine if the position of the head and eyes when oriented away from the target would lead to a decrease in localization ability over time. It was expected that when head and eyes were oriented toward the target a strong perceptual reference would be maintained for the target and little decrease in accuracy over time would result. In Experiment 1, it appeared that the positions of the head and eyes gave directional orientation that resulted in constant directional errors (bias) for localization and movement reproduction but that for movement reproduction this bias was uninfluenced by an interpolated retention interval. In addition, it appeared that, in terms of variability (absolute error), movement reproduction was uninfluenced by the positions of the head and eyes. This finding would indicate that the positions of the head and eyes determine accuracy of the perceptual processes involved in target localization and movement reproduction (measured by constant error) but that the functioning of the effector processes (as measured by absolute error) is relatively independent of these perceptual processes. In essence, it appears that once the perceptual decision has been made as to where the target is, the effector processes execute the movement in the intended direction and are uninfluenced by any bias inherent in the perceptual decision. The present experiment was designed so that a replication of this finding could be made.

For this experiment a within-subject design was used where 10 subjects performed all experimental conditions. The experimental conditions involved (a) section of the working space where the visual targets had to be localized or movements reproduced; (b) retention intervals of a 0- or 30-sec delay either after presentation of the visual target to be localized or after the attempted movement to the target; and (c) positions of the head and eyes in relationship to the target. In this latter condition, the head and eyes were oriented either toward the target (head same, HS) or away from the target (head different, HD).

The experimental procedures were similar to those of Experiment 1 except for the following. Only two sections of the working space (Sections 1 and 3) were used. Targets were randomly placed within these sections and no target was presented twice. For the HS condition, subjects were shown the target and told to orient their eyes and head to the target and to maintain the direction of the gaze but to close their eyes 2 sec after fixation. They then either immediately attempted to localize the target or were required to sit quietly (rest) for 30 sec and then attempt localization. After their attempt, the cursor was returned to the starting position by the experimenter. Then either immediately or after a 30-sec interval, during which subjects quietly rested, they were told to reproduce the movement they had initially made in localizing the target. In the HD condition all procedures were identical to the HS condition except that, after the subjects had oriented their heads and eyes to the target and had held this position for 2 sec, they were required to turn their heads and eyes to the opposite side of the table from which the target was located. After this they closed their eyes and then, depending on the specific retention interval, attempted to localize the target and reproduce the movement made in the localization attempt. For example, if the target had been presented in Section 1 (to the left of the subject) the subject was required to orient his head and eyes to the upper right-hand corner of the table, close his eyes, and then maintain this orientation while he executed the required movements. If the target was presented in Section 3 (to the right of the subject) his head and eyes were oriented to the upper left-hand corner while he produced the required movements.

For each of the eight possible combinations [i.e., HS–HD, section in which target was presented (Section 1 or 2), and the two retention intervals] four targets were given, making for a total of 32 target presentations per subject. The same 32 targets were used for all 10 subjects, but the order in which the various combinations of the three conditions were presented was randomized for each subject. As in Experiment 1, only directional constant and absolute error, averaged for the four targets per condition, were analyzed.

Tables III and IV present the statistically significant ($p < 0.05$) effects for both the localization (Table III) and movement reproduction (Table IV) results of Experiment 2. For constant errors in target localization the interaction of location of target (table section) × position of head and eyes was caused by the HD condition, similar to the head-fixed group Experiment 1, demonstrating an overcompensation effect, whereas the HS condition demonstrated more of a central tendency effect. In this latter condition, errors in Section 3 were definitely influenced toward the center of the subjects' working space, whereas, in Section 1, the central tendency effect is only apparent on a relative basis when compared to the same condition of the HD condition.

In terms of the stability of the processes involved in localizing the targets, it is interesting to note that the HS and HD conditions were completely independent of the retention interval condition. Whatever caused the differential errors of the

Table III

Effects of Positions of Eyes and Head
(Same or Different as Target) on the
Ability to Localize a Target

	Bias (constant directional error in degrees)	
	Section 1	Section 3
Head same	− 1.15	− 3.82
Head different	− 2.23	1.00

Retention interval (sec)	Variability (absolute directional error in degrees)
0	5.66
30	6.96

Table IV

Effects of Positions of Eyes and Head (Same or Different as Target) on the Ability to Reproduce Movement

	Bias (constant directional error in degrees)	
	0 sec	30 sec
Head same	0.03	− 0.29
Head different	− 0.62	0.32

Retention interval (sec)	Variability (absolute directional error in degrees)
0	3.12
30	3.53

HS and HD conditions appears to be relatively stable, at least over the time period studied in the present study. However, as indicated by the overall increase in absolute error, there is an increase in variability for all conditions, which, as in Experiment 1, probably is reflective of a deteriorating effector process over the 30-sec retention interval.

The analysis of the significant ($p < 0.05$) effects from the movement reproduction phase of the experiment (Table IV) gave almost exactly the same results, in terms of trend, as in the localization phase. The only difference was one of magnitude of effect. The central tendency effect of the HS condition was present, as was the overcompensation effect of the HD group, but the size of these constant errors was considerably reduced as compared to the localization results. In addition, the constant effects occurring in movement reproduction were completely independent of the interpolated retention interval, with only overall variability increasing with time.

These results offer a relatively good replication of the main findings from Experiment 1 in terms of the influence that positions of the head and eyes have on bias (constant error) in localizing a target and reproducing a movement. There was a difference in the results of the two experiments in terms of the head-free group of Experiment 1 and the HS condition of Experiment 2. If one examines Tables I and IV in terms of constant error, it is apparent that the trend of bias over the different working areas is somewhat different for these two experimental groups. There were two differences in experimental design that may account for these differences. In Experiment 1, the head-free group was an independent group (the head-fixed condition was performed by a different group of subjects) and the subjects performed localizations and movement reproduction in all three sections of the working space. In Experiment 2, the design was completely within subjects so that all subjects performed the HS and HD conditions and, in addition, these subjects worked only in Sections 1 and 3 of the working space. The within-subject design may have been responsible not only for changing the perceptual bias over the different sections of the working space but also, because of a larger number of trials, for decreasing the magnitude of the constant errors in the movement reproduction phase of Experiment 2 (Table IV as compared to Table II).

Regardless of not being able to replicate exactly the bias effects over the two experiments, there is enough evidence to suggest that the positions of the head and eyes definitely affect the ability of subjects to localize targets in space and to reproduce movements. The fact that the overcompensation effect was present in both experiments (i.e., in the head-fixed group and in the HD condition) and that this bias was substantially different from the head-free group and the HS condition leads to the conclusion that the observed effect is a real one. The cause of this effect, however, is not quite as clear. The two explanations offered in the discussion of the results of Experiment 1 (i.e., a perceptual illusion effect versus the reflexive tuning hypothesis) are still both quite capable of explaining the results, and further experimentation is needed to discriminate between those explanations.

Whatever the explanation, it appears that the positions of the eyes and head are of central importance to the ability to make spatially oriented slow movements. In addition, it appears from the results of Experiment 2 that this spatial reference system is quite stable over at least 30 sec. This was demonstrated by the fact that the bias of target localization and movement reproduction was not influenced by the retention interval condition. This stability over time suggests that the spatial reference system is probably based on an individual's long-term experiences. In particular, it is argued here that the system being utilized in these experiments is the same system that an individual uses in the everyday experience of reaching for objects in his immediate environment. Thus, it is reasonable to assume that this system has been developed since early childhood and overlearned to a very great extent by the countless experiences that every individual encounters. If this is the case, one would expect that any bias a system introduces into target localization or movement reproduction would be rather stable and would not be influenced by the interpolation of any relatively short time interval.

The final aspect of Experiment 2 that deserves discussion, and is a partial replication of the results of Experiment 1, concerns the variability (absolute error) of the target localization and movement reproduction responses. In Experiment 1, variability of target localization was influenced by the positions of the head and eyes, with the head-fixed condition producing significantly greater variability. However, this was the only case in the two experiments (Tables I–IV) where variability was a function of the positions of the head and eyes. In all other cases, variability was only a function of retention interval, where significantly greater variability was associated with the 30-sec retention interval. These results are consistent with those of Foley and Held (1972), who investigated several parameters that affected visually directed pointing. They showed that bias (directional constant error) in visually directed pointing was a function of the sighting eye and handedness and they concluded that these types of variables influence the perception of objects in space. Moreover, they found that along with this bias there was a variance in the pointing response that could not be attributed to the perceptual process, but rather was attributable to response variance.

The results of the present experiments are also suggestive of two components to the response of target localization or movement reproduction. One component has to do with spatially defining the target through some perceptual process that creates a directional bias depending on the position of the head and eyes. The other component, although not quite as dramatic in nature, has to do with variability of the response in attempting to carry out the perceived spatial location. While it was argued earlier that the movement component of these types of responses is rather small, evidently there is a large enough component to cause some variability that is identifiable in the total response. Furthermore, it appears that this variability is only influenced by the interpolation of a time interval. Thus, for localizing targets in near space or for reproducing movements, it appears that the bias established by the positions of the head and eyes remains constant over time but that the variability of the movement used in localization or reproduction becomes larger. This finding argues for two separate mechanisms in the total response of target localization and movement reproduction.

C. Experiment 3

This experiment was designed to investigate further the nature of the spatial reference system underlying localization of targets in the immediate environment and movement reproduction. One view of this system is Hein's (1974) concept of a body-centered map of visual space. As mentioned previously in Section II, such a view holds that past visual and proprioceptive experiences in reaching for objects in near body space result in an integrated store of visual and proprioceptive information that can then serve to spatially code not only objects in space but also the position of the reaching limb. The individual's task is to reduce the discrepancy between these two positions, and he does this by comparing feedback from the limb, as it moves toward the object in space, to the spatially coded position of the object. Since the positions of the head and eyes have been shown to be a central reference point to this system, it appears that these judgments are always made in reference to the information received from the positions of the head and eyes. Thus, the information from the positions of the head and eyes serves to calibrate this space coordinate system and to allow calculation of the coordinates of objects in space and the positions of the limbs relative to the body and the object to be reached for. From this viewpoint, then, it can be predicted that orienting the head and eyes toward a target in space is like an executive function that maps out the necessary spatial coordinates on which movement is based. Furthermore, such an executive system would be wholly dependent on the set positions of the eyes and head and would be relatively immune to any interfering activity.

Another view of the spatial reference system would be a system that is more dependent on the anticipation and reception of proprioceptive and visual feedback for the accurate spatial mapping of the limbs and objects in the immediate environment. Rather than acting in an executive role, this system would act, through past experience, only in terms of the present situation. It would map the spatial coordinates of the limbs and objects in space in terms of the expected sensory consequences for localization and in terms of actual sensory consequences for movement reproduction. In other words, such a view is based more on feedback than is the previously outlined executive function. The feedback view could also incorporate the positions of the head and eyes as a central part of the decision process in that the performer would still need a central reference point to which to refer the anticipated or actual feedback. However, unlike the prediction made from the executive function viewpoint, one would predict that, in the present case, such a system would be very susceptible to interfering activity designed to structurally interfere with the anticipated or actual feedback.

The present experiment was designed to test between the executive function and feedback-based viewpoints of the spatial reference system. Only movement reproduction was studied and the positions of the head and eyes were manipulated in a manner identical to that used in Experiment 2. The executive function viewpoint predicts that, if the head and eyes are oriented toward the end location of the movement to be reproduced, interfering activity designed to structurally interfere with movement reproduction would not have a deleterious effect on performance. However, the opposite prediction would hold from the feedback-based viewpoint. If the head and eyes are oriented away from the end location of the movement to be produced, both viewpoints would predict a deleterious effect on performance from interfering activity.

The conditions of this latter prediction (i.e., head and eyes oriented away from the intended direction of movement) also serve to test the reflexive tuning notion of Turvey (1977) as described in the discussion of Experiment 1 (Section III,A). If the orienting of the head and eyes away from the direction of the intended movement serves to reflexively pretune a set of neural pathways different from the pathways that are required for the movement, one would expect the resulting bias to be uninfluenced by any structurally interfering activity. However, a perceptual interpretation of the role of the position of the head and eyes in spatial judgments predicts a disruption of the bias normally attributable to the influence of head and eyes.

The procedures of this third experiment were similar to those of Experiment 2 except that target localization was not studied. The subjects were presented with a visual target by the experimenter pointing to a location on the tabletop. The subject moved the cursor out to the indicated location with full vision. Once there, he held this position for 2 sec, after which the various experimental conditions began.

The design was completely within subjects, with the 10 subjects reproducing three different movements in each of 12 conditions. The conditions comprised the 12 combinations of (a) head and eyes oriented toward or away from the end location of the to-be-reproduced movement; (b) three retention intervals; and (c) sections of the working space in which movements were made (Sections 1 and 3). The conditions of orientation of head and eyes were identical to those described in Experiment 2 for the HS and HD conditions except that in the HD condition subjects did not turn their heads until the cursor had been at the target location for 2 sec. Sections 1 and 3 of the working space were also identical to those used in Experiment 2.

For the retention intervals, 0- and 30-sec intervals were used in the same manner as in Experiment 2. The procedures for the 0- and 30-sec rest retention intervals were that (a) the subject moved the cursor to the target location and held this position for 2 sec; (b) he either kept his head and eyes oriented toward the target or oriented them to the opposite corner of the table; (c) he then closed his eyes, released the cursor, and returned his hand to the starting position; and (d) the experimenter returned the cursor to the starting position. If an immediate movement reproduction was required, the subject regrasped the cursor and moved it, with his eyes closed, to where he thought the target location was. For the 30-sec rest interval the subject sat quietly and then regrasped the cursor and attempted to reproduce the target location with his eyes closed.

The third retention interval condition was 30 sec in duration and involved subjects making two movement reproductions in Section 2 of the working space. When the subject returned his hand to the starting location after initially moving out to the criterion target location, he was instructed to regrasp the cursor. The experimenter then *passively* moved the cursor and the subject's hand to a target location somewhere (randomly determined) in Section 2 of the working space. The experimenter held this position for 2 sec, and the subject released the cursor and, after the experimenter returned it to the starting position, immediately attempted to actively reproduce the target location. After this, another target location in Section 2 was again passively presented and the procedure was repeated. These two movement reproductions took 25–28 sec on the average. After 30 sec the subject regrasped the cursor and attempted to reproduce the criterion target location that had been presented about 30 sec earlier. It is important to note that,

Table V

Effects of Positions of Eyes and Head (Same or Different as Target) and Retention Interval on the Ability to Reproduce Movement

	Bias (constant directional error in degrees)	
	Section 1	Section 3
0 sec		
Head same	−3.01	0.04
Head different	−4.57	1.93
30-sec rest		
Head same	−2.78	1.18
Head different	−4.76	2.34
30-sec filled movement		
Head same	−3.65	0.60
Head different	−9.87	5.30

Retention interval (sec)	Variability (absolute directional error in degrees)
0	5.23
30	6.92
30 (filled movement)	7.58

while subjects were either resting or making movements during the two 30-sec retention intervals, their heads and eyes were still oriented in the direction required by the particular condition (i.e., HS or HD).

Table V presents the relevant results of Experiment 3. For constant error the main effect of section of working space, the interaction of retention interval × section of working space, and the interaction of position of head and eyes × section of working space were all statistically significant ($p < 0.05$), but since these are all involved in the significant ($p < 0.05$) triple interaction presented in Table V they will not be individually presented. However, if the above two double interactions are recovered from Table V, it becomes immediately apparent that they were caused by the large increase in the overcompensation effect of the HD condition in the 30-sec filled retention interval. That is, when subjects were required to reproduce passively presented movements during the 30-sec retention interval, this activity significantly increased the bias (overcompensation) in the two sections of the working space. In addition, it is interesting to note that the results for the 0- and 30-sec (rest) intervals are surprisingly similar in trend to the results of Experiment 2 (see Tables III and IV). In essence, the range of constant errors over Sections 1 and 2 is smaller for the HS conditions (this holds for the 30-sec filled retention interval as well) than for the HD conditions. It is apparent that the overcompensation effect is magnified by the HD condition.

For absolute error, the only significant finding was for the main effect of retention intervals. This was also consistent with Experiments 1 and 2 not only with respect to the increasing variability over time (and in this case also because of interfering activity) but also because that position of the head and eyes was again independent of any systematic changes in variability.

The above results can be taken as support for the notion that the orientation of the head and eyes toward a target in immediate space not only serves as a central reference point upon which the reaching limb and target are spatially coded but also acts in the form of an executive for spatial decisions. It appears that once the head and eyes are oriented toward a target in the immediate environment, this acts to lock in the spatial coordinates of the intended movements and thus makes the whole process relatively impervious to structurally interfering activities.

It also appears from the present results that the idea of reflexive tuning resulting from the orientation of the head and eyes (Turvey, 1977) is not supported. From this viewpoint one would not have predicted any influence of structural interference in either the HS or the HD conditions. The reflexive tuning idea would predict that in the HD condition a bias would result because of the pre-tuning and activation of an inappropriate set of neural pathways, but, once these pathways are determined, the prediction would be, as in the HS condition, that structural interference would have no effect on directional bias. That such was not the case speaks in favor of a perceptual interpretation for the function of the position of head and eyes in spatial judgments. When the head and eyes are oriented toward a target, the coordinates of the limbs and target are spatially determined as coordinates in the body-centered spatial reference system. The coordinates then act as reference points to guide ongoing slow movements in a closed-loop fashion. When the orientation of the head and eyes is different from the direction of the target, a perceptual illusion is created that causes systematic biases to occur in localization and movement reproduction responses. These biases probably result from an incorrect spatial coding of the target or the reaching limb or both.

IV. Implications of the Experimental Evidence for Head and Eye Orientation

The results of the three experiments described above are quite conclusive in implicating the orientation of the head and eyes toward a target as an executive function in determining the spatial requirements of slow, graded types of movements. When the head and eyes are oriented toward a target in the immediate environment, the processes involved in localization of the target and in reproduction of the movement made in the localization attempt are stable over time and, in the case of movement reproduction, are not affected by structural interference. Evidence from other research has been presented that suggests that the positions of the head and eyes may be the central part of a spatial reference system that is developed early in life and used extensively in everyday activities. The implication is that this system is similar to what Hein (1974) calls a body-centered map of visual space. Hein (1974) and Held and Bauer (1974) have shown that with animals it is developed from visual feedback of a limb being correlated with active movement of the same limb. In addition, other evidence (Gazzaniga, 1969; Paillard, 1971; Paillard & Beaubaton, 1976) supports the contention that proprioceptive reafferents from the position of the head and eyes play a central role in the successful operation of the spatial reference system. The exact way in which this type of information becomes so central in spatial judgments is not known, but it is probably due to countless pairings of the head and eyes being used to guide the arms and hands to visual targets in the immediate environment.

The import of the above for the work in studying the underlying mechanisms of slow, graded movements is that much can be gained by understanding that subjects, in a laboratory task, use a system (in this case the body-centered map of visual space) that has been developed since early childhood and used in everyday life. In essence, the point is that much of the research on slow, graded movements has ignored this system; as a result, variables that are not based on any ecologically valid principle have been studied. Placing work on slow, graded movements into a context that is related to how individuals acquire the ability to move their limbs naturally to objects in their near space will undoubtedly lead to a more fruitful approach to understanding the mechanisms by which individuals make such movements.

Another implication arising from the results of the research presented here concerns the issue of memory for slow, graded movements. More particularly, the question raised by the present results is whether there is a *motor* short-term memory for these types of movements. This chapter has established the idea that slow movements are dependent on spatial (perceptual) processes and that movement per se plays a relatively minor role in successful target localization and movement reproduction. Since the spatial reference system is developed early in life, it follows that college-age subjects, who are normally used in the majority of studies investigating the short-term memory of slow, positioning movements, probably use this system when executing slow, graded movements. If this is the case, what is actually being studied is not memory of *movement* per se but rather a set of variables that are related to the well-developed spatial reference system. The implication here is that these latter variables would not be related to any motor memory system. It may be, for instance, that deterioration of performance (whether due to a "lack of central processing capacity" or "structural interference") is nothing more than the subjects' spatial reference system becoming disoriented. Certainly, all studies that have not controlled for position of the head and eyes would be open to this alternative explanation in that, while some subjects may automatically orient their heads and eyes to the desired end location of the movement, other subjects, without specific instructions, may orientate their heads and eyes in any one of many possible directions.

This does not mean to imply, however, that there is no such thing as motor short-term memory. Certainly for young children there might be a memory store for sensations arising from produced movements as well as for efferent commands. In addition, for people of all ages, where novel movements depend on timing, force production, and perhaps velocity and acceleration cues, some type of short-term memory may exist where afferent as well as efferent information is coded and subject to the limitations of such a system.

The final point to be made, related to above issue, concerns the use of "efference" as a variable in influencing the accuracy with which slow, graded movements are reproduced. The position here is that such movements have a relatively small effector component and, as such, can be seen as a series of steps with each step resembling a small motor program for which conscious utilization of feedback occurs after each step. The feedback in this case would be spatial information used by the spatial reference system in determining the relationship between the moving limb and the desired end location. From this description of slow positioning movements it is difficult to conceptualize what would be the relevant "efferent" information for use in subsequent reproduction of the criterion movement. At best it would be a series of relatively minor movement commands stored as a corollary discharge for later use. However, this type of information does not seem to be detailed enough for a subject to use in recalling the relevant extent or end position of his movement. From this reasoning, it is proposed here that the models of motor short-term memory that have utilized "efference" as an explanation for their experimental findings (e.g., Jones, 1974; Kelso & Stelmach, 1976) based on the use of slow positioning movements must reevaluate their notion of "efference."

Acknowledgments

The author wishes to thank John Sullivan for assistance in collecting and analyzing the data. In addition, thanks go out to Christie MacKenzie, Dick Schmidt, John Sullivan, and Ian Williams for the helpful reviews they made of an earlier draft of this chapter.

Reference Notes

1. Marteniuk, R. G., & Sullivan, S. J. *Role of visual information and head position in localizing a target and in movement reproduction in two-dimensional space.* In preparation, 1977.
2. Tooley, M. J. *The role of trace decay, structural interference, and capacity interference in motor short-term memory.* Unpublished M.S. thesis, University of Waterloo, 1976.

References

Brooks, V. B. Some examples of programmed limb movements. *Brain Research*, 1974, *71*, 299–308.

Cohen, L. A. Role of eye and neck proprioceptive mechanisms in body orientation and motor coordination. *Journal of Neurophysiology*, 1961, *24*, 1–11.

Foley, J. M., & Held, R. Visually directed pointing as a function of target distance, direction, and available cues. *Perception & Psychophysics*, 1972, *12*, 263–268.

Gazzaniga, M. S. Cross-cueing mechanisms and ipsilateral eye-hand control in split-brain monkeys. *Experimental Neurology*, 1969, *23*, 11–17.

Hein, A. Prerequisite for development of visually guided reaching in the kitten. *Brain Research*, 1974, *71*, 259–263.

Held, R., & Bauer, J. A. Development of sensorially-guided reaching in infant monkey. *Brain Research*, 1974, *71*, 265–271.

Jones, B. Role of central monitoring of efference in short-term memory for movement. *Journal of Experimental Psychology*, 1974, *102*, 27–43.

Kelso, J. A. S., & Stelmach, G. Central and peripheral mechanisms in motor control. In G. E. Stelmach (Ed.), *Motor control: Issues and trends*. New York: Academic Press, 1976.

Lashley, K. S. The problem of serial order in behavior. In L. A. Jeffress (Ed.), *Cerebral mechanisms in behavior: The Hixon symposium*. New York: Wiley, 1951.

Marteniuk, R. G. Cognitive information processes in motor short-term memory and movement production. In G. E. Stelmach (Ed.), *Motor control: Issues and trends*. New York: Academic Press, 1976.

Marteniuk, R. G., & Sullivan, S. J. Utilization of information in learning and controlling slow and fast movements. In *Proceedings of the International Congress of Physical Activity Sciences*, Quebec City, 1976.

Neisser, V. *Cognition and reality*. San Francisco: Freeman, 1976.

Paillard, J. Les determinants moteurs de l'organization de l'espace. *Cahiers de Psychologie*, 1971, *14*, 261–316.

Paillard, J., & Beaubaton, D. Triggered and guided components of visual reaching. Their dissociation in split-brain studies. In M. Shahani (Ed.), *The motor system: Neurophysiology and muscle mechanisms*. Amsterdam: Elsevier, 1976.

Schmidt, R. A. A schema theory of discrete motor skill learning. *Psychological Review*, 1975, *82*, 225–260.

Schmidt, R. A. Control processes in motor skills. *Exercise and Sport Sciences Reviews*, 1976, *4*, 229–261.

Shapiro, D. C. A preliminary attempt to determine the duration of a motor program. In D. M. Landers & R. W. Christina (Eds.), *Psychology of motor behavior and sport* (Vol. 1). Urbana, Illinois: Human Kinetics, 1977.

Turvey, M. T. Preliminaries to a theory of action with reference to vision. In R. Shaw & J. Bransford (Eds.), *Perceiving, acting, and comprehending: Towards an ecological psychology*. Pontiac, Maryland: Erlbaum, 1977.

14

Hemispheric Lateralization and Orientation in Compensatory and Voluntary Movement

Waneen Wyrick Spirduso

I. Introduction

Many motor tasks require that decisions be made with regard to side of body, direction (right or left), and amplitude or intensity of the task. When these tasks must be completed as rapidly as possible, the relative contribution that each of these decisions makes to the information-processing time consumed can be inferred. The decision as to which side of the body must respond is a very important decision, in that uncertainty in this dimension serves to lengthen reaction time more than uncertainty with regard to direction or extent of movement (Glencross, 1973). Rosenbaum (in press) claims that when these three decisions must be made, the decision with regard to side of body is made first and consumes the most time, followed by the decision for direction, and finally for extent.

Although an enormous amount of attention has been focused on the organization of voluntary movement to visual and auditory stimuli, very little attention

Information Processing in
Motor Control and Learning

has been turned to the organization of a response with regard to side of body when the stimulus is a kinesthetic stimulus. A kinesthetic stimulus in the context of this chapter is a sudden change in joint angle and muscle length. This is a type of stimulus, unlike visual and auditory stimuli, that changes the neurophysiological state of spinal levels and, in addition, projects to different cortical areas.

II. A Kinesthetic Stimulus–Response Paradigm

It will be helpful at this point to digress long enough to describe our experimental findings and our questions of interest. Our instrumentation allows us to study reflex and voluntary responses to a displacement of limb position (Duncan, Wyrick, & Miller, 1974). Subjects are seated with one or both arms straight, abducted at a right angle, and attached to a wooden support by an electromagnet held in place by a wrist cuff. When the magnet on the wooden support is energized, the subject's arm is supported through the iron disk on the cuff. When the current is discontinued, the magnetic field collapses and the subject's arm begins to fall at a constant acceleration predicted by gravitational force. An accelerometer on the cuff records the acceleration of the limb as it drops from the magnet. Wire electrodes are inserted into the middle deltoideus muscle of both limbs, and a surface ground electrode is placed on an earlobe. Subjects are trained via EMG responses to maintain the deltoid in a quiescent state and to maintain electrical silence until the stimulus occurs. The segmental or stretch reflex latency is defined as the time release of the magnet to the first deflection of the EMG response. The premotor latency is defined as the time between the break of the magnet and the recording of continuous muscle action potentials in the stimulus arm, as well as in the nonstimulus arm. The stimulus arm always contains a stretch reflex in conjunction with a voluntary response, whereas the nonstimulus arm contains only the voluntary response.

We have been investigating the effects of various instructional sets on the total response to limb displacement. Under one set of instructions, subjects responded to the falling of just one arm (stimulus limb condition) by resisting its fall, to the falling of one arm by abducting both arms (bilateral condition), or to the falling of one arm by abducting the opposite arm (nonstimulus limb) (Ducan, 1975). The significant finding in that study was that the response by the falling limb was faster under bilateral conditions that when the stimulus limb only was released. This was presumably due to central facilitation generated by the presence of a raised contralateral arm and with the intention to move both limbs. However, an even more interesting finding was that when one limb was displaced and response was to be a bilateral response, the nonstimulus limb reacted faster than the stimulus limb; that is, the side opposite the falling limb was able to initiate a premotor response faster than the arm in which the stimulus was generated (Duncan, 1975; Duncan & Spirduso, 1975). This seemed to be a strange state of affairs, since the pathway from the displaced limb to the controlling contralateral hemisphere has to be a circuitous and time-consuming route to initiate efferents to the nonstimulus limb. At first we speculated that, since the stimulus limb was the only limb in which a stretch reflex occurred, the presence of the reflex might be delaying the vountary response. That seemed reasonable, in light of the known possible sources of inhibition that follow a stretch reflex, until we realized that in all of our experimental protocols the subjects were always aware of which limb was to be displaced; in other words, the subjects were always able to prepare for the stimulus, preprogram the command, and generate sensory consequences. The task of responding bilaterally to the falling of one limb involves, after all, two different mechanisms for each limb. The response of the falling limb is modulated by motoservo actions, whereas the contralateral limb is probably controlled by α–γ coactivation. From the subject's perspective, his falling limb has a kinesthetic stimulus to use as a cue, whereas the opposite limb must be controlled entirely by central command. Modulation of the central command might be more influential than modulation of peripheral commands, and it seemed necessary to examine the supraspinal mechanisms in more detail.

In this chapter, then, the way that an individual organizes a voluntary bilateral response to a kinesthetic stimulus such as a load disturbance in one limb will be discussed in terms of the nature of the response and the commands necessary to evoke it. Several models, such as hemispheric input/output coupling, hemispheric specialization and dominance, and hemispheric orientation, will be discussed in terms of their appropriateness with regard to our findings (Duncan, 1975; Duncan & Spirduso, 1975; Spirduso, Baylor, & Lee, Note 1).

III. Components of a Kinesthetic Stimulus–Response in the Stimulus Limb

Let us turn our attention first to the components of a response to a kinesthetic stimulus that occurs on one side of the body. When the nature of the response is known to the subject, he structures a command to be evoked in response to the stimulus. Simplifying greatly in order to emphasize levels of control, the command for a voluntary movement may be categorized into three components: a central command that signals the intent to move to the pyramidal tract cells in the motor cortex, a pyramidal tract command that sends impulses down descending fibers from pyramidal tract neurons to the spinal cord, and peripheral commands or the efferent impulses from the spinal cord to the muscle (Houk, 1972). The mechanical properties of muscle interacting with spinal reflex influences alter the temporal features of the command signals as they travel their pathways. Pro-

WANEEN WYRICK SPIRDUSO

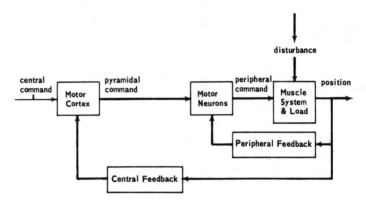

Figure 1 Model showing different levels of motor control mechanisms. [From Crago *et al.* (1976, p. 49). Reprinted by permission.]

prioceptive feedback occurs peripherally from muscle spindles and Golgi tendon organs, which have a short latency. Joint and visual afferents, and perhaps cutaneous afferents, provide feedback that is processed centrally as well.

The kinesthetic stimulus that elicits the response may be evoked in a number of ways, but another common strategy that relates to our limb displacement strategy has been to elicit a normal resisting contraction by the subject against a resistance and then provide, during the course of the movement, an unexpected change in the resistance [see Crago, Houk, and Hansan (1976) for a diagram of the apparatus]. This either loads or unloads the primary agonist muscle and sets into play a series of segmental and supraspinal events that have been analyzed in a number of provocative ways. EMG responses from these paradigms are quite similar to our model (see, for example, Evarts & Tanji, 1976, p. 1071). The important point to bear in mind is that the kinesthetic stimulus unleashes both segmental and supraspinal reflexes that modulate the central command (Conrad, Matsunami, Meyer-Lohmann, Wiesendanger, & Brooks, 1974; Evarts, 1973; Evarts & Tanji, 1974; Hammond, 1956; Hayes, 1976; Marsden, Merton, & Morton, 1972; Tatton, Forner, Gerstein, Chambers, & Liu, 1975; Wisendanger, 1973). Immediately following the unloading, or change in muscle length, a segmental stretch reflex is elicited of about 18–25 msec, and this in turn is followed by a silent period (see Figure 8) of varying lengths that has been attributed to (*a*) Renshaw cell inhibition; (*b*) Golgi tendon organ inhibition; and/or (*c*) a synchronizing effect of simultaneous discharge on the α motorneuronal pool (Agarwal & Gottlieb, 1972; Angel, 1974; Jansen & Rudjord, 1964).

Following the stretch reflex is a second component, about 45–70 msec, that has been described as a long-loop or transcortical reflex. Long-loop reflexes particularly are observable in the special case when there is a strong and direct path to the areas of the contralateral cortex that control the output of a triggered movement. A triggered movement has been defined as a preprogrammed response that is triggered by input to the limb and is quite different and substantially faster than movement from a response that is triggered by input from visual or auditory input (Crago et al., 1976). A fascinating aspect of the supraspinal reflex is that it is heavily influenced by the instructional set preceding the voluntary response and is influenced by practice. When monkeys are first faced with a perturbation of their limb while making a response, for instance, they drop the handle and withdraw in fright. It takes many trials before the well-practiced load disturbance response with the appearance of the cortical loop occurs (Evarts, 1973). In humans, the long loop becomes less variable with practice (Crago et al., 1976).

The cortical nature of the long loop has been further substantiated by investigators who found these reflexes to be substantially lengthened and more variable under instructional conditions to humans to "let go" in the pulled limb than when they were instructed to "resist" (Evarts & Tanji, 1974, 1976; Hammond, 1956). In humans a choice stimulus evokes more variable and slower long-loop reflex responses (Crago et al., 1976).

The mechanism by which these long-loop reflexes are mediated in a voluntary movement is conceived to be a transcortical spindle circuit whose projection from precentral cortex to spinal motoneurone reinforces servo loops that include the cerebellum and postcentral cortex. When the muscle is suddenly changed in length, signals from muscle spindle afferents (Group II), which are know to project to precentral cortex in times fast enough to be within those latencies observed, evoke a synchronous and well-defined burst in the precentral cortex (Conrad et al., 1974). The influence of these Group II afferents is partially dependent upon interaction of cutaneous and joint afferents accompanying the volley (Evarts & Tanji, 1976; Marsden et al., 1972; Meyer-Lohmann, Conrad, Matsunami, & Brooks, 1975; Tatton et al., 1975; Wisendanger, 1973). The anatomical pathways suggested have been spinocerebellar–spinal and spinothalamic–cerebrospinal. These anatomical pathways describe a relay via the sensory cortex, corticocortical projections from sensory to motor cortex, or pathways from muscle receptors directly to motor cortex, bypassing the sensory cortex (Murphy, Wong, & Kwan, 1975). In other words, there is a strong functional linkage in the motor cortex between input from and output to muscles *in which the stimulus occurs,* and this linkage is spatially organized with a great deal of specificity for single muscles (Murphy et al., 1975; Asanuma & Rosen, 1972; Asanuma & Fernandez, 1974).

Long-loop reflexes, then, as well as segmental reflexes, occur as a result of the sudden change in muscle length and enter into the total response. In addition, Evarts and Tanji (1974) have shown that motor cortex neurons were clearly active 200 msec prior to an expected stimulus, and the cortical activity is substantially different depending upon the instructions received regarding the response to be made. Instructions of different movements, whether they are in direction or in terms of amount of information about the movement to be made,

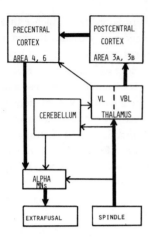

Figure 2 Basic structures involved in the supraspinal reflex. The darkened line represents the path of the fastest responses.

modify the nature of the motor cortex activity prior to the movement. Thus, afferent impulses from triggered movements arrive upon a different state of cortical activity. This has been described as "gating" of neural control by Evarts and Tanji (1973).

Thus, it can be seen that the control mechanisms operative in just a simple load disturbance stimulus in one limb are enormously complex, and we have yet to consider the situation in which these stimuli might be presented in either limb, reacted to by either limb or by both simultaneously, and under different instructional sets. In our experiments, when subjects were instructed to respond bilaterally, we saw that nonstimulus limb responses were faster than stimulus limb latencies. What mechanism would produce these results? When both limbs respond to a unilateral stimulus, do the cortical hemispheres process the stimulus simultaneously? Does one hemisphere receive the afferent input before the other? Is the left hemisphere in controlling the right hand more dominant?

IV. Bilateral Response to a Unilateral Kinesthetic Stimulus

To answer these questions, we must examine cortical influences, and three factors seem to be of importance: (*a*) hemispheric input/output coupling; (*b*) hemispheric dominance and specialization; and (*c*) hemispheric orientation. Each will be considered as a possible mechanism to explain response latencies of the limbs under bilateral response conditions.

A. Hemispheric Input/Output Coupling

Unlike visual afferents, 50% of which go to each hemisphere of the cerebral cortex, and auditory afferents, about 60% of which project to the contralateral hemisphere, almost 85% of proprioceptive afferents travel to the contralateral hemisphere (Gardner, 1963; Ruch, 1965). Although there may be ipsilateral projections, they are weak and questionable as to function. If a split-brain cat learns to discriminate between two surfaces of different roughness with one paw, the discrimination does not transfer to the other paw (Stamm & Sperry, 1957). In humans the ipsilateral proprioceptive input is very crude, serving primarily as a cueing mechanism and not relaying information about quality (Gazzaniga, 1967). At least two independent systems project to the motor cortex: one carrying specific information from the periphery and the other nonspecific (Asanuma & Fernandez, 1974).

Discrete neural colonies in the motor cortex receive peripheral afferent impulses specifically related to the contraction of the muscle to which the colony projects (Asanuma & Rosen, 1972). These colonies have been shown, when electrically stimulated, to cause extension, flexion, abduction, and adduction of a single finger, especially the thumb, and they produce various movements of given joints located close together. The columns respond to light touch, skin pressure, and/or passive joint movement, with about one-half of the cells activated by passive joint movement. The peripheral afferents project to more superficial and higher layers of the cortex, however, where the threshold for eliciting movement is higher. It is speculated that the downward directed impulses from superficial to deep cortical layers must be predominantly excitatory and serve the function of positive feedback, which reinforces the activity of the corticofugal cells.

The motor control from each hemisphere is predominantly contralateral, but bilateral projections are also present. Descending corticospinal fibers terminate (a) on the dorsal horn of the cord where they modulate sensory transmission; (b) directly on the contralateral motoneurons of the ventral horn; and (c) on the intermediate zone of the cord where they influence the ventral horn neurons as well. The descending terminations on the intermediate zone are on the dorsolateral part or the ventromedial part of the intermediate zone. Those terminating on the dorsolateral part are contralateral terminations that distribute preferentially to motoneurons of distal musculature and provide a high degree of fractionation of movement. Those terminating on the ventromedial part of the intermediate zone terminate bilaterally and influence motoneurons of axial and proximal limb muscles. So each hemisphere is connected both directly and indirectly with the dorsolateral part of the spinal intermediate zone contralaterally and with its ventromedial parts bilaterally (Brinkman & Kuypers, 1972). Each hemisphere strongly and in a specific fashion controls the contralateral arm, hand, and finger movement, and gross arm movement ipsilaterally (Gazzaniga, 1970). In a person with a left hemispherectomy, for instance, the right hands and fingers are paralyzed but the right arm can be controlled (Wiley, 1975).

In our motor task, although the muscle being monitored is proximal and has some ipsilateral control, the fact that our subjects had both hemispheres intact means that contralateral pathways were selectively used.

B. Hemispheric Dominance and Specialization

In terms of cerebral dominance, it can be stated with some degree of certainty that at least 90% of humans are right-handed (Hicks & Kinsbourne, 1976; Thompson & Marsh, 1976). Hand preference for motor tasks is most apparent when timing or serial organization is important (Beaumont, 1974), and in skilled acts the nonpreferred hand may operate under the control of the dominant hemisphere exerted across the corpus callosum (Heilman, Coyle, Gonyea, & Geschwind, 1973, p. 26). Sensory information has generally been shown to be detected at lower threshold levels on the nonpreferred side (Ghent, 1961; Green, Reese, Pegues, & Elliott, 1961; Semmes, Weinstein, Ghent, & Teuber, 1960; Weinstein, 1962; Weinstein & Sersen, 1961), although some slight doubt has been cast on this general conclusion (Carmon & Benton, 1969). However, although the two hemispheres are anatomically asymmetrical they are not isolated units. A more cohesive way to conceive of the functioning of the two hemispheres in controlling movement is in terms of hemispheric specialization, rather than dominance.

The fact that the left hemisphere is specialized for processing speech or verbal related tasks (Perl & Haggard, 1975; Risberg, Halsey, Hills, & Wilson, 1975; Springer & Gazzaniga, 1975; Gazzaniga & Young, 1967; Aitken, 1976; Kleinman, Carron, Cloninger, & Halvachs, 1976; Cohen, 1975) and that the right hemisphere is specialized in spatial analysis (Benton, 1967; Carmon, 1970; Carmon & Benton, 1969; Carmon, Bilstrom, & Benton, A.L. 1969; Corkin, 1965; Fontenot & Benton, 1971; Sperry, 1968) has been documented many times. Milner (1974) has suggested a principle of "complementary specialization" in which the left hemisphere's specialization of verbal material goes hand in hand with the right hemisphere's specialization for spatial processing. Kimura (1973) has also assigned the process of nonvisual location to the right hemisphere. These specializations have been identified on the basis of studies that show verbal or spatial processing reaction times to be much faster when completed in the left or right hemisphere, respectively. Leision studies have complemented the reaction time findings by showing that when leisions appear in one or the other hemisphere the impaired abilities reflect the specialization location (Provins & Jeeves, 1975). Hemispherectomy patients also reflect these specializations. Jeeves and Dixon (1970) propose that the left motor cortex is more efficient than the right in initiating a reaction response, whereas the sensory area in the right hemisphere processes unpatterned light stimuli faster than the corresponding area in the left hemisphere.

Risberg *et al.* (1975), by using the xenon inhalation method, also showed that regional cerebral blood flow increased 16% in the left hemisphere during verbal processing and 10% in the right hemisphere during spatial processing. In both cases the cerebral blood flow increase in the specialized hemisphere was significantly greater than in the nonspecialized hemisphere.

More important to our problem, however, is specialization of each hemisphere for processing afferent information regarding body position or tactual information, or for controlling motor output. At least four investigators have suggested that the processing of proprioceptive information concerning the position of body parts is comparable to the analysis of spatial relations, and consequently the right hemisphere is more specialized at processing proprioceptive information (Carmon & Benton, 1969; Corkin, 1965; Levin, 1973). Although this concept is contrary to the preponderance of literature regarding kinesthetic processing, these investigators came to this conclusion by finding that brain-damaged patients who had an intact right hemisphere were able to use high-intensity proprioceptive feedback to improve their ability to press and hold a button within a target range, whereas right hemisphere-damaged subjects made no improvements with practice. Unilateral damage in either hemisphere caused impairment at low-intensity feedback conditions, but at the higher intensities only those with right hemispheres intact were able to use the feedback. These studies dealt primarily with tactile discrimination rather than with latencies, but they bear indirectly upon our findings.

Kimura (1973) has suggested that the left hemisphere may be essential for some types of movements, particularly those related to speech, such as copying hand movements of others or writing. She observed that a deaf mute, after left hemisphere damage, displayed disturbances of hand movements analogous to disturbances of speech. In addition, free gesturing movements made by normal individuals during speech are primarily made by the hand opposite the hemisphere controlling speech.

Lateral specialization may also be specific to the input/output modalities, as suggested by Sussman in a series of tracking studies (MacNeilage, Sussman, & Stolz, 1975; Sussman & MacNeilage, 1975). He has proposed a "cursor-to-control" hypothesis that predicts superior performance when direct contralateral transmission of an auditory feedback tone from the cursor is sent to the hemisphere that is to control ongoing movements. This specialization is modality specific, in that performance was significantly better when the tone controlled by a speech articulator was presented to the right ear, but not if the tone was controlled by hand. Similarly, subjects could track a visual target better when the feedback from the tracking hand was also sent to the hemisphere controlling the hand. The lateralized sensorimotor integration mechanism for eye–hand coordination was not as clear-cut in the nonpreferred hand, perhaps because the sensorimotor integration mechanism for contralateral hand control is less well developed in the right hemisphere than in the left (Kutas & Donchin, 1974) or because more "higher-order" aspects of movement conceptualization and planning for the nonpreferred left hand may reside in the left hemisphere. At any rate, the fact that Sussman found a laterality effect tracking with articulators only when the target was an auditory one, and with the hand only when the target was a visual one, suggested strongly that the laterality effect was not due to some general property of the nervous system but to a speech-related or eye–hand-related sensorimotor integration mechanism.

A basic assumption of Sussman's hypothesis is the use of direct contralateral pathways over which the sensory information travels. Sensory information traveling to a hemisphere over contralateral pathways does not have to cross the corpus callosum and thus travels along a direct path, whereas information traveling to the ipsilateral hemisphere must go by way of ipsilateral fibers (of which there are few in the case of proprioceptors) or cross the callosum, thus consuming time. The time taken to cross the callosum is called interhemispheric transmission time (IHTT). In the study of IHTTs by reaction time paradigms, there have been a great many confounding variables and substantial confusion, but IHTT, in a reaction time task to a verbally oriented stimulus, ranges from 3 to 5 msec. Higher values may be found, but these will be discussed in Section IV,C. The general finding has been that information sent on direct paths is processed faster (Brewer, 1958; Blumstein, Goodglass, & Tartter, 1975; Bryden, 1976; Filbey & Gazzaniga, 1969; Grafstein, 1959; Kleinman et al., 1976; Majkowski, Bochenck, Bochenck, Knapik-Fijalkowska, & Kopec, 1971; Provins & Jeeves, 1975).

C. Hemispheric Orientation Model

Recapitulating momentarily, we have discussed an anatomical model and hemispheric dominance and specialization models have been proposed largely to explain visual and auditory lateral asymmetries, but which also may elucidate the control processes occurring when a subject responds to a kinesthetic stimulus. Before we return to our findings regarding these responses, one more model should be discussed, and that is a hemispheric orientation model, most prominently espoused by Kinsbourne (1970). The models discussed previously have been structural models comprised of anatomical pathways with the corpus callosum viewed as a barrier to be crossed. According to Kinsbourne (1970), a response is facilitated in relation to the direction of orientation. Any simple response controlled by the left hemisphere will benefit from environmental stimulation that elicits an orientation to the right side of space. When the focus of attention must be straight ahead, the hemispheres are mutually inhibited. An eccentric stimulation elicits a corresponding orientation response in one hemisphere and inhibits a contralateral orienting response in the other. Large lateral differences that have been reported for IHTT represent in Kinsbourne's model not a crossing of a structural barrier but a stimulus-directed compatibility effect (Swanson, Ledlow, & Kinsbourne, in press). Basically, then, the orientation model is an expectancy model, which indicates that, when subjects know where and what type of stimulus to expect, IHTTs are reduced to an almost negligible nerve conduction time across the callosum. It is instructive to view several studies on IHTTs from this perspective in terms of randomly presented or blocked trials (Table I). The

Table I

Interhemispheric Transmission Times (IHTTs) Categorized According to Method of Stimulus Presentation

IHTTS [a]	Investigators	Year	Modality	Presentation
4.0	Poffenberger	(1912)	Visual–manual	Blocked
2.6	Jeeves and Dixon	(1970)	Visual–manual	Blocked
10.0	Moscovitch and Catlin	(1970)	Visual–verbal	Blocked
2.7, 3.3	Berlucchi et al.	(1971)	Visual–manual	Blocked
3.0	Swanson and Kinsbourne	(1976)	Visual–manual	Blocked
30.0	Filbey and Gazzaniga	(1969)	Visual–verbal	Random
20.0	Bradshaw and Perriment	(1970)	Visual–manual	Random
27.0	Swanson and Ledlow	(1974)[b]	Visual–verbal	Random
28.5	Swanson and Ledlow	(1974)[b]	Visual–manual	Random
20.0	Swanson and Kinsbourne	(1976)[c]	Visual–manual	Random
13.6	Aitken	(1976)	Auditory–manual	Random
20.0	Kleinman et al.	(1976)	Visual–verbal	Random
5.0	Kleinman et al.	(1976)	Visual–manual	Random

[a] In milliseconds.
[b] Reference Note 2.
[c] Reference Note 3.

great variability in IHTTs can be attributed to the varying degrees of uncertainty of stimulus and response location across the several studies. Thus, hemispheric specialization may be exaggerated or obscured merely by shifting attention between hemispheres. If the left hemisphere is cued, its superiority in the processing of linguistic material is more dramatic; if the right hemisphere is cued, the advantage of the left hemisphere is diminished or eliminated.

Other evidence exists that hemispheric orientation provides a mechanism of selective inhibition that influences lateral responses. When split-brain subjects were alerted by a signal to the right hemisphere but were given the signal requiring a right-hand reaction, the right-hand reactions were almost three times longer, presumably because the left hemisphere had been inhibited (Gazzaniga & Hillyard, 1973). This effect was not seen in the left hemisphere–left hand combination because the left hand is controlled bilaterally much more than the right hand is. Gazzaniga, Bogen, & Sperry (1963) also reported the blocking of somesthetic sensations from one-half of the body as a function of attentional and response sets in split-brain patients. In the normally interconnected brain, information undergoing processing extraneous to the dominant cognitive activity under consideration is inhibited at the collosum, and ipsilateral pathways are also suppressed. The ipsilateral ear cortex pathways have been shown to be suppressed in split-brain subjects and in normal individuals participating in a dichotic listening task (Springer & Gazzaniga, 1975; Mononen & Seitz, 1977; Milner, Taylor, & Sperry, 1968).

V. Application of Hemisphere Models to the Bilateral Response Paradigm

Returning to our kinesthetic stimulus–response paradigm, we can test three models: the hemisphere input/output coupling model, the specialization/dominance model, and the orientation model.

1. The hemispheric input/output coupling model predicts that the kinesthetic load disturbance (stimulus) initiates central feedback directly to the contralateral motor cortex, which also controls the response movement, thus initiating a very fast long-loop reflex response. The hemisphere contralateral to the nonstimulus limb, however, must initiate its response from the command structure. In this model the nonstimulus limb receives a stimulus that has crossed the callosum, and thus will always be slower, regardless of limb dominance (Figure 3).

2. The hemispheric specialization model predicts that since the left hemisphere is more specialized for motor control of the right hand (in terms of a right-hander being more skilled with one hand than the other), and the right hemisphere is specialized for processing kinesthetic stimuli (as shown by the thresholds of the nondominant side being lower), then when the nondominant limb is the stimulus, the information travels to the right hemisphere specialized to process it, and the left verbal–motor specialized hemisphere is the one that has to initiate a nonstimulus arm response. A stimulus in the dominant limb, though, travels to the left hemisphere, which is not specialized for kinesthetic stimuli, and the nonstimulus limb must be activated by the right hemisphere, which is the hemisphere with less-refined motor control. In this model, the stimulus in the nondominant limb would always produce the faster latencies.

3. The orientation model in which the hemisphere responsible for a decision is facilitated and produces the faster latencies predicts faster times when the stimulus location is known, regardless of stimulus limb dominance or hemispheric specialization. In our previous studies, the stimulus side was always known to the subjects; thus, they had the opportunity to facilitate the hemisphere that was to make an active command.

One way to test the three models is to make stimulus location uncertain, across

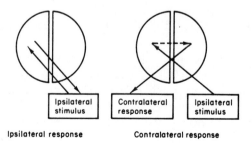

Figure 3 Hemispheric input/output coupling model.

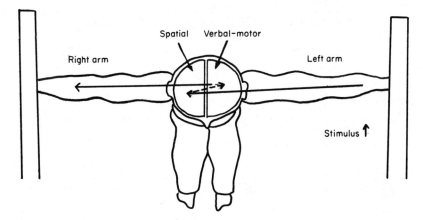

Figure 4 Hemispheric specialization model.

the nondominant and dominant side. In the certain condition we told our subjects which arm would be released, and in the uncertain condition we told them either arm would be released.

A summary of our findings (Spirduso *et al.*, Note 1) is shown in Figure 6. As might be expected, an interaction of models explains the findings more efficiently. The response of the stimulus limb to the sudden release is uninfluenced by limb dominance or stimulus certainty (Figure 6A). Simple reaction time, although it was substantially faster when the stimulus was in the dominant limb, was generally uninfluenced by stimulus location certainty (Figure 6B). This apparent lack of effect of the certainty conditions on simple reaction time is masking the most interesting influence of stimulus location certainty, however: the differences that occur in the nonstimulus limb premotor times (Figure 6C).

The nonstimulus limb response varied dramatically with the instructional set

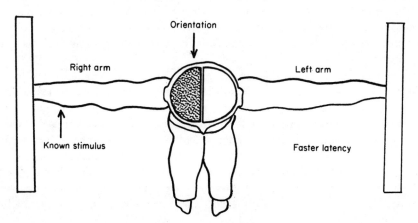

Figure 5 Hemispheric orientation model

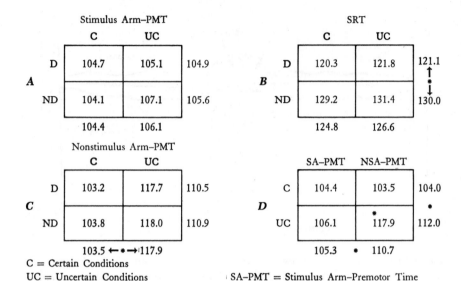

C = Certain Conditions
UC = Uncertain Conditions
SRT = Simple Reaction Time
SA–PMT = Stimulus Arm–Premotor Time
NSA–PMT = Nonstimulus Arm–Premotor Time

Figure 6 Means and main-effect means for stimulus location certainty-by-dominance factors. [From Spirduso *et al.* (Note 1). Reprinted by permission.]

even though the task was to produce a bilateral response. Premotor latencies were drastically different under different stimulus location certainty conditions. The nonstimulus limb response latencies for both dominant and nondominant limbs were fast and not significantly different under "certain" conditions but were considerably slower under "uncertain" conditions. When the stimulus location is known, the nonstimulus limb premotor latency is the same as or faster than the stimulus limb premotor latency, but when stimulus location is not known, the nonstimulus latency trails the stimulus limb latencies. This direct comparison may be seen in Figure 6D. Going back to our earlier modification of Houk's (1972) command level model, we see now that we can combine parts of all three models to explain our results.

The stimulus limb may be controlled by, or is at least strongly influenced by, a more reflexive long-loop process, in which a central command is not issued. Thus, stimulus limb latencies are uninfluenced by stimulus location certainty and, since they involve a direct transmission to the motor cortex that also controls the limb, are not significantly different in dominant and nondominant limbs. The stimulus limb utilizes the load disturbance as the primary cue to initiate the motor command. Even when the subject's *uncued* arm is released and he finds himself having to react to the displaced limb that he was not expecting, the stimulus limb responds as fast as or faster than under known stimulus location conditions. In this case, the response in the stimulus limb appears to be a transcortical spindle

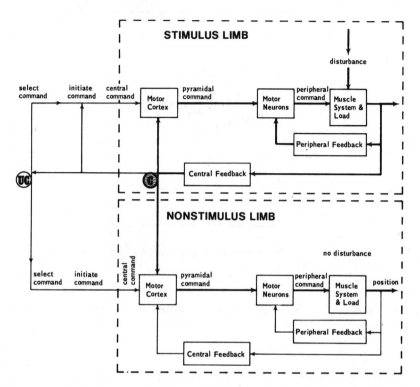

Figure 7 Modification of Houk's (1972) model of control; modified to account for stimulus and nonstimulus arm responses to a kinesthetic stimulus. In the case shown, the darkened lines indicate the control pathways when the stimulus location is known (©, certain). When stimulation location is uncertain, UC, the central feedback path leads to the "select command" component of the decision. [From Houk (1972). Reprinted by permission.]

loop in which the cortical component is also in the hemisphere that was oriented for a voluntary command to be made for the nonstimulus limb. Thus, the servoloop is activated in a previously facilitated hemisphere.

The nonstimulus limb, however, must await a cue from the stimulus limb. Thus, it operates from a select command status (see Figure 7). If the stimulus location is known, central feedback may travel directly to the pyramidal level of the motor cortex contralateral to the nonstimulus limb so that it either precedes by a few milliseconds or is concurrent with the stimulus limb response. The known location of the stimulus can allow for the initiate program to be readied and for spinal tuning mechanisms to enhance the awaited command. When stimulus location is unknown, however, central feedback must provide information upon which a decision must be made (right or left limb) and an initiate command must precede the pyramidal command. Thus, considerable delay is

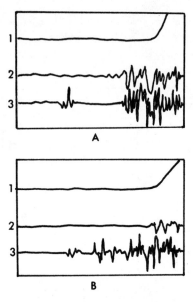

Figure 8 Comparison of a stimulus location "certain" condition and a miscued condition. In A, channel 2 of the oscilloscope reveals a nonstimulus arm response that is faster than the stimulus arm (channel 3) response. Channel 1 is the accelerometer recording, representing simple reaction time. Both arms appear to be under voluntary control. In B, the stimulus arm (channel 3) responds to the unexpected stimulus faster than in A; the response is not compact and is quite dissimilar from that of A. The nonstimulus arm response (channel 2) is quite delayed.

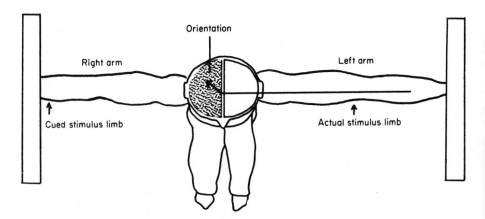

Figure 9 Hemispheric orientation in a miscued trial. In this figure, since the subject expects the left limb to drop, he facilitates the right hemisphere for the voluntary nonstimulus arm command. Instead, the left arm is the stimulus and responds with a long-loop reflex that projects to a previously facilitated hemisphere.

encountered under certain stimulus location, a delay that is exaggerated under uncertain conditions when the nonstimulus limb is the nondominant limb (see Figure 6C). This implies that the afferent information travels to the left hemisphere where it may be less efficiently processed and crosses to the right hemisphere where motor control is less refined. There the right–left decision is made, and a command is initiated to the nondominant limb. This finding corroborates that of Jeeves and Dixon (1970).

In summary, hemispheric input/output coupling seems to explain the data very nicely for a response of one limb to a kinesthetic stimulus in that limb, but the bilateral response to a unilateral stimulus is much more complex because it requires both the notion of hemispheric specialization and dominance as well as Kinsbourne's (1970) concept of hemispheric orientation.

We are in the process of preparing to study the rectified and averaged EMG interference patterns that result from the experimental conditions of stimulus location, handedness, and stimulus location certainty. Through the analysis of these factors, we hope to elucidate the interaction between reflexive and voluntary control and the conditions under which subjects use different strategies. We have found the experimental paradigm of subjects responding bilaterally to a unilateral kinesthetic stimulus to be an extremely useful one that promises opportunities to analyze types of responses under different command levels and the influence of hemispheric dominance on spatial selection of movement.

Reference Notes

1. Spirduso, W. W., Baylor, A. M., & Lee, W. A. *Effects of stimulus certainty and limb dominance on simple and premotor characteristics to a kinesthetic stimulus.* Paper presented at the North American Society for Psychology of Sport and Physical Activity conference, Ithaca, New York, 1977.
2. Swanson, J. M., & Ledlow, A. *Unilateral input, attention, and performance in RT experiments.* Paper presented at American Psychological Association meeting, New Orleans, 1974.
3. Swanson, J. M., & Kinsbourne, M. *S–R compatibility and interhemispheric transfer time.* Paper presented at American Psychological Association meeting, Washington, D.C., 1976.

References

Agarwal, G. C., & Gottlieb, G. L. The muscle silent period and reciprocal inhibition in man. *Journal of Neurology, Neurosurgery and Psychiatry*, 1972, *35*, 72–76.
Aitken, P. G. The effects of contralateral noise on reaction time to monaural stimuli. *Perception & Psychophysics*, 1976, *19*, 206–210.
Angel, R. W. Electromyography during voluntary movement: the two-burst pattern. *Electromyography and Clinical Neurophysiology*, 1974, *36*, 393–398.
Asanuma, H., & Fernandez, J. J. Organization of projection from the thalamic relay nuclei to the motor cortex in the cat. *Brain Research*, 1974, *71*, 515–22.

Asanuma, H., & Rosen, I. Functional role of afferent inputs to the monkey motor cortex. *Brain Research*, 1972, *40*, 3–5.

Beaumont, J. G. Handedness and hemisphere function. In S. J. Diamond & J. G. Beaumont (Eds.), *Hemisphere function in the human brain*. London: Elek Science, 1974.

Benton, A. L. Constructional apraxia and the minor hemisphere. *Conference of Neurology*, Basel, 1967, *29*, 1–6.

Berlucchi, G., Heron, W., Hyman, R., Rizzolati, G., & Umilta, C. Simple reaction times of ipsilateral and contralateral hand to lateralized visual stimuli. *Brain*, 1971, *94*, 419–430.

Blumstein, S., Goodglass, H., & Tartter, J. The reliability of an advantage in dichotic listening. *Brain and Language*, 1975, *2*, 226–236.

Bradshaw, J. L., & Perriment, A. D. Laterality effects and choice reaction in a unimanual two-finger task. *Perception and Psychophysics*, 1970, *7*, 185–188.

Brewer, F. Physiology of the corpus callosum. *Research Publications of the Association for Nervous and Mental Diseases*, 1958, *36*, 424–448.

Brinkman, J., & Kuypers, H. G. J. M. Splitbrain monkeys: Cerebral control of ipsilateral and contralateral arm, hand, and finger movements. *Science*, 1972, *176*, 535–539.

Bryden, M. P. Response bias and hemispheric differences in cat localization. *Perception and Psychophysics*, 1976, *19*, 23–28.

Carmon, A. Impaired utilization of kinesthetic feedback in right hemispheric lesions. *Neurology*, 1970, *20*, 1033–1038.

Carmon, A., & Benton, A. L. Dominance of the right cerebral hemisphere for stereopsis. *Neuropsychologia*, 1969, *7*, 29–39.

Carmon, A., & Benton, A. L. Tactile perception of direction and number in patients with unilateral cerebral disease. *Neurology*, 1969, *19*, 525–532.

Carmon, A., Bilstrom, D. E., & Benton, A. L. Thresholds for pressure and sharpness in the right and left hands. *Cortex*, 1969, *5*, 27–35.

Cohen, G. Hemisphere differences in the effects of cueing in visual recognition tasks. *Journal of Experimental Psychology*, 1975, *1*, 366–373.

Conrad, B., Matsunami, K., Meyer-Lohmann, J., Wiesendanger, M., & Brooks, V. B. Cortical load compensation during voluntary elbow movements. *Brain Research*, 1974, *71*, 507–514.

Corkin, S. Tactually-guided maze learning in man: Effects of unilateral cortical excisions and bilateral hippocampal lesions. *Neuropsychologia*, 1965, *3*, 339–351.

Crago, P. E., Houk, J. C., & Hansan, Z. Regulatory actions of human stretch reflex. *Journal of Neurophysiology*, 1976, *39*, 925–935.

Duncan, A. M. Electromyographical study of unilateral and bilateral measurement conditions of reflex, premotor, and simple reaction time to joint displacement. *American Journal of Physical Medicine*, 1975, *54*, 132–41.

Duncan, A. M., & Spirduso, W. An electromyographical study of stimulus limb dominance and measurement conditions on fractional response variables. *Mouvement*, 1975, *7*, 55–62.

Duncan, A. M., Wyrick, W., & Miller, E. L. Instrumentation for obtaining fractionated electromyographical response times to a joint displacement stimulus. *Research Quarterly*, 1974, *45*, 452–459.

Evarts, E. V. Motor cortex reflexes associated with learned movement. *Science*, 1973, *179*, 501–503.

Evarts, E. V., & Tanji, J. Gating of motor cortex reflexes by prior instruction. *Brain Research*, 1974, *71*, 479–494.

Evarts, E. V., & Tanji, J. Reflex and intended responses in motor cortex pyramidal tract neurons of monkey. *Journal of Neurophysiology*, 1976, *39*, 1069–1080.

Filbey, R. A., & Gazzaniga, M. S. Splitting the normal brain with reaction time. *Psychonomic Science*, 1969, *17*, 335–336.

Fontenot, D. J., & Benton, A. L. Tactile perception of direction in relation to hemispheric locus of lesion. *Neuropsychologia*, 1971, *9*, 83–88.

Gardner, E. O. *Fundamentals of neurology*. Philadelphia: Saunders, 1963.

Gazzaniga, M. S. The split brain in man. *Scientific American*, 1967, *217*, 24–29.

Gazzaniga, M. S. Sensory-motor control mechanisms. In *The bisected brain*. New York: Appleton-Century-Crofts, 1970.

Gazzaniga, M. S., Bogen, J. E., & Sperry, R. W. Laterality effects in somesthesis following cerebral commisurotomy in man. *Neuropsychologia*, 1963, *1*, 209–215.

Gazzaniga, M. S., & Hillyard, S. A. Attention mechanisms following brain bisection. In S. Kornblum, (Ed.), *Attention and performance IV*. New York: Academic Press, 1973.

Gazzaniga, M. S., & Young, E. D. Effects of commisurotomy on the processing of increasing visual information. *Experimental Brain Research* 1967, *3*, 368–371.

Ghent, L. Developmental changes in tactual thresholds on dominant and nondominant sides. *Journal of Comparative Physiological Psychology*, 1961, *54*, 670–673.

Glencross, D. J. Response complexity and the latency of different movement patterns. *Journal of Motor Behavior*, 1973, *5*, 95–104.

Grafstein, B. Organization of callosal connections in suprasylvian gyrus of cat. *Journal of Neurophysiology*, 1959, *22*, 504–515.

Green, J. B., Reese, C. L., Pegues, J. J., & Elliott, F. A. Ability to distinguish two cutaneous stimuli separated by a brief time interval. *Neurology*, 1961, *11*, 1007–1009.

Hammond, P. H. The influence of prior instruction to the subject or an apparently involuntary neuro-muscular response. *Proceedings of the Physiological Society*, 1956, 17P–18P.

Hayes, K. Functional significance of the supraspinal stretch reflex. In D. M. Landers & R. W. Christina (Eds.), *Psychology of motor behavior and sport* (Vol. 1) Champaign, Illinois: Human Kinetics Publishers, 1976.

Heilman, K. M., Coyle, J. M., Gonyea, E. F., & Geschwind, N. Apraxia and agraphia in a left hander. *Brain*, 1973, *96*, 21–28.

Hicks, R. E., & Kinsbourne, M. Human handedness: A partial crossfostering study. *Science*, 1976, *192*, 908–910.

Houk, J. C. On the significance of various command signals during voluntary control. *Brain Research*, 1972, *40*, 49–53.

Jansen, J. K. S., & Rudjord, T. On the silent period and Golgi tendon organs of the soleus muscle of the cat. *Acta Physiologica Scandinavica*, 1964, *62*, 364–379.

Jeeves, M. A., & Dixon, N. F. Hemisphere differences in response rates to visual stimuli. *Psychonomic Sciences*, 1970, *20*, 249–251.

Kimura, D. The asymmetry of the human brain. *Scientific American*, 1973, *228*, 70–80.

Kinsbourne, M. The cerebral basis of lateral asymmetries in attention. In A. F. Sanders (Ed.), *Attention and performance III*. Amsterdam: North Holland, 1970.

Kleinman, K. M., Charron, R., Cloninger, L., & Halvachs, P. A comparison of interhemispheric transmission times as measured by verbal and manual reaction time. *International Journal of Neuroscience*, 1976, *6*, 285–288.

Kutas, M., & Donchin, E. Studies of squeezing: Handedness, responding hand, response force and asymmetry of readiness potential. *Science*, 1974, *186*, 545–548.

Levin, H. S. Motor impersistence and proprioceptive feedback in patients with unilateral cerebral disease. *Neurology*, 1973, *23*, 823–841.

MacNeilage, P. F., Sussman, H. M., & Stolz, W. Incidence of laterality effects in mandibular and manual performance of dichoptic visual pursuit tracking. *Cortex*, 1975, *11*, 251–258.

Majowski, J., Bochenck, Z., Bochenck, W., Knapik-Fijalkowska, D., & Kopec, J. Latency of averaged evoked potentials to contralateral and ipsilateral auditory stimulation in normal subjects. *Brain Research*, 1971, *25*, 416–419.

Marsden, C. D., Merton, P. A., & Morton, H. B. Servoaction in human voluntary movement. *Nature*, 1972, *238*, 140–143.

Marsden, C. D., Merton, P. A., & Morton, H. B. Latency measurements compatible with a cortical pathway for the stretch reflex in man. *Proceedings of the Physiological Society*, 1972, 58–59P.

Meyer-Lohmann, J., Conrad, B., Matsunami, K. & Brooks, V. B. Effect of dentate cooling on precentral unit activity following torque pulse injections into elbow movements. *Brain Research*, 1975, *94*, 237–251.

Milner, B. Hemispheric specialization: Scope and limits. In F. O. Schmitt & F. G. Worden (Eds.), *The neurosciences: Third study program*. Cambridge, Massachusetts: MIT Press, 1974.

Milner, B., Taylor, L., & Sperry, R. W. Lateralized suppression of dichotically presented digits after commissural section in man. *Science*, 1968, *161*, 184–186.

Mononen, L. J., & Seitz, M. R. An AER analysis of contralateral advantage in the transmission of auditory information. *Neuropsychologica*, 1977, *15*, 165– 173.

Moscovitch, M., & Catlin, J. Interhemispheric transmission of information: Measurement in normal man. *Psychonomic Science*, 1970, *18*, 211–213.

Murphy, J. T., Wong, Y. C., & Kwan, H. C. Afferent-efferent linkages in motor cortex for single forelimb muscles. *Journal of Neurophysiology*, 1975, *38*, 990–1014.

Perl, N., & Haggard, M. Practice and strategy in a measure of cerebral dominance. *Neuropsychologia*, 1975, *13*, 347–352.

Poffenberger, A. T. Reaction time to retinal stimulation with special reference to the time lost in conduction through nerve centers. *Archives of Psychology*, 1912, *23*, 1–73.

Provins, K. A., & Jeeves, M. A. Hemisphere differences in response time to simple auditory stimuli. *Neuropsychologia*, 1975, *13*, 207–211.

Risberg, J., Halsey, J. H., Wills, E. L., & Wilson, E. M. Hemispheric specialization in normal man studied by bilateral measurements of the regional cerebral blood flow. *Brain*, 1975, *98*, 511–524.

Rosenbaum, D. Stages of human movement initiation. *Quarterly Journal of Experimental Psychology*, in press.

Ruch, T. C. The cerebral cortex: Its structure and motor functions. In T. C. Ruch, H. D. Patton, J. W. Woodbury, & A. L. Towe (Eds.), *Neurophysiology*. Philadelphia: Saunders, 1965.

Semmes, J., Weinstein, S., Ghent, L., and Teuber, H. L. Somatosensory changes after penetrating brain wounds in man. Cambridge: Harvard University Press, 1960.

Sperry, R. W. Hemispheric deconnection and unity in conscious experience. *American Psychologist*, 1968, *23*, 723–733.

Springer, S. P., & Gazzaniga, M. S. Dichotic testing of partial and split-brain subjects. *Neuropsychologia*, 1975, *13*, 341–346.

Stamm, J. S., & Sperry, R. W. Functions of corpus callosum in contralateral transfer of somesthetic discrimination in cats. *Journal of Comparative Physiological Psychology*, 1957, *50*, 138–143.

Sussman, H. M., & MacNeilage, P. F. Studies of hemispheric specialization for speech production. *Brain and Language*, 1975, *2*, 131–151.

Swanson, J., Ledlow, A., & Kinsbourne, M. Lateral asymmetries revealed by simple reaction time, in press.

Tatton, W. G., Forner, S. D., Gerstein, G. L., Chambers, W. W., & Liu, C. N. The effect of postcentral cortical lesions on motor responses to sudden upper limb displacements in monkeys. *Brain Research*, 1975, *96*, 108–113.

Thompson, A. L., & Marsh, J. F. Probability sampling of normal asymmetry. *Neuropsychologia*, 1976, *14*, 217–223.

Weinstein, S. Tactile sensitivity of the phalanges. *Perceptual and Motor Skills*, 1962, *14*, 351–354.

Weinstein, S., & Sersen, E. A. Tactual sensitivity as a function of handedness and laterality. *Journal of Comparative Physiological Psychology*, 1961, *54*, 665–669.

Wiesendanger, M. Input from muscle and cutaneous nerves of the hand and forearm to neurones of the precentral gyrus of baboons and monkeys. *Journal of Physiology, London*, 1973, *228*, 203–219.

Wiley, J. Hemispherectomy and consequent motor behavior. In W. W. Spirduso & J. D. King (Eds.), *Proceedings: Motor Control Symposium*. Austin, Texas: The University of Texas, 1975.

Index

A
B
C 8
D 9
E 0
F 1
G 2
H 3
I 4
J 5